Working Life

Critical Perspectives on Work and Employment

Series editors:
Irena Grugulis, Bradford University School of Management, UK
Caroline Lloyd, School of Social Sciences, Cardiff University, UK
Chris Smith, Royal Holloway University of London School of Management, UK
Chris Warhurst, University of Strathclyde Business School, UK

Critical Perspectives on Work and Employment combines the best empirical research with leading edge, critical debate on key issues and developments in the field of work and employment. Extremely well regarded and popular, the series is linked to the highly successful *International Labour Process Conference*.

Formerly edited by David Knights, Hugh Willmott, Chris Smith and Paul Thompson, each volume in the series includes contributions from a range of disciplines, including the sociology of work and employment, business and management studies, human resource management, industrial relations and organisational analysis.

Further details of the *International Labour Process Conference* can be found at www.ilpc.org.uk.

Published:
Paul Thompson and Chris Smith
WORKING LIFE

Maeve Houlihan and Sharon Bolton
WORK MATTERS

Alan McKinlay and Chris Smith
CREATIVE LABOUR

Chris Warhurst, Doris Ruth Eikhof and Axel Haunschild
WORK LESS, LIVE MORE?

Bill Harley, Jeff Hyman and Paul Thompson
PARTICIPATION AND DEMOCRACY AT WORK

Chris Warhurst, Ewart Keep and Irena Grugulis
THE SKILLS THAT MATTER

Andrew Sturdy, Irena Grugulis and Hugh Willmott
CUSTOMER SERVICE

Craig Prichard, Richard Hull, Mike Chumer and Hugh Willmott
MANAGING KNOWLEDGE

Alan Felstead and Nick Jewson
GLOBAL TRENDS IN FLEXIBLE LABOUR

Paul Thompson and Chris Warhurst
WORKPLACES OF THE FUTURE

More details of the publications in this series can be found at
http://www.palgrave.com/business/cpwe.asp

Critical Perspectives on Work and Employment Series
Series Standing Order ISBN 978–0230–23017–0

You can receive future titles in this series as they are published by placing a standing order. Please contact your bookseller or, in case of difficulty, write to us at the address below with your name and address, the title of the series and the ISBN quoted above.

Customer Services Department, Macmillan Distribution Ltd, Houndmills, Basingstoke, Hampshire RG21 6XS, England

Working Life

Renewing Labour Process Analysis

Edited By
Paul Thompson

And

Chris Smith

First published 2010 by
PALGRAVE MACMILLAN

Palgrave Macmillan in the UK is an imprint of Macmillan Publishers Limited,
registered in England, company number 785998, of Houndmills, Basingstoke,
Hampshire RG21 6XS.

Palgrave Macmillan in the US is a division of St Martin's Press LLC,
175 Fifth Avenue, New York, NY 10010.

Palgrave Macmillan is the global academic imprint of the above companies
and has companies and representatives throughout the world.

Palgrave® and Macmillan® are registered trademarks in the United States,
the United Kingdom, Europe and other countries.

ISBN: 978-0-230-22223-6

This book is printed on paper suitable for recycling and made from fully
managed and sustained forest sources. Logging, pulping and manufacturing
processes are expected to conform to the environmental regulations of the
country of origin.

A catalogue record for this book is available from the British Library.

A catalog record for this book is available from the Library of Congress.

10 9 8 7 6 5 4 3 2 1
19 18 17 16 15 14 13 12 11 10

Printed and bound in Great Britain by
CPI Antony Rowe, Chippenham and Eastbourne

Contents

List of Illustrations

Tables

Figures

Acknowledgements

The editors would like to thank all the contributors for their indulgence in allowing us to harry them to get chapters produced to ridiculously tight deadlines. Most of the papers have been presented at International Labour Process Conferences over the past two years, in Dublin and Edinburgh, and all contributors would like to acknowledge the comments they received on preliminary drafts at these sessions. We would like to acknowledge the speed and efficiency of Deepa Chennat, the Chennai-based copy editor for the book. Finally we would like to thank Eleanor Kirk (Strathclyde University) and Lynette Maton (Royal Holloway) for their excellent work on the subject and name indexes, respectively.

Notes on Contributors

Jacques Bélanger
Professor of Industrial Relations in the Département des relations industrielles at Université Laval, in Quebec City. His research has focused on workplace relations and, more generally, on the evolution of employment relations. The results of field research that he has conducted within multinational firms have appeared in various industrial relations and sociological journals, in both English and French. He recently published (with Paul Edwards) two complementary articles on social compromise in the workplace in the *British Journal of Industrial Relations* (2006 and 2007). He is Co-director of the Centre de recherche interuniversitaire sur la mondialisation et le travail (CRIMT).

Sharon C. Bolton
Professor of Organisational Analysis at Strathclyde University Business School, Glasgow, UK. Her research interests include the emotional labour process, public sector management, the nursing and teaching labour process, gender and the professions, dignity in and at work, and the human in human resource management. Her research is published widely in leading sociology and management journals. A sole authored book *Emotion Management in the Workplace* was published by Palgrave Macmillan in 2005, followed by three edited collections: in 2007, *Searching for the Human in Human Resource Management* (with Maeve Houlihan) (Palgrave Macmillan) and *Dimensions of Dignity at Work* (Elsevier) and, in 2009, *Work Matters: Critical Reflections on Contemporary Work* (with Maeve Houlihan) (Palgrave Macmillan). In her previous life, Sharon worked as a Senior Administrator in the public and private sectors.

Hazel Conley

Hazel Conley is a senior lecturer in HRM in the School of Business and Management and a member of the Centre for Research in Equality and Diversity (CRED) at Queen Mary University of London. Her research interests include labour market 'flexibility', its impact on equality and diversity and the role of the State and trade unions. Her research has been published in leading journals and she is the co-editor, with Tessa Wright, of *A Handbook of Discrimination at Work* (Gower forthcoming).

Rick Delbridge

Professor of Organizational Analysis and Associate Dean (Research) at Cardiff Business School. His research interests include workplace relations, theorizing organization and the management of innovation. He is author of *Life on the Line in Contemporary Manufacturing*, co-author of *The Exceptional Manager* (both published by Oxford University Press) and an Associate Editor of *Organization*. He is a Senior Fellow of the ESRC/EPSRC Advanced Institute of Management Research and a Fellow of the Sunningdale Institute.

Susan Durbin

Senior Lecturer, Centre for Employment Studies Research, Business School, University of the West of England, Bristol, UK. Susan's research interests are in the areas of senior women's careers, networking and work-life balance; the career trajectories and networking behaviours of female part-time managers; the gendering of knowledge and knowledge work; equality, diversity and intersectionality; and employee involvement and participation in high performance workplaces. Recent publications have appeared in *Gender, Work and Organization*; and books include *Women in Engineering, Science and Technology: Education and Career Challenges* (IGI Global) and *Gendering the Knowledge Economy* (Palgrave Macmillan, 2007)

Paul Edwards

Professor of Industrial Relations, Industrial Relations Research Unit, Warwick Business School, University of Warwick. His research interests include new forms of work organization, the employment relationship in small firms, and personnel policy in multinational companies. Recent publications include *Social Theory at Work* with Marek Korczynski and Randy Hodson (Oxford University Press, 2006) and *The Politics of Working Life* with Judy Wajcman (Oxford University Press, 2005).

Peter Fleming

Professor of Work, Organisation and Society, School of Business and Management, Queen Mary, University of London. His research focuses on the political economy of corporations, power, cultural politics of work organizations, and the modes of ideological control that operate to enlist the participation of labour. He also researches corporate corruption and the social dynamics that characterize it. He has published the following books: *Authenticity and the Cultural Politics of Work* (Oxford University Press, 2009); with Fleming and Zyglidopoulos *Charting Corporate Corruption: Structure, Agency and Escalation* (Edward Elgar, 2009); and with Fleming and Spicer *Contesting the Corporation: Struggle, Power and Resistance in Organizations* (Cambridge University Press, 2007).

Irena Grugulis

Professor of Employment Studies at Bradford University School of Management and an AIM/ESRC Services Fellow. Her research has been funded by the ESRC, EPSRC and EU and focuses on all areas of skill, including soft skills, technical skills and national skill formation systems; recent projects have covered the retail sector as well as work in film and TV and she is currently conducting an ethnography of work in computer games. Her latest book is *Skills, Training and Human Resource Development* published by Palgrave Macmillan. She sits on the expert panel for the UK Commission for Employment and Skills.

Richard Hall

Associate Professor of Work and Organisational Studies, University of Sydney. His research interests include new technology at work, organizational discourse and international and comparative aspects of political economy, industrial relations and human resource management. He regularly and enthusiastically attends the International Labour Process Conference. His most recent book is *New Technology @ Work* (Routledge, 2008) with Paul Boreham, Paul Thompson and Rachel Parker.

Andrew Herod

Professor of Geography, Adjunct Professor of International Affairs, and Adjunct Professor of Anthropology, University of Georgia, USA. He has written widely on issues of globalization and labour politics. He is author of *Labor Geographies: Workers and the Landscapes of Capitalism* (Guilford Press, 2001); editor of *Organizing the Landscape: Geographical Perspectives on Labor Unionism*, (University of Minnesota Press, 1998); and co-editor of *The Dirty Work of Neoliberalism: Cleaners in the Global Economy* (Basil Blackwell, 2006 – with Luis Aguiar), *Geographies of Power: Placing Scale* (Basil Blackwell, 2002 – with Melissa Wright) and of *An Unruly World? Globalization, Governance and Geography* (Routledge, 1998 – with Gearóid Ó Tuathail and Susan Roberts). His latest book is *Geographies of Globalization* (Basil Blackwell, 2009). He is also an elected member of the government of Athens-Clarke County, Georgia, USA.

Stephen Jaros

Professor of Management and Organizational Behavior, College of Business, Southern University, USA. His research interests are in labour process theory, commitment and identity in organizations, and the relationship between knowledge transfer and value creation. He has been active on the International Labour Process Conference for many years. His work has recently been published in *Commitment in Organizations* (Klein, Becker, & Meyer, 2009); ICFAI *Journal of Organizational Behavior* and in the *Journal of Workplace Rights*.

Caroline Lloyd

Reader, School of Social Sciences, Cardiff University and Senior Research Fellow at the Economic and Social Research Council centre on Skills, Knowledge and Organisational Performance (SKOPE). Her research interests focus on the relationship between product markets, labour markets, work organization and skills. She has written widely on issues related to the political economy of skill and has recently participated in a US-European research project on low-waged work, co-editing the book *Low-Wage Work in the United Kingdom* (Russell Sage Foundation, 2008). Her current research involves a European comparative study of work organization, skills and performance in the service sector.

Susan McGrath-Champ

Senior Lecturer in Work and Organisational Studies, University of Sydney. Susan's research interests include the geographical aspects of the world of work, employment relations in the coal and construction industries, and international human resource management. Her recent work has been published in *Work, Employment and Society; Economic and Industrial Democracy,* and *Construction Management and Economics.* She is the first editor of the *Handbook of Employment and Society: Working Space* (with Andrew Herod and Al Rainnie, 2010).

Abigail Marks

Reader in Work and Employment at Heriot-Watt University. Her research interests include workplace identities, class and stratification, employability and the construction of professions. She has previously worked in the University of Edinburgh and the University of Strathclyde and published in a number of leading journals including *Work, Employment and Society*; *Human Relations* and the *British Journal of Industrial Relations*.

Al Rainnie

Professor in the Graduate School of Business, Curtin University, Perth, Western Australia, formerly Professor and Director of Research at the Centre for Labour Market Studies at the University of Leicester. He is co-editor (with Andy Herod and Susan McGrath-Champ) of the *Handbook of Employment and Society: Working Space* (Edward Elgar, 2010).

Chris Smith

Professor of Organisation Studies and Head of the School of Management, Royal Holloway, University of London. His research interests are in labour process theory, knowledge transfer through the transnational firm, comparative analysis of work and employment and professional labour. He is currently researching the organization of the labour process in Chinese factories and the Chinese Business Model abroad. He has been active in the International Labour Process Conference for many years. His recent publications include *Creative Labour – Working in the Creative Industries* with Alan Mckinlay, (Palgrave Macmillan, 2009); *Remaking Management: Between Global and Local* with Brendan McSweeney and Robert Fitzgerald (Cambridge University Press, 2008); and *Assembling Work* with Tony Elger (Oxford University Press, 2005).

Andrew Sturdy

Professor of Organizational Analysis and Head of Department of Management, the University of Bristol. His research interests focus on the introduction, use and impact of management ideas and practices. Currently, he is studying the role of management consultants. He has had a long involvement in the International Labour Process Conference and co-edited two of its books – *Skill and Consent* (with David Knights and Hugh Willmott) and *Customer Service* (with Irena Grugulis and Hugh Willmott). His most recent book is *Management Consultancy* (Oxford University Press, 2009) with Tim Clark, Robin Fincham and Karen Handley.

Phil Taylor

Professor of Work and Employment Studies in the Department of Human Resource Management at Strathclyde Business School in Glasgow. He has researched and published extensively on work organization, labour process and employment relations in call/contact centres. Latterly, several studies have focused on the offshoring of 'voice' and other business services (BPO) to India and other international destinations. Other ongoing research interests include occupational health and safety, prison privatization, trade union organizing, information and consultation regulations and sickness absence management. He is currently co-editor of *Work, Employment and Society* as part of a team based at the University of Strathclyde.

Paul Thompson

Professor of Organizational Analysis, Department of Human Resource Management, the University of Strathclyde. He is currently researching, with colleagues, creative labour in the visual effects part of the film industry, and the work and employment dynamics of supermarket supply chains. He has been active in the International Labour Process Conference for many years. His recent books include *New Technology @ Work* (Routledge, 2008) with Paul Boreham, Rachel Parker and Richard Hall; *A Handbook of Work and Organization* (Oxford University Press, 2004) with Stephen Ackroyd, Pam Tolbert and Rose Batt; and the 4th edition of *Work Organisations* (Palgrave Macmillan 2009) with David McHugh.

Christian Thuderoz

Professor of Sociology at INSA, Institut National des Sciences Appliquées, Lyon, France. His research has focused on trade unionism and workplace sociology, and he has also published widely on the firm as an institution of advanced modern society and, more recently, on social negotiation as a way of decision-making. He has published various articles and books including "Travail et individualisme coopératif" (1997), "La recodification de la relation d'emploi" (1998, with Jacques Bélanger), and *Sociologie des entreprises* (1997), *Négociations. Essai de sociologie du lien social* (2000) and *Histoire et sociologie du management* (2006).

Steve Vincent

Senior Lecturer in Industrial Relations and Human Resource Management at the University of Leeds. He is also a member of the Centre for Employment Relations, Innovation and Change at Leeds University Business School. His research interests include inter-organizational relations and their consequences for employment outcomes, issues surrounding freelancer networks, new public management practices and skills at work. He is also interested in labour process theory, critical realism and the implications of these theoretical frameworks for applied social research. He has published 15 book chapters and journal articles, including articles in *Human Relations; Journal of Management Studies; Work, Employment and Society; Public Administration* and *New Technology, Work and Employment*.

Chris Warhurst

Professor of Labour Studies at the University of Sydney. His research interests focus on labour process and labour market issues and developments. Specific expertise centres on the areas of aesthetic labour, knowledge work, creative work and low-wage work. He has been a regular co-organizer of the Annual International Labour Process Conference and is an editor of the accompanying book series for Palgrave, *Critical Perspectives on Work and Employment*. Recently co-edited books for the series include *Work Less, Live More?* (with Doris Eikhof and Axel Haunschild, 2008) and *The Skills That Matter* (with Irena Grugulis and Ewart Keep, 2004). He is also co-editor of the journal *Work, Employment and Society*.

Carol Wolkowitz
Reader in the Department of Sociology, University of Warwick. Her publications include *Bodies at Work* (Sage 2006), *A Glossary of Feminist Theory* (with Terry Lovell and Sonya Andermahr (Arnold 2000) and co-authored books on gender and homeworking. She is currently co-editing, with Julia Twigg, Sarah Nettleton and Rachel Cohen, a Sociology of Health and Illness Monograph on 'Body Work in Health and Social Care'.

Introduction: Labour Process Theory in Retrospect and Prospect

Paul Thompson and Chris Smith

A number of chapters in this volume begin by referring back to an earlier book in the series (of publications of edited books) associated with International Labour Process Conference, *Labour Process Theory* (Knights and Willmott, 1990). This is not surprising as the book was an important means of 'taking stock' of an extremely fruitful period from the late 1970s and through the 1980s that became known as post-Braverman 'second wave' writing. Since then, though the influence of labour process analysis and research has waxed and waned, the various manifestations of the book series has produced 16 further volumes on themes both traditional (skills, resistance, participation), new (work-life boundaries, creative labour, knowledge and its management) and specialist (management of quality, trade union organizing). This publication output is a more or less faithful reflection of the durability and diversity of the annual International Labour Process Conference (ILPC), now in its 28th year, from which most of the chapters in this collection are drawn.

The 'international' in the conference title was added in 1993 to indicate that the event had long been attracting scholars with a critical interest in the workplace from a variety of countries. That trend has accelerated in recent years. Oddly, given the origin of the species, the conference has never attracted North American delegates in substantial numbers. That is ironic given that this volume is being launched at our first ever US-based event. This is not the occasion to explain the absence, but it is worth remarking briefly perhaps on some its effects. In the absence of an equivalent institutional support, American research explicitly informed by Labour Process Theory (LPT) has been smaller and the debate (and 'outsiders' perceptions of it) has remained more Braverman-focused. This was certainly the case in two notable earlier contributions from Vicki Smith (1994) and Mark Wardell (1999) that seek to assess Braverman's (1974) legacy and how to move beyond it.[1] It also means that scholars in the UK (and elsewhere) and in the US who have much in common in terms of their basic theoretical and methodological approaches – notably a commitment to realist social science and progressive, pro-labour public policy – have often not seen such commonalities or been part of the same debates.[2] A recent Canadian volume inspired by LPT (Shalla and Wallace, 2007) showed how a parallel, but essentially similar, evolution of debate to the UK-based variant and common materialist, political economy perspectives could take place, yet with minimal interaction Shalla and Clement (2007).

All this is a way of saying that we have to be aware of the exigencies and effects of time and place on what we write. This matters more to the actual content than the forums it is expressed through. Too few of Braverman's observations, for example, showed any recognition of the specifically American context. The same cannot be said for the contributions in this volume. Whilst some may draw on predominantly 'domestic' evidence, there is appropriate recognition of the comparative dimension and a broad range of international evidence (see for example the chapter on skills from Grugulis and Lloyd).

Such observations bring us back to the purposes of this book. Like its 1990 predecessor, we see it as an exercise in taking stock. So, what is the difference in intent and outcome between the two volumes? The content of *Labour Process Theory* can be primarily divided between chapters seeking to consolidate the advances of second wave theory into some kind of revised 'core' (Littler, Thompson, Paul Edwards) and those that wanted to reconstruct it with theoretical resources 'that have been largely absent from labour process literature' (Knights and Willmott, 1990: 33). Whereas the former was geared towards traditional materialist concerns with work relations and political economy, the latter sought new post-modern territories with an emphasis on subjectivity, identity and power. This division thus foreshadowed the debates that were to dominate the following decade.

In contrast, what is *Working Life: Renewing Labour Process Analysis* taking stock *of*? The simplest answer would be that it is examining debates and research in the intervening 20 years. And of course, there is some truth in that. There is a strong body of work in traditional areas such as resistance and new ones such as emotions and work, reflected in the chapters from Bélanger and Thuderoz (Chapter 7), and Bolton (Chapter 10) respectively. Such bodies of work reflect what Ackroyd has recently described as the 'normal science' dimension of the lively and long running 'labour process debate' over the past 30 years.

Today, of course, LPT is the basis for a fertile approach to the study of contemporary work and organisation, in which a large number of researchers are currently participating. It is, in a full sense of the term, a research community. The numbers engaged in the work are large enough to provide sufficient critical mass for serious research to be undertaken on many related subjects, but small enough for most of the contributors to be known to each other and for researchers with similar interest to be aware of parallel activities to their own. ... In short, contemporary LPT has become the basis for a species of 'normal science'. (2009: 263)

Part of the brief given to chapter authors was to set out 'what we know' from these research programmes and indeed from the wider social science community. Whilst the outcomes are inevitably varied, we are happy that, by and large, the chapters have achieved this objective. But a qualification has to be made at this point. Despite the numerous volumes from the conference and other sources, LPT has largely failed to develop from its conceptual insights and empirical observations a serious theory-building project that has elucidated 'testable' core propositions that elucidate patterns and propositions discovered through relevant research programmes.[3]

To explain this limitation we have to return to the nature of that previous labour process debate. In the 1990s, too much of its content became in practice, a variant of paradigm wars. Some of these were with varieties of post-Fordism and other paradigm break perspectives. Others were with post-structuralists and post-modernists. The latter were the most divisive because the standard bearers (Knights, Willmott and their followers) saw themselves, initially at least, as part of the labour process community. This is a question of perspectives not personality. Much of the divisiveness arose from incompatible epistemological and ontological assumptions that made the differences very hard to resolve. Debates thus tend to repeat to nobody's benefit, to say nothing of producing a 'labour process debate' that mostly wasn't about the labour process. Though there will inevitably be some requirement for meta-theoretical debates with post-structuralists, as well as critiques of new economy perspectives of various kinds, we were determined that this volume would move on from paradigm wars, to focus less on what things are not, and more on what they actually are or might become. To give some account of those debates, we decided to reprint a recently published article from the editors (Thompson and Smith, 2009). This also has the added bonus that we would not be repeating ourselves to nobody's benefit in this short introduction. Given that we wrote the piece in the same period as preparing this book, its more positive agenda concerning the remapping and remaking of labour power chimes with many of the chapters herein.

Moving on does not preclude a more positive engagement with post-structuralist perspectives. This reflects, in part, contributors who are more sympathetic. In Part I, Jaros argues that differences between the contending positions is exaggerated and has been partially resolved through 'productive cross-pollination' in areas such as identity, resistance and control. Meanwhile in Part II, Sturdy, Fleming and Delbridge combine traditional labour process and (post-) Foucauldian concepts on control to argue for the relevance of a new regime – neo-normative control; whilst Hall argues that LPT can learn from social constructivist writings on the role of discourse and micro-agency in explaining the enactment and experience of technology. Other chapters are much more critical, but in all cases there is an orientation towards what can be learned from debates in terms of theory-building, rather than repeating old arguments. This can be particularly seen in the chapter from Marks and Thompson (Chapter 15) that is very sceptical of discourse-based accounts of identity, but recognizes the importance of the issue and the role played by post-structuralists in raising its profile.

However, as we said, this book is not a series of extended debates with 'post' perspectives of any kind. The structure of the book divides the content into chapters that address the core concepts and traditions of LPT; classic issues associated with labour process research programmes in which clear propositions are more likely to have been developed and newer issues where labour process approaches are pertinent, but unevenly developed. What follows is not an attempt to provide chapter summaries, but some observations on overlapping themes.

An outline of the book

Part I contains four chapters that provide accounts of the state of general debate concerning labour process analysis. Aside from the previously mentioned reprinted article from the editors, the other contributions focus on the issue of what a 'core theory' of the labour process does or might consist of. As we indicated earlier, the idea of a core theory developed from attempts to bring together propositions from second wave theory and research. The conclusion drawn by Thompson (1990) and Edwards (1990) was that such a core should be based on a specific and differentiated set of empirical objects (the labour process as a specific site of the production process of capital, rather than general social production). The labour process should be regarded as having a relative autonomy within the wider capitalist political economy and society. To quote Ackroyd again,

> LPT is, in this conception, an account of a key inner mechanism of capitalism, which, while it does require a broader analysis of the systemic features of its context, the form this takes cannot be entirely derived from theoretical postulates. Thus research is central to this approach and takes

in the nature of the connections between labour process and the wider context. (2009: 264)

This position continues to be misunderstood by some commentators on LPT. In a recent piece, Frenkel complains of the narrowness of an 'isolated niche community' that focuses mainly on themes such as technology, control, skill, worker resistance and identity, then goes on to criticize attempts by Thompson and others to discuss 'big theory' of capitalist political economy, on the grounds that 'why should the labour process be privileged?'(2009: 526). Setting aside the contradictory statements, the point is that the 'narrow' version of core theory privileges the labour process only to answer research questions relevant to that sphere and 'works with' other compatible theoretical resources to answer the kind of mid-range problems and issues Frenkel rightly highlights. This has not been easy for us. Whilst there is probably a great deal of consensus in mainstream labour process analysis about the 'relative autonomy' position, it left unresolved a whole set of empirical and conceptual boundary issues. In different ways, this is what the three chapters from Edwards (Chapter 2), Thompson and Vincent (Chapter 3), and Jaros (Chapter 4) seek to address. Thompson and Vincent invoke the 'layered ontology' of critical realism as an aid resolving those boundary issues, but reach similar conclusions to Jaros about why and how additional theoretical resources can be combined with labour process analysis. Edwards takes a similar view about scope and objects of inquiry, but advances a broader agenda that suggests a variety of methodological and conceptual means for researchers to do better labour process and related theory. The idea and content of core theory is also addressed in some later chapters. Hall revisits a traditional, but now somewhat neglected theme – technology and work relations – to produce a revised conception of core theory, with an appropriately modified form of technology analysis back in. In contrast, in a chapter on gender regimes (Chapter 9), Durbin and Conley challenge the 'narrow' conception, arguing that LPT would benefit from explicit theorization of issues such as the relations between different kinds of inequalities, or the state, and recommend intersectionality as the conceptual means to do so.

Part II begins with Grugulis and Lloyd's chapter on skill. Whilst they make reference to the continuing relevance of some of Braverman's critiques of upskilling, this is not a revisiting of past debates as much as a consideration of the consequences of what they describe as 'the dramatic increase in the lexicon of skill and the increasing emphasis on social and soft skills'. These are not merely the outcome of (re)labelling, but a reflection of real changes in what employers want from labour power through more demanding work. The chapter also contains the first of a number of discussions on emotions and work (see also Durbin and Conley, Bolton, and Wolkowitz and Warhurst in Part III), signifying its growing centrality to labour process research. We have already referred to the chapters from Hall and Durbin/Conley. The other two chapters in Part II are concerned with another traditional labour process theme – control and resistance. Contrary to the deluded few who still nonsensically repeat claims that LPT believes that Taylorism is the dominant/only form of control used by employers, Sturdy, Fleming and Delbridge revive a long-standing tradition of identifying a new form, in this case a hybridized extension of normative control, that, they claim, chimes with a number of developments within capitalism. In the second half of their chapter and drawing on French and English-language literatures, Bélanger and Thuderoz also appear to reclaim a labour process tradition – the integrated model of control and resistance characteristic of second wave research. However, that appearance is partly deceptive. Resistance is opened out into a wider repertoire of oppositional (and cooperative and consensual) employee behaviours and the modes of control are appropriately contextualized to take account of those parts of the world characterized by a post-industrial context.

Finally, the chapters in Part III are a recognition that facts as well as fashions change. There are new realities and new understandings of how those realities may be understood. Though other chapters discuss emotions and labour, Bolton's contribution is a systematic effort to map the different categories of emotions at work and the potential role of LPT in explaining them. There are overlaps with the following chapter from Wolkowitz and Warhurst on embodying labour. But this has a wider intent as an ambitious and persuasive attempt to link more established labour process concerns with aesthetic labour and the complex literatures on the production and reproduction of the body.

The three chapters by Taylor (Chapter 12), Smith (Chapter 13) and Rainnie et al. (Chapter 14) can be discussed together in that they share common concepts – space, place, scale and flow. Consistent with the broader mission of the book, the three chapters look outwards to other disciplines and frameworks, but with a strong urge to integrate and not simply add-on concepts to LPT in order to empirically better capture workplace dynamics within a more globalizing capitalism. Taylor is the most concrete, bringing together and extending more than a decade's worth of research and theorizing on call centres. Focusing on call centre offshoring, especially to India, he offers a valuable interrogation of commodity, value and production chain concepts which have developed to capture the nature of transnational integration of production and services beyond the limitations of the simple linearity of MNC HQ-Subsidiary hierarchy. The chapter by Smith is more wide-ranging in its review of impact of changes in work, contracts, technology, labour supply, mobility of capital and labour on labour power and labour processes within a more globalized capitalism. But it is also narrower, in that he attempts to map these changes onto an approach to labour power that emphasizes the uncertainties of both use (effort) and movement (mobility) as a power calculus for both workers and employers. Space, discussed in both the Taylor and Smith chapters, is at the centre of the chapter by Rainnie, McGrath Champ and Herod which aims to champion a spatial approach to the labour process, by reviewing the theoretical and empirical insights into work offered by economic geographers.

Finally, if one issue has been used to define a territory closed to mainstream LPT, it has been identity. This is challenged by the chapter by Marks and Thompson (Chapter 15), but with a materialist twist – the need to integrate a conception of interests alongside identity as equally plausible explanations of behaviour in and out of work. The book ends with some appendices that list influential chapters and journal articles informed by labour process theory. Aside from any intrinsic interest for the reader, a key rationale is that you can't theory-build without being aware of what we already know. As Edwards illustrates in his chapter, there is a continual tendency to reinvent the conceptual wheel. Listing such resources might occasionally help to offset that.

Conclusion

Many of these chapters began as papers to theory streams at the annual International Labour Process Conference at Dublin (2008) and Edinburgh (2009). We are grateful for the work put in by authors in revising their chapters and responding to our comments and suggestions. Of course, there are issues we should have covered, but did not eventually appear. Equally, not every conceptual problem has been addressed, let alone resolved. However, we are convinced that the main purpose of this book has been achieved – to systematically set out and explore what we have learned and need to learn within (one branch of) the labour process tradition. Of the authors who contributed to the 1990 volume, only two 'survive' in this one. There is a new and diverse generation of scholars that indicates that LPT is alive and well.

Notes

1   It was also evident from a conference organized to celebrate *Labor and Monopoly Capital* held at the State University of New York at Binghamton, in May 1998.

2 Breaking down such barriers was one of the purposes of *The Oxford Handbook of Work and Organization* (Ackroyd, S., Batt, R., Thompson, P. and Tolbert, P., 2005).

3 A partial exception is Thompson and Harley's (2007) preliminary mapping of what some of those propositions might look like with respect to control, work organization and skill formation.

REFERENCES

Ackroyd, S. (2009) 'Labor Process Theory as "Normal Science"', *Employee Responsibilities and Rights (Symposium on Labour Process Theory)*, 21: 263–72.

Ackroyd, S., Batt, R., Thompson, P. and Tolbert, P. (eds) (2005) *The Oxford Handbook of Work and Organization*, Oxford: Oxford University Press.

Braverman, H. (1974) *Labor and Monopoly Capital*, New York: Monthly Review Press.

Edwards, P. K. (1990) 'Understanding Conflict in the Labour Process: The Logic and Autonomy of Struggle', in Knights, D. and Willmott, H. (eds) *Labour Process Theory*, London: Macmillan, 125–52.

Frenkel, S. (2009) 'Critical Reflections on Labour Process Theory, Work and Management', in Alvesson, M., Bridgman, T. and Willmott, H. (eds) *The Oxford Handbook of Critical Management Studies*, Oxford: Oxford University Press.

Knights, D. and Willmott, H. (eds) (1990) *Labour Process Theory*, London: Macmillan.

Shalla, V. and Clement, W. (eds) (2007) *Work in Tumultuous Times: Critical Perspectives*, London: McGill-Queens University Press, 227–61.

Smith, V. (1994) 'Braverman's Legacy: The Labor Process Tradition at 20', *Work and Occupations* 21.4: 403–21.

Thompson, P. (1990) 'Crawling from the Wreckage: The Labour Process and the Politics of Production', in Knights, D. and Willmott, H. (eds) *Labour Process Theory*, London: Macmillan.

Thompson, P. and Harley, B. (2007) 'HRM and the Worker: Labor Process Perspectives', in Boxall, P., Purcell, J. and Wright, P. (eds) *The Oxford Handbook of Human Resource Management*, Oxford: Oxford University Press.

Thompson, P. and Smith, C. (2009) 'Labour Power and Labour Process: Contesting the Marginality of the Sociology of Work', *Sociology*, 43(5): 913–30.

Wardell, M. (1999) 'Labor Processes: Moving beyond Braverman and the Deskilling Debate', in Wardell, M., Steiger, T. L. and Meiksins, P. (eds) *Rethinking the Labor Process*, Albany: NY: State University of New York Press.

The Core Theory

Debating Labour Process Theory and the Sociology of Work[1]

Paul Thompson and Chris Smith

Introduction

In June 1978 many of Britain's leading industrial sociologists met to debate Braverman's (1974) *Labor and Monopoly Capital*. This was the beginning of a development in which, 'During the late 1970s, studies of the "labour process", inspired by the work of Marglin, Edwards and Braverman, virtually redefined British "industrial sociology"', (Ingham, 1996: 562). The research programme of Labour Process Theory (LPT) – an emphasis on the dynamics of control, consent and resistance at the point of production – was also consistent with the writings of a new generation of radical industrial sociology and industrial relations writers such as Huw Beynon (1973), Theo Nichols and Peter Armstrong (Nichols and Armstrong, 1976; Nichols and Beynon, 1977). Popularizing extended theoretically informed case-study methods against an early generation of more quantitative assessment (Bechhofer et al., 1968), their books combined an emphasis on the limited effects of new managerial practices, such as job enrichment, with the practical and ideological problems of trade union organization. LPT, therefore, strengthened those tendencies in workplace research that sought to reach beneath institutional, formal patterns and to discover and explore hidden or informal realms of industrial relations and workplace conflict.

Yet, why did British industrial sociology need to be 'redefined'? After all, as one later study noted: 'in the early 1960s industrial sociology looked as though it had arrived. Its special task was the study of social relations in work situations and to develop an understanding of the links between industrial systems and the wider society' (Eldridge, Cressey and MacInnes, 1991: 202). A decade later the situation had changed. It was argued that industrial sociology had fragmented, and had become less able to explain the new trends in economic life and the world of work such as new forms of conflict, labour market segmentation and work organization (Brown, 1992: 168–74; Hyman, 1982). More importantly, industrial sociology's influential accounts had come to view the factory as the recipient of external orientations to work rather than as a source of conflict and identity, becoming more concerned with orientations *to* work than work itself (Thompson, 1989).

LPT was attractive because it had the capacity to connect different dimensions of work, employment and industrial relations, and therefore counter the tendency to fragmentation. It had a theoretical narrative – the degradation of work under the impact of new forms of capitalist production and management – attuned to a radical decade and based on Marxist accounts of labour and capital within capitalism. LPT's focus on the 'objective' conditions of work contrasted positively with the somewhat exhausted attention paid to subjective meanings, worker attitudes and class-consciousness in mainstream and radical sociology (Bechhofer et al., 1968; Bulmer, 1975). However, there was also methodological continuity with the long-standing traditions of 'plant sociology' stretching back to Donald Roy in the USA (1952) and the 'Liverpool school' of industrial sociology that influenced a diverse range of researchers from Lupton to Banks, Blackburn to Beynon.

In sum, as capitalism and work were changing, LPT offered to British industrial sociology the analytical and empirical tools to maintain the historic interest in the dynamics of work relations and the connections between workplace and the wider social system. Of course, this is not the whole story of the sociology of work in Britain during the past 25 years. Debates have continued on other territories such as work, gender and the family. Indeed, complaints of narrow agendas influenced by LPT have occasionally surfaced from the peak of second wave research to more recent times (Bradley, 2000; Salaman, 1986). Such objections have recently been reassembled by Strangleman (2005). His case would have been more credible if the paper had actually referred to *any* contemporary research and writings from this perspective (the last relevant reference is to Hyman in 1987). Given that 14 widely read volumes of papers derived primarily from the labour process conference have been published since 1990 on topics as diverse as resistance and power, global Japanization, customer service, white-collar work and work-life boundaries, narrowness is not the word that comes immediately to mind (for a full list of titles see http://www.ilpc.org.uk/BookSeries.aspx).

However, there is a kernel of truth about scope and boundaries of analysis contained in such complaints. Selectivity is inherent in any distinctive conceptual framework. Some things are studied and others are not (see also Edwards, this volume, on the boundary question). The orientation of LPT to the waged workplace and to some extent the case-study methods of analysing that workplace meant that it was less equipped to address, amongst other things, issues such as the varieties of (often informal or unwaged) types of work, temporal and spatial dimensions (see Rainnie et al. this volume), and what Glucksmann calls the 'total social organisation of labour' (Pahl, 1988; Pettinger et al., 2005; though see Taylor and Bain, 2007 for a critique of Glucksmann). The research programme of LPT utilizes particular theoretical resources to explain specific empirical problems. A conceptual and empirical focus on the labour process only becomes a problem if privileging those social relations becomes a means of denying the significance of others. That has never been the case. LPT is neither paradigmatic nor a complete sociology of work in terms of concepts and coverage. Whatever the limitations in its scope, our contention in this chapter is that LPT has played a necessary and positive purpose in maintaining a space for a critical sociology of work. We want to make an argument that the core propositions of LPT provide it with resources for *resilience* (to counter claims of rival perspectives) and *innovation* (to expand the scope and explanatory power of the sociology of work).

Second wave theory: A reconsideration

Constructed from the responses to Braverman and a fresh range of research from the late 1970s to the end of the 1980s, a second wave of LPT came into being that had a strong base in the UK. Whilst a varied range of studies were undertaken, not least into the extent of and limits to deskilling, '...the core of their research programme consists of a series of historically informed empirical studies focused on managerial control strategies and practices in work organisations' (Reed, 1992: 155). These studies (especially Edwards, 1979; Friedman, 1977; Littler, 1982) are well known and their details need not be repeated here. At one level they shared a similar sense of scope of analysis, developing causal and sequential patterns of management control, seeking to make connections between workplace, industrial relations, the state and broader social structures, though with some focus on struggle at the micro level and how this related to broader management regimes. Beyond conditions of sale of labour power, detailed attention was paid to the myriad of job controls, wage-effort bargains, individual and informal, collective and organized, especially in the work of Edwards and Scullion (1982). Elaboration of this dialectic of control and resistance became a central feature of the approach, but was modified through the pioneering work of Burawoy (1979) over the question of *consent* of the worker to managerial controls inside the labour process.

Also notable during this period were a series of factory case studies of women production workers by a new generation of feminist industrial sociologists (Cavendish, 1982; Pollert, 1981; Westwood, 1984). Ethnographic methods not only allowed a close observation of the conditions and informal practices of female wage labour, but the very marginalization of the concerns of women workers by the local and national trade union apparatus stimulated a focus on the dual sources of resistance and consent in gender-based modes of control and shop-floor cultures (see Durbin and Conley this volume).

The new generation of theory-led case studies illustrate how 'matters at the point of production' are indicative not just of battles over the frontier of control, but also of 'how workers are persuaded to release their labour power' (Edwards and Scullion, 1982: 151). Whilst labour power is clearly reproduced inside and outside the workplace, the distinctive and innovatory nature of second wave theory was facilitated by the concept of the dynamics of workplace regulation having a 'relative autonomy' (Edwards, 1990). The implication is that similar external situations can produce different internal labour process outcomes, because of the distinctiveness and peculiarities of particular points of production. However, this does not mean some infinite variety of workplaces isolated from capital accumulation, but rather that labour processes have common and specific features. Selecting and shaping labour power, or determining work effort are necessarily variable given differentiation and competition between capitals and between workers as socially and historically diverse owners and sellers of labour power. The special, indeterminate status of labour power as human, embodied, mobile and active ensure common imperatives of control are tried, but also that any settlement between labour and capital is temporary and diverse.

Building on the relative autonomy concept, a related theoretical shift was to retain focus on the problematic of labour power through materialist accounts of conflicts between capital and labour, but that sought to move beyond the limitations of existing debates on class struggle and industrial relations. The work of many second wave writers has tried to disentangle LPT from Marxism; or more precisely those elements that pertain to the relations between production and political economy, from the complete baggage of assumptions about society and social transformation (Edwards, 1990; Thompson, 1990). The central argument was that the dynamics of relations between capital and labour as actors in the workplace cannot be assumed to be continuous with capital and labour as societal actors. In other words, labour process struggles might have diverse, not predictable or singular, outcomes at the level of the political and the political within work.

Challenges to and for Labour Process Theory

New economies for old?

The mid-1980s saw the emergence of paradigm break theories such as post-Fordism and flexible specialization (Piore and Sabel, 1984). Leading contributors have tended to proclaim the end or at least decentring of work or work *society* (Bauman, 1998; Lash and Urry, 1994). Post-Fordist or post-modern variants of a 'new economy' are based on individualized, consumption-oriented actors rather than collectivities with interests and identities rooted in the employment relationship. Two strands are inter-meshing here. On the one hand, post-modernists following the cultural turn are asserting the centrality of identity and consumption (Pakulski and Waters, 1996). On the other, social theorists such as Beck (2000) are rehears-ing new versions of 'end of class' or end of capital-labour conflict arguments (Gorz, 1999). The other influential new economy narrative is based on the centrality of knowledge. In the informational or knowledge economy, the traditional factors of production are displaced by weightless or immaterial sources of competitive advantage (Castells, 1996). Rather than the accumula-tion of capital, socio-economic life is characterized by the flow or circulation of ideas and information.

This is not the place for a critique of new economy narratives (see Bradley, 2000; Henwood, 2005; Thompson, 2003) but to make three observations with important implications for a sociology of work. First, given that, as Crompton (2008) notes, classical sociology has strongly linked class and work, the latter has been a conceptual casualty of the perceived decline of the former. Second, marginalization is a consequence of misrepresentation. Dominant social theory retains a sociology of the economy, but without a substantive sociology of work. New economies are conceived either as not centred on work relations, or having largely benign consequences for the people *at* work. The combined effect of these two strands of social theory has been to render large sections of the economy, workforce and work relations invisible.

What marked these approaches was an unshakeable optimism with respect to trends in work and employment. More recently the new economy baton has been passed to proponents of the knowledge economy from man-agerial writers (Despres and Hiltrop, 1995) to high-profile social theorists (Castells, 1996). Details of the plot (knowledge as driver of change) and some of the characters (expert labour, independent subcontractors) change, but the optimistic message about a move from command and control to collaborative high-trust, high-commitment work relations remains the same.

This has led to a return of upskilling arguments. Indeed the proclamation of the existence of or need for a high skills model is an unquestioned feature of public policy across all OECD countries. Labour process research drawing on case studies and wider skill surveys has repeatedly questioned this myth (Thompson, Warhurst and Callaghan, 2000). Whilst there will be growth at both ends of the spectrum, most new jobs in the UK and US are in low-skill, low-wage parts of the service sector (Henwood, 2005; Nolan and Wood,

2003). Many of the signifiers of high skill – qualifications, the spread of information and communication technologies, and investment in research and development – are merely proxies that have little relationship to actual skill and knowledge work*ed* on the job (Warhurst and Thompson, 2006; see Hall this volume). For example, the main UK skill survey has shown a marked decline in task discretion and job influence (Felstead, Gallie and Green, 2004). Whilst autonomy might appear to be distinct from skill, discretion in tasks is a core feature of the capacity of employees to utilize their skills (see Grugulis and Lloyd, this volume).

The supposed need for skills in the new economy and paradigm shifts in production and markets were seen to have positive implications for workers in the labour process. As such, the 1990s meant labour process research fought a necessary, if somewhat defensive, battle to analyse the continuities and constraints associated with 'lean production', 'flexibility' and other new management practices. In contrast to the optimistic claims of workplace transformation that remained stubbornly persistent in much of the managerially orientated literature, a wealth of qualitative case-study research from North America (Parker and Slaughter, 1988; Rinehart, Huxley and Robertson, 1997) and the UK (Delbridge 1998; Elger and Smith, 1994) emerged to illustrate the 'dark side' of these lean production regimes. These accounts, heavily reliant on the control/resistance framework for their theoretical resources, reviewed the opportunities these new workplace regimes present to actively extend labour control. Far from providing a replacement to the mind-numbing stress of mass production, flexibility systematically intensifies work by finding yet new ways to remove obstacles to the extraction of effort. Moreover, by restoring an emphasis on the experience of employees, such research also demonstrated that workers continue to adopt an array of resistive responses to this extension of control (see Sturdy et al. this volume).

LPT is, however, concerned with the transformation of labour power rather than a particular means, such as deskilling. As an important collection of studies largely from the International Labour Process Conference (Warhurst, Grugulis and Keep, 2004) has shown, whilst there is a persistent trend towards the maintenance of low-skill jobs, that has been accompanied by significant shifts in the definition and nature of skills. The most prominent of these has been the rise of 'generic' skills with the shift to service work – adaptability, motivation, cooperativeness – many of which are attitudes, social predispositions and character traits. In other words, LPT has been at the forefront of research into new sources of labour power.

A good example is the way that Bolton (2005) has built on and from Hochschild's (1983) work on emotional labour (see also Bolton, this volume). Whilst Hochschild drew on Braverman as part of her attempt to show how the profit motive 'slipped in under acts of emotion management' (1983: 119), her account of the 'transmutation' of worker neglects the indeterminacy of labour. Bolton uses a 'partnership' of LPT and Goffman to develop a 'detailed realist account of workplace emotion' (2005: 3) that considers emotions to the contested nature of the emotional effort bargain. In a similar vein, writers sympathetic to LPT have developed the concept of aesthetic labour (first used in Warhurst et al., 2000). Whilst there is now an extensive range of writing about the body, materialist accounts focus on managerial interventions with respect to workers' corporeality and consideration of how the body becomes 'a focus of diverse labour processes' (Wolkowitz, 2006: 2; see also Wolkowitz and Warhurst, this volume).

Another conceptual innovation concerns knowledge and skills. While we may not be seeing an increased demand for high-autonomy knowledge workers (see critique from Warhurst and Thompson, 2006), management have become more interested in the knowledge*ability* of employees. In pursuit of the 'high-performance workplace', firms need to move beyond the limits of Taylorism and Fordism to introduce organizational structures and practices that facilitate initiative and innovation in the form of creativity and continuous improvement on the part of workers. Yet, many of these skills are social rather than technical. As a result, employers, particularly in the service sector, may be choosing to invest more in recruitment and selection processes to identify workers with the personal characteristics than skill development and learning (Callaghan and Thompson, 2002). The expanded definition of skill benefits capital rather than labour. Employees or the education system are given the responsibility for 'skill' development and maintaining employability; social skills carry no wage or other premium in the occupational hierarchy; and mobilizing the *whole person* rests on a qualitative intensification of labour.

This argument is consistent with more general evidence of work intensification. Insecurity in the labour market may have been overstated (see Fevre, 2007), but sources of insecurity and pressure in the labour process – linked to increased responsibilities and falling staffing levels in response to heightened market pressures; subjection to greater accountability, measurement and appraisal; and emotional exhaustion – is attested to in a growing range of studies (Burchell, Ladipo and Wilkinson, 2002; Green, 2001; Heery and Salmon, 2000). Overwork, time squeeze and 'negative job-to-home spillover' from high-performance practices have also been noted in extensive UK surveys (Hogarth et al., 2000).

Capital's expanded use of labour power can be a source of consent and common interests. That is certainly the line that emerges from discourses of high-performance work systems (see Lloyd and Payne, 2006). But current conditions make that unlikely. Discretionary effort is being asked for from employees, including taking over responsibility for career development, when many employers are making less investment in training and skill development, and workers feel insecure in their jobs, despite relatively stable figures for job tenure (Beynon et al., 2002; Cappelli, 1999). This collectivization of effort and decollectivization of risk (Burchell, Ladipo and Wilkinson, 2002) frequently applies just as much to core workers and firms that develop track records of high performance (Konzelmann and Forrant, 2002). Labour process and other theorists have been rebuilding connections between workplace dynamics and the broader political economy by trying to conceptualize these new conditions that bear little resemblance to any variety of post-Fordism. Such outcomes point to the dominance of financial circuits of capital and to the impact of capital markets driven by the pursuit of shareholder value (Froud et al., 2006; Lazonick and O'Sullivan, 2000; Thompson, 2003), as well as profitability from the whole value chain through systematic rationalization (Altmann and Deiß, 1998). Successive waves of downsizing and delayering are undertaken as firms seek ways of cutting costs to improve financial performance (see also Thompson and Vincent, this volume).

New identities for old interests?

If arguments for upskilling and the end of Taylorism drew inspiration from different *owners of capital* and their production regimes (the Japanese especially), another source of attack on LPT came from an attention to the existential character of *owners of labour power* within new service and professional contexts. In the 1990s the influence of post-modernism peaked in most of the social sciences. This was manifested in what became known as the 'cultural turn' – the argument that the reproduction of everyday life and the basis of domination had shifted from the material to the symbolic (Lash and Urry, 1994). Such arguments were taken into the labour process debate by Hugh Willmott and David Knights, who were centrally involved in the Labour Process Conference which has acted as a key source for disseminating labour process research and ideas from the early 1980s.

Willmott and Knights led an assault on the critical materialist or modernist orthodoxy that had characterized second wave thinking. Drawing in Foucauldian notions of power and identity, their aim was to understand how (post) modern individuals are constituted by and subjugated to the discourses and disciplines within the modern corporation (Knights and Willmott, 1989; see Jaros, this volume). At one level, such arguments can be seen as a radical version of the mainstream argument in the business and management literature that culture and the management of commitment have displaced control and bureaucracy. The outcome that individuals 'buy into' the system is held in common, but the explanation is sought in processes of seduction, surveillance and self-discipline.

In this version of LPT, identity rather than labour becomes the site of indeterminacy (see Marks and Thompson, this volume). Post-modern perspectives in the labour process debate have also been developed through Foucault-influenced case studies on work organization and new management practices (Barker, 1993; Sewell, 1998). In both variants of the post-modern position worker resistance and self-organization is seen as diminished or defunct. In contrast to the post-modernist view that subjectivity is no longer a significant source of resistance, a substantial body of workplace research has identified that employees remain knowledgeable about management intentions and outcomes and retain the resources to resist, misbehave or disengage (e.g. Ackroyd and Thompson, 1999; McKinlay and Taylor, 1996; see Belanger and Thuderoz, this volume). Whilst traditional qualitative case-study research supplied sources of resilience concerning labour agency, it added little to the analytical armoury of LPT.

That was provided, in part, by Ackroyd and Thompson's (1999) work on organizational misbehaviour. As was explicitly recognized in the book, there is a long and fruitful tradition in British sociology that explores the informal and recalcitrant side of employee (mis)behaviour from the effort-bargain studies of Baldamus (1961) to the workplace deviancy studies of Ditton (1977) and Mars (1982), and the classic account of control and resistance patterns by Edwards and Scullion (1982). It is also worth noting that attempts to defend and extend conceptions of agency were paralleled in Hodson's (1995, 2001) exploration of the role of resistance in maintaining employee dignity at work.

However, the misbehaviour perspective did bring something distinctive to the table. This involved a systematic and distinctive mapping of worker action and agency based on four distinct loci of struggle over working time, working effort, the product of work and work identities. Each dimension of misbehaviour is described as a *form of appropriation* underpinned by group self-organization around a variety of interests and identities. This framework constitutes a conceptual innovation in two ways. First, it moves beyond the control and resistance model. Referring to the term appropriation, Fleming comments that, 'rather than resistance being conceived as a negative reaction to power the authors instead frame misbehaviour as an active set of practices that attempt to recover a degree of autonomy at work' (2001: 190–1). Clearly, this argument extends the view that the workplace has a degree of 'relative autonomy' within which struggles over divergent interests and identities takes place. Second, it seeks to resolve some of the disputes about subjectivity through an explicit focus on identity: 'Interests and identities are not opposites. They reciprocally and discursively form one another...' (Ackroyd and Thompson, 1999: 55).

The defence of the core idea of indeterminacy of labour and provision of new categories of employee action significantly expanded conceptions of agency available to researchers in the sociology of work. New research from a labour process perspective is putting flesh on that argument, for example, Taylor and Bain's (2005) graphic account of how call centre workers are using humour as a tool of both informal and formal resistance. Linking back to the previous section, we can say that enhanced managerial efforts to mobilize the whole person through teamworking, corporate culture, customer care programmes and the like meet worker identities and interests on a new, more contested terrain or emotional effort bargain.

Limitations and moving on: Remapping labour power in a globalizing economy

We have sought to demonstrate that LPT has been a source of resilience and innovation in thinking about work and its contexts. That is not to say that the approach is without limitations. Given the nature of the above two debates, engagement with other dimensions of a broader sociology of work were neglected, notably the employment and reproduction of labour power, community, class and professions, kinship and external linkage (see for example, Crompton, 2006, 2008). Sociological writings using labour market and workplace survey data, exploring the interplay between markets, organizations and intensification of labour are particularly important (Green 2006; McGovern et al., 2007). This ties in with a previous 'methodological' weakness we have identified.

Second wave theory began with broadly based, historical accounts of workplace change, then put through the critical filter of numerous workplace case studies to test propositions about management control and skill formation strategies and practices; and more sophisticated typologies of conflict and consent. Whilst much of value was generated, the danger is that the research programme can disappear into micro-level case studies whose causal chain ends at the office door. This trend was accentuated by the idea of a 'relative autonomy' of the labour process. Whilst this opened a space to see distinctive workplace dynamics, when the 'relativity' becomes the dominant focus, it created the potential, if unintended, legitimation of a narrower frame of analysis.

A great strength of LPT is its capacity to connect the workplace to a broader political economy (see Taylor's and Edwards' chapters in this volume). In too much labour process research, distinctions about moments in political economy (exchange, production, circulation, realization) have been lost or subordinated to a general focus on the labour process as *work organization* – an empirical site of employment. The focus on the workplace to research the labour process is empirically logical. Workplaces as a rule do not walk around but are spatially set pieces of physical capital, with inputs (labour and capital) flowing into sites with fixed abode. Empirically, however, this leaves out those who contribute but are not workplace located, or have recently left or even future workers and managers that have yet to enter the abode of production. In other words pre-production, reproduction and post-production tend to be excluded or less well examined when we only look at what occurs in actually existing workplaces. Multi-site, multilayered research studies can overcome some of these issues, but these often end up disconnected from actual labour processes. Longitudinal research also challenges problems of stasis and the tendency to construct case-study stories on the basis of limited temporal investigations.

Whilst new thinking about financialized or disconnected capitalism, discussed earlier, are important attempts to restore links to a bigger picture, there have been other innovations in creating a less 'organization-centric' frame of analysis. Elger and Smith's (2005) work on Japanese-owned companies in the UK used repeat visits to factories over a number of years which revealed interesting interactions between the labour market, employment relations and work organization. In some factories the size of the workforce could vary by as much as 500 within a few months (Smith et al., 2004) which had major implications for 'work discipline' and 'work effort', as these interacted with such mercurial labour flows. Despite the need for temporal and spatial dynamic to be introduced back into the LPT, there is requirement to see how ICTs *decentre work* from a single physical site and open up working to any space with communication facilities which have implications for 'workplace-civic society-home' reconfigurations (Felstead and Jewson, 2005; see Smith, this volume).

These empirical shifts also require a theoretical adjustment in how LPT conceptualizes labour power, so that it can encompass the transnational flows of workers and capital, and the shifts in the responsibility for maintaining workers ready for the market. It is useful to think about labour power as possessing two components or indeterminacies: *effort power* and *mobility power* (Smith, 2006). The first indeterminacy emerges from the distinction between labour and labour *power* made by Marx. Hiring labour power does not guarantee an automatic outcome or product for the buyer; as the capacity to work remains within the person of the worker, and the imperative to realize or extract this capacity as work or labour is the very *raison d'etre* of the management function. The second indeterminacy reflects the decentralization of the authority over the disposal of labour power to the individual worker who has the burden and freedom (constraint and choice) as to *where* and to *which* employer the individual sells his or her labour services. This can be called *mobility power*, which is indeterminate in the sense that the decision on which employer the worker chooses to park his or her labour power is given to the individual and therefore remains a source of uncertainty for the employing firm in calculating whether the workers will remain with them. It is also an uncertainty for the worker as to whether the employing firm will continue to require their labour services, and where it will locate to get these resources. The explosion of remote services, especially call or contact centres, highlights this spatial expansion of the mobility power of employers in sectors, such as financial services, previously tied to national economies (Taylor and Bain, 2005; see Taylor, this volume).

Conclusion: Beyond industrial sociology

In many ways, LPT retained its influence because, intentionally or unintentionally, it played to and built on the strengths of British industrial sociology. That is, a 'plant-based' approach focusing on the dynamics of formal and informal workplace relations, with some sensitivity to a broader macro context (see Edwards, this volume). However, if an *industrial* sociology was ever empirically and intellectually viable, it is not now. Various factors, some discussed in this chapter, are redrawing the boundaries of skills and controls: the firm, the nation and the global economy; and between the public and private domains.

There are those who will see LPT as somehow outdated or out of sync with whatever version of the 'new economy' is currently fashionable. But we are not in the middle of a crisis of the knowledge economy or post-modern society, but of financialized capitalism. The orientation of LPT towards capturing and connecting work/place dynamics and their multiple forms of embeddedness in the broader political economy, makes it highly relevant for our times. The remaking and remapping of labour power is central to this conception and remains integral to the contemporary contradictions in the management of the firm. Whilst we associate crises of financialized capitalism with banking failures and the credit crunch, there are equivalents at the level of the employment relationship. Capital, particularly in a service-based economy, relies on the intensive use of a broader range of worker capacities and tacit knowledge, expressed through the ideas of discretionary effort and high-performance practices. However, the dominance of capital markets and shareholder value mean that employers are seldom willing to pay for that enhanced effort through a stable and inclusive workplace mutual gains bargain. Financial pressures on the contemporary state mean that governments are often unwilling or unable to adequately plug that gap in terms of skill formation, childcare support and the like.

A further barrier to LPT being part of the solution rather than the problem is raised by Strangleman: 'The interdisciplinary nature of the Labour

Process forum (*sic*) can be seen to undermine a more explicitly sociological account of work by occupying such a dominant position in the field' (2005: 5). Aside from the fact that this does not sit easily with the view in the previous sentence that the debate has produced 'a very narrow set of interests', he has a point. This does reflect, as Strangleman previously notes, the fragmentation of the disciplinary base of sociology, including the fact that many sociologists of work, supportive of LPT, are located in business schools. This UK trend actually has mixed outcomes. Certain themes, such as total quality management, team working, lean production, flexible specialization, management strategies and a tendency to focus on management as the most important agency in work are, anecdotally, more typical of work research in business schools. It might also be the case that some themes are harder to raise – trade unions, social class, social community, social movements connected to work, unemployment and the unemployed, divisions within the working class. However, studying work and employment relations within management schools is core business; the same cannot be said for sociology departments.

In the UK at least, the fragmentation genie is unlikely to be put back in the sociology bottle. The wider range of contributions and debates reflects this and is, in many ways, a positive feature of LPT. Whilst, undoubtedly, more needs to be done to feed back more of the workplace research and middle range theorizing into the disciplinary foundations of sociology, is interdisciplinarity really the main threat to a healthy sociology of work? We think not. The real problem has been the marginalization of work and the employment relationship in mainstream social theory, which is reflected in its weak position in most sociology departments. Oddly enough, this division has been reproduced within labour process debates, with the orthodox majority rejecting the post-modernist attempt to construct an identity-based analysis that is rooted in organization theory rather than the employment relationship (see the debate between Thompson and O'Doherty in Alvesson et al., 2009 and Marks and Thompson, this volume). The latter group now put their energies into Critical Management Studies.

Whatever the undoubted limitations of its contribution to the discipline, LPT is rooted in classical sociology, particularly in Marx and Weber. To reiterate an earlier point, LPT alone cannot be the engine for a reinvigorated sociology of work. But with its orientation to the dynamics of capitalist political economy, it is well placed to engage with new and welcome perspectives in economic sociology, as well as maintaining friendly relations with others who continue with a focus on the multiple layers of work and the employment relation. In expanding its conceptualization of labour power, LPT is bringing something distinctive to a new and enhanced sociology of work that is being developed in and beyond Britain.

Note

1   This is an abridged version of a paper by Thompson and Smith (2009) 'Labour Power and Labour Process: Contesting the Marginality of the Sociology of Work', *Sociology*, 43(5):—913–930. We are grateful to the publishers, Sage, for permission to reproduce in this form. Whilst that paper was written for a special issue of *Sociology* on the decline of the sociology of work in Britain, and our perspective on this from within the labour process tradition in the UK that we have both been part of for more than two decades, we thought this was sufficiently focused on contemporary themes addressed in this book for it to act as an opening overview chapter. Abridging from the original paper has been limited to removing text specifically related to the special issue, but this has been 10 per cent at most. We have inserted some references to themes picked up by chapters within this book, but have avoided adding any additional text as this would detract from the character of an abridged paper. The focus of the paper has a British orientation, given the aim of special issue, but we think the British debate does have some wider applications to developments of the labour process more generally, and we make these linkages in the chapter – although it was not the intention of the paper to be in any sense comparative or international in an explicit way.

REFERENCES

Ackroyd, S. and Thompson, P. (1999) *Organizational Misbehaviour.* London: Sage.
Altmann, N. and Deiß, M. (1998) 'Productivity by Systemic Rationalization: Good Work, Bad Work, No Work?', *Economic and Industrial Democracy*, 19(1): 137–60.
Baldamus, W. (1961) *Efficiency and Effort: An Analysis of Industrial Administration.* London: Tavistock.
Barker, J. R. (1993) 'Tightening the Iron Cage: Concertive Control in Self-Managing Teams', *Administrative Science Quarterly*, 38: 408–37.
Bauman, Z. (1998) *Work, Consumerism and the New Poor,* Cambridge: Polity.
Bechhofer, F., Goldthorpe, J., Lockwood, D. and Platt, J. (1968) *The Affluent Worker: Political Attitudes and Behaviour,* New York: Cambridge University Press.
Beck, U. (2000) *The Brave New World of Work,* Cambridge: Polity.
Beynon, H. (1973) *Working for Ford.* Harmondsworth: Penguin.
Beynon, H., Grimshaw, D., Rubery, J. and Ward, K. (ed.) (2002) *Managing Employment Change,* Oxford: Oxford University Press.
Bolton, S. (2005) *Emotion Management,* London: Palgrave.
Bradley, H. (2000) *Myths at Work,* London: Blackwell.

▶

▶

Braverman, H. (1974) *Labor and Monopoly Capital,* New York: Monthly Review Press.

Brown, R. (1992) *Understanding Industrial Organizations,* London: Routledge.

Bulmer, M. (ed.) (1975) *Working Class Images of Society,* London: Routledge and Kegan Paul.

Burawoy, M. (1979) *Manufacturing Consent: Changes in the Labor Process under Monopoly Capitalism,* Chicago, IL: Chicago University Press.

Burchell, B., Ladipo, D. and Wilkinson, F. (eds) (2002) *Job Insecurity and Work Intensification,* London: Routledge.

Callaghan, G. and Thompson, P. (2002) 'We Recruit Attitude: The Selection and Shaping of Call Centre Labour', *Journal of Management Studies,* 39(2), 233–54.

Cappelli, P. (1999) *The New Deal at Work,* Boston, MA: Harvard Business School Press.

Castells, M. (1996) *The Rise of the Network Society: The Information Age Economy, Society and Culture,* vol. 1, Oxford: Blackwell.

Cavendish, R. (1982) *Women on the Line,* London: Routledge.

Crompton, R. (2006) *Employment and the Family,* Cambridge: Cambridge University Press.

Crompton, R. (2008) *Class and Stratification,* 3rd edition, Cambridge: Polity.

Delbridge, R. (1998) *Life on the Line in Contemporary Manufacturing,* Oxford: Oxford University Press.

Despres, C. and Hiltrop, J. (1995) 'Human Resource Management in the Knowledge Age: Current Practice and Perspectives on the Future', *Employee Relations,* 17(1): 9–23.

Ditton, J. (1977) *Part-Time Crime: An Ethnography of Fiddling and Pilferage,* London: Macmillan.

Edwards, P. K. (1990) 'Understanding Conflict in the Labour Process: The Logic and Autonomy of Struggle', in Knights, D. and Willmott, H. (eds) *Labour Process Theory,* London: Macmillan.

Edwards, P. K. and Scullion, H. (1982) *The Social Organization of Industrial Conflict: Control and Resistance in the Workplace,* Oxford: Blackwell.

Edwards, R. (1979) *Contested Terrain: The Transformation of the Workplace in the Twentieth Century,* London: Heinemann.

Eldridge, J. E. T., Cressey, P. and MacInnes, J. (1991) *Industrial Sociology and Economic Crisis,* Hemel Hempstead: Harvester Wheatsheaf.

Elger, T. and Smith, C. (2005) *Assembling Work: Remaking Factory Regimes in Japanese Multinationals in Britain,* New York: Oxford University Press.

Elger, T. and Smith, C. (eds) (1994) *Global Japanization? The Transnational Transformation of the Labour Process,* London: Routledge.

Felstead, A. and Jewson, N. (2005) *In Work, At Home: Towards an Understanding of Homeworking,* London: Palgrave.

Felstead, A., Gallie, D. and Green, F. (2004) 'Job Complexity and Task Discretion: Tracking the Direction of Skills at Work in Britain', in Warhurst, C., Grugulia, I. and Keep, E. (eds) *The Skills That Matter,* London: Palgrave.

Fevre, R. (2007) 'Employment Insecurity and Social Theory: The Power of Nightmares', *Work, Employment and Society,* 21(3): 517–36.

▶

▶

Fleming, P. (2001) 'Beyond the Panopticon?', *Ephemera*, 1(2): 190–4.

Friedman, A. (1977) *Industry and Labour: Class Struggle at Work Monopoly Capitalism*, London, Macmillan.

Froud, J., Johal, S., Leaver, A. and Williams, K. (2006) *Financialization and Strategy: Narratives and Numbers*, London: Routledge.

Gorz, A. (1999) *Reclaiming Work: Beyond the Wage-Based Society*, Cambridge: Polity Press.

Graham, L. (1995) *On the Line at Subaru-Isuzu: The Japanese Model and the American Worker*, Ithaca, NY: ILR Press.

Green, F. (2001) 'It's Been a Hard Day's Night: The Concentration and Intensification of Work in Late Twentieth-Century Britain', *British Journal of Industrial Relations*, 39(1): 53–80.

Green, F. (2006) *Demanding Work: The Paradox of Job Quality in the Affluent Economy*. Princeton, NJ: Princeton University Press.

Heery, E. and Salmon, J. (eds) (2000) *The Insecure Workforce*, London: Routledge.

Henwood, D. (2005) *After the New Economy*, New York: The New Press.

Hochschild, A.R. (1983) *The Managed Heart: Commercialisation of Human Feeling*. London: University of California Press.

Hodson, R. (1995) 'Worker Resistance: An Underdeveloped Concept in the Sociology of Work', *Economic and Industrial Democracy*, 16(1): 79–110.

Hodson, R. (2001) *Dignity at Work*, Cambridge: Cambridge University Press.

Hogarth, T., Hasluck, C., Pierre, G., Winterbotham, M. and Vivian, D. (2000) *Work-Life Balance 2000: Basline Study of Work-Life Balance Practices in Great Britain: Summary Report*, London: Department for Education and Employment.

Hyman, R. (1982) 'Whatever Happened to Industrial Sociology?', in David Dunkerley and Graeme Salaman (eds) *International Yearbook of Organization Studies 1981*, London: Routledge and Kegan Paul.

Ingham, G. (1996) 'The "New Economic Sociology"' *Work, Employment and Society*, 10(3): 549–64.

Knights, D. and Willmott, H. (1989) 'Power and Subjectivity at Work: From Degradation to Subjugation in Social Relations', *Sociology* 23(4): 535–58.

Konzelmann, S. J. and Forrant, R. (2002) 'Creative Work in Destructive Markets', in Burchell, B., Deakin, S., Michie, J. and Rubery, J. (eds) *Systems of Production: Markets, Organization and Performance*, London: Routledge.

Lash, S. and Urry, J. (1994) *Economies of Signs and Space*, London: Sage Publications.

Lazonick, W. and O'Sullivan, M. (2000) 'Maximising Shareholder Value: A New Ideology for Corporate Governance', *Economy and Society*, 29(1): 13–35.

Littler, C. R. (1982) *The Development of the Labor Process in Capitalist Societies*, London: Heinemann.

Lloyd, C. and Payne, J. (2006) 'Goodbye to All That? A Critical Re-Evaluation of the Role of the High Performance Work Organization within the UK Skills Debate', *Work, Employment & Society*, 20(1): 151–65.

Mars, G. (1982) *Cheats at Work: An Anthropology of Workplace Crime*, London: Counterpoint.

▶

▶

McGovern, P., Hill, S., Mills, C. and White, M. (2007) *Market, Class and Employment*, Oxford: Oxford University Press.

McKinlay, A. and Taylor, P. (1996) 'Power, Surveillance and Resistance inside the Factory of the Future', in Acker, P., Smith, C. and Smith, P. (eds) *The New Workplace and Trade Unionism*, London: Routledge.

Nichols, T. and Armstrong, P. (1976) *Workers Divided*, Glasgow: Fontana.

Nichols, T. and Beynon, H. (1977) *Living With Capitalism*, London: Routledge and Kegan.

Nolan, P. and Wood, S. (2003) 'Mapping the Future of Work', Special Edition of *British Journal of Industrial Relations*, 41(2): 165–74.

Pahl, R. E. (ed.) (1988) *On Work: Historical, Comparative and Theoretical Approaches*, Oxford: Blackwell.

Pakulski, J. and Waters, M. (1996) *The Death of Class*, London: Sage.

Parker, M. and Slaughter, J. (1988) *Choosing Sides: Unions and the Team Concept*, Boston, MA: South End Press.

Pettinger, L., Parry, J., Taylor, R. and Glucksmann, M. (eds) (2005) *A New Sociology of Work?* Oxford: Blackwell.

Piore, M. J. and Sabel, C. F. (1984) *The Second Industrial Divide: Possibilities for Prosperity*, New York: Basic Books.

Pollert, A. (1981) *Girls, Wives, Factory Lives*, London: Macmillan.

Reed, M. (1992) *The Sociology of Organisations*, London: Harvester.

Rinehart, J., Huxley, C. and Robertson, D. (1997) *Just Another Car Factory?: Lean Production and Its Discontents*, Ithaca, NY and London: ILR Press.

Salaman, G. (1986) *Working*, Chichester: Ellis Horwood.

Sewell, G. (1998) 'The Discipline of Teams: The Control of Team-Based Industrial Work through Electronic and Peer Surveillance', *Administrative Science Quarterly*, 43: 406–69.

Smith C., Daskalaki, M., Elger, T. and Brown, D. (2004) 'Labour Turnover and Management Retention Strategies in New Manufacturing Plants', *International Journal of Human Resource Management*, 15(2): 365–90.

Smith, C. (2006) 'The Double Indeterminacy of Labour Power: Labour Effort and Labour Mobility', *Work, Employment and Society*, 20(2): 389–402.

Strangleman, T. (2005) 'Sociological Futures and the Sociology of Work', *Sociological Research Online* 10(4), URL (consulted June 2009): http://www.socresonline.org.uk/10/4/strangleman.html.

Taylor, P. and Bain, P. (2005) 'India Calling to the Far Away Towns: The Call Centre Labour Process and Globalisation', *Work, Employment and Society*, 19(2): 261–82.

Taylor, P. and Bain, P. (2007) 'Reflections on the Call Centre – a Reply to Glucksman', *Work, Employment and Society*, 21(2): 349–62.

Thompson, P. (1989) *The Nature of Work, 2nd ed.*, London: Macmillan.

Thompson, P. (1990) 'Crawling from the Wreckage: The Labour Process and the Politics of Production', in David Knights and Hugh Willmott (eds) *Labour Process Theory*, London: Macmillan.

Thompson, P. (2003) 'Disconnected Capitalism: Or Why Employers Can't Keep Their Side of the Bargain', *Work, Employment and Society*, 17(2): 359–78.

▶

►

Thompson, P. and O'Doherty, M. (2009) 'Debating Labor Process Theory and Critical Management Studies', in Alvesson, M., Bridgman, T. and Willmott, H. (eds) *The Oxford Handbook of Critical Management Studies*, Oxford: Oxford University Press.

Thompson, P., Warhurst, C. and Callaghan, G. (2000) 'Human Capital or Capitalising on Humanity? Knowledge, Skills and Competencies in Interactive Service Work', in Pritchard, C., Hull, R., Chumer, M., and Willmott, H. (eds) *Managing Knowledge: Critical Investigations of Work and Learning*, London: Macmillan.

Warhurst, C. and Thompson, P. (2006) 'Mapping Knowledge in Work: Proxies or Practices?' *Work, Employment and Society*, 20(4): 787–800.

Warhurst, C., Grugulis, I. and Keep, E. (eds) (2004) *The Skills that Matter.* Houndmills: Palgrave.

Warhurst, C., Nickson, D., Witz, A. and Cullen, A. (2000) 'Aesthetic Labour in Interactive Service Work: Some Case Study Evidence from the "New Glasgow"', *Services Industries Journal*, 20(3): 1–18.

Westwood, S. (1984) *All Day Every Day: Factory and Family in the Making of Women's Lives*, London: Pluto Press.

Wolkowitz, C. (2006) *Bodies at Work*, London: Sage.

Developing Labour Process Analysis: Themes from Industrial Sociology and Future Directions

2

Paul Edwards

Philip Larkin famously and ironically declared that sexual intercourse began in 1963. Compare this with the following two statements, presumably intended without irony.

> [Study of resistance started] with the Labour Process analyses of worker resistance in the 1970s. Here, the antecedents of workplace resistance were derived from essentialist expressions of class-consciousness and the outcome of a capitalist mode of production. This [was an] 'all or nothing' view of resistance, as acts and behaviours, driven purely by class conflict. (Thomas and Davies, 2005a: 711–12)

> We aim to break out of the dualistic debate of 'compliance with' versus 'resistance to', to offer a more generative understanding of resistance at the micro-level. ... Analysis of resistance has tended to focus on reactions by a homogenous and genderless body to forms of control imposed upon it, thus reducing individuals to empirically and structurally, or discursively, determined phenomena. (Thomas and Davies, 2005b: 683, 685)

Similar themes emerge in the work of Fleming and Spicer (2007) among others. If these statements were true, we would have to reach a depressing conclusion about the 'labour process debate', for it would have begun only in the 1970s, would have taken a plainly unsatisfactory view of the nature of workplace relations, and would have needed rescuing by those offering an alternative point of view grounded in post-modern or post-structuralist positions. They are, however, either (a) untrue, or (b) statements with which 'labour process theory' would readily agree, for example, that compliance and resistance cannot be rigidly separated. This point has been made by many authors (Ackroyd and Thompson, 1999; Thompson, 1990; Thompson and Ackroyd, 1995), and it is not substantiated in detail here. As Friedman (2004) shows, much post-structural work has a straw man picture of labour process analysis: it attributes positions to authors that they do not hold, or it rediscovers what they in fact said, or both.

Just one theme will be highlighted: the fact that many of the 'new' points made by critics of labour process analysis were well established in industrial sociology. The purpose of labour process analysis was to remove some of the deficiencies of industrial sociology while retaining its key insights. The critics misunderstand this, and end up in many ways where industrial sociology started. No effort will be made here to explain why the critics make such repeated errors; Armstrong and Lilley (2008) address this question.

The chapter begins by recovering some themes from industrial sociology and showing how labour process writers built on them. The main purpose of the chapter is to suggest how labour process analysis can be developed further. This is done in the following four sections. The conclusion draws together the implications with some remarks on concrete research design issues.

Industrial sociology and the labour process

Two of the labour process debate's triumvirate, Braverman and Burawoy, were very clear about the industrial sociology that preceded their work and about its limitations, as indeed was the other leading theorist of the 1970s, Richard Hyman, though for unclear reasons his work never seems to have been included in the debate. The third of the triumvirate, Richard Edwards, paid less attention to this heritage. Burawoy (1979), for example, engaged constructively and respectfully with the work of writers such as Lupton (1963), Gouldner (1955) and, of course, Roy (1952, 1953, 1954), while Hyman (1972, 1975) drew extensively on a very wide reading of the relevant literature to develop an alternative view. Their point was to take some themes recognized in industrial sociology and to deepen the analysis.

Industrial sociology was strong on the specifics of workplace situations. Gouldner (1955), for example, compared what would now be called resistance among miners and surface workers in a gypsum mine. He explained higher levels among the former in terms of the technology of the workplace and the resulting state of worker-manager relations. A different, and less technologically driven, strand asked about 'restriction of effort' – plainly a form of 'resistance' – and sought its origins in work group dynamics (Lupton, 1963). Conflict was also plainly well known, and analysed without treating it as some fixed category. The works of Gouldner and of Lupton are very clear on this point, for they relate workplace behaviour to the complex and contradictory nature of workplace regimes, as has been explained repeatedly (e.g. Edwards, 1988).

As for the point about 'homogeneous and genderless' workers, there is an element of truth here in that the focus tended to be on male-dominated occupations, with the explanation turning on technology rather than gender. Lupton (1963) is the most interesting example here, for he studied women as well as men and considered, and rejected, the argument that the differences that he observed could be explained in terms of gender. His explanation was that women in one of his male-dominated cases behaved much as did the men, and that in the other, now female-dominated, case men had formerly been more prominent and had behaved as the women now did. This was not a very satisfactory approach, for it reduced each factor to a single dimension and did not ask how gender might interact with other influences (Edwards, 1986). It nonetheless did not treat workers as homogeneous. Moreover, it compared cases and sought causal analysis, an approach that informed much similar work of the time (e.g. Brown, 1973) and one that has been abandoned by the post-structuralists.

Such work produced clear insights, and it was also possible to show how these built on each other, for example, in the refinement of the concept of 'restriction' and improved analysis of its causes (Edwards, 1988; Lupton, 1963). What concerned writers such as Burawoy and Hyman was that the analysis remained at the level of particular cases: the existence of conflict was assumed and not demonstrated, and there was no effort to relate it to underlying features of the organization of work in capitalism (see, notably, Hyman, 1989). In seeking a deeper analysis, they did not start from Marxist categories and generate some crude model of workplace conflict as being driven by class-consciousness. They aimed to use these categories to offer a deeper account of empirical observations.

The post-structuralists have drawn attention to certain important issues such as the negotiation of identity and the ways in which workplace regimes are constituted. They have not, however, replaced labour process analysis except the plainly inadequate form which exists only in their imaginings. In some ways, moreover, they have retreated from the concerns of industrial sociology, which set out to explain why workplace behaviour took the form that it did through comparative study; such causal and explanatory analysis seems to have been largely abandoned. The treatment of 'contesting the corporation' by Fleming and Spicer (2007), for example, could embrace the ways in which consumer and green movements and anti-globalization protesters have challenged modern capitalism. But these authors focus in practice on workers' struggles, and very micro-level ones at that. They also lack a boundary to show how far these relate to the employment relationship and how far they are part of people's wider creation of identities, in which the workplace is no more than a stage. Consider their analysis of sexuality. This discusses the various ways in which call centre workers related to managers and colleagues in sexual ways. But do these ways pertain to the employment relationship? In some respects, they do. Thus, Fleming and Spicer show that management in the firm used a culture of freedom and fun to enhance control over workers. But – even if we leave aside issues as to the weight of evidence here and how far this practice is generic to all firms or is in some way distinctive to the context studied – it is not clear how this linkage between management and sexuality is viewed. Other aspects of behaviour may have no implications for how workers relate to managers.

Perhaps most strikingly, post-structural discussion shows little interest in causal analysis in the senses of either tracing some feature of the workplace to context or explaining variation between workplaces. Fleming and Spicer do not say why freedom and fun characterized the workplace studied or consider how this workplace might differ from others in terms of the organization of work. The rest of this chapter attempts to say what such analysis should look like.

Boundary of the labour process

We need a way to demarcate the object of inquiry of labour process analysis. The solution is to treat the employment relationship as to do with the means by which labour power is translated into labour. Braverman (1974) and those who debated his work initially were clear that the labour process is that part of the mode of production in which workers' productive capacity is deployed in order to produce use-values and at the same time surplus value; there was an interest in the nature of the valorization process and in the dynamics of struggle. Without some delimitation of this kind, analysis becomes excessively broad. To avoid covering everything, the labour process needs to be seen as that activity in which the capacity to work is turned into concrete labour, together with the relevant relations between managers and workers. It thus embraces the effort-reward bargain of industrial sociology, with this bargain being seen as part of a struggle over the terms of exploitation. Worker identity and other issues are relevant to the extent that they affect the terms of the struggle, but they are not a constituent part of the analysis in their own right.

Various aspects of worker characteristics are inserted into this relationship. As Lupton found, in some circumstances religious affiliation affects the relationship directly, whereas in others it does not. It is thus possible to consider what dimensions of sexuality have implications, and what do not. Rather than treating sexuality in an undifferentiated way, we can ask when and why it enters struggle around the employment relationship. As such scholars as Pollert (1981) and Westwood (1984) showed, sexual banter can be a way for female workers to establish distance from managers and to mock their authority. We can then ask how far, in these specific situations, this acted to sustain some distinct strategy of struggle (e.g. demonstrating collective solidarity and thus making managers nervous of exerting authority) and how far it was merely a form of accommodation. We can then ask about the meaning of such banter in other settings. We would, for example, expect the style of the relevant relationships in call centres to differ from that in factories.

Both use-value and exchange value are important. One concomitant of this distinction is that worker resistance is not reduced to a narrow economistic struggle over the price of labour power. Workers produce use-value as well as surplus value, and they take pride in their work. As Friedman (2004) stresses, a sense of justice and fairness is an important driver of behaviour: once some boundary of unfairness is breached, formerly quiescent workers may engage in collective protest – a theme, of course, clear in Gouldner (1955). Workplace struggles are thus about the meaning and value of work as well as wages, though, as many Marxists stress, the functioning of capitalist markets makes it hard to sustain arguments about the former, as workers learn the 'rules of the game' and are reduced to economistic struggles by the terrain on which they find themselves (Hobsbawm, 1964: chapter 17).

A focus on the labour process and valorization may help to avoid an undue interest in the specific concept of resistance and whether it is (still) important. Such a question is, arguably, unanswerable: it is not as though in some mystical past there was a mass of 'resistant' workers (and indeed a great of industrial sociology specified why there was not); there is no way of comparing evidence in a reliable way; and whether any given act is a case of resistance requires careful scrutiny. On the last point, going absent, for example, may be a conscious act of hostility to management; it may be a pragmatic taking of benefits on offer; it may reflect 'excess' conformity if physical and emotional exhaustion make the worker unfit to work; and so on (Edwards and Scullion, 1982). And absence will have different implications for fellow workers (shared expression of resistance, a cause of lateral conflict because those at work have extra work to do...) and for managers (a cost if work cannot be reorganized easily, or something relatively costless if other workers cover the relevant duties).

The solution is to look at the organization of the labour process and the way in which a frontier of control is created and sustained. Thus workers may not 'resist' but may obtain benefits, for example, through legal rights. Thus Burawoy (1983) notes that workplace regimes are located in national contexts and that states take different views of the regulation of the labour process.

To take a simple example, in the UK since 1971 there have been legal protections against unfair dismissal and indeed the number of issues on which employees can bring claims against employers has risen from 1 to 90. The operation of the rights is plainly far from automatic, but the terms of the labour process have changed. We thus need to look at workplace regimes and how they produce packages of costs and benefits for workers, and not seek out resistance for its own sake.

This does not mean that the focus is solely on direct producers, but it does mean that distinct tools are needed to understand different groups. To take the key instance of managerial jobs, these are different from the jobs of direct producers because they are defined fundamentally in terms of an agency relationship with capital (Armstrong, 1989). Armstrong underlines contradictions in the agency relationship between controlling the agent through performance management and allowing trust and discretion. These contradictions might seem to be identical to those of control and autonomy that pertain to 'real' labour processes. But for Armstrong they arise within an agency relationship, and there are cases where management has not been deskilled; in his view, the agency approach can explain this while alternatives cannot.

A stronger argument would certainly be needed to sustain the point. Armstrong asks why, if the result of the organization of managerial and non-managerial labour is the same, there is any point making the distinction. His answer is that it is not always the same: managerial work is not necessarily 'deskilled' even when this is technically feasible (1989: 320). This seems a rather weak answer, since not all *non-managerial* labour is deskilled. An answer more consistent with Armstrong's analysis turns on the nature of the agency relationship. There is thus evidence that 'management' retains its core supervisory nature; in other words, management is about the control of subordinates and not just about the technical coordination of work (Hales, 2005Similarly, Watson (2001) shows that middle managers recognize their distance from shop-floor employees even though they are also aware that they are removed from higher corporate decision-making. The wider theoretical point is that managers are agents of capital, and that they gain from this to the extent that they can move closer to the principals but lose if their role as agents can be performed in some other way. Thompson (2005) has restated the agency view of managers and used it to address some of the contradictions in the management process. To some extent, managers such as those studied by Watson share interests with workers, in that both groups' jobs are dependent on decisions taken by more senior managers well away from local production units. But in other respects they do not: managers' interests are driven by their ability to meet, as agents of other managers, their performance targets by controlling the work of others; and they have much clearer means to move further up the hierarchy than do those whom they control.

For present purposes, the key is that a labour process perspective can say some distinctive things about management, and that we need to understand the labour process, not as work in general, but as a form of human activity that takes a particular character under capitalism. Here, managers and workers meet in a relationship of 'structured antagonism', and they define themselves in this relationship: there can be no manager without a worker, and the basics of social class lie in the dynamics and contradictions of the relationship (Armstrong, 1989, 1993). Managerial work becomes problematized in terms of its connection to the generation of use-values and surplus value. Is it the case, for example, that changing the role of the supervisor to that of coach and facilitator alters relationships with workers? Such a shift can be seen as one that stresses use-values (achieving a productive task) over surplus value (controlling workers) though the latter will of course have to be secured by other means. This does not mean that (1) the analyst directly wishes to place all behaviour in either the use-value or the surplus value box or (2) some view is taken as to what a use-value really is. Let us suppose that the supervisor just imagined works is a weapons factory, and that becoming a coach means that workers are trained better and that weapons are produced more efficiently. We need to treat efficiency here in its technical sense of producing more output for a given set of inputs. The production process is coordinated in a way that is technologically superior to its previous form. Workers are not working any harder. The argument does not necessarily mean that weapons are inherently useful. It simply means that under current social and political arrangements, there is demand for these products, that they have a use under these arrangements and that there are more and less efficient ways of providing the products. That deals with point (2). As for point (1), the idea of the two types of values is an analytical one, which allows us to ask about the ways in which work is configured and the changing composition of jobs. For example, what is the balance between the activities or control and coordination among a group of managers, and how is the agency relationship managed (e.g. in terms of performance targets or a reliance on other mechanisms such as trust)?

A labour process analysis thus places clear boundaries around the object of inquiry. It also has a distinct way of analysing the relationships of workers and managers. It does not thereby reduce everything to the fundamentals of class relationships or read off concrete behaviour from these relationships; it sees these fundamentals as underpinning the nature of workplace relations, but the specifics of any particular workplace regime reflect many other factors and contingencies.

Categorization of behaviour and explanation of variation

We then need some categories of different types of workplace regime. Mumby (2005) dismisses one attempt – that of Hodson (1991) – to identify types of worker behaviour as tending towards the sin of reification. That is, such types reduce empirical complexity to formal categories. He seems to prefer to stress the deeply embedded connections between control and resistance. But there is a deep irony here. If we abandon categories and types of behaviour, we end up discovering particular instances of resistance, or cynicism, or whatever, and we end up imposing categories chosen by the analyst – which is just what the post-structuralist claims to avoid. Hodson's types may be useful, or not, but they aim to capture the range of experience within a distinct analytical framework. As Gabriel (1999: 186) had noticed, a focus on organizational control as a 'defining feature of post-modernity has tended to obscure the possibility that different organizations employ different strategies of control'.

These strategies can be placed in a wider explanatory framework that formally characterizes the relations between capital and labour and then addresses the causal conditions generating different positions (Bélanger and Edwards, 2007). There is necessarily a limit to this endeavour, for we lack details on published cases, and information is missing on enough cases of different kinds to be decisive. But progress has clearly been made. This mode of analysis is different from that of Hodson (1991, 2001) in treating workplace regimes as complex wholes rather than reducing their features to variables (Edwards and Bélanger, 2008). It thus tries to respect the richness of cases while also developing a causal account.

At this level of the point of production one may wish to contrast different types of worker ideology as Hodson (1991) did. The point of this is not to reify behaviour, but to deploy some ways of capturing variation, rather than simply finding out the essence of worker behaviour anywhere. The categories will depend on the topic at hand. Thus Mars (1982) made very effective use of a different set of four categories, Burawoy (1983) offers another set of four types of workplace regime, and so on. Now, any of these categories can be interrogated for their logic and completeness. But they certainly take us quite a long way. The reader of Mars will have a much clearer view of different types of 'fiddles' and the conditions generating them than would have been possible without these analytical ideal types.

Similar moves can be identified in more recent analyses of contemporary work, notably that of service employees. Understanding of this work began with accounts of the distinct nature of the service encounter, and has more recently identified different types of service work. Frenkel (2005), for example, speaks of mass service and mass customized types of work. Related to this, there is now a huge amount of work on call centres, which is increasingly differentiating types of such work according to the market segment in which the firm is engaged and hence different levels of pay and different degrees of worker autonomy (Batt, Holman and Holtgrewe, 2009).

Once we have categories of types of work situation, we can begin to ask about causal influences on them. Mars (1982) provided an extended and in many ways exemplary explanation of the four patterns of 'fiddle' that he identified, which turned on the structure of the work tasks. We would also now want to give more attention to managerial strategies and the operation of the capitalist economy. Thus one of Mars's types was the 'wolf' fiddle, practised by gangs of workers with a strong sense of collective identity; dockers were his archetypal example. They were able to sustain their position because of a set of factors: their work was hard to monitor; they worked in gangs; and it was hard for management to find substitute labour. Containerization of dock work has challenged all these conditions and has led to major redefinitions of the job of a docker. This development in turn reflects competition between ports, the role of the state in allowing work that in many countries was legally defined as dockers' work to be carried out by other workers, often well away from ports themselves, and so on (Turnbull and Weston, 1993). Certain sorts of fiddle may have been squeezed out, but this has not removed workers' collective organization: international coordination can provide an effective challenge to changed work practices (Turnbull, 2006). In short, changing structural conditions shape events within the politics and production, and at this level people make choices as to how to respond to these conditions, and out of the resulting actions, bargains and compromises a new pattern of workplace politics emerges. We might also wish to apply Mars's method to other features of a financialized economy. Thus Mars spoke of 'hawks', who are powerful people who act individually to secure benefits for themselves; the many scandals of the financial system since 2007 provide neat illustrations, and also means to test Mars's explanation of fiddle-proneness.

A related issue is the placing of a work regime in its organizational and economic context. As Thompson (2003) argues, we need to locate a workplace in corporate strategies and the development of the economy as a whole. A call for multiple levels of analysis is increasingly common, and rightly so given the pressures of globalization and the way in which market rationality impinges on the workplace. Some of the early studies, such as those of Friedman (1977), were explicitly concerned with the historical evolution of forms of labour and the connections between workplace practices and competitive conditions. There is, though, an issue of practical research design: if we are interested in the dynamics of workplace relations, we need a relatively micro focus, albeit one that is sensitive to material conditions – and it is reasonable to ask, as argued below, that researchers give explicit attention to these conditions. But a 'complete' placing of a workplace regime in the circuit of capital would be too much to ask.

A reasonable approach is to pursue causal influences as far as needed for the task at hand. Thus, Delbridge (1998) argued that the pattern of workplace relations that he observed at 'Valleyco' reflected the fact that this factory was a supplier to others and was therefore under distinct kinds of customer pressure. Studies of small firms have also addressed how 'exogenous' influences such as ethnicity and family shape the labour process (Ram, Jones and Sanghera, 2001). They show that co-ethnic ties influence the effort bargain by establishing relations of mutual dependence and moderating managerial control. Now, such research might be read as saying that ethnic and family identities are key, and that studies privileging the labour process are in error. But such a view makes sense only if one operates without analytical distinctions and wishes to treat social life as undifferentiated. If the research question is people's sense of identity and meaning, then the intersections of class, race, and gender are central. But if we are concerned with the production of surplus at the point of production, then gender, ethnicity and so on can be treated as factors that shape particular labour processes but which are analytically separate from the labour process itself. Future research might take this theme further. From the Delbridge example, one might wish to explore supply chain effects more directly, and also to compare workplaces in different locations in a supply chain. From the ethnicity example, the obvious point is to try to compare otherwise similar workplaces with differing ethnic mixes. As recent research in this tradition has argued, there is the danger of essentialism in treating ethnic categories as fixed; they are in fact variable and open to interpretation (Jones and Ram, 2007). The analytical need, therefore, is to consider to what extent external factors impinge on the workplace and how far they are negotiable by workplace actors.

Effects of worker behaviour

It is important to continue to ask explicitly about the implications of worker activity. This is one important qualification to Ackroyd and Thompson's (1999) insistence on the continued presence of worker 'misbehaviour'. As well as showing that it exists, and that managerial claims to secure control and commitment are empirically hollow and conceptually impossible, we need to continue to ask what it does. Does it represent Burawoyian consent to one's own exploitation and even if it does, what might the practical implications be? Burawoy's workers (in mid-1970s US manufacturing) were doing reasonably well in having secure and relatively well-paying jobs. At the time, their interests may well have lain – in the sense of the balance of costs and benefits of alternative lines of action – in continuing as they were. We now know with the benefit of hindsight that many threats were on the horizon, and it is a perfectly proper question to ask whether these might have been anticipated and what if anything might have been done about it. It is also analytically important to ask how patterns of behaviour reproduce existing relationships. Thus, high rates of quitting in low-wage and insecure jobs tend to undermine any worker collectivity and, along with other factors, to reproduce this form of labour process (Edwards, Sengupta and Tsai, 2009).

In other circumstances, worker action has clear effects. Among the most common noted in labour process studies is some kind of tacit disobedience that means that a managerial initiative fails to achieve its ends. Another is the exploitation of space to bend rules. Thus call centre studies reveal workers who spend longer than they are supposed to on calls (Korczynski, 2002). This gives them some personal satisfaction and is not necessarily consciously 'resistance' against 'management'. It may also have the result – in an echo of Roy's (1953, 1954) finding that workers break formal rules to achieve substantive objectives – of improving customer service. It is within such ambiguities that 'resistance' takes its meaning.

It is also important to note longer-term effects. Ackroyd and Thompson (1999) focus on specific and small-scale acts of misbehaviour, as do Noon and Blyton (2002) in their discussion of five survival strategies. These acts may in themselves come to shape how a workplace regime is defined. This was the burden of many of the classic studies, which demonstrated that there was an established space for workers that managers attempted to change at their peril. Such clearly established custom and practice may be less common than it was, but it illustrates the wider point that socially constructed expectations shape the extent to which managerial objectives can be met. Overt 'resistance' may be limited, but, as the limited effectiveness of numerous managerial initiatives shows, management intentions are often not realized. The reasons turn on the contradictions inherent in the organization of work: establishing control while eliciting consent, meeting customer 'needs' while also hitting financial targets, and so on.

Beyond specific acts that come to define workplace regimes there are more deliberate efforts to alter the terms of the labour process. These embrace bargaining over pay and conditions, strikes, and at the extreme quasi-revolutionary protests. Such acts, or the threat of them, can come to define a certain terrain of workplace relations. Terrains cannot necessarily be ordered in terms of whether they are better or worse from the worker's (or the manager's) point of view. Gallie (1978: 300–17), in his classic comparison of French and British oil refineries, showed that in some respects – for example, shift work and manning levels – the French workers were the more militant, but also that French management retained much greater freedom of action than did its British counterparts. In some circumstances, an ordering may be possible if the frontier of control is unambiguously more in favour of workers in one place than in another. But it may also be that workers who have won workplace battles thereby expose themselves to counterattack, and so on. The point is that we need to address such issues directly if the significance of misbehaviour, resistance, and so forth is to be grasped.

Comparative analysis

The key future development, which draws together the preceding three themes, is comparative analysis. The most effective studies have always been comparative in at least one of several senses: direct comparison within the same study (Lupton, Gouldner, Mars, Gallie); comparison of one study with specifically comparable data from other studies (Burawoy); or a use of a new study in the light of previous expectations in the literature (e.g. Ditton's (1979) study of the control of time by workers paid flat rate, taking as its foil evidence of the practices of workers paid by the piece). As noted above, Hodson (2001) and his collaborators have drawn together workplace ethnographies into a comparative data set, now numbering 204 cases. Yet this exercise can reveal as much about what is not known as what can in fact be gleaned from the ethnographies (Edwards and Bélanger, 2008). It has also been possible, in more discursive fashion, to extract from studies of teams or Total Quality Management some factors that seem to explain patterns of variation (Edwards, Geary and Sisson, 2002. But more planned and systematic comparisons would have obvious benefits of generating directly comparable data. The logic of Qualitative Comparative Analysis (QCA) (Ragin, 2008) may be of use here. The core of the logic is to treat cases as wholes and to ask what sets of conditions are sufficient or necessary to produce a given result (say, success in teamwork). QCA's development in terms of fuzzy logic also allows degrees of success or whatever to be identified. Such logic may assist in asking more careful and rigorous questions than has been the practice in the past. That is, we may have an outcome in relation to teamwork, and specify the degree to which it meets certain objectives from workers' and managers' points of view; note that fuzzy logic allows explicitly for cases to be partially but not wholly within a set such as 'fully meeting managerial goals'. We can then ask about conditions that generate the results in terms of necessary and sufficient conditions. Having done this, we might find gaps or puzzles which should inform the selection of further cases; for example, if it appears to be uncertain what role a particular pattern of product market conditions plays, we can then seek out cases that vary on this dimension. QCA may not be fully applicable, for it needs modestly large numbers of cases, and data that are common across the cases – requirements that workplace studies may find hard to meet. But its underlying logic can be applied, at it may encourage researchers to generate comparable data so that workplaces can be compared directly with each other across relevant dimensions.

Comparative analysis in this field is bound to be hard because the phenomena of interest do not vary independently of each other or in ways that are easily observable in advance. Studies of TQM have in fact found it hard to find firms that clearly 'had' or 'did not have' the relevant practice; quality principles need not go under a particular label. There is no simple solution to this issue, but sensitivity to previous studies and to likely sources of variation can give some pointers. Recent studies of call centres throw a great deal of light on this issue. A comparative study across 17 countries concludes that change is multilayered (Batt, Holman and Holtgrewe, 2009). There is, for example, commonality in terms of management organization and technology but variation at several institutional levels: coordinated market economies generally offer better jobs than liberal market economies; there is notable variation within both of these groups; and there is intra-country variation between in-house call centres and subcontractors. Yet this study relies on management respondents, and might be complemented with analyses of work experience from the employees' point of view.

Studies in this vein have made useful advances in deploying quantitative surveys within case studies of particular settings. This has been of great value in demonstrating the representativeness of the results and also in showing that claimed differences between cases are real. None the less, there are limits to the value of self-report data on such things as work intensification, and independent direct observation can also be valuable. It is, for example, common to read that performance management systems (PMS) put new pressures on workers and run counter to claims about empowerment. This is a perfectly sensible argument. But there are benefits in substantiating it in more detail. In any particular case, the exact ways in which the effect works needs demonstrating, and the extent to which the effect is real – in the sense of being substantial and affecting a significant number of workers – needs evidence. Illustrative quotations do not show just how important the effect really is. And across cases it is important to know whether all PMSs have this effect, or only some, and if the latter why.

The classic studies were able to address these issues through the presence of the researcher in the workplace for a substantial amount of time, so that it was possible to find out what 'really' happened as opposed to what respondents might report. Some were based on structured observation, as in the work of Batstone, Boraston and Frenkel (1977, 1978) and, with a different focus, the work of Blackburn and Mann (1979). Observation is time consuming and expensive, and there are also issues of access for such studies as firms become leaner and outcome-oriented. But the pay-offs are considerable and the demands on those being researched are less, in terms of time if not exposure, than is the case with survey and interview methods.

Conclusions: Role of labour process analysis

A distinctively *labour process* analysis of work needs to retain its core strengths. These include an empirical interest in the experience of work at the point of production and a theoretical concern with the contradictory relationships between capital and labour. And, in terms of method, detailed case studies and ethnographies have been, and should be, the preferred approach. Large-scale comparative surveys do not fit well with these preferences – though it certainly makes sense for them to be *informed* by labour process issues in terms of the questions that they ask.

Within the labour process tradition, I would argue, first, for more explicit comparative analysis, which can be within a country as well as being inter-nationally comparative. Second, it would be a great help if analysts took it upon themselves to collect and report key data on such things as pay levels, quit rates, local unemployment rates, and the labour market experience of employees. Third, systematic observation can reveal important information about the nature of the work task and other key issues such as the ways in which managerial controls are deployed (e.g. extent of direct supervision, frequency of reporting of data). It would also be desirable, if difficult, to observe processes such as performance appraisals. There are now useful stud-ies that give workers' self-reports of how far performance targets are agreed or imposed, and what the effects of the targets on subsequent behaviour are. But it is also desirable to have direct evidence on what goes on, how far workers talk among themselves about appraisals and develop some collect-ive norms about them, and if possible how far appraisal really shapes the effort bargain. Fourth, the time dimension is central. A question about the large number of one-off case studies that now exist naturally concerns how stable the relationships reported are. Understanding a workplace over time can surely reveal a great deal about processes of change and continuity (e.g. Ahlstrand, 1990).

As for multi-level analysis, a basic need is that the context of a workplace be described in terms of such features as the type of product, the inten-sity of competition, and the place of the workplace in the (exchange) value chain. We can then obtain some view of the causal forces at work. Just how much further one should go in developing a multi-level analysis must then surely depend on the task at hand. The danger of being too ambitious is that analysis becomes superficial. Influences from outside the workplace itself need to be traced to the extent that they are likely to shape events.

As to what might be studied, there is a huge range of choice but also challenges. Workplace sociology developed from studies of large groups of workers assembled in distinct work sites. As the character of work changes, the idea of a fixed work place also loses resonance. A solution may lie less in multi-level approaches and more in the use of multiple methods embracing interviews and systematic observation. To mention just two candidates: understanding the restructuring of work at the bottom of the labour market, in the light, for example, of migration to developed economies, is an important issue; and the nature of managerial work continues to deserve attention. On the latter, we know something of 'middle managers' but it would also be very instructive to learn more about higher levels of management, for example, how identities and loyalties are created and the way in which the agency relationship with capital is understood and played out. Sklair (2001), for example, identifies a 'transnational capitalist class' of elites in multinational companies and state agencies, though his work seems largely a hypothesis about the presence of such a class rather than detailed substantiation of its existence as an economic category, still less as a class with shared awareness and interests. It would be extremely valuable, if challenging, to analyse the work of putative members of this class, their agency relationships, their roles in planning corporate reorganizations, and so on. At the time of writing, work organized via the Centre de recherché sur la mondialisation et le travail (CRIMT: www.CRIMT.org) is taking this agenda forward, suggesting that there are important divisions within the putative class and that it is often constrained by nationality rather than being truly transnational in the sense of losing its spatial constraints.

There is some well-established research on the structures of corporate power and managerial elites that could offer some foundations here (Fidler, 1981; Scott, 1997). A less challenging study might take some occupational groups and examine their positions within management and how they define the nature of the managerial task – pursuing the agenda on these issues established by Armstrong (1993). Such a study would take the Foucauldian interest in 'knowledge' and render it in a reasonably precise way by asking about knowledge claims and how they are *sustained*, through the effective assertion of claims to knowledge and expertise, together with the relationship between these claims and the material demands of a capitalist enterprise: some claims to knowledge are more successful than others and it is important to understand why. Plainly, comparative analysis would be of central value here, for example, between groups or between similar groups in different countries. Is it the case that American managers assert their knowledge in different ways from those from other countries, and has a sense of crisis weakened such claims, or possibly reinforced them if managers are seen as having a technical competence that can be distinguished from the machinations of finance capital?

In short, the labour process debate, *qua* debate, has entailed a fair number of false starts, reinventions of wheels, and attempts to establish stark differences between perspectives where there is also common accord. It has also generated important empirical evidence and sustained critical engagement with major changes in the experience of work over many years. Analysis now needs to build on these strengths by examining workplace regimes and their costs and benefits, and placing such examination in the context of capitalism as a mode of production.

REFERENCES

Ackroyd, S. and Thompson, P. (1999) *Organizational Misbehaviour,* London: Sage.

Ahlstrand, B. (1990) *The Quest for Productivity,* Cambridge: Cambridge University Press.

Armstrong, P. (1989) 'Management, Labour Process and Agency', *Work, Employment and Society,* 3: 307–22.

Armstrong, P. (1993) 'Professional Knowledge and Social Mobility', *Work, Employment and Society,* 7: 1–22.

Armstrong, P. and Lilley, S. (2008) 'Practical Criticism and the Social Sciences of Management', *Ephemera,* 8: 353–70.

Batstone, E., Boraston, I. and Frenkel, S. (1977) *Shop Stewards in Action,* Oxford: Blackwell.

Batstone, E., Boraston, I. and Frenkel, S. (1978) *The Social Organization of Strikes,* Oxford: Blackwell.

Batt, R., Holman, D. and Holtgrewe, U. (2009) 'The Globalization of Service Work: Comparative Institutional Perspectives on Call Centers', *Industrial and Labor Relations Review,* 62: 453–89.

Bélanger, J. and Edwards, P. (2007) 'The Conditions Promoting Compromise in the Workplace', *British Journal of Industrial Relations,* 45: 713–34.

Blackburn, R. and Mann, M. (1979) *The Working Class in the Labour Market,* London: Macmillan.

Braverman, H. (1974) *Labor and Monopoly Capital,* New York: Monthly Review Press.

Brown, W. (1973) *Piecework Bargaining,* London: Heinemann.

Burawoy, M. (1979) *Manufacturing Consent,* Chicago: Chicago University Press.

Burawoy, M. (1983) *The Politics of Production,* London: Verso.

Delbridge, R. (1998) *Life on the Line in Contemporary Manufacturing,* Oxford: Oxford University Press.

Ditton, J. (1979) 'Baking Time', *Sociological Review,* 27: 157–67.

Edwards, P. (1986) *Conflict at Work,* Oxford: Blackwell.

▶

▶

Edwards, P. (1988) 'Patterns of Conflict and Accommodation', in Gallie, D. (ed.) *Employment in Britain,* Oxford: Blackwell.

Edwards, P. and Bélanger, J. (2008) 'Generalizing from Workplace Ethnographies', *Journal of Contemporary Ethnography,* 32: 291–313.

Edwards, P. and Scullion, H. (1982) *The Social Organization of Industrial Conflict,* Oxford: Blackwell.

Edwards, P., Geary, J. and Sisson, K. (2002) 'New Forms of Work Organization in the Workplace', in Murray, G. Bélanger, J., Giles, A. and Lapointe, P-A. (eds) *Work and Employment Relations in the High Performance Workplace,* London: Continuum.

Edwards, P., Sengupta, S. and Tsai, C-J. (2009) 'Managing the Low-Skills Equilibrium', *Human Resource Management Journal,* 19: 40–58.

Fidler, J. (1981) *The British Business Elite,* London: Routledge.

Fleming, P. and Spicer, A. (2007) *Contesting the Corporation,* Cambridge: Cambridge University Press.

Frenkel, S. (2005) 'Service Workers in Search of Decent Work', in Ackroyd, S. Batt, R., Thompson, P. and Tolbert, P. (eds) *The Oxford Handbook of Work and Organization,* Oxford: Oxford University Press.

Friedman, A. L. (1977) *Industry and Labour,* London: Macmillan.

Friedman, A. L. (2004) 'Strawmanning and Labour Process Analysis', *Sociology,* 38: 573–91.

Gabriel, Y. (1999) 'Beyond Happy Families', *Human Relations,* 52: 179–203.

Gallie, D. (1978) *In Search of the New Working Class,* Cambridge: Cambridge University Press.

Gouldner, A. (1955) *Patterns of Industrial Bureaucracy,* New York: Free Press.

Hales, C. (2005) 'Rooted in Supervision, Branching into Management', *Journal of Management Studies,* 42: 471–506.

Hobsbawm, E. (1964) *Labouring Men,* London: Weidenfeld and Nicolson.

Hodson, R. (1991) 'Good Soldiers, Smooth Operators and Saboteurs', *Work and Occupations,* 18: 271–90.

Hodson, R. (2001) *Dignity at Work,* Cambridge: Cambridge University Press.

Hyman, R. (1972) *Strikes,* London: Fontana.

Hyman, R. (1975) *Industrial Relations: A Marxist Introduction,* London: Macmillan.

Hyman, R. (1989) *The Political Economy of Industrial Relations,* Basingstoke: Macmillan.

Jones, T. and Ram, M. (2007) 'Re-embedding the Ethnic Business Agenda', *Work, Employment and Society,* 21: 439–57.

Korczynski, M. (2002) *Human Resource Management in Service Work,* Basingstoke: Macmillan.

Lupton, T. (1963) *On the Shop Floor,* Oxford: Pergamon.

Mars, G. (1982). *Cheats at Work,* London: Counterpoint.

Mumby, D. K. (2005) 'Theorizing Resistance on Organization Studies: a Dialectical Approach', *Management Communication Quarterly,* 19: 19–44.

Noon, M. and Blyton, P. (2002) *The Realities of Work,* 2nd edn., Basingstoke: Palgrave.

▶

▶

Pollert, A. (1981) *Girls, Wives, Factory Lives,* London: Macmillan.

Ragin, C. C. (2008) *Redesigning Social Inquiry,* Chicago: University of Chicago Press.

Ram, M., Jones, T. and Sanghera, B. (2001) 'Making the Link: Households and Small Business Activity in a Multi-ethnic Context', *Community, Work and Family,* 4: 237–52.

Roy, D. (1952) 'Quota Restriction and Goldbricking in a Machine Shop', *American Journal of Sociology,* 57: 427–42.

Roy, D. (1953) 'Work Satisfaction and Social Reward in Quota Achievement', *American Sociological Review,* 18: 507–14.

Roy, D. (1954) 'Efficiency and the "Fix"', *American Journal of Sociology,* 60: 255–66.

Scott, J. (1997) *Corporate Business and Capitalist Classes,* Oxford: Oxford University Press.

Sklair, L. (2001) *The Transnational Capitalist Class,* Oxford: Blackwell.

Thomas, R. and Davies, R. (2005a) 'What Have the Feminists Done for Us? Feminist Theory and Organizational Resistance', *Organization,* 12: 711–40.

Thomas, R. and Davies, R. (2005b) 'Theorizing the Micro-politics of Resistance: New Public Management and Managerial Identities in the UK Public Services', *Organization Studies,* 26: 683–706.

Thompson, P. (1990) 'Crawling from the Wreckage', in Knights, D. and Willmott, H. (eds) *Labour Process Theory,* Basingstoke: Macmillan.

Thompson, P. (2003) 'Disconnected Capitalism', *Work, Employment and Society,* 17: 359–78.

Thompson, P. (2005) 'Introduction: Unmanageable Capitalism?', in Ackroyd, S., Batt, R., Thompson, P. and Tolbert, P. (eds) *The Oxford Handbook of Work and Organization,* Oxford: Oxford University Press.

Thompson, P. and Ackroyd, S. (1995) 'All Quiet on the Workplace Front?' *Sociology,* 29: 615–33.

Turnbull, P. (2006) 'The War on Europe's Waterfront', *British Journal of Industrial Relations,* 44: 305–26.

Turnbull, P. and Weston, S. (1993) 'Co-operation or Control?', *British Journal of Industrial Relations,* 31: 115–34.

Watson, T. (2001) *In Search of Management,* London: Thomson.

Westwood, S. (1984) *All Day, Every Day,* London: Pluto.

Labour Process Theory and Critical Realism

3

Paul Thompson and Steve Vincent

This chapter explores the potential synergies between labour process theory (LPT) and critical realism (CR). Its purpose is not to suggest that using CR is a substitute for theorizing within the LPT tradition. Rather it is to set out the view that CR conceptions of a layered ontology may help to address and resolve some long-standing issues about the scope and character of LPT, particularly those associated with the idea of a 'core' theory, as discussed below and in several chapters within this volume (see also Edwards, 2005).

In the earlier volume *Labour Process Theory* (Knights and Willmott, 1990), essays from Littler, Thompson and Paul Edwards sought to develop conceptual commonalities from second wave LPT and research. A number of purposes can be discerned within such efforts. The main one was to identify a set of core propositions concerning some strong and important tendencies encompassing the capitalist political economy, work and employment relations. These tendencies stem, in part, from empirically consistent features of the capitalist labour process, such as the 'control imperative' (see below). In turn, developing such 'higher order' statements acted to offset two general criticisms of the field. The first associated LPT with contingent claims, mostly associated with Braverman, such as the deskilling thesis or the dominance of Taylorism as a control system. The second, partly as a reaction to the first, was an accumulation of counter-contingencies, arising from the welter of case-study research that of the 'I studied office x or factory y and I couldn't find deskilling' kind.

The content of a core was outlined most explicitly by Thompson (1989, 1990) and has been developed only incrementally since then, most recently in Thompson and Newsome (2004) and Jaros (2005, see also this volume). The former restate the argument that the core begins from the unique character of labour as a commodity – its indeterminacy – and thus 'the conversion of labour power (the potential for work) into labour (actual work effort) under conditions which permit capital accumulation' (Littler, 1990: 48). Four principles flow from this:

1. Because the labour process generates the surplus and is a central part of human experience in acting on the world and reproducing the economy, the role of labour and the capital-labour relationship are privileged in our analysis.
2. There is a logic of accumulation that compels capital to constantly revolutionize the production of goods and services. This arises from competition between capitalists and between capital and labour. This logic has no determinate effects on any specific feature of the labour process (such as use of skills), but it does place constraints on the willingness and ability of capital to dispense with hierarchical relations, empower employees and combine conception and execution.
3. Because market mechanisms alone cannot regulate the labour process, there is a control imperative as systems of management are utilized to reduce the indeterminacy gap. Again, this imperative specifies nothing about the nature or level of control or the efficacy of particular management strategies and practices, nor does it preclude the influence of control mechanisms that originate from outside the workplace.
4. Given the dynamics of exploitation and control, the social relations between capital and labour in the workplace are of 'structured antagonism' (P. Edwards, 1990). At the same time, capital, in order to constantly revolutionize the work process, must seek some level of creativity and cooperation from labour. The result is a continuum of possible situationally driven and overlapping worker responses – from resistance to accommodation, compliance and consent.

This core has been widely used as a framing device to guide research (e.g. S. Taylor, 1998; P. Taylor and P. Bain, 2003). But it should be understood that this was a deliberately 'narrow' formulation of the scope and purposes of LPT. Paul Edwards (1990) articulated this orientation through the idea of the 'relative autonomy' of the labour process and the workplace within capitalism. The most direct consequence was a distinction between the class struggle at work and in the wider society. Whilst the structured antagonism between labour and capital created potentially divergent interests that are manifest in a continually contested terrain, no wider class struggle or social transformation could be 'read off' from such relations. As the teleological claims of Marxism that the working class became the gravedigger of capitalism by virtue of its location in the social relations of production were rejected, mainstream LPT became a variety of post-Marxist materialism (Elger, 2001).

Observing that at the peak of its influence, LPT was applied to an increasing range of social phenomena (such as housework) and criticized for not having a theory of, for example, the state (Ramsay, 1985), it was argued that an expansive theory was mistaken. Nevertheless, such arguments do reveal a genuine problem about interconnections of events, structures and the concepts to explain them. If theorists try to exclude 'external' factors from influencing the labour process, as Burawoy (1979) did in his early work when trying to explain the nature of worker subordination, we end up with an incomplete analysis. Thompson's solution was a 'transaction' model in which a 'narrow' core theory 'intersects with analyses and practices deriving from other social relations to provide explanations of given phenomena' (1990: 112). Totalizing explanations were rejected in favour of 'theories reflecting the complex and interrelated layering of social experience' (112–13). As we shall see later, this is consonant with a critical realist perspective.

Contesting the core

Predictably, the core has proven contentious and faced challenges from post-structuralists, orthodox Marxists and some friendly critique from within mainstream LPT (see Jaros, 2001, 2005 and this volume). The first set of challenges focused on two issues: first, the significance and understanding of the subjectivity of labour, initially in the light of Braverman's omission of such questions. This 'missing subject' debate is well-trodden territory and footsteps still continue (see Jaros this volume and Thompson and O'Doherty's 'debate', 2009). We will only step in them briefly here. In our view, this is or should be a debate about the agency of labour. All major players in the debate agreed that the hole left by Braverman needed to be filled. Those in the materialist mainstream tended to think that this explanation gap was at least partly addressed within core understandings of the nature of labour power as a commodity and labour's creative and resistive responses to it. As the 'missing subject' debate rolled on through the 1990s, the post-structuralist wing increasingly spoke in terms of a general theory of subjectivity based on the indeterminacy of human agency, which they defined largely in terms of the general characteristics of human subjects (such as feelings of insecurity and unachievable search for 'inner coherence'). Any connection to the specific characteristics of labour under capitalism was lost and theoretical resources drawn wholly from outside the labour process tradition, from Foucault and others, came to be dominant. However, there are issues of subjectivity and agency that LPT lacks the theoretical resources on its own to address, notably identity. Willmott and Knights have been fond of quoting Thompson's argument that a full theory of the missing subject was (at that time) a key task for LPT, but never mention the subsequent line that given the available conceptual tools, 'it cannot be fulfilled by that theory alone' (1990: 114). We shall return to this issue at various points in this chapter. For now, it is sufficient to state that a core was not only rejected by post-structuralists in substance (the theory is about the wrong thing), but in principle – such a project is essentialist and privileges certain voices over others. But a theory must be about *something* and all resources have a core territory and propositions. It is both disingenuous and difficult to envisage any viable *labour process* theory that does not have its roots within the conditions of labour power in a capitalist economy. In this light, the missing subject debate could not be resolved because there was insufficient commonality in its empirical objects and theoretical resources.

Turning to the next types of objections, whilst most of the Marxists working within a labour process framework came to accept the relative autonomy argument, at least to the extent that they were willing to explore the contingent connections between the two types of class struggle, others were more hostile (e.g. Rowlinson and Hassard, 2001; Spencer, 2000). The relative autonomy argument is seen as giving too much discretion to agents of capital (managers and control strategies) and underplaying the links between the economic laws of capitalism (the law of value/labour theory of value, the tendency of the rate of profit to fall) and workplace outcomes. Spencer also wants to restore a further 'law of motion' of capitalist society – the gravedigger thesis – berating Thompson and others for political pessimism and neglecting Braverman's injunction that the purpose of Marxian critique is to generate a theory of revolution and a tool of combat (2000: 225).

Spencer makes some valid points about ambiguities in the core concerning levels of analysis and hierarchies of concepts, but fails to demonstrate any convincing alternative propositions. Instead we get vague statements about movements from essence to appearance and abstract to concrete, and reference to, 'The categorical progression from value as socially necessary labour time through valorization and surplus value production to realization marks the unifying moment of capitalist production' (2000: 233). Such arguments are typical of a wider problem that for all that it is used as a stick to beat Thompson, Edwards, Burawoy and others, nowhere do these authors show how value theory or any other 'law of motion' actually makes a difference. The link between the 'value theoretic approach' and labour processes is simply not demonstrated – indeed, there is no real attempt to demonstrate it. It lacks explanatory power and functions more as an article of faith or theoretical fidelity.

Moving to 'in-house' critique, in detailed and closely argued commentaries Elger (2001) and Jaros (2005) offset their defence of much LPT and research by observing that the core is 'underspecified' and that insufficient attention has been paid to refining it. Elger (2001: 2) notes that a key issue is how work and the workplace articulate with other loci of social relations, including product markets, the state, inter-corporate relations, the labour market and households. Given the concerns of LPT, particular attention is given to the dynamics of labour markets as work histories increasingly span multiple workplaces. Connections between labour power and labour markets are also central to Smith's (2006 and this volume) argument that in modern capitalism labour mobility is a second indeterminacy of labour. If, as Jaros (2005) observes, too much (analytical) autonomy was granted to the labour process, it is unsurprising that core theory has to leave room for institutional and other factors to help explain variations in the strategies of economic actors and labour processes.

Before we discuss how this has and might be done, we need to consider how CR can aid this rethinking of boundary issues. The general lesson from the above discussions is that beyond the immediate core, the labour process does not occur within a vacuum and other levels of causal phenomenon are important both to maintaining capitalism and explaining local outcomes. As such, whilst the phrase 'core' implies a centre, this is not meant in to imply 'spatial' relationships in which an independent labour process is surrounded by an external capitalist political economy. External relations are already present in various features of the core, albeit in differential form and influence. This endeavour is also consistent with the call in Chapter 2 by Edwards for a multi-levelled explanation that considers how different types of phenomena combine to affect outcomes within specific labour processes. What we are arguing is that the layered ontology offered by CR implies an approach to social inquiry that encourages us to identify the dynamics of these interrelations, making more meaningful connections between the various layers of the political economy and the forms of social agency situated within specific labour processes. The key question is how can we map these connections and what implications does it have for the core in doing so?

Critical realism and social inquiry

CR developed from Roy Bhaskar's philosophy of science (1978, 1986; see also Collier, 1994), that sees the universe as a naturally multilayered open-system of interrelated parts or entities that interact over time. All entities, whether natural or social, are viewed as *really constituted* in that they have *causal powers* – to affect outcomes in specific ways – and *susceptibilities* – to be affected by the powers of other entities in specific ways. Furthermore, the powers and susceptibilities of entities are irreducible to their constituent parts and are best viewed as a condition of their *articulation*, or how entities are internally and externally related to one another over time. Thus, in terms of their internal relations, it is the articulation of an entire body, and not organs in isolation, that reproduces a complex organism and it is the articulation of the production line and not the effort of workers alone that determines the rate of production. And equally, within these examples external relations within ecosystems, product markets and the like are vital to making accurate explanations of why matters are as they are and not otherwise.

This position can be contrasted with the social constructionist view that the social world is emergent from discursively constructed human subjects. Whilst protagonists of CR do not deny the language-based 'character of all seeing' (Deetz, 2003: 424), they assert that social formations have powers that are separate from their constituent subjects and that these powers do not need to be recognized within language to be *really* influential. So, our internal, discursive and transitive theories more or less accurately correspond to and explain the external and intransitive causal powers observed.

In developing theories about 'the way things are', natural scientists typically use experimental methods to isolate phenomena in the effort to understand how 'lower level' entities (atoms, molecules, etc.) are constituted within 'higher level' entities (compounds, organisms, etc.). Similarly, social analysts consider how local ideologies, subjects and social groups (and others) are reconstituted within their workplaces, cultures and nations (and others). In either case, evidence can be used to logically determine the mechanism or collection of powers that explains an empirical regularity observed in the patterns of events. However, social research is not as amenable to experimental methods due to the cognitive, reflexive and social character of its research subject, so social inquiry has a logic of its own.

Outside of the laboratory, the powers of differently layered entities (organizations, subjects, ideologies, etc.) interact and can variously obscure, prevent, encourage and overlay one another as they constitute the mechanism that explains observed regularities. Where mechanisms are particularly complex, our language forms can become a barrier to knowledge development. Experts tend to concentrate and specialize on the powers and susceptibilities of particular types of entity, honing specific methods, theories and frameworks in ways that are useful for exploring a specific class or classes of phenomenon. This analytical specialism results in specific jurisdictions and departments (biology and physics, human resource management and accountancy, for example) that reflect or correspond to the different strata of phenomenon that we investigate (Collier, 1994). As a result of specialization, specific discursive forms (jargon) and vested academic interests are also created. Different academic discourses can refer to the same or similar phenomenon using different conceptual resources. As a result, theoretical resources are often contested, confused and constrained due to misinterpretations, tunnel vision and academic empire-building.

This suggests that our inquiries require sensitivity to language's *transitive* conceptual schemas and intransitive objective phenomenon – as both influence outcomes within *any* knowledge domain. This point can be illustrated by considering the role of feminist narratives about workplace relations. It is impossible to deny that gendered work relations and their associated subjective interests existed before the use of sophisticated concepts that represent these relations and interests, such as patriarchy, institutional discrimination and feminization, for example. In this regard, gendered work relations are intransitive – they exist outside language and subjects do not need a critical awareness of them to be affected by them. However, as actors have used their agency to explore the reality of women's economic position and experiences of work, they have developed and created new and critical *transitive* concepts (patriarchy, etc.) to communicate these intransitive experiences.

Subsequently, these transitive constructs have causal potentials within social processes. This is because they are *ideally real* and represent a stratum of antecedent conditioning related to 'the received wisdom' that independently affects the evolution of social processes (see Fleetwood, 2005). In this case, the articulation of new critical concepts about women's work has created new conceptual *structures* (words) in the discursive *mechanism* (language) used to convey an understanding of the world. So, actors' effort at discovering and conceptualizing their intransitive social world has stimulated new forms of understanding, and these have altered *the balance of power* within inter-subjective social processes (such as debates about women's work), informing the social struggles of the feminist movement as they campaign to produce structured counter *tendencies* to women's subjugation (such as equality legislation and family-friendly policies). In short, it would seem that the inter-actions between the various strata of phenomenon affect the development of knowledge and society (see Bhaskar, 1998) and that the discursive practices and activities of individuals, agencies (and for that matter critically minded researchers) are *both* structurally mediated *and* potentially transformational (Archer, 1995).

Those who apply CR to social inquiry assert that our analytical approach should reflect this structure-agency dualism, with analyses of the powers and susceptibilities of social agents integrated with an appreciation of the antecedent contexts that inform activities. Specifically, '(i) that structure [and for that matter culture] necessarily pre-dates action(s) which transform it (...), and; (ii) that structural [and cultural] elaboration necessarily post dates those actions which transform it' (Archer, 1995: 375; added notes, and see Archer, 2006). This suggests a *morphogenetic cycle* in which agency is limited, constrained and influenced by multifaceted antecedent structural and cultural circumstances. Subsequent to this conditioning, social agents have the inde-pendent causal power to shape and change the world in ways that recondi-tion and alter circumstances. As a result, it is important that we understand how individuals and groups *tend* to react to specific circumstances in order to assess whether relative social stability or change is likely at any level (see Vincent, 2008).

In workplaces, for example, individuals and groups tend to identify them-selves as workers, managers, shareholders, business owners, trade unionists, and so on, at different moments in social processes. As a result of identifying themselves, they also tend to associate with a distinctive set of material and symbolic interests (prestige, pay, profits, promotion, skills, business stabil-ity, etc.), and identify themselves relative to other subjects (colleagues and competitors, 'us' and 'them'). Social agents have to choose which of their distinctive interests they represent in opposition to their other interests and those of other groups. As a result, 'choices' do not need to be consistent and tend to be based on individual experiences, preferences and, perhaps most importantly, antecedent possibilities and opportunities. Inconsistencies arise because the material and symbolic interests identifiable in social formations, such as labour processes, are so complex, nested, overlapping and multifa-ceted that competing tensions about 'what to do' and for that matter 'who I am' are inevitable (see also Emirbayer and Mische, 1998). This suggests a *pluralism of the self and agency* in which there is no easy downward fit between locations, interests and normativities.

If actors are indeed searching for 'inner coherence', they do this by finding ways to justify their activities and seeing what they do as worthwhile rela-tive to structured situations, with emergent social value systems becoming collectively held within the 'lay normativity' of distinctive social groupings (Sayer, 2005). However, getting inside lay normativity is no easy matter because collectively held schemas are often overlapping and contradictory. Their manifestation is also very much dependent on the 'inner conversa-tions' of social subjects and how people understand their situatedness and potentials (see Archer, 2000). For example, individuals and groups often redefine their structured inequalities as 'desired' even when they were not chosen for themselves, because this can be a less alienating way to experi-ence the world than more active defiance to a situation that is beyond their control (Bhaskar, 1986, see also Sen, 1997). Such belief systems often sustain inequalities. Furthermore, as a result of residing in structured locations from which divergent and potentially contradictory interests and values emerge, there will inevitably be moments in which specific interests and values can-not be reconciled, such as when demands for 'fair pay' compromise the prof-itability of one's workplace, for example. In these circumstances, people must either (1) find a way of dealing with inconsistencies through 'containment strategies' that suppress one set of values within socio-cultural interactions, and/or (2) engage in more open ideological conflict that results in either the elimination of one set of ideas or the general acceptance of cleavage within one's world (Archer, 2006: 28–33).

In this regard, Archer (2000) argues that tensions within interest-based social values systems, such as those inherent to labour processes, can be usefully explored using the heuristic distinction between *corporate* and *primary* agency. The former has the material and symbolic resources required to pursue sectional interests whilst the latter often does not. Arguably, all agents within the labour process are to an extent corporate agents in one capacity or another, albeit with many groups lacking a strongly articulated ideological position from which to voice their concerns. In this regard, countervailing forces, restrictive social practices and institutional mechanisms, such as those inherent to labour processes, can result in substantive vested interests (such as increased pay, relative autonomy or promotion) remaining *primary* for long periods. Also, beyond these structured constraints, interest groups may not be able to articulate their concerns because they lack the conceptual resources and/or moral rationales required, so opportunities exist to develop new conceptualizations of situations that may have beneficial transformative potentials.

Critical realism at work

In our view, this general analytical framework has much appeal. In the following sections, CR acts as both an ontological framework and an approach to social inquiry in a (non-exhaustive) exploration of different conceptual tools that, alongside and in combination with LPT, can credibly claim explanatory power with respect to the broader political economy. Our argument is that the apparent empirical (and corresponding theoretical) diversity indicates that the multilayered causal interrelationships which exist across capitalism are simply too complex for any one theoretical tool/resource to claim jurisdiction over the entire territory. In this regard, our principal assertion is that grounding our analyses within CR offers opportunities to develop more fine-grained appreciation of the usefulness of the different theoretical resources available for understanding the labour process under capitalism.

This argument is extended over the remaining sections of this chapter. Following this, a further section extends the logic of morphogenetic cycles to consider social agency within the labour process, connecting this agency with an appreciation of its structured context. Our general argument is that useful explanations of specific event regularities within the labour process, as well as across the political economy more generally, can be generated by drawing variously on the theoretical resources available, with the particular conceptual mix derived and dependent on the *articulation of powers* within the specific and empirically bounded focal point of our investigations.

Reconnecting the political economy

One of the main prerequisites of conforming with CR ontology is the general acceptance that many differently stratified and antecedent causal powers exist and that these interact as they affect the pattern of events at any location. This is broadly consonant with mainstream LPT which has always incorporated empirical sensitivity to the interaction among structural, national and other institutional dynamics. But despite such forms of connection, supporters of LPT have bemoaned the tendency to lose sight of phases of valorization or capital accumulation as a key motor of the transformation of work relations (Elger, 1979; Rainnie, 1984; Thompson and Smith, 2001). Existing research utilizing workplace-based case studies tended to make use of a variety of contextual framing. These included sectoral approaches that place transformations of work in the context of industrial restructuring and the conditions of competition that shape the strategies of economic actors (Rainnie, 1984); the elaboration of institutional conditions that influence the actions of firms, particularly of labour markets; and reference to types of capitalism, or stages in capitalist development, from Braverman's (1974) emphasis on monopoly capitalism to numerous studies utilizing concepts of Fordism, neo-Fordism and post-Fordism.

None of these directions has ultimately provided an independently durable model of the conceptual 'connective tissue' between the labour process and the broader political economy. So how then, should the connectivity gap left by the idea of relative autonomy be filled? One of the earliest attempts critiqued accounts that reduced workplace change to the outcome of labour-capital relations at work, rather than the 'full circuit of capital' in a variety of market contexts (Kelly, 1985). Kelly argued that we have to consider the role of competition between capitals, but it is worth noting that it was explicitly confined to *industrial* capital: (the purchase of) labour, extraction of surplus value in the labour process and realization of surplus value in product markets (1985: 32–3). Whilst the observation that the dis/articulation of different moments in the circuits of capital shapes firm behaviour is perfectly sensible, it is difficult to see how this is very different from contingency arguments about the fit between firm structure and environment, with added Marxist language. Tellingly, though the circuits concept is often referred to in passing, its application has been extremely limited. One of the few studies to do so was another account of industrial restructuring in the clothing industry

(Peck, 1990). Peck rightly argues that LPT needs to 'look over the factory gates' to understand the broader dynamics of capitalism. Pressure for structural change in the clothing industry arise from product and labour markets, but the subsequent tightening of profit margins have to be (largely) secured through reducing labour costs in the production process. Whilst such arguments were a useful corrective to the small number of theorists who confined their analysis to what Peck called the 'internal logic of the labour process' (such as control and resistance patterns), the most influential studies were already taking into account the broader conditions of competition that influenced workplace relations (Edwards and Scullion, 1982).

Arguably, the most obvious place to look for a broader contextual frame for analyses for specific labour processes was regulation theory (Aglietta, 1979; Lipietz 1986). This perspective was developed largely by French Marxists and utilizes a distinctive conceptual language to create a unified account of the basic features of capitalism (such as the wage relation and commodity form), the stages of capitalist development, the specific institutional configurations associated with such stages and the motors of change (such as class struggle) that lead to conjunctural crises and systemic change. Labour power and its reproduction is held to be central to capitalist development, enabling regulationists to place the labour process at the heart of their analyses. The key concept is regime of accumulation, constituted primarily by particular patterns of production, consumption, circulation and distribution such as the Fordist 'virtuous circle' of mass production and consumption. However, such structures require 'guidance' through modes of regulation, encompassing institutional structures and norms governing intra- and inter-firm relations, relations between capitals and between capital and labour (such as industrial relations systems).

The approach became associated with particular claims about the crisis of Fordism and emergence of post-Fordism or further refinement through neo-Fordism. This may partially account for its limited take up by British labour process researchers, who tended to be sceptical of paradigm break perspectives and particularly critical of claims for the emergence of a more collaborative, high-skill variant of capitalist work systems. Such scepticism has proven to be correct and post-Fordist perspectives have largely faded from view. A related problem has arisen from the 'unified account' itself. Regulation theory is an extremely ambitious attempt to link phenomena such as macro-economic structures, monetary systems, state formations, political parties, labour markets and processes within the same explanatory framework. Despite references to particular national 'modes of growth' or largely retrospective attempts to distinguish between different objects of regulation at macro and micro levels (Jessop, 1990), when applied to actual conditions in particular national or sector contexts, the overdetermined explanation breaks down or collapses in a welter of exceptions and variations (e.g. see Jessop, 1992). In sum, this kind of framework imposed too many conceptual costs for LPT that operated with assumptions of more loosely coupled relations among economic, political and workplace spheres.

There is, of course, an ostensibly less restrictive alternative – the varieties of capitalism approach (Hall and Soskice, 2001; Whitley, 1999). This is presented as a form of comparative political economy that makes distinctions between liberal, coordinated and other varieties. The question is, what are such national entities influencing and at which level? The answer, overwhelmingly, is that nation states influence firm market-relations in business systems, labour markets, education and industrial relations institutions, and so on. Whichever is the case, the institutional logics identified are located in 'stylized typologies of national economies as discrete and internally consistent "models"' (Deeg and Jackson, 2006: 150), so the independent causal powers of those entities that constitute and transcend nation states appear neglected or of secondary significance.

National institutional logics are important and have been particularly useful in labour process research. However, labour processes – where they are located and how they are organized – are less likely to be so embedded in circumstances where globalizing firms can transfer and replicate practices across their networks (Smith, 2005). But institutionalists have been so concerned to counter populist accounts of globalization with their overemphasis on convergence that they have been unable to address questions of how capitalist production is constituted increasingly through global networks. Within institutionalist debates, there has been increased recognition of the resultant tendency towards static analysis that is unable to explain change within and across national economies (Crouch, 2007; Deeg and Jackson, 2007). Unfortunately, the preferred corrective is to move to a more actor-centred, micro-level approach or to a greater engagement with national and international politics. In other words, there would be more emphasis on the political than the economy. Whilst that may generate particular insights, it does nothing to address the problem of stronger connections between workplaces and capitalist development.

Beneath more lofty theoretical insights concerning national systems and regimes of accumulation, other theoretical resources can be used to address the 'too much variety, not enough capitalism' problem. Specifically, global value chain (GVC) analysis of inter-firm relations and the dynamics of global industries have a long history with a variety of earlier incarnations, such as global commodity chain research (Gereffi, 1994, 1996). More recent frameworks have developed from a focus on power relations between dominant and subordinate buyers and producers to a fuller account of changing, varied patterns of governance and the associated mechanisms of coordination and control (markets, hierarchies and networks) across the whole chain, from conception of a product or service to its consumption (Gereffi, Humphrey and Sturgeon, 2005). Though this conceptual schema takes in objects of analysis wider than the core concerns of LPT, it should, intuitively, appeal given the emphasis on studying the mechanisms of value creation and capture across the chain.

GVC analysis has received some friendly criticism recently from those seeking to pursue a global production network (GPN) approach, on the grounds that the former focuses too much on linear, inter-firm structures and too little on 'all relevant sets of actors and relationships' that may impinge on the nexus of interconnected functions, operations and transactions involved in the production, distribution and consumption of a product and service (Coe, Dicken and Hess, 2008). Opening out GVC analysis would certainly enable the incorporation of a labour process focus, given that GVC frameworks are currently deficient in focusing almost wholly on capital-capital, rather than capital-labour-capital relations. From our perspective, it would be limited and misleading to analyse mechanisms of value creation and capture without a substantive focus on the labour process, and research sympathetic to LPT are beginning to make links to GVC and GPN perspectives (Flecker et al., 2008; Thompson, Parker and Cox, 2009; Taylor, this volume).

Where does this leave us with respect to the connective tissue between workplace labour processes and the broader stratified layers of the political economy? The most important observation is that these contextual framings are not necessarily incompatible, but may refer to the specific causal mechanisms influencing conditions of competition. This is not to deny that distinctive theoretical resources underpin the conceptualizations, but the latter are not reducible to the former. The key issue is what the particular analysis is seeking to explain. For example, whatever weaknesses regulation theory may have, the concept of regime of accumulation is potentially useful in addressing macro-level shifts in the political economy and the circuits of capital. Equally, whilst notwithstanding the intricacies of specific labour processes, research seeking to explain skill utilization in nationally based service industries is more likely to find useful connections with variety of capitalism than GVC perspectives. But, as Taylor argues in this volume, GVC/GPN concepts are particularly pertinent in developing meso-level accounts of governance mechanisms and value capture within industries. In other words, the logic of our argument is that specific subjects of investigation will have different susceptibilities in relation to the different causal mechanisms we observe within their surrounding context.

Let us take Thompson's (2003) disconnected capitalism thesis as a more detailed illustration. Within the categories we have discussed, this would correspond most closely to the idea of a regime of accumulation. Briefly, the argument is that shifts in the dynamic of capital accumulation have produced a new regime that we can designate as financialized capitalism, whose drivers are focused more on enhanced returns in capital markets than competition in product markets. Using previous terminology, we might say that this represents a shift in powers from industrial to financial circuits of capital, involving new focal agents including investment banks, private equity firms and global consultancies. Growth strategies for firms are directed to a simultaneous squeezing of labour and more active management of corporate assets, manifested in delayering, disaggregation, downsizing and divestment. Empirically, the argument depends on the assertion of a number of observations about actual and potential event regularities concerning the adverse impact of shareholder value 'regimes' on the sustainability of progressive work and employment relations at workplace level. However, Thompson's paper was careful to note that such tendencies do not equally apply across all economies, introducing variety of (national) capitalism arguments into the picture. Drawing on our other categories, it might also be observed that the tendencies might not apply equally or in the same way across industries, thus opening up links to a GVC analysis.

In sum, whilst the labour process remains a key focus for new forms of accumulation, its dynamics are not necessarily the driver of them. The 'credit crunch' illustrates that the first systemic crisis of financialized capitalism originated largely outside the industrial circuit of capital, but has profound consequences for it. The task of LPT is to develop an account of the potential causal powers of new structures and their varied effects in differentially embedded workplaces. As we indicated earlier, this needs to reveal the particular dis/articulation of causal powers, but rests on an ordering of specific explanations, rather than a totalizing framework such as regulation theory.

Reconnecting the agent within the politics of production

In the previous section we made a case for connecting LPT to wider theoretical resources for a fuller picture of the political economy. Deciding what the equivalent is at a more micro level depends on identifying the problem. We noted at the beginning of the chapter that post-structuralist participants in earlier LP debates focused on the 'missing subject'. However, assertions that this dimension of agency is the primary explanation for the reproduction of capitalist (or other) social relations fails to understand that intransitive social structures have independent causal powers that cannot be reduced to the identities and subjectivities of the actors who constitute them. As Armstrong

(2008: 3) notes in his critique of Willmott's arguments about existential character of managerial agency in reproducing capitalism:

> ... if the social structures of capitalism are so pliable that they can be transformed by the micro processes of interaction ... one's first impulse is to question whether they are social structures at all, and to wonder what they might consist. Certainly Willmott cannot be referring to the ownership by capital of the means of production nor to the exchange of labour power against capital.

Contra CR, post-structuralism does not deal adequately with the causal powers of *collective* agency and 'lay normativity' inside and acting on the workplace. If we consider, for example, agency issues arising from discussion in the previous section, focal actors and their agential projects would include transnational firms (GVC/GPN); fractions of capital (accumulation regimes); and, business associations and labour movements (varieties of capitalism). Consideration of such issues would constitute part of developing a broad account of the politics of production within which workplaces are influenced and influence (Burawoy, 1985).

Most of the attention to agency issues within recent labour process debates has been on *labour* agency. Reflecting this, we focus our attention on this sphere, using the logic of morphogenetic cycles to consider how social agents are connected to the broader antecedent structures of the political economy. The labouring subjects conceived within mainstream LPT are attributed potential causal powers, as can be seen in classic accounts of the dialectical relations between control and resistance (R. Edwards, 1979; P. K. Edwards and Scullion, 1982) and misbehaviour and managerial regimes (Ackroyd and Thompson, 1999). Worker self-organization is conceptualized at both formal and informal levels, and labour as socially diverse sets of actors rather than homogenous class warriors. Furthermore, agency is not confined to recalcitrant behaviour, evidenced in Burawoy (1979) and other accounts of workplace consent. This is not to say that theorizations of labour agency are without problems. As spelt out in other chapters from Edwards and Bélanger and Thuderoz, existing analyses need to do more to expand the repertoire of employee oppositional practices and more systematically explain their logics, conditions and consequences.

Returning to the theme of connectivity, there are analytical challenges in making links between workplace action (the distinctive sphere of competence of LPT) and broader structures and practices where a variety of interest groups (such as unions, professional and occupational associations) are part of that action. The International Labour Process Conference regularly debates papers on union organizing, but there has been limited attempt to integrate those studies with traditional concerns about labour agency. Part of the problem is changes to real structures, with a gradual disconnect between the kind of informal job controls and union organization that underpinned key aspects of worker power, but there are also analytical disconnects. The most obvious source for making such connections is mobilization theory (Kelly, 1998), which seeks to outline the structural and agential conditions that enable grievances that begin in work relations to become collectively directed towards asserting wider labour interests.

However, this is not the end of the story. The subjectivity of labour cannot be contained within the workplace and we suggested in an earlier section that CR insights into social enquiry and social agents as purposeful if constrained actors can add explanatory power. With this in mind, the labour process can be viewed as an antecedent structure within which various agents are located, but the various interests and identities 'in play' are also shaped by extra-organizational influences (class, gender, ethnicity, etc.) that require broader conceptualizations. Post-structuralists are right that the agential properties of the subject are (in part) generic and that we can address some questions through concepts of the self and identity. A detailed consideration of these issues are beyond our scope, though see the chapter from Marks and Thompson. What we want to suggest is that whilst social constructionists of various types have made some significant contributions that usefully illustrate how the search for 'inner coherence' affects choices (see Erickson, 1995; Knights, 2001), other theoretical resources to be found in critical realist social inquiry are needed to make more meaningful connections with the broader political economy.

More specifically, whilst CR social inquiry offers a set of general propositions for analysing social agency across different empirical locations, it says little about specific social formations, such as labour processes. In contrast, whilst the core theory is open to the possibility of multiple influences, it is more specifically concerned with intransitive conditions of wage labour and the structural/agential tendencies that result from these conditions. The salient point of connectivity is that social inquiry informed by CR encourages researchers to consider how labour processes are affected by the transitive (the conditions of 'knowing' and 'being') and the intransitive (external conditions, including any interactions between structured mechanisms beyond the labour process). For example, broader institutional imperatives have been observed to affect aggregate levels of trust at a societal level (see Lane and Bachmann, 1998), and employment relations are no exception to this rule. But this does not prevent trust-based niches developing in ostensibly distrusting institutional environments and vice versa (see Marchington and Vincent, 2004). Outcomes will be very much dependant on a combination of actors' 'feel for the game' and the latent or realized potentials of regulatory mechanisms that condition actors' behaviour. In short, structure-agency dualisms are ongoing, whether or not actors are aware of their own influences or the influence and conditions of the structures that surround them.

Reflecting on the (re)connections

In our view, the different conceptual schemas posited above correspond to different constellations of entities and causal forces, all of which may be seen to interact according to the logic of interdependent, spatially and temporally sequenced morphogenetic cycles. In Figure 3.1 these theoretical resources are synthesized in relation to the levels of the political economy they represent and around a core concern with labour processes. This sketch offers a stylized map of capitalist political economy that helps theoretically locate the various strata of phenomena that significantly affect labour processes. For expediency, we have crudely divided the map into five generally recognized and used categories or levels of entities. In this regard, we are not offering an exhaustive exploration of theoretically interesting matters (specific discourses, cultures, ethnicities, genders, geographies, etc.) that also have causal implications for specific labour processes, but instead have the goal of beginning to articulate a more systemic conception of the multiple embeddedness of labour processes.

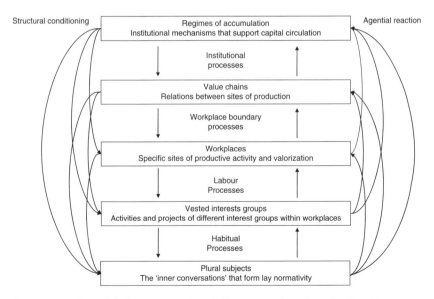

Figure 3.1   The political economy of capitalism as a series of stratified entities

'Above' labour processes, regimes of accumulation, the positions of firms within value chains and the antecedent structure of workplace social relationships all impact on agential projective tendencies by conditioning actor and workplace orientations and strategies. 'Within' labour processes the negotiation of plural interests result in a variable mixture of accommodation, compliance, resistance and consent, with the collective outcome of these relations necessarily conforming with expectations about profitability and performance in lieu of real possibility of organizational dissolutions and restructuring. Each of the layers identified signifies an independent strata of causal conditioning within the political economy. So, the distinctive articulations of different regimes of accumulation as a whole result in them competing in different ways for relative prosperity within the international division of labour. Likewise, the articulations of supply-chains, firms and interrelations therein affect how they compete with one another for market share within and across markets and regimes of accumulation. Similarly, the articulation of interest groups within and between firms affects how they vie for the symbolic and material resources required to extend their separable and often competing interests.

It is also useful to view each level as linked to the others via specific temporally emergent processes. So, for example, extending from regimes of accumulation, *institutional processes* ensure the long-term stability of the economic order by enabling competing capitals to restructure their investments – institutionalizing the extraction of value within an 'iron cage' that perpetuates cycles of capital. Yet other institutional processes recondition company laws, industrial relations mechanisms and impose sanctions and penalties on those who digress from normally 'acceptable' practice. Similar constraints are imposed by value chains that inform workplace boundary processes, workplaces that inform the labour processes and vested interest groups that inform habitual processes. Finally, plural agents respond to these broader conditions, with responses dependent on the real and imagined potentials of these various causal forces. And ultimately, the activities of plural agents combine through the entities they relate to, resulting in specific forms of articulation that condition broader processes of social reproduction and transformation.

Final comment: The core revisited

This chapter has placed the core theory under critical scrutiny to consider both its contribution and limitations. In our view, the core theory will remain an important reference point. It offers a significant contribution to the development of LPT in terms of a materialist framework for considering the dynamics and development of workplace social relations. It connects significant antecedents inherent to capitalism – specifically, the indeterminacy of labour and broader competitive conditions – to specific agential tendencies at the level of the workplace – specifically, the necessity of reorganization, the need for control and 'structured tension'. But the tightness of controls, the degree of reorganization and the level of tension are left relatively unspecified due to the implicit recognition that broader conditions elsewhere in the political economy also affect the labour process, as do the understandings and actions of the people who constitute them.

Given this conclusion, we have argued that there is much potential for fruitful dialogue between the core theory and other theoretical resources, albeit one framed within a broadly CR ontology. For example, if we can accept that there is something about social structures that cannot be reduced to subjectivity alone, the insights about identity and subjectivity developed by post-structuralist and mainstream labour process writers can inform and trade with each other in a more productive and less debunking way. Thus, beyond the boundary of the core theory, we have sought to highlight how other modes of theorizing are essential (1) to explain the other antecedent conditions that affect the evolution of specific labour processes, and (2) to explain the general and specific conditions of the agency of capital and labour. Whilst existing conceptualizations of the core could and probably should be revisited to examine whether they adequately express the requisite structural tendencies, the discussion in this chapter is generally supportive of the idea of a 'narrow' interpretation. Indeed, by filling in some of the connective conceptual tissue, the idea of relative autonomy is rendered more defensible because we have identified theoretical resources that help to answer the question: relative to what?

As labour processes are constantly evolving, it is important that our theories and conceptualizations of them are systematically scrutinized and interrogated, preferably via interdisciplinary and collaborative investigations, in order to clarify those mechanisms that are explained by any given theoretical resource and, more importantly, for limits to jurisdictions. Ultimately, as theoretical schemas and models are confirmed by event regularities within specific domains social scientists can be more confident about their representation within that domain and move on to consider the relations between one domain and another – the movement being towards better conceptions of 'the systems' we study. In this regard, whilst we acknowledge the need to proceed with cautious reflexivity, we should not deny our potential to develop more accurate and revealing explanations of the features of emergent labour processes, and we should acknowledge that our insights can make a positive difference to purposive political activities, as the previous example of feminist research arguably demonstrates.

As a result, continuity in the tradition of detailed qualitative, longitudinal and comparative research would seem to be essential to discover more about the evolving antecedents of the labour process and its multiple forms of embeddedness. In this regard, we promote a form of labour processes analyses that appreciates the independent causal powers of (1) the stratified political economy (2) discourses/normative systems within workplace relations (thus connecting workplace relation to broader societal narratives, such as those connected with ethnicity, neoliberalism or consumerism, for example), and (3) the fallibilities/susceptibilities of human subjects. Such contributions are timely, since the potential coherence and influence of labour process analyses and its capacity for long-term theory building (Thompson and Harley, 2007) have been muted by the debate about what is and what is not 'proper' LPT. This lack of unity has only slowed progress and lessened the impact of important analyses which seek to connect a critique of the capitalist modes of production to the specific policies and practices that affect work.

REFERENCES

Ackroyd, S. and Thompson, P. (1999) *Organizational Misbehaviour*, London: Sage.

Aglietta, M. (1979) *A Theory of Capitalist Regulation: The US Experience*, London: New Left Books.

Archer, M. (1995) *Realist Social Theory: The Morphogenic Approach*, Cambridge: Cambridge University Press.

Archer, M. (2000) *Being Human: The Problem of Agency*, Cambridge: Cambridge University Press.

Archer, M. (2006) 'Structure, Culture and Agency', in Jacobs, M. and Weiss Harahan, N. (eds) *The Blackwell Companion to the Sociology of Culture*, Oxford: Blackwell.

Armstrong, P. (2008) 'Existential Struggle and Surplus Value: Hugh Willmott on Managerial Subjectivities', Paper presented at the Conference of Practical Criticism in the Managerial Social Sciences, Leicester University Management School, 15–17 January.

Bhaskar, R. (1978) *A Realist Theory of Science*, Hassocks: Harvester Press.

Bhaskar, R. (1998) *The Possibility of Naturalism: A Philosophical Critique of the Contemporary Human Sciences*, London: Routledge.

Bhaskar, R. (1986) *Scientific Realism and Human Emancipation*, London: Verso.

Braverman, H. (1974) *Labor and Monopoly Capital*, New York: Monthly Review Press.

Burawoy, M. (1979) *Manufacturing Consent*, Chicago: Chicago University Press.

Burawoy, M. (1985) *The Politics of Production*, London: Verso.

Coe, N., Dicken, P. and Hess, M. (2008) 'Global Production Networks: Debates and Challenges', *Journal of Economic Geography*, 8(3): 267–9.

▶

▶

Collier, A. (1994) *Critical Realism: An Introduction to Roy Bhaskar's Philosophy*, Verso: London.

Crouch, C. (2007) 'Institutional Change and Globalization: How to "Do" Post-determinist Institutional Analysis', *Socio-Economic Review*, 5: 527–67.

Deeg, R. and Jackson, G. (2006) 'The State of the Art: Towards a More Dynamic Theory of Capitalist Variety', *Socio-Economic Review*, 5: 149–79.

Deetz, S. (2003) 'Reclaiming the Legitimacy of the Linguistic Turn', *Organization*, 10(3): 421–9.

Edwards, P. (2005) 'The Challenging but Promising Future of Industrial Relations: Developing Theory and Method in Context-Sensitive Research', *Industrial Relations*, 36(4): 264–82.

Edwards, P. K. (1990) 'Understanding Conflict in the Labour Process: The Logic and Autonomy of Struggle', in Knights, D. and Willmott, H. (eds) *Labour Process Theory*, London: Macmillan.

Edwards, P. K. and Scullion, H. (1982) *The Social Organization of Industrial Conflict: Control and Resistance in the Workplace*, Oxford: Blackwell.

Edwards, R. (1979) *Contested Terrain*, London: Heinemann.

Elger, T. (1979) 'Valorisation and Deskilling: A Critique', *Capital and Class*, 7: 58–99.

Elger, T. (2001) 'Critical Materialist Analyses of Work and Employment: A Third Way?', *Sociologie del Livoro*, 34: 61–84.

Emirbayer, M. and Mische, A. (1998) 'What Is Agency?', *American Journal of Sociology*, 103(4): 962–1023.

Erickson, R. (1995) 'The Importance of Authenticity for Self and Society', *Symbolic Interaction*, 18(2): 121–44.

Flecker, J., Holtgrewe, U., Schönauer, A., Dunkel, W. and Meil, P. (2008) 'Restructuring across Value Chains and Changes in Work and Employment. Case Study Evidence from the Clothing, Food, IT and Public Sector', FORBA Research Report 1/2008, Vienna, download: http://www.worksproject.be/documents/D10.1.pdf.

Fleetwood, S. (2005) 'Ontology in Organization and Management Studies: A Critical Realist Perspective', *Organization*, 12(2): 197–222.

Gereffi, G. (1994) 'The Organization of Buyer-Driven Global Commodity Chains: How U.S. Retailers Shape Overseas Production Networks', in Gereffi, G. and Korzeniewicz, M. (eds) *Commodity Chains and Global Capitalism*, Westport, CT: Praeger.

Gereffi, G. (1996) 'Global Commodity Chains: New Forms of Coordination and Control Among Nations and Firms in International Industries', *Competition and Change*, 1(4): 427–39.

Gereffi, G., Humphrey, J. and Sturgeon, T. (2005) 'The Governance of Global Value Chains', *Review of International Political Economy*, 12(1): 78–104.

Hall, P. A. and Soskice, D. (eds) (2001) *Varieties of Capitalism: The Institutional Foundations of Comparative Advantage*, Oxford: Oxford University Press.

Jaros, S. (2001) 'Labour Process Theory: A Commentary on the Debate', *International Studies of Management and Organization*, 30: 25–40.

Jaros, S. (2005) 'Marxian Criticisms of Thompson's (1990) Core Labour Process Theory: An Evaluation and Extension', *Ephemera*, 5(1): http://www.ephemeraweb.org.

▶

▶

Jessop, B. (1990) 'Regulation Theories in Retrospect and Prospect', *Economy and Society*, 19(2): 153–216.

Jessop, B. (1992) 'Fordism and Post-Fordism: A Critical Reformulation', in Storper, M. J. and Scott, A. J. (eds) *Pathways to Regionalism and Industrial Development*, London: Routledge.

Kelly, J. (1985) 'Management's Redesign of Work: Labour Process, Product Market and Labour Market', in Knights, D., Willmott, H. and Collinson, D. (eds) *Job Redesign*, London: Routledge: 30–51.

Kelly, J. (1998) Rethinking Industrial Relations: Mobilization, Collectivism and Long Waves, London: Routledge.

Knights, D. (2001) 'Hanging Out the Dirty Washing: Labor Process Theory and Its Dualistic Legacies', *International Studies of Management and Organization*, 30(4): 68–84.

Knights, D. and Willmott, H. (eds) (1990) *Labour Process Theory*, London: Macmillan.

Lane, C. and Bachmann, R. (eds) (1998) *Trust within and between Organizations: Conceptual Issues and Empirical Applications*, New York: Oxford University Press.

Lipietz, A. (1986) 'Behind the Crisis: The Exhaustion of a Regime of Accumulation', *Review of. Radical Political Economics*, 18: 13–32.

Littler, C. (1990) 'The Labour Process Debate: A Theoretical Review, 1974–1988', in Knights, D. and Willmott, H. (eds) *Labour Process Theory*, London: Macmillan.

Marchington, M. and Vincent, S. (2004) 'The Role of Institutional Forces, Employer Choice and Boundary Spanning Agents in the Formation and Maintenance of Inter-organisational Relations', *Journal of Management Studies*, 41(6): 1029–56.

Peck, J. (1990) 'Circuits of Capital and Industrial Restructuring: Adjustment in the Australian Clothing Industry', *Australian Geographer*, 21(1): 33–52.

Rainnie, A. (1984) 'Combined and Uneven Development in the Clothing Industry: The Effects of Competition and Accumulation', *Capital and Class*, 22: 11–29.

Ramsay, H. (1985) 'What Is Participation For: A Critical Analysis of Labour Process Analyses of Job Reform', in Knights, D., Willmott, H. and Collinson, D. (eds) *Job Redesign: Critical Perspectives on the Labour Process*, Aldershot: Gower.

Rowlinson, M. and Hassard, M. (2001) 'Marxist Political Economy, Revolutionary Politics, and Labour Process Theory', *International Studies of Management and Organization*, 30: 85–112.

Sayer, A. (2005) *The Moral Significance of Class*, Cambridge: Cambridge University Press.

Sen, A. (1997) *Development as Freedom,* Oxford: Oxford University Press.

Smith, C. (2005) 'Beyond Convergence and Divergence: Explaining Variations in Organizational Practices and Forms', in Ackroyd, S., Batt, R., Thompson, P. and Tolbert, P. (eds) *The Oxford Handbook of Work and Organization*, Oxford: Oxford University Press.

▶

▶

Smith, C. (2006) 'The Double Indeterminacy of Labour Power: Labour Effort and Labour Mobility', *Work, Employment and Society*, 20(2): 389–402.

Spencer, D. (2000) 'Braverman and the Contribution of Labour Process Analysis to a Critique of Capitalist Production – 25 Years On', *Work, Employment and Society*, 14: 223–43.

Taylor, P. and Bain, P. (2003) 'Subterranean Worksick Blues: Humour as Subversion in Two Call Centres', *Organization Studies*, 24(9): 1487–509.

Taylor, S. (1998) 'Emotional Labour and the New Workplace', in Thompson, P. and Warhurst, C. (eds) *Workplaces of the Future*, London: Macmillan.

Thompson, P. (1989) *The Nature of Work: An Introduction to Debates on the Labour Process*, London: Macmillan.

Thompson, P. (1990) 'Crawling from the Wreckage: The Labour Process and the Politics of Production', in Knights, D. and Willmott, H. (eds) *Labour Process Theory*, London: Macmillan.

Thompson P. (2003) 'Disconnected Capitalism: Or Why Employers Can't Keep Their Side of the Bargain', *Work, Employment and Society*, 17(2): 359–78.

Thompson, P. and Harley, B. (2007) 'HRM and the Worker: Labour Process Perspectives', in Boxall, P., Purcell, J. and Wright, P. (eds) *The Oxford Handbook of Human Resource Management*, Oxford: Oxford University Press.

Thompson, P. and Newsome, K. (2004) 'Labour Process Theory, Work and the Employment Relation', in Kauffman, B. (ed.) *Theoretical Perspectives on Work and the Employment Relationship*, Ithaca, NY: Cornell University Press.

Thompson, P. and Smith, C. (2001) 'Follow the Red Brick Road – Reflections on Pathways into and out of the Labour Process Debate', *International Studies of Management and Organization*, 30: 40–67.

Thompson, P., Parker, R. and Cox, S. (2009) 'Networks in the Shadow of Markets and Hierachies: Calling the Shots in the Visual Effects Industry', Paper to EGOS Conference, Barcelona 2–4 July.

Vincent, S. (2008) 'A Transmutation Theory of Inter-organizational Exchange Relations and Networks: The Application of Critical Realism to Analysis of Social Agency', *Human Relations*, 61(6): 875–99.

Whitley, R. (1999) *Divergent Capitalisms: The Social Structuring and Change of Business Systems*, Oxford: Oxford University Press.

The Core Theory: Critiques, Defences and Advances

4

Stephen Jaros

Core theory is perhaps the four-stroke internal combustion engine of labour process analysis.

Damian O'Doherty

Labour process theory...research projects are routinely undertaken and considered by investigators as modular contributions; produced, as it were, as bricks in a wall.

Stephen Ackroyd

These extracts from O'Doherty (2009a) and Ackroyd (2009a) imply that core labour process theory (core LPT) has contributed to the formation of a cohesive intellectual community successful in generating insightful accounts of workplace dynamics. Yet the author of the first quote would probably disagree with this interpretation, since O'Doherty's intention was to highlight a belief that core LPT is an intellectual straitjacket producing myopic, under-theorized accounts of work. And perhaps the second quote, though from an author much more sympathetic to core LPT, could prompt one to think of Pink Floyd's *Another Brick in the Wall*, a dystopian vision of intellectual conformity. Thus, the contribution of this chapter is to describe and extend debates about core LPT: Its adequacy in helping or hindering theoretical and empirical inquiry into the workings of labour processes, their linkages with broader political economies and the possibility of 'emancipating' employees from at least some of the harsher realities of life at work.

The term 'core LPT' refers to the guiding principles for labour process research originally described by Thompson (1990). While others contributed to its development (cf. Littler, 1990; Edwards, 1990) and later refinement (cf. Thompson and Smith, 2001; Elger, 2001; Jaros, 2005; Thompson, 2009), Thompson's original formulation remains the most formally explicit and impactful. And since none of these later elaborations fundamentally alter the core's main tenets, it will set the parameters of my analysis. In a nutshell, core LPT holds that capitalist labour processes are characterized by capital's need to *control* labour; a logic of *accumulation* that impels refinements in technology and administration; a fundamental, *structured antagonism* between capital and labour; and because it is the place where labour is valorized, the 'labour process', the point of production, is *privileged* for analysis. Importantly, Thompson (1990) emphasized that while core LPT draws heavily on Marx's categories, it is not a Marxist theory, because core LPT rejects the idea that there is an automatic progression from struggle within the workplace to broader struggles of societal transformation. While this theoretical decoupling of workplace conflict from social conflict freed core LPT from the albatross of Marx's failure to predict the overthrow of capitalism in Western countries, it seemingly leaves the core without a mechanism for linking what happens in workplaces to the broader political economy, a problem that the editors of this volume describe as perhaps the most salient issue for contemporary labour process researchers. The rejection of Marxism more generally also left core LPT bereft of a 'meta-theoretical' foundation, an ontological and epistemological grounding, that has contributed to core LPT's perceived vulnerability to Marxian and post-modernist attacks, and which has arguably led to the engagement of core LPT with Critical Realism as a possible antidote (see Thompson and Vincent, this volume).

These are issues I have addressed in part before. Jaros (2001) provided a '10th anniversary' update on core LPT's impact on the study of work, while Jaros (2005) provided a defence (and some critique) of core LPT against Marxian attacks on its usefulness. Here, I extend those analyses in light of practical and theoretical developments since. Specifically, core LPT confronts an ongoing post-modernist critique (cf. O'Doherty and Willmott, 2001a,b; O'Doherty, 2009a,b) and calls for revision from friendly analysts as well (cf. Elger, 2001). My strategy is to describe these critiques and evaluate their implications for core LPT. The editors of this volume have argued that it is time for LPT to move beyond 'paradigm wars', and my assessment leads me to believe that this is possible, because on important issues, there is actually considerably less difference between core LPT and post-modern (PM) perspectives than meets the eye. I conclude by combining the insights from my evaluation of the PM critique with concerns raised by commentators friendly to core LPT (e.g. Ackroyd, 2009a; Elger, 2001; Jaros, 2005) to develop ideas on what role, if any, core LPT can best play in addressing issues such as employee emancipation and understanding capitalist political economy.

Core LPT and post-modernism

Calls for an end to 'paradigm wars' notwithstanding (Thompson and Smith, 2001), PM and core LPT advocates have continued to joust. At the meta-theoretical level, the PM position has broadened its intellectual resources, moving beyond its original Foucauldian roots to incorporate ideas drawn from thinkers such as Lacan, Zizek, and Laclau and Mouffe (O'Doherty, 2009a; Willmott, 2005). At the same time, as discussed in Chapter 2, core LPT has linked itself to the Critical Realist (CR) philosophy of science (cf. Ackroyd and Fleetwood, 2000; Reed, 2009) and these perspectives have clashed (cf. Reed, 2005a and 2005b; Contu and Willmott, 2005). And at the meso-theoretical level, the two perspectives have debated the relevance of core LPT in guiding research into issues such as identity and resistance (Contu, 2008; O'Doherty, 2009a and 2009b; Thompson, 2009; Webb, 2006). Here, I turn my attention to this 'meso-theoretical' aspect of the debate.

Meso-theory: PM and the relevance of a 'core theory' to analysis of labour processes

I call this debate 'meso-theoretical' because although the antagonists draw upon meta-theoretical concepts derived from CR and PM as weapons of combat, the battle is over theorizing what happens within labour processes as specific, middle-range 'sites', the dynamics of behaviour within workplaces, where structure and agency interact and where multiple discourses converge. A recent clash between Thompson (2009) and O'Doherty (2009a,b) is exemplary of the current status of the debate, so I focus on them as champions of the respective sides.

Reading both Thompson (2009) and O'Doherty (2009a,b), one gets the impression that things haven't changed much over the years since this debate unfolded. According to Thompson, the PM approach rejects core LPT because PM believes that capital and labour are not 'real', but merely signifiers in language games, still relying primarily on the deconstructive method rather than empirical research, and uncritically accepting that new forms of control (i.e. concertive, cultural) have superseded older ones, creating self-disciplining, non-resistant subjects – or more recently it views 'everything', even innocuous behaviours like 'farting' as resistance, trivializing the term.

O'Doherty (2009a,b) has a similarly grim view of core LPT. O'Doherty (2009b) argues that it is reductionist, largely confining itself to analyses of wage-effort bargaining among male, blue-collar workers; is an 'increasingly hegemonic' discourse characterized by methodological and theoretical conformity and still dualistically pits agency against structure. In an explicitly humorous account, researchers who utilize core theory are depicted by

O'Doherty (2009a) as 'automatons' working on the core LPT 'production line' under the watchful, controlling eye of 'manager' Paul Thompson.

The exchange between Thompson and O'Doherty certainly makes it seem as if nothing has changed in the past decade; that the paradigm war is as firmly entrenched as ever. But in my view, the differences are at least somewhat exaggerated. For example, Thompson (2009) argues that PM methodology is oriented towards the analysis of texts, not of actual workplaces, as its primary source of data, and cites O'Doherty and Willmott (2001a) to that effect. Indeed, O'Doherty and Willmott (2001a,b) do recommend the deconstructive method and call for more analyses of 'orthodox' labour process texts to surface the dualisms and essentialisms lying within. However, later developments suggest that this call was *not* heeded. During the 2000s, PM-inspired labour process research has moved in a decisively empirical direction: O'Doherty and Willmott (2001a,b) were the *last* such prominent deconstructive studies in the PM-LPT domain. At the least, the number of studies that deconstruct other texts is dwarfed by the number of PM-inspired case studies of identity, control and resistance in actual workplaces (e.g. see Collinson, 2003, 2008; Gagnon, 2008; Knights and McCabe, 2003; McDonald, Harrison and Checkland, 2008; Sturdy et al., 2006; Winiecki, 2004, 2007; Zanoni and Janssens, 2007), indicative of the move within PM towards taking empirical reality, the 'extra-discursive' aspects of capitalism, seriously.

Furthermore, these PM case studies have not generally assumed or found that cultural forms of control produce docile 'subjects' at work. This stance, which Taylor and Bain (1999) and Bain and Taylor (2000) incisively critiqued, has largely been disowned by post-modernist writers. For example, in Knights and McCabe's (2003) empirical study of call centre workers, we see an explicit acknowledgement of the indeterminacy of the capital-labour dynamic with respect to control and resistance. As another PM writer, Collinson (2003, 2008), finds struggles for control may result in conformist/compliant, disguised/dramaturgical, or resistant 'selves'. There is no assumption of an inescapable Foucauldian prison.

Also, consistent with core LPT's emphasis on continuity in managerial control strategies, recent PM research tends to acknowledge that new forms of cultural/normative control interact with and reinforce traditional hierarchical methods. For example, McDonald, Harrison and Checkland's (2008) study of medical personnel experiencing the implementation of government-mandated 'employee empowerment' found that 'far from eradicating or reducing bureaucracy, the expansion of "enterprise" takes place alongside new forms of bureaucracy; despite the growth in self-surveillance, the introduction...has, at the same time, increased the use of top-down surveillance' (367). Thus, this newer line of PM research recognizes the continuity and layering of control strategies within organizations and institutions.

Recent trends in PM-inspired research also recognize the need to incorporate the broader political economy into an account of what happens at work and thus move beyond authorial reflexive 'navel-gazing' and towards formulation of an emancipatory politics. In their overview of PM-inspired identity research, Alvesson, Ashcraft and Thomas (2008) argue that this research typically focuses on perceptions and practices of the author and thus misses 'the bigger picture'. Spicer, Alvesson and Karreman (2009), in calling for a more overtly activist political orientation for CMS, argue that '...by placing itself into a consistently negative position, CMS is unable to put forward a firm claim about what it actually wants and desires' (541). Thus, PM-inspired research, like core LPT, is grappling with how to explain interrelationships between what happens at the workplace and the broader, global political economy, and how to construct an impactful critical political stance.

Finally, Thompson cites Fleming and Spicer (2007) to support his view that recent PM research has adopted an 'anything goes' mentality about resistance. But since these authors are *PM* writers, this critique is coming from within the PM community. Similarly, another post-modernist writer, Contu (2008), recently critiques both Ackroyd and Thompson's (1999) impactful concept of misbehaviour and PM researchers who look to the Foucauldian 'care of the self' as a path to liberation for making too much of trivial forms of 'resistance'. Contu calls these acts 'decaf' resistance, which 'do not constitute a threat to the dominant order of the workplace' (369). Thus, there is evidence that post-modernist writers are well aware of the risk of trivializing resistance, and are working the problem. In my view, this closely parallels the recent work of core-LPT researchers such as Thompson and Ackroyd (2009) and Ackroyd (2009b), who are also struggling to define exactly what the concept of resistance should entail.

Overall, my contention is that Thompson (2009) is an accurate depiction of the state of post-modernist research during the 1990s, but on issues such as identity, resistance and control, it misses the degree to which PM research has moved away from totalizing, deconstructionist approaches, and towards an 'extra-discursive', materialist frame of reference (cf. Collinson (2003). Furthermore, my reading is that core LPT played a significant role in this movement: Works by Taylor and Bain (1999; Bain and Taylor, 2000) and Ackroyd and Thompson (1999) among others were influential in swaying post-modernists away from the excesses of the 1990s. Therefore, to a significant extent, Thompson's (2009) insistence that an impasse exists strikes me as an example of refusing to take 'yes' for an answer.

However, just as Thompson's account exaggerates the differences between core LPT and PM, so does O'Doherty's. O'Doherty (2009a and b) claims that LPT researchers are trapped in an intellectual straitjacket that focuses myopically on the effort bargain, and yet the 2000s have seen a significant amount of core-LPT inspired research that has investigated employee identity and has taken an expansive perspective on the influences that shape employee agency.

For example, Webb's (2006) comprehensive assessment of identity rejects totalizing accounts, arguing that people resist being defined by a single, categorical social identity, whether 'marked by class, race, or gender' (145). Also, core-LPT researchers have taken seriously the PM notion that identity and self-construction are important, not peripheral, aspects of the labour process (cf. Marks, 2009). Leidner (2006) argues that identity influences many aspects of the employment relationship, including the 'design of jobs, workplace relations, and the exercise of power at work' (433). This renewed interest in identity within the core-LPT community as a central aspect of the labour process is also reflected in the structure of recent Labour Process Conferences, which for at least the past four years have featured a dedicated 'stream' to identity and agency at work.

As Jaros (2009) notes, recent core-inspired identity research also recognizes that employee identities are multiple, contingent and 'fragile', having both work and non-work influences; and like Collinson's (2003) PM-inspired argument that employee behaviour might reflect role-playing – the display of 'dramaturgical' selves – core-LPT identity work has investigated how employees may present compliant selves while secretly resisting managerial rhetoric (Thompson, 2003). Likewise, both PM and core-LPT identity research has begun to investigate the notion that even if an employee seeks to maintain an 'inner' resistant identity, overt displays of conformity may result in reinforcement of managerial hegemony anyway (cf. Zizek, 2000) and the degree to which employee 'distancing' and 'dis-identification' with management discourses constitutes effective resistance or serves to reinforce managerial hegemony (cf. Contu, 2008; Costas and Fleming, 2009; Marks, 2009; Thompson and Ackroyd, 2009).

This is not to say that there are no differences between PM and core-inspired identity research. Core-LPT research problematizes the PM notion that existential (or even 'materialist') anxiety concerns are *the* deep-rooted motivation for identity work, and argues that perceptions of interests are more salient (Marks, 2009). Nevertheless, similarities between these bodies of work significantly outweigh the differences. And importantly, the contending beliefs that interests or anxiety reduction act as motivators of identity work are theoretical propositions that can be tested via empirical research (cf. Jaros, 2009). It is likely that contextual factors might mean either or both will play a causal role in 'crafting of self' processes.

Likewise, recent core-LPT associated work is not characterized by limitations characteristic of intellectual straitjackets; on the contrary, it has been theoretically and methodologically innovative. For example, core-LPT writers have recently explored the impact of management's deployment of furniture and artwork to foster employee commitment to management strategies (Baldry and Hallier, 2007); Vallas (2003) conducted comparative case studies at multiple workplaces to investigate the extent to which team-based normative controls would shape worker identities and their capacity for individual and collective resistance; Marks and Scholarios (2007) supplemented their qualitative analysis with survey-feedback to gain a fuller picture of competing organizational and professional identities in the minds of employees; while Ellis and Richards (2009) used internet surveys and interviews to study the anonymous 'blogging' habits of public service workers as an opposition technique for contesting management policies.

Also, contrary to the PM notion that core LPT focuses solely or even largely on the experience of male, blue-collar factory workers, this more recent work has investigated identity and resistance among diverse categories of employees. For example, Bolton and colleagues (e.g. Bolton, 2005; Bolton and Muzio, 2008; Bolton and Wibberley, 2007) have utilized core-LPT concepts to study emotional labour, gender dynamics, resistance and dignity at work amongst legal secretaries, doctors, nurses, interactive service workers and primary school teachers.

Thus, O'Doherty's (2009a,b) critique largely misses the extent to which core LPT-inspired research has developed in the 2000s. And importantly, PM-inspired research deserves a significant amount of credit: it was the work of Knights, Willmott and others, via their deconstructive problematizing of core-LPT concepts and insistence on the central role of subjectivity in understanding the labour process that compelled core LPT to take seriously issues of identity and agency at work. As Elger (2001) states 'post-modernist theorists...prompted fresh thinking about the salience of the formation and contestation of identities within workplaces' (10). Likewise, in the 1990s, it was PM-inspired researchers who led the way in recognizing the emergence of new team-based, normative, emotional and cultural forms of control.

Finally, O'Doherty (2009a) argues that the emergence of rival Critical Management Studies (CMS) and LPT camps has reduced the quality of debate. However, my account shows that the 2000s have seen a productive cross-pollination of PM, core LPT, and Marxian ideas, as reflected in the works cited above, and in special issues of journals dedicated to various aspects of the controversies described herein (e.g. *ISMO's* special issue on the labour process debate in 2001; the 2007 special forum on Paleo-Marxism in *Organization Studies*, the 2005 special forum on CR versus PM ontology in *Organization*; the 2008 special issue on Identity research in *Organization*, and the forthcoming *Oxford Handbook of CMS* from which the Thompson/O'Doherty exchanges are derived). O'Doherty (2009a) might resent Thompson's 'pugnacious' writing style, but this clash of personalities hasn't prevented a fruitful exchange of ideas, one that has, in my view, dramatically closed the gap between the two perspectives.

The future of core theory

Beyond the issues raised by the PM/core-LPT debate, analysts have also raised concerns about the adequacy of core LPT with respect to the following issues: (1) how core LPT fits within the broader 'critical management studies' community (2) articulating linkages between workplaces and the broader socius and (3) the role of core theory in developing an emancipatory politics. It is to these issues that I now turn.

Core LPT and the broader Critical-Management community

Many PM-inspired writers believe that core LPT has been enforced as a kind of 'hegemonic orthodoxy' (O'Doherty, 2009a), and this perception has driven some of them away from the LPT community and towards Critical Management Studies (CMS). I have argued that the conceptual differences between core LPT and PM-LPT are actually small enough to reject the hypothesis of fundamental incommensurability. This leads to the conclusion that advancing our understanding of the labour process would benefit from collaborative research by PM and core-LPT writers, an example being the insightful article on conflict and resistance by Collinson and Ackroyd (2005). The emergence of competing CMS and LPT 'brands', vying for the hearts and minds of critically inclined researchers, may seem to be solely about conflicting theories, but personality clashes are also at work here.

This isn't to say that substantive issues do not still play a role in the schism. Just as PM comes in 'hard' and 'soft' forms, the former oriented towards making CMS the 'brand name' for post-modernist research only, the latter more consistent with a 'big tent' CMS that welcomes all critically oriented workplace scholarship, no matter what the intellectual pedigree (cf. Thompson, 2004); so might we characterize core LPT. To me, the key to not only its past success in helping develop a robust empirical research program but also in fostering a stronger intellectual community is emphasizing the *general* nature of core-LPT principles. When viewed in their best light, these principles do not reflect hard, deterministic, totalizing aspects of capitalist employment relations, but tendencies. As an example of the latter approach, Ackroyd (2009b), whilst accepting the core-LPT concept of 'structural antagonism' between capital and labour, argues that it does not 'provide the basic explanation of every kind of observed conflict' (3) at work. Consistent with CR notions of causal contingency, these core principles should be viewed as creating general tendencies that may be moderated or counteracted by other tendencies in specific workplaces.

Thus, while boundary-maintenance is inevitable and necessary within any intellectual community (cf. Parker, 1999), we should be modest in patrolling the boundaries of core LPT, eschewing language that harshly rejects the application of non-core theories and intellectual resources as 'distractions' or as indicative of a lack of serious interest in the nature of work. Looking back at my own work (Jaros, 2004 and 2005), I see evidence of being guilty of this. A respectful, collegial tone in our writing and personal interactions would go a long way to healing schisms and rifts between some in the CMS community and LPT, paving the way for re-engagement and even collaborative research. O'Doherty's invitation to debate issues of reflexivity at the most recent (2009) LPC is a hopeful step in that direction.

Core LPT and global linkages

The problem of apprehending the relationships between what happen in particular workplaces and the broader political economy is something the editors of this volume call LPT's greatest current challenge. This is the problem that Adler (2007) tried to address via his Paleo-Marxian theory. Other writers more sympathetic to core theory have done the same. Elger (2001) is in this regard exemplary, so in this section I engage with his work to draw conclusions about core LPT's role in addressing this critical issue.

Elger (2001) characterizes core LPT as a 'regional' theory of the labour process, in that it is a conceptual framework designed to explain the capital-labour relation dynamic 'within the enterprise, rather than developing a general critique of the social relations of capitalist societies' (3). This formulation poses questions about how what happens at the workplace 'articulate' with other aspects of capitalism, such as product markets, the state, culture and the broader political economy. Elger is thus referencing the 'boundary problem' in core LPT (Jaros and Jermier, 1995), the meaning of the term 'relative autonomy' (Thompson, 1990) that has captured the attention of LPT theorists since the core was first delineated.

Elger (2001) also argues that the core-LPT concept of 'structural antagonism' is underspecified, in that it is compatible with a broad range of conflict-behaviours, from minor, arguably trivial acts of individual misbehaviour up to collective activities aimed at altering the capital-labour relation at the societal level, and as such it can't practically inform a politics of production. He notes that it 'may be that core LPT must remain analytically indifferent to these varied emphases, or it may be that the propositions of core theory are insufficiently developed but with further work might give more support to one than the other' (12). Elger concludes by arguing that core LPT remains a progressive research programme '...in the ambitious sense that it has the potential to inform an emancipatory politics within and about the workplace' (20) but fulfilling that potential means re-entering the terrain of political economy to articulate linkages with broader social forces.

Elger's (2001) concerns have been reiterated by other theorists. Thompson and Newsome (2004) share Elger's (2001) optimism about core LPT's potential, arguing that 'a great strength of (core) LPT is its capacity to connect the workplace to a broader political economy' (7); while Ackroyd (2009a) says that 'a key question for LPT...concerns what is known and needs to be known beyond the labor process itself, of the wider pattern of institutions which constitute the economy' (1). And similarly, Thompson (2003) attempts to reclaim a 'bigger picture' for core LPT, one that tries to tie what happens at workplaces to a broader canvas whilst avoiding the totalizing tendencies of orthodox Marxism and the 'non-empirical meta-theorizing' of post-modernist approaches. In doing so he argues for an ascending analysis: 'The pursuit of a complete picture of capitalist political economy and its relations with the spheres of work and employment, may, in other words, have inherent limitations and to the extent that it can be achieved, come, not from *a* total analysis, but the combination of smaller pictures, and from analyses that start at different levels' (22). In this passage, one can sense Thompson (2003), like Elger (2001) before him, straining to resolve the difficulty of modelling linkages between the 'labour process' and the broader political economy while maintaining the boundary-integrity of a middle-range theory. This is the conundrum of the 'relative autonomy' concept.

So, is there a solution? In Jaros (2005), I suggested methodological approaches: the use of 'meta-ethnography' techniques, and/or quantitative methods, were proposed as means to aggregate data collected via case-study research across many workplaces and thus grasp trends and tendencies that characterize the global political-economic canvas. Four years later, I still think that these recommendations have some merit, and there is a modicum of supportive evidence. For example, Littler and Innes (2003) quantitatively analysed data from over 4000 Australian banks and were thus able to draw conclusions about broad patterns of skills-changes among organizations in that country. Core-LPT empirical research, like post-modern LP research, is overwhelmingly done using qualitative, case-study methods, and if data are gathered only from a particular workplace, or a handful of workplaces, it is unlikely that one will be able to draw conclusions that reliably extend beyond those boundaries.

However, in thinking about the possible solutions Elger (2001) discusses, the correct one is that core LPT should be 'analytically indifferent' about the broader political economy, and about worker 'emancipation'. The reason for this is that the boundaries of any social theory can, indeed must, for the theory to be coherent, be delimited along two dimensions, *scope* and *level*. The former refers to the aspect of social reality addressed by theory. Examples include gender, ethnicity, religion and class relations. Level refers to the scale of analysis, ranging from the local to the global, micro to meso to macro. In my view, core LPT is properly bounded by a focus on capital-labour relations (its scope) at the workplace (its level). What this means is that core LPT should not be re-conceptualized so as to attempt to account for broad, global, political, economic or cultural dynamics. These lie beyond its proper scope and/or level, which is that of a middle-range theory of capitalist employment relations.

The urge to extend core-LPT analysis towards an account of the broader political economy (an extension of level) is a relic of LPT's Marxian heritage. The reason I say this is because core-LPT writers, such as the ones cited above (including myself), typically do not express consternation that core LPT does not account for *every* dimension of broader society, just those that constitute 'political economy', which was Marx's primary concern. There is seemingly no concern within the LPT community about core LPT's limited scope, its focus on the capital-labour relation, only its limited level, a focus on the workplace to the 'neglect' of the broader political economy.

For example, when discussing female subjugation at work, Thompson (1990) characterizes gender theory as addressing another 'sphere of analysis', patriarchy, which is distinct from the labour process in the content of its concerns (in my terms, 'patriarchy' is a different scope-foci). Still, because patriarchal structures and discourses are manifested in, influence, and are in part reproduced in the gender dynamics of the workplace, LP theorists must be literate in gender theory, and know how to apply its insights when conducting studies of the labour process. But crucially, Thompson (1990) doesn't argue that core LPT is responsible for extrapolating observed gender dynamics within a workplace to claims about how these influence societal-level patriarchal structures and discourses. This would be an 'intrusion' into the theoretical domain of a separate social sphere, an unwarranted extension of LPT's scope and level.

Thompson (1990) emphasizes that theories are developed to address particular phenomenon, 'social spheres', and have tools that are designed specifically for that purpose. Thus, it is inappropriate to apply conceptual tools developed for one purpose (studying capital-labour dynamics) to another social sphere (e.g. gender relations). It would be like trying to use a hammer to saw a piece of wood. Theorizing gender dynamics is the responsibility of gender theory, while theorizing capital-labour relations is the province of LPT. In my view, this same logic of theoretical responsibility that limits the scope of core LPT to capital-labour relations should also apply to the issue of level: Theorizing capital-labour relations at a macro, societal level is the responsibility of fields such as political-economics and sociology, not core LPT. In the social sciences division of labour, core LPT's role is that of a middle-range theory of capital-labour dynamics. Its proper theoretical level is that of 'the organization', or at most networks of organizations. In saying this, I do not believe that I am calling on core LPT to abdicate responsibility. Expecting core-LPT concepts to explain what happens beyond its level is no more appropriate than expecting it to explain what happens beyond its scope. Core LPT's 'core' responsibility is to account for (a) capital-labour dynamics (b) at work.

Importantly, this does not mean that LPT *researchers* must limit themselves to 'micro-level' analyses of single workplaces or abandon efforts to describe relationships between what happens inside the firm and broader social institutions. This would only be the correct view if workplaces are empirically autonomous from broader social forces, and of course they are not. Comparative research at workplaces in multiple industrial sectors and/or in different countries can be conducted to show how these core-LPT tendencies play out in different political-economic contexts. Teams of researchers, some of whom are experts in LPT and others who grasp theories that address other social spheres/levels, can collaborate on multi-level projects to investigate mutual influence processes. Understanding linkages between and among social spheres and at different levels of analysis is important, and the critical social scientist has obligations to investigate them. But that's a responsibility of the researcher, not the core LP *theory*.

Nor does it mean that theoretically, core LPT should be isolated from other social theories. For example, when studying labour processes, the LPT researcher must be aware of gender theory and the implications of that theory for the study of work relations, and the gender theorist should be mindful of LPT research of gender dynamics in specific workplaces, and its implications for understanding social-level gender dynamics. Over time, insights from LPT might thus reinforce or refute aspects or propositions of gender theory, and vice versa.

This is what 'relative autonomy' should mean, in an analytical sense: each theory focusing on that aspect of the socius for which it was developed, and at its proper level, while at the same time incorporating into its analysis the insights and concepts of theories from other spheres and levels of analysis that address the empirical interpenetration of both in 'real life'. I think this perspective reflects the notion that capitalist society is, as Elger (2001) states, 'a complex structure of linked but relatively autonomous loci of social relations, rather than...a tightly integrated totality' (8). If this model of society is correct, than each locus of social relations requires its 'core theory', but these core theories should not, in their analytical formulation, intrude upon the domains of other social loci. The task of explicating the linkages among social loci X, Y and Z requires the simultaneous application of theoretical concepts from the specific theories that have been developed to explain each social locus, either by teams of researchers or by a single researcher who has mastered the several theories.

Thus, we should not expect to find the empirical interpenetrations between different social spheres and levels fully reflected in our theories of those relatively autonomous spheres, until or unless the time arrives when the process of inter-theory interaction described above generates enough empirical evidence that a merging of theories, in terms of both scope and level, is warranted, or because social conditions have changed and now warrant it. Only under these circumstances can we hope to derive a 'grand theory of everything', such as physicists are searching for. This is a process that in my view can only unfold 'naturally' through the normal science process of iterative empirical research-theory building; and only if societies change such that the concept of relatively autonomous social spheres is no longer an accurate description of empirical reality. It cannot be 'forced' or hastened by grand-theorizing built on empirically unsupported leaps of faith.

Core LPT and emancipation

Similarly, I believe core LPT must, at least for now, be *analytically* indifferent towards the forms that worker 'emancipation' can and should take. This is contrary to what Bhaskar (2002), a founder of Critical Realism, has stated. Bhaskar argues that while CR is not designed to support the interests of any particular political tendency, 'through Critical Realism positive values are generated by rational argument which show that capitalism is evil and immoral' (190). But in my view, the ascription of 'evil' to a social institution cannot be proven via scientific inquiry, because any definition of evil is inherently subjective.

However, this does not mean that core LPT must abandon its critical dimension. To the contrary, core LPT should continue to espouse an anti-capitalist political view, and seek to find ways to help workers 'emancipate' themselves from oppressive working conditions. Core LPT has proven a fruitful basis for surfacing and analysing exploitative working conditions and explaining how conditions in particular workplaces are the result not just of the personal ethical failings of 'bad' managers and owners, but of systemic tendencies and pressures that compel capital to fail to live up to its side of the effort-bargain (cf. Thompson, 2003; Newsome, Thompson and Commander, 2009). LPT researchers can and should use these findings to engage with academic, organized labour, left-political, and social constituencies in the fight to implement public policies that eliminate or at least ameliorate 'hard times at work' (Warhurst and Thompson, 1998).

My contention is merely that the justification for our political positions, for specific definitions of 'emancipation' that we adopt, cannot be derived from core *analytical* principles of LPT, since these principles are by definition scientific in nature. The contention that business owners face a 'control imperative' or that the capital-labour relation is characterized by antagonistic tendencies, two of the four principles of core LPT, are theoretical proposals that can be supported or undermined empirically. On the other hand, the idea that workers deserve to be 'emancipated' is a moral/ethical claim that cannot be objectively supported or refuted by evaluation of evidence (cf. Parker, 1999).

Probably the closest we can get to a universal definition of emancipation is that the concept necessarily implies some kind of removal of constraints *from something*, it cannot leave social inequality undisturbed (Armstrong, 2009). But beyond this threshold, if a neoliberal researcher defines 'worker emancipation' to mean the freedom to sell one's labour power to the highest bidder or as entrepreneurship (Rindova, Barry and Ketchen, 2009), unconstrained by laws that regulate wages or working conditions, while a core-LPT researcher defines it as being free from capitalist control over wages or working conditions, there is no scientific way to prove that either one is the 'true' definition of worker emancipation in any objective sense. Its definitional indeterminacy also suggests that the content of the principle should be broadly defined. It should be a 'big tent' definition, not a narrow, 'hard' conceptualization that, for example, counts only mass-scale, social transformation as 'real' emancipation.

Note that this definitional indeterminacy does not apply to the researcher's advocacy of political tactics to achieve whatever concept of emancipation they adopt. These claims cannot be given a 'free pass' with regard to being evaluated by scientific procedures because they imply cause-effect relationships. So, for example, a researcher who adopts the Alvesson and Willmott (1992) concept of 'micro-emancipation' as their definition of emancipation and argues that self-reflexivity on the part of the employee is a viable method to achieve it has to be able to support that claim with empirical data showing that this method is both usable by employees and produces the emancipatory results claimed for it, and their interpretation of the data has to withstand challenge by others who doubt the efficacy of the self-reflexive method (e.g. Armstrong, 2009). Likewise, if one believes that setting up workshops to tutor workers on organizing strategies for forming labour unions will lead to successful union organizing efforts and ultimately improvements in wages and benefits, then doing so should be the occasion for conducting case-study research that evaluates the usefulness of the workshops. Thus, rather than merely calling for the adoption of certain political tactics to help workers achieve some kind of emancipation, these tactics should be implemented, and simultaneously subject to empirical validation so that LPT accumulates knowledge on the emancipatory-efficacy of various political tactics, just as it accumulates knowledge on issues such as resistance, skill dynamics and identity. As of now, core LPT is not in a position to advocate a defined set of political tactics because the empirical work needed to validate them has not been done.

Conclusion: Core LPT as normal science

Thompson (2009) performs a useful service in reminding us of why a 'core theory' of the labour process was developed, tracing this back to the late-1980s belief that LPT had run aground. At that time, while a welter of empirical studies had generated insights about control, resistance and exploitation at work, this research took place in a context in which key aspects of the Braverman-era theoretical edifice, such as deskilling and an emphasis on structure over worker and managerial agency, had been discredited to the point that it was no longer clear what the 'theory' in 'labour process theory' stood for. Thompson (1990) developed 'core LPT' as an antidote to this problem. It was an attempt to consolidate the knowledge generated by the previous decade's empirical studies, and distil them in to a set of theoretical principles and conceptual tools that capture systemic features of capitalist labour processes so as to provide a focus and direction for future empirical research and theory-building. It also would serve the organizational purpose of allowing researchers with like-minded interests to more easily recognize each other's work, facilitating the formation of a cohesive intellectual community.

My analysis of the post-modernist critiques of core theory and friendly defences of it leads to the conclusion that, by and large, core theory has proven successful in fulfilling these roles. The delineation of four general features of capitalist employment relations has provided a robust foundation for analysing important dimensions of the labour process, such as control, resistance, identity/agency, and skills in a wide variety of occupational, industrial and service sectors. And these principles have stood the test of time as underlying 'generative mechanisms' that have allowed the LPT community to recognize patterns and commonalities among surface-level differences across workplaces, and to recognize continuity in labour process dynamics amidst seemingly profound changes in technology and administrative strategies. Thus, core-inspired LPT has made progress in advancing from a 'field' towards that of a 'normal science' project (Ackroyd, 2009a).

Building on that framework, this chapter has attempted to clarify the challenges core LPT faces from competing points of view within the critical intellectual community, separate the wheat from the chafe, and identify points of commonality that could lay the groundwork for integrative theory-building that would thereby make core LPT an even more robust perspective from which to study capital-labour dynamics at work, and thus provide better theoretical and empirical descriptions of the 'hard times at work' that currently characterize the lives of labour in a turbulent technological, political and financial world. Progress in addressing these issues might be made by adopting the proposals offered herein.

REFERENCES

Ackroyd, S. (2009a) 'Labour Process Theory as Normal Science', *Employee Responsibilities and Rights Journal*, 21: 263–72.

Ackroyd, S. (2009b) 'Organizational Conflict', in Cooper, C. and Clegg, S. (eds) *The Handbook of Macro Organizational Behaviour*, London: Sage.

Ackroyd, S. and Fleetwood, S. (eds) (2000) *Realist Perspectives on Management and Organizations*, London: Routledge.

Ackroyd, S. and Thompson, P. (1999) *Organisational Misbehaviour*, London: Sage.

Adler, P. (2007) 'The Future of Critical Management Studies: A Paleo-Marxist Critique of Labour Process Theory', *Organization Studies*, 28: 1313–45.

Alvesson, M. and Willmott, H. (1992) 'On the Idea of Emancipation in Management and Organizational Studies', *Academy of Management Review*, 17: 432–54.

Alvesson, M., Ashcraft, K. and Thomas, R. (2008) 'Identity Matters: Reflections on the Construction of Identity Scholarship in Organization Studies', *Organization*, 15: 5–28.

Armstrong, P. (2009) 'Small Expectations: Critical Management Studies Does Emancipation', Paper presented at the annual conference of the *British Sociological Association*, Cardiff, UK.

Bain, P. and Taylor, P. (2000) 'Entrapped by the "Electronic Panopticon"? Worker Resistance in the Call Centre', *New Technology, Work and Employment*, 15(1): 2–18.

Baldry, C. and Hallier, J. (2007) 'Who Am I? Work Space and Social Identity', *25th Annual International Labour Process Conference*, the University of Amsterdam, Holland.

Bhaskar, R. (2002) *From Science to Emancipation: Alienation and the Actuality of Enlightenment*, London: Sage.

Bolton, S. (2005) *Emotion Management in the Workplace*, London: Palgrave Macmillan.

Bolton, S. and Muzio, D. (2008) 'The Paradoxical Processes of Feminization in the Professions: The Case of Established, Aspiring, and Semi-professions', *Work, Employment, and Society*, 22: 281–99.

Bolton, S. and Wibberley, G. (2007) 'Best Companies, Best Practice and Dignity at Work', in Bolton, S. (ed.) *Dimensions of Dignity at Work*, London: Butterworth Heinemann, 134–53.

▶

▶

Collinson, D. (2003) 'Identities and Insecurities: Selves at Work', *Organization*, 10: 527–47.

Collinson, D. (2008) 'Conformist, Resistant and Disguised Selves: A Post-structuralist Approach to Identity and Workplace Followership', in Riggio, R., Chaleff, I. and Lipmen-Blumen, J. (eds) *The Art of Followership*, New York: Jossey-Bass, 309–24.

Collinson, D. and Ackroyd, S. (2005) 'Resistance, Misbehaviour and Dissent', in Ackroyd, S., Thompson, P., Batt, R. and Tolbert, P. S. (eds) *The Oxford Handbook of Work and Organization*, Oxford: Oxford University Press, 305–26.

Contu, A. (2008) 'Decaf Resistance: On Misbehavior, Cynicism, and Desire in Liberal Workplaces', *Management Communication Quarterly*, 21: 364–79.

Contu, A. and Willmott, H. (2005) 'You Spin Me Round: The Realist Turn in Organization and Management Studies', *Journal of Management Studies*, 42: 1645–62.

Costas, J. and Fleming, P. (2009) 'Beyond Dis-identification: A Discursive Approach to Self-alienation in Contemporary Organizations', *Human Relations*, 62: 353–78.

Edwards, P. (1990) 'Understanding Conflict in the Labour Process: The Logic and Autonomy of Struggle', in Knights, D. and Willmott, H. (eds) *Labour Process Theory*, London: Macmillan, 125–52.

Elger, T. (2001) 'Critical Materialist Analyses of Work and Employment: A Third Way?', *Sociologie del Livoro*, 34: 61–84.

Ellis, V. and Richards, J. (2009) 'Creating, Connecting, and Correcting: Motivations and Meanings of Work-Blogging amongst Public Service Workers?', in Bolton, S. and Houlihan, M. (eds) *Work Matters: Critical Reflections on Contemporary Work*, London: Palgrave.

Fleming, P. and Spicer, A. (2007) 'Beyond Power and Resistance: New Approaches to Organizational Politics', *Management Communication Quarterly*, 21: 301–9.

Gagnon, S. (2008) 'Compelling Identity: Selves and Insecurity in Global, Corporate Management Development', *Management Learning*, 39: 375–91.

Jaros, S. (2001) 'Labour Process Theory: A Commentary on the Debate', *International Studies of Management and Organization*, 30: 25–40.

Jaros, S. (2004) 'Jacques's (2000) Call for a Knowledge Theory of Value: Implications for Labour Process Theory', *Electronic Journal of Radical Organization Theory*, 8: November.

Jaros, S. (2005) 'Marxian Criticisms of Thompson's (1990) Core Labour Process Theory: An Evaluation and Extension', *Ephemera: Theory and Politics in Organization*, 5(1): www.ephemeraweb.org.

Jaros, S. (2009) 'Identity in the Workplace: An Assessment of Contextualist and Discursive Approaches', Paper presented at the *2009 International Labour Process Conference*, Edinburgh, UK.

Jaros, S. and Jermier, J. (1995) 'Labor Process Analysis and the McDonaldization of Society Thesis: Revisiting Boundary Problems', Paper presented at the 13th annual International Labour Process Conference, Blackpool, UK.

▶

Knights, D. and McCabe, D. (2003) 'Governing through Teamwork: Reconstituting Subjectivity in a Call and Processing Center', *Journal of Management Studies*, 40: 1587–619.

Leidner, R. (2006) 'Identity and Work', in Korcyznski, M., Hodson, R., and Edwards, P. (eds) *Social Theory at Work*, London: Oxford.

Littler, C. (1990) 'The Labour Process Debate: A Theoretical Review, 1974–1988', in Knights, D. and Willmott, H. (eds) *Labour Process Theory*, London: Macmillan, 46–94.

Littler, C. and Innes, P. (2003) 'Downsizing and De-knowledging the Firm', *Work, Employment, and Society*, 17: 73–100.

Marks, A. (2009) 'The Missing Self: Debating the Conceptualization and Role of Identity in the Workplace', Paper presented at the *2009 Labour Process Conference*, Edinburgh, UK.

Marks, A. and Scholarios, D. (2007) 'Revisiting Technical Workers: Professional and Organizational Identities in the Software Industry', *New Technology, Work, and Employment*, 22: 98–117.

McDonald, R., Harrison, S. and Checkland, K. (2008) 'Identity, Contract, and Enterprise in a Primary Care Setting: An English General Practice Case Study', *Organization*, 15: 355–70.

Newsome, K., Thompson, P. and Commander, J. (2009) 'The Forgotten Factories: Supermarket Suppliers and Dignity at Work in the Contemporary Economy', in Bolton, S. and Houlihan, M. (eds) *Work Matters: Critical Reflections on Contemporary Work*, London: Palgrave.

O'Doherty, D. (2009a) 'Revistalising Labour Process Theory: A Prolegomenon to Fatal Writing', *Culture and Organization*, 15: 1–19.

O'Doherty, D. (2009b) 'Perspectives on Labour Process Theory', in Alvesson, M., Bridgman, T. and Willmott, H. (eds) *The Oxford Handbook of Critical Management Studies*, London: Oxford, 108–21.

O'Doherty, D. and Willmott, H. (2001a) 'The Question of Subjectivity and the Labour Process', *International Studies of Management and Organization*, 30: 112–31.

O'Doherty, D. and Willmott, H. (2001b) 'Debating Labour Process Theory: The Issue of Subjectivity and the Relevance of Poststructuralism', *Sociology*, 35(2): 457–76.

Parker, M. (1999) 'Capitalism, Subjectivity, and Ethics: Debating Labour Process Analysis', *Organization Studies*, 20: 25–45.

Reed, M. (2005a) 'Reflections on the "Realist Turn" in Management and Organization Studies', *Journal of Management Studies*, 42: 1621–44.

Reed, M. (2005b) 'Doing the Loco-motion: Response to Contu and Willmott's Commentary on the "Realist Turn" in Organization and Management Studies', *Journal of Management Studies*, 42: 1663–73.

Reed, M. (2009) 'Critical Realism in Critical Management Studies', in Alvesson, M., Bridgman, T. and Willmott, H. (eds) *The Oxford Handbook of Critical Management Studies*, London: Oxford.

Rindova, V., Barry, D. and Ketchen, D. (2009) 'Entrepreneurship as Emancipation', *Academy of Management Review*, 34: 477–91.

▶

Spicer, A., Alvesson, M. and Karreman, D. (2009) 'Critical Performativity: The Unfinished Business of Critical Management Studies', *Human Relations*, 62: 537–60.

Sturdy, A., Brocklehurst, M., Winstanley, D. and Littlejohns, M. (2006) 'Management as a (Self) Confidence Trick: Management Ideas, Education and Identity Work', *Organization,* 13(6): 841–60.

Taylor, P. and Bain, P. (1999) 'An Assembly Line in the Head: Work and Employee Relations in the Call Centre', *Industrial Relations Journal*, 30: 101–17.

Thompson, P. (1990) 'Crawling from the Wreckage: The Labour Process and the Politics of Production', in Knights, D. and Willmott, H. (eds) *Labour Process Theory*, London: Macmillan, 95–124.

Thompson, P. (2003) 'Disconnected Capitalism, or Why Employers Can't Keep Their Side of the Bargain', *Work, Employment, and Society*, 17: 359–78.

Thompson, P. (2004) 'Brands, Boundaries, and Bandwagons: A Critical Realist Reflection on Critical Management Studies', in Fleetwood, S. and Ackroyd, S. (eds) *Critical Realist Applications in Organization and Management Studies*, 54–70.

Thompson, P. (2009) 'Perspectives on Labour Process Theory', in Alvesson, M., Bridgman, T. and Willmott, H. (eds) *The Oxford Handbook of Critical Management Studies,* London: Oxford.

Thompson, P. and Ackroyd, S. (2009) 'Reclaiming Resistance', Paper presented at the *2009 International Labour Process Conference,* Edinburgh, UK.

Thompson, P. and Newsome, K. (2004) 'Labour Process Theory, Work, and the Employment Relation', in Kauffman, B. (ed.) *Theoretical Perspectives on Work and the Employment Relationship,* Ithaca, NY: Cornell University Press.

Thompson, P. and Smith, C. (2001) 'Follow the Red Brick Road – Reflections on Pathways into and out of the Labour Process Debate', *International Studies of Management and Organization*, 30: 40–67.

Vallas, S. (2003) 'The Adventures of Managerial Hegemony: Teamwork, Ideology, and Worker Resistance', *Social Problems*, 50: 204–25.

Warhurst, C. and Thompson, P. (1998) 'Hands, Hearts, and Minds: Changing Work and Workers at the End of the Century', in Thompson, P. and Warhurst, C. (eds) *Workplaces of the Future*, London: Macmillan, 1–24.

Webb, J. (2006) *Organisations, Identities, and the Self,* London: Palgrave.

Willmott, H. (2005) 'Theorizing Contemporary Control: Some Post-structuralist Responses to Some Critical Realist Questions', *Organization*, 12: 747–80.

Winiecki, D. (2004) 'Shadowboxing with Data: Production of the Subject in Contemporary Call Centre Organisations', *New Technology, Work and Employment,* 19, 78–95.

Winiecki, D. (2007) *Discipline and Governmentality at Work: Making the Subject and Subjectivity in Modern Tertiary Labour,* London: Free Association Books.

Zanoni, P. and Janssens, M. (2007) 'Minority Employees Engaging with Diversity Management: An Analysis of Control, Agency, and Micro-emancipation', *Journal of Management Studies*, 44: 1371–97.

Zizek, S. (2000) *The Ticklish Subject: The Absent Centre of Political Ontology,* London: Verso.

Classic Themes Revisited

Skill and the Labour Process: The Conditions and Consequences of Change

5

Irena Grugulis and Caroline Lloyd

Skill has always been the pivotal aspect of Labour Process theory. Central to the relationship between capital and labour at the workplace is how workers are deployed and managed. Questions such as what workers do, how they do it, how decisions are made about work and by whom have at their heart the issues of skill and the way that skills are distributed. These aspects of the labour process are subject to ongoing pressures for change, as organizations seek to cut costs, adjust quality standards or introduce new products and services. However, skill does not simply reflect managerial requirements; it is an arena of conflict within and beyond the workplace, over the organization of work, control and wages.

The starting point for many of the debates and analysis of skill and the labour process was the publication of Harry Braverman's (1974) *Labor and Monopoly Capital*. His argument that deskilling was an inevitable tendency within capitalism was both a political and academic challenge to the conventional views of the 1960s and early 1970s that work was becoming more skilful, more knowledgeable and more creative. Taking examples from across the US economy, Braverman showed again and again how, in practice, work was deskilled with preset routines, tight supervision and a detailed subdivision of labour.

While Braverman's 'deskilling thesis' has been widely criticized (see, e.g. Cockburn, 1983; Friedman, 1977; Thompson, 1983; Wood, 1982) his work has been extremely influential. Initially it provoked considerable debate over how to develop a historical analysis of the interrelations between the capitalist labour process, issues of control and skill, developments in production and the requirements of capital accumulation (Wood, 1982). Critical discussion also focused on Braverman's explicit neglect of many of the subjective aspects of work and the need to integrate worker resistance into the analysis (Thompson, 1983; Wood, 1982). Others argued that Braverman had a 'romanticized' view of the skill levels and control possessed by craft workers (Cutler, 1978) and, although recognizing the looseness of the term skill, failed to explore the extent to which skills are socially constructed (Cockburn, 1983). These debates and critiques produced a far more nuanced analysis of the relationship between developments in the labour process, work organization, skill formation and skill utilization (see also Thompson and McHugh, 2009: 219–28).

Over time, there has been a shift away from attempts to locate skill within a broader analysis of capitalist development, towards a narrower exploration of particular trends and concepts. Debates over the existence, extent and nature of deskilling and upskilling remain a central theme (Grugulis, Warhurst and Keep, 2004), but the emphasis has been more on detailed empirical research at the workplace rather than theoretical development. The more complex and contingent view of skill changes that has emerged led Adler (2007) to argue that labour process academics had abandoned 'the challenge of theorizing long-term skill trends' (see Thompson, 2007 for a response). However, the resurgence of claims that a generalized upskilling of the workforce was taking place, linked to notions of the knowledge economy, has provided the impetus for more empirically informed analysis of skill trends, as well as alternative conceptualizations of a high-skills economy (Lloyd and Payne, 2005; Thompson, 2004)

This chapter explores two mains themes that have developed over recent years around the issue of skill. First, as a response to renewed 'upskilling' claims, there has been a focus on refuting these claims through exploring more generalized patterns of skill changes. In addition, attempts have been made to develop and utilize more sophisticated indices of skill in order to empirically measure skill changes over time. Second, there has been an escalating interest in re-conceptualizing skill, in part to reflect the growing focus of research on the service sector. The aim has been to develop and extend the notion of skill itself, theorizing skill in ways that move beyond knowledge, technical know-how and autonomy towards ideas of social, aesthetic and emotional skills. While there is general agreement that there are three dimensions of skill – skill of the worker, skill required of the job and the social construction of skill (Cockburn, 1983: 113) – there is little consensus about whether and how to incorporate 'soft' or 'social' skills.

The chapter begins by examining the resurgence of the upskilling thesis, and the way that labour process research has been used to refute such a proposition. This section outlines the longitudinal findings of a series of surveys undertaken in the UK and identifies some of the difficulties and contradictions associated with interpreting the results. The chapter then moves on to consider how the notion of skill has been redefined, and focuses on some of the problems raised by the widespread use of the term 'social skills' and the tendency to separate aspects of skill from the quality of jobs. The final section explicitly moves away from these concerns over measurement and definitions to a broader examination of the role of national institutional and regulatory factors in shaping the nature of the labour process. It considers whether a focus on different patterns of work processes, skill and pay across countries will encourage a return to concerns over the broader political economy.

Upskilling – here we go again

During the 1990s a new upskilling thesis emerged in popular and academic discourse, linked to developments in information technology and promises of a new knowledge economy (Leadbeater, 2000; Reich, 1991). Policy-makers from across the industrialized world welcomed the tantalizing prospect of an inevitable progression towards higher-skilled jobs (European Commission, 2000; OECD, 1996).

> While we don't yet know what the jobs of the future will be, we do know that more and more jobs will demand high skills. Our analysis tells us we can expect almost 20 million new high skilled jobs by 2020 and 13 million medium-level jobs. Routine jobs will tend to disappear – creative skills will be in demand (Speech by the President of the European Commission, José Manuel Barroso, 2008).

> The workforce is 'upskilling', both in terms of the average educational level of workers and the types of job that they are performing... This is not just a question of growth in knowledge 'sectors'. Work is becoming more skilled across industries and within individual occupations. (OECD, 2001: 99)

The decline of manufacturing, the continued expansion of the service sector, and in particular, the rise of dot.com businesses and financial services were seen to offer a vision of a promising, if not utopian, future (for a discussion see Warhurst and Thompson, 1998; Lloyd and Payne, 2003). Evidence of a growth in the numbers working in professional and managerial occupations, and the rising qualification levels of the workforce have been continually deployed to support the idea of a generalized upward shift in skill levels (see, e.g. Brinkley, 2008; Leitch, 2006; Reich, 1991). The increasing number of jobs that require higher education qualifications and the robustness of wage returns have been used as further confirmation of a general upward shift in the skill demands of advanced industrialized economies (Elias and Purcell, 2004; Machin and McNally, 2007).

Braverman's criticisms of the upskilling mantra in the 1960s have considerable resonance to contemporary debates, particularly in relation to the difficulties that arise in trying to measure skill changes. Braverman insisted that measures based on occupational classifications and time spent in education were far from self-evident indicators of skill levels. These classifications were 'neither "natural" nor self-evident, nor is the degree of skill a self-evident quality which can simply be read from the labels' (428). Years of education, Braverman also argued, failed to reflect the deterioration in the quality of that education and the role that employers play in raising 'their screening requirements for job applicants' (438). While he conceded that developments in science and technology meant that the skill content of many labour processes is 'much greater now than in the past' (425), the important question was whether the 'content of labor tends towards *averaging*, or, on the contrary, towards *polarization*' (425). If it is towards polarization,

> to then say that the 'average' skill has been raised is to adopt the logic of the statistician who, with one foot in the fire and the other in ice water, will tell you that 'on the average', he is perfectly comfortable. The mass of workers gain nothing from the fact that the decline in their command over the labor process is more than compensated for by the increased command on the part of managers and engineers. (425)

Contemporary critics of the upskilling thesis have used similar arguments about the problems of occupational categories, 'qualification inflation' and the use of 'averaging'. UK statistics, for example, show that 15 per cent of the workforce are managers, while Germany is able to make do with 5 per cent and France 8 per cent. We are unable to tell whether there are simply different ways of categorizing professional workers across countries or if in the UK 'relatively low paid, low skill jobs [are] being described as managers' (Brinkley, 2008: 52).

A good example of these problems can be seen in relation to the growth in jobs demanding degree level qualifications. Elias and Purcell (2004) re-categorized numerous UK jobs as 'graduate occupations' and then attempted to show that these jobs had expanded and upskilled to match the growing number of graduates.. However, their approach has been heavily criticized for creating 'a definitional trap, wherein any job now being done by a graduate has become a graduate job' (Keep and Mayhew, 2004: 300), regardless of the skills actually required. The concern is that with the advent of mass higher education, the US and the UK have experienced 'credential inflation' (Brown and Hesketh, 2004), with employers raising the qualifications bar without changing the content of jobs. Rather than jobs being upskilled to match rising qualification levels, Brown and Hesketh argue that there is a jobs queue in which qualifications are simply a vital element in securing positional advantage in the competition for the limited number of 'good jobs'. Although 'average' incomes of graduates has been increasing, the underlying figures indicate a growing dispersion in wages and rising levels of overqualification (Brown and Lauder, 2006: 326; Green and Zhu, 2008).

The resurgence of new versions of the upskilling thesis has sparked renewed interest in skill trends within the labour process tradition although the response has been, according to Thompson and Smith, a 'somewhat defensive battle' (2009: 7). Considerable effort has focused on revealing the contradictory changes in workers' skills, the continued existence of substantial numbers of low-skilled workers, and the limited scale of the new 'knowledge jobs'. There has also been a return to the issue of skill polarization, reflecting empirical evidence of a growing inequality in pay and working conditions, particularly in the UK and the US. Job growth at both the top and bottom of the occupational hierarchy has taken place, alongside a hollowing out of the middle (Brown and Hesketh, 2004; Goos and Manning, 2003; Lawton, 2009; Nolan and Wood, 2003).

This 'battle' over skill trajectories, however, is not just an academic debate; it is also political. For the UK government, skills policy has become the principal 'lever of choice' to solve a whole array of social and economic problems (see Keep and Mayhew, 2009). Faced with rather gloomy evidence about the state of the labour market, the response from politicians and policy-makers has been largely to ignore anything that does not match their 'world view' or which indicates the need for unpalatable interventions (Lloyd and Payne, 2002). This unwillingness to engage is demonstrated by the government's lack of reaction to the Commission for Employment and Skills' recent report (UKCES, 2009) which concludes that the skills deficit is predominantly one of low demand for skills from employers.

One of the problems for researchers in this area has been the lack of robust data that can provide evidence of changing skill levels over the long-term. In the UK, a series of surveys[1] have been conducted which now cover a 20-year period and provide a data set that uses a number of different measures of skill. In the following section, some of the key results are outlined before moving on to consider why a definitive answer to the question of 'how are skills changing' continues to remain elusive.

Surveying skills

The Skills Surveys (Felstead et al., 2007), and their predecessors, provide a unique data set for the UK using a range of standardized indicators, including perceptions of skills, qualifications, training times and levels of discretion and work effort. Some of the indices cover 20 years, while others are only available for the most recent 10-year period. These types of trend data give a much more nuanced picture of skills than is available simply from occupational and qualification proxies. Key results show that when individuals are asked about their perceptions of the skills they use at work, more than half of the respondents consistently reported increases in skills compared with five years earlier and only a small minority (approximately 10 per cent) expressed an overall loss of skills (Felstead et al., 2007). Broad skills – as measured through qualification requirements, learning and training times – were found to have 'risen significantly' over the 20-year period (see Figure 5.1). In addition, between 1997 and 2006, the surveys found an increase in the use of all generic skills except physical skills (Felstead et al., 2007).

The trends from the 20-year period have been used by the surveys' authors to support the idea of a general steady upskilling of the UK workforce (Felstead et al., 2007). Nevertheless, they concede that two indicators, qualification entry requirements and learning time to do the job, 'have reached a plateau' (ibid.: 66), suggesting a 'deceleration of the pace of upskilling' (ibid.: 167).

These are without doubt the most robust survey evidence that exists for the UK in relation to measures of skills in work. However, there remains a concern as to what exactly the surveys are measuring and what they really tell us about the nature of generalized skill trends. The use of individual recall about perceptions of skill changes has been criticized (see Claydon,

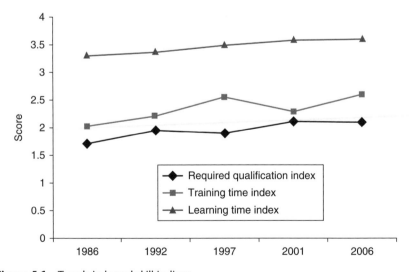

Figure 5.1 Trends in broad skill indices
Source: Felstead et al., 2007: 54.

1994) and even the surveys' authors use it as a supportive, rather than a strong, indicator of upskilling. Instead, considerable reliance is placed upon the use of qualifications, learning times and training times indices as proxies for broad skill levels; yet these indicators face the same methodological issues that were identified by Braverman in the 1970s.

A couple of contemporary examples illustrate the problematic nature of these proxies for skills. One underlying assumption is that what is 'within the qualification box' remains the same over time. In practice, over the past 20 years, the English education and training system has undergone numerous reforms and changes that have shifted the landscape of how skills are formed (Keep, 2006). Government policy has focused on ratcheting up the qualification levels of workers with corresponding incentives for organizations to provide recognized qualifications. Changes in funding regimes have shifted the uptake of qualifications and the time spent in training. For example, training times for a sales assistant may be extended from one week to six months in order to incorporate a level 2 National Vocational Qualification in retail that is now financed by the state through Train to Gain. The length of the training period does not necessarily mean that the training itself is more extensive and in-depth than before, but the outcome is a job that 'requires' increased training and learning times and a level 2 qualification. All three indices, therefore, can rise without any necessary changes to the job itself.

Qualifications change over time – see the debates over falling standards of academic qualifications (BBC, 2009; Frean, 2007), as do perceptions by employers and workers over what is regarded as 'necessary' to do the job. These requirements may reflect changes in the nature of the job but alternatively they may be an outcome of developments in the education system or the labour market. The UK Skill Surveys do have more direct measures of skill that combine job activities into a number of generic skills. But the majority of these skills are measured by the extent to which they are deemed important in an individual's job rather than on their relative complexity. The surveys' authors admit that their method is limited in its ability to pick up occupation-specific technical skills (Felstead et al., 2007: 11).

While measuring skills is clearly difficult, it is also crucial that there is clarity about how skills are being defined. A central conceptual assumption of the Skills Surveys is about the relationship between discretion and skill. One finding that does not fit easily with a generalized upskilling trend is the declining level of task discretion. The survey data show that between 1992 and 2001, levels of task discretion declined substantially, stabilizing only from 2001 (see Figure 5.2). This decline in discretion was found to be matched by a rise in external sources of control, in particular through other workers, clients and customers (Felstead et al., 2007: 125). Green (2006: 109) explains that those subject to increased use of new technology experienced

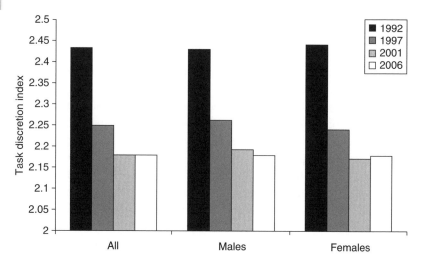

Figure 5.2 Employee task discretion index
Source: Felstead et al., 2007: 121.

the greatest decline in their discretion, which is 'consistent with the view that new technologies are part of the reason for declining discretion'. However, he argues that a decline in the level of discretion is not inconsistent with average upskilling because of the loose connection between discretion and skill. Within a low trust environment where workers have limited market power, 'it is possible to have low levels of discretion ... even when the work is highly skilled' (ibid.: 94).

The attempt to disconnect discretion from skill has a long history and has been a contested issue within labour process literature. There is some support for Green's approach. Noon and Blyton (1997: 84) present 'skill as discretion', as an alternative to 'skill as complexity' as a way of assessing skill. They are critical of discretion as a measure of skill arguing that it focuses on the visible and fails to take account of the significance of the task and the consequences of mistakes. It evokes a notion of craft workers, they argue, that fails to recognize the interdependency of jobs today. Brown (1992: 219) also claims that analytically it is 'more satisfactory to regard skill and discretion as distinct attributes'. Others, however, identify discretion as one of the central components of skill (Littler, 1982; Rolfe, 1990). Littler stressed that it is 'not possible to define "skill" independently of organizational control and control processes' (1982: 9).

Take an example of schoolteachers in England. On a narrow definition of skill that excludes issues of discretion, it could be argued that they have been upskilled over the past 20 years. Schoolteachers have had to cope with constant changes in the curriculum, assessment and teaching methods, all of which require them to continually learn new things. Levels of continuous professional development have risen substantially, while proposals are being put forward for teaching to become a Masters level profession (DCSF, 2008). On the other hand, evidence indicates that the introduction of a national curriculum and a range of highly prescriptive teaching strategies have meant that teaching jobs have become more tightly prescribed with considerably lower levels of professional autonomy (see Sinclair, Ironside and Seifert, 1996). A recent House of Commons Select Committee conceded that the result had been a 'deskilling' of teachers.

> the level of central prescription and direction through the National Curriculum and National Strategies has de-skilled teachers. At times schooling has appeared more of a franchise operation, dependent on a recipe handed-down by Government rather than the exercise of professional expertise by teachers. (House of Commons, 2009: 4)

This case shows the difficulties that arise in trying to separate measures of discretion, control and autonomy from a definition of skill. It is also makes clear that the concept of skill is highly contested.

The ongoing problem of defining and measuring skills fundamentally questions the ability of large-scale surveys to provide a convincing picture of generalized skill trends that can somehow resolve the ongoing debates about how skills are changing. These issues become even starker when we delve a little closer into what we actually mean by skill and how the notion of skill has changed over time. The Skill Surveys show that there are a considerable number of jobs in the UK, estimated at 7.4 million in 2006 (Felstead et al., 2007), that do not require any qualifications for entry. On the surface, these jobs appear to demand little technical skill or knowledge, are highly routine, lack discretion and have low material rewards in terms of pay and benefits (Lloyd, Mason and Mayhew, 2008). Many are in the service sector and, as we see in the next section, one strand of labour process research has argued that the old concepts and measures of skill are simply not recognizing the real skills that are involved in these types of jobs.

More skills and better skills?

A second trend that has evolved both within the labour process tradition and popular discourse has been the dramatic increase in the lexicon of skills and the increasing emphasis on social and soft skills (Payne, 2000). Self-confidence, communications, problem solving and customer service, among many others, are now commonly referred to as skills. This shift has been met by some protest and criticism from academic commentators and soft skills have been accused of legitimizing discrimination, individualizing responsibility, conflating disparate and dissimilar practices and generally confusing the whole skills debate (see, e.g. Grugulis, 2007; Keep, 2001; Payne, 2006). Given the focus of this chapter, we concern ourselves largely with the effect on workers and consider whether calling more things skills *increases* their power in the workplace by, for example, explicitly acknowledging practices which might otherwise be taken for granted, bringing additional elements into job evaluations and providing richer dimensions to narrow and impoverished tasks. Alternatively, does it *decrease* workers' power by bringing more aspects of work under management control, expecting workers to compensate for poor job design and working environments, trivializing broader discussions of skill or exaggerating the importance and complexity of minor actions?

Analytically it may help to consider soft skills in context and, particularly, in the context of the technical skills and status possessed by job holders. This approach is significant because, despite the common terminology, soft skills are not generic and may vary markedly in different environments. For example, problem solving, a skill which appears on numerous lists, is clearly very different when the problems to be solved are complex and technical than when they are straightforward and informational. Asaf Darr's (2004, 2002) detailed ethnographic study of computer sales people reveals the way that systems and software were configured to clients' unique requirements sometimes over months, in ways that the technical sales staff developed as they worked (often in collaboration with experts from the clients' side). Problem solving here was complex, unpredictable and innovative and required high levels of technical know-how. Contrast this type of problem solving with that undertaken by post room workers who receive a parcel addressed to an unknown recipient. They might check for new or visiting staff, hold the goods for a set period or return it to sender but the process is much swifter requiring little technical knowledge and may simply involve following set routines. In this instance, the problem solving undertaken by Darr's technical salesforce is vastly different to that done by the post room staff.

The importance of the context in which soft skills are deployed helps to explain why many call centre workers in Lloyd and Payne's (2009) study did not accept that their jobs were 'skilled' despite managers insisting that high levels of soft skills were required. The majority of workers considered that the work was either low or unskilled due to the limited technical skills required and the routine nature of the customer interactions. The issue is that most of the new skill lists neglect to consider that many soft skills are transitive; communication requires a message, problem solving demands a problem. As a result, soft skills and technical skills are likely to be interdependent.

In general, technical skills not only provide the substance that soft skills require to be meaningful, but they also fundamentally affect the nature of the soft skills themselves.

The evidence on the ways in which soft skills impact on the nature of work is mixed. Intensive, alienating work has a long history (it was, indeed, a particular concern of both Marx and Braverman) and, as noted above, it has not ceased. It may be that a focus on emotion management and soft skills, particularly in customer facing jobs, makes them more pleasurable by increasing their complexity, providing openings for workers to exhibit generosity or simply by mimicking the actions of genuine friendships. There is some evidence for this. Wharton (1996) observes higher levels of job satisfaction in workers who were required to work with their emotions than those who were not, while Bolton (2000) notes the philanthropy extended to callers by call centre workers. However, although Korczynski reports his informants pleasure in pleasant exchanges with callers, he goes on to note that workers 'were so satisfied with the job that they were leaving in considerable numbers' (2001: 92). While emotional links to customers, colleagues and bosses may indeed make work meaningful for some workers (Macdonald, 1996; Pierce, 1996), it would be both unrealistic and managerialist to extend this to all. Resistance, criticism and misbehaviour may provide just as much pleasure (Ackroyd and Thompson, 1999; Paules, 1991) without ever being listed as skills.

Do soft skills advantage women? Women are often disadvantaged in employment. They earn less money, are promoted less readily and are often confined (or confine themselves) to less prestigious jobs than their male counterparts. If part of the reason for this discrimination is because many soft skills are unrecognized or dismissed as 'natural' when exercised by women (Cockburn, 1987) then it may be that the more enthusiastic labelling of soft skills will advantage these workers: they will have a language of performance against which to claim, gauge and assess skills.

This argument sounds feasible except that, as numerous empirical studies have shown, the problem lies not in a lack of *recognition* of women's skills, but in the very low *valuation* placed on them. Soft skills involve a wide (and often confusing) range of qualities, behaviours, virtues and skills, many of which are highly subjective. In practice, these can all too easily slide into gendered norms with rather counterproductive effects, since the norms women are judged against are often more demanding than those set for men. Women workers are often expected to demonstrate a range of skills and behaviours not required (or required to differing extents) from their male colleagues; but find that these skills and behaviours are not highly rewarded in terms of pay, status or job prospects. The women call centre representatives observed by Taylor and Tyler (2000) were expected to reach targets on both soft skills and sales, their male colleagues were expected only to reach sales targets. Women paralegals were required to 'mother' or flirt with male bosses, their male colleagues were expected only to be courteous (Pierce, 1995). Unfortunately, many women workers seem to be caught in a Catch-22 situation where 'feminine' behaviours are both an expected part of 'good' performance in low-level work and a bar to promotion (Grugulis, 2007). Jobs are redesigned with gendered norms in mind and pay rates are geared accordingly (Skuratowicz and Hunter, 2004). Despite repeated employer protests about the shortages of soft skills among low-graded staff, no additional rewards are offered (Bolton, 2004; Felstead et al., 2007).

However, at the other end of the labour market, Green et al. (2007) observe clear premia available to highly technically skilled ICT staff who also possess soft skills. Grugulis and Vincent (2009) also found that considerable financial rewards were available to highly technically skilled, and mainly male, workers who possessed the requisite soft skills. The issue in all of these studies is not that 'women's skills' are not recognized, they are and in consequence many women are expected to achieve more at work, it is that there are no financial rewards. It is not clear that simply expanding the vocabulary of skills will advantage women, while in some cases it seems to actively disadvantage them.

Conversely, the expansion of the notion of skill may actually have a number of negative effects, possibly contributing to the trend of declining discretion observed above. Emphasizing soft skills serves to supply a new range of performance indicators for workers with individuals appraised on how well, how emotionally, how convincingly they act and on the feelings they provoke in others (often in jobs that are already demanding, see Bolton, this volume). Although these traits have only recently been labelled skills, this concern with workers' moral characters, their behaviours in and out of the workplace and the effort they put into work is not new (Keep, 2001; Pollard, 1965). However, labelling these attributes as skills pushes the responsibility for their formation and application onto the individual worker and the education and training system. The role of management in providing a conducive working environment is overlooked as workers are expected to show their own motivation or team-working skills irrespective of context (see Grugulis, Warhurst and Keep, 2004).

There is also the additional danger that expanding the meaning of skill obscures the existence of a large number of jobs which are routine, repetitive, highly controlled and are learnt in a short space of time. Braverman argued that with the development of capitalism, 'the very concept of skill becomes degraded' (444), 'so long as he or she is *adequate to the needs of capital* the worker is no longer to be considered or called unskilled' (447; emphasis in original). Similar concerns have been raised over attempts to define many low-paid service sector jobs as skilled, with claims that it is a 'rhetorical device that carries with it no material benefits' (ibid.: 12). As Payne has identified, 'One potential casualty is the concept of skill itself, which becomes so loosely defined that it ceases to have any real analytical or operational meaning or significance...This not only makes it much harder to talk about job quality, or what we mean by a skilled job, but there is a danger that it may leave unchallenged the dull, highly routinized and monotonous nature of many front-line service jobs' (2009: 362–3). The 'degradation' of the concept of skill, therefore, provides a serious challenge to those attempting to explore the concrete nature of the labour process and, in particular, the material conditions of work.

Following the discussions to date, it would seem that there is a need for more research that focuses on an integrated account of skills: one which is set into a societal and workplace context; which combines discretion and complexity; which allows an explanation of the counter-intuitive and apparently contradictory trajectories of different types of skill; and which enables an engagement with the varied language and meaning of skills. Such accounts exist, but they are rare and are mostly qualitative and ethnographic explorations (see, among others Hochschild, 1983; Hurrell, Scholarios and Thompson, 2009; Paules, 1991), with a number also dealing with the impact of external categories such as class, gender and race (Cockburn, 1983). Although time consuming and lengthy, such analyses can make a disproportionate contribution to understanding the nature of skill in the workplace.

Institutionalized skills

These ongoing debates about what skills actually are, how they are measured and what they really mean in terms of the work process and the material conditions of the job, are likely to continue. One of the problems, however, with this focus on skill trends and attempts to extend and develop the notion of soft skills is that jobs are often examined in isolation with little consideration of the broader political economy. As Thompson and Smith (2009) have argued, '[i]n too much labour process research, distinctions about moments in political economy...have been lost or subordinated to a general focus on the labour process as *work organization*'. The result is that often skills are simply portrayed as a reflection of new technology, management strategy and/or changing patterns of consumer demands. Examining firm product strategies, the environment within which organizations operate and the nature of inter-firm competition is rarely considered, neither (more surprisingly) is the imperative to cut labour costs.

An alternative approach to a focus on the workplace has been to explore workers' skills across countries and to link differences to the broader political economy. Resonating with earlier research (Finegold and Soskice, 1988; Streeck, 1992), a key concern has been the disproportionate number of low-skilled, low-paid jobs in the US and the UK when compared with many continental European countries (Brown, Green and Lauder, 2001; Lloyd, Mason and Mayhew, 2008). Braverman was based in the US and his examples of work, institutional structures, management and organization are all drawn from there. The large, relatively homogeneous domestic market and rapid industrialization that characterized the US are neither natural, nor inevitable features of capitalism (Thelen, 2004). Neither is the industrial relations system, with its weak collective institutions: a lack of formal institutions for employer organizations and relatively weak organized labour that lacks political representation (Ferner, 2000). Within such a context, workers have been unable to obtain the kind of welfare institutions and labour market regulations that are typically found in Europe. The US political economy, no doubt, influenced Braverman's analysis of the nature and development of capitalism and the implications for skills.

Other economies have developed very differently, with diverse outcomes for skills (Thelen, 2004; Whitley, 1999). The close cooperation between state, unions and employers that characterized the German system supported extensive skill building to intermediate level through high-quality apprenticeships, secured pay premia for skills, discouraged employer freeloading and funded long-term industrial development (Rubery and Grimshaw, 2003). This 'cooperative' German approach, found predominantly in manufacturing, was based on a relatively powerful labour movement that was able to ensure strong regulation of the labour market and skill formation systems at national, industry and workplace level. A conducive economic environment and an embedded form of long-termism within capital markets enabled employers to achieve competitive advantage through producing higher-quality products. In effect, under this system, labour has been comparatively expensive and difficult to make redundant, so employers had incentives to use workers differently (Lane, 1987; Streeck, 1992).

Similar outcomes can also be found in other countries. In Denmark, institutionalized high wages and low-income differentials substantially limit the cost advantages gained from deskilling work (Westergaard-Nielson, 2008). With low unemployment and a high reservation wage, recruiting workers to dull, routine positions is problematic. As a result, upskilling may take place, not as some inevitable process of capitalist development and the introduction of new technology, but as an outcome of the particular configurations of the political economy.

The emphasis of much labour process literature and research on skills has focused on the US and the UK, where neoliberalism, substantially weakened trade unions and lightly regulated labour markets have left employers with considerable discretion in how they organize their production systems, their workforce and their skill levels. As a result, the constraints that exist on capital in more regulated institutional environments where labour has substantially more power tend to be marginalized. The different skill systems found across countries does not mean that employers may not prefer to utilize a lower-skilled, lower-paid workforce that is more controllable. However, this approach is not always possible, as employers have to work within a set of constraints that may be difficult to challenge. In Germany, the evidence indicates that these 'beneficial constraints' (Streeck, 1997) are being seriously weakened following reunification and the rise of mass unemployment, and the corresponding deterioration in the power of labour. In the context of a more competitive international environment, employers have increasingly sought to undermine skill levels and reduce wages (Bosch and Weinkopf, 2008; Streeck and Hassel, 2004; Tuselmann and Heiss, 2000).

More broadly, the emergence of debates over the extent and nature of globalization (see Hirst and Thompson, 1999 for a review) has led to a concern that these types of nationally based constraints may become increasingly redundant as more firms operate within a global production process. Rather than the knowledge economy and the further diffusion and application of information technology upskilling workers, Brown, Lauder and Ashton (2008b) argue that a broad range of multinational companies are intent on leveraging new technologies to standardize functions and jobs. 'Digital Taylorism' – a new form of deskilling – is being applied to managerial and professional work by 'translating *knowledge work* into *working knowledge* through the extraction, certification and digitisation of knowledge into software prescripts that can be transmitted and manipulated by others regardless of location' (ibid.: 139). The claim is that these processes 'depend on reducing the autonomy and discretion of the majority of managers and professionals' (Lauder, Brown and Ashton, 2008: 25). One of their examples reports the experience of a bank manager who previously had discretion over the amount of money he could lend to a customer:

> The bank relied on his expertise and judgement in making decisions. Now he no longer has that discretion, as it is all done by computer algorithms. He had become a sales person and he had a whole series of manuals as to how to sell particular kinds of products.

The argument is that employers are increasingly looking to segment their higher-skilled service workers, deskill many of them and shift their work (where possible) to lower-cost locations. This reading of changing technology and the knowledge economy offers a far more pessimistic vision of both likely skill trajectories and the material rewards for what were once considered middle-class jobs. The evidence for these types of changes, however, are limited and we still know little about differences in skills across countries, why they exist and whether it might be possible to shift towards a higher-skilled economy (see Lloyd and Payne, 2005).

Conclusion

The optimistic hype of the knowledge economy, general upskilling of the workforce and the end of unskilled work has been a prominent feature of policy debates over the past ten years across a range of industrialized economies. Despite criticisms from sections of the academic community, many seem to accept willingly the evidence of shifting occupational structures, rising qualification levels and rhetoric from managers about new skill requirements. Through an exploration of the evidence of generalized skill changes and the way that skills are being radically redefined, it becomes clear that much of Braverman's critique remains relevant today, in particular, the challenge to the optimistic 'upskilling' arguments, the caution required in using data and in the 'misuse' of the term 'skills'. Perhaps more significantly it reminds us of the importance of going beyond the minutiae of skill to consider the material conditions experienced by workers, the way they are controlled, homogenized, degraded and alienated (Thompson, 1990).

In the UK, much of the heralded job growth at the higher-skilled end of the labour market has been in the IT sector, financial services and the public sector. The resulting vulnerability of the UK to the current global recession has been well documented and is reflected in rapidly rising levels of unemployment. The loss of jobs in these sectors, and the likely contraction of public sector expenditure over the next ten years, may well lead to a renewed debate about the extent and nature of future skill trajectories. The recent recognition by government bodies that employer demand for skill in the UK has been relatively low – even before the recession (Scottish Government, 2007; UKCES, 2009) – social mobility has stagnated (Cabinet Office, 2009) and income inequality has increased (Brewer et al., 2009) adds further cracks to the belief that 'things can only get better'.

A major deficiency of much of the research on skill and the labour process has been the lack of recent systematic comparisons of the skill content of jobs in different countries (see Finegold, Wagner and Mason, 2000; Mason, Osborne and Voss-Dahm 2007; Winch, Clarke and Brockmann, 2009 for notable exceptions). It is only by comparing across countries that we can really begin to identify the role of institutions, regulations and the broader political economy in shaping skills and their associated rewards within the workplace (see Gautié and Schmitt, 2009). Another notable absence has been much engagement with the debates over globalization, the 'race to the bottom' in global labour standards (Coates, 2000) and whether we will see the widespread emergences of a 'high skilled, low waged workforce' (Brown et al., 2008). Adopting a more comparative research process would allow an appreciation of the possibilities of different skill outcomes and could help identify the kinds of actions and interventions that are required to achieve improvements.

Skill is both complex and contested. Rather than seeking to identify generalized skill trajectories, a pursuit which has an uneasy relationship with the expanding notion of skill, researchers would be well advised to widen their remit to cover broader aspects of job quality. A focus on skill to the detriment of other elements of the jobs, such as pay and conditions, work intensity, progression opportunities and so on, risks the danger of being side tracked into an ever-narrowing agenda. Highlighting where job quality is deteriorating – the degradation of work – where jobs are already low quality and whether and how these can be improved would be a way of reintegrating the academic and political debates in this area. Such an approach might see a shift in the balance of research away from a desire to uncover an ever-growing array of new skills towards a greater focus on the conditions and actions required to make work better.

Note

1 SCELI 1986 (Gallie, 1994), the Employment in Britain Survey 1992 (Gallie and White, 1993) and the UK Skills Survey 1997, 2001 and 2006 (Felstead et al., 2007).

REFERENCES

Ackroyd, S. and Thompson, P. (1999) *Organizational Misbehaviour*, London: Sage.

Adler, P. (2007) 'The Future of Critical Management Studies: A Paleo-Marxist Critique of Labour Process Theory', *Organization Studies* 28(9): 1313–45.

BBC (2009) 'GCSE Science Concerns Explained', news.bbc.co.uk, 27 March, accessed 15 September 2009.

Bolton, S. (2000) 'Emotion Here, Emotion There, Emotional Organisations Everywhere', *Critical Perspectives on Accounting*, 11: 155–71.

Bolton, S. (2004) 'Conceptual Confusions: Emotion Work as Skilled Work', in Warhurst, C., Grugulis, I. and Keep, E. (eds) *The Skills That Matter*, Basingstoke: Palgrave Macmillan.

▶

▶

Bosch, G. and Weinkopf, C. (eds) (2008) *Low Wage Work in Germany*, New York: Russell Sage Foundation.

Braverman, H. (1974) *Labor and Monopoly Capital*, New York: Monthly Review Press.

Brewer, M., Muriel, A., Phillips, D. and Sibieta, L. (2009) 'Poverty and Inequality in the UK 2009', London: IFS.

Brinkley, I. (2008) 'The Knowledge Economy: How Knowledge Is Reshaping the Economic Life of Nations', London: The Work Foundation.

Brown, P. and Hesketh, A. (2004) *The Mismanagement of Talent: Employability and Jobs in the Knowledge Economy*, Oxford: Oxford University Press.

Brown, P. and Lauder, H. (2006) 'Globalisation, Knowledge and the Myth of the Magnet Economy', in Lauder, H., Brown, P., Dillabough, J-A. and Halsey, A. H. (eds) *Education, Globalisation and Social Change*, Oxford: Oxford University Press, 317–40.

Brown, P., Ashton, D., Lauder, H. and Tholen, G. (2008) 'Towards a High-Skilled, Low-Waged Workforce? A Review of Global Trends in Education, Employment and the Labour Market', Cardiff: SKOPE Monograph 10, Cardiff: SKOPE, Cardiff University.

Brown, P., Green, A. and Lauder, H. (2001) *High Skills: Globalization, Competitiveness and Skill Formation*, Oxford: Oxford University Press.

Brown, P., Lauder, H. and Ashton, D. (2008) 'Education, Globalisation and the Future of the Knowledge Economy', *European Educational Research Journal*, 7(2): 131–56.

Brown, R. (1992) *Understanding Industrial Organisations*, London: Routledge.

Cabinet Office (2009) 'Unleashing Aspiration: The Final Report on the Panel on Fair Access to the Professions', London: Cabinet Office.

Claydon, T. (1994) 'Employee Commitment and the Skills Revolution. Book Review', *British Journal of Industrial Relations*, 32(2): 289–91.

Coates, D. (2000) *Models of Capitalism: Growth and Stagnation in the Modern Era*, London: Polity Press.

Cockburn, C. (1983) *Brothers: Male Dominance and Technological Change*, London: Pluto Press.

Cockburn, C. (1987) *Two-Track Training: Sex Inequalities and the YTS*, Basingstoke: Macmillan.

Cutler, T. (1978) 'The Romance of "Labour"', *Economy and Society*, 7(1): 74–95.

Darr, A. (2002) 'The Technicization of Sales Work: An Ethnographic Study in the US Electronics Industry', *Work, Employment and Society*, 16(1): 47–65.

Darr, A. (2004) 'The Interdependence of Social and Technical Skills in the Sale of Emergent Technology', in Warhurst, C., Grugulis, I. and Keep, E. (eds) *The Skills That Matter*, Basingstoke: Palgrave Macmillan.

DCSF (2008) 'Being the Best for Our Children: Releasing Talent for Teaching and Learning', Sheffield: Department for Children, Schools and Families.

Elias, P. and Purcell, K. (2004) 'Is Mass Higher Education Working? Evidence from the Labour Market Experiences of Recent Graduates', *National Institute Economic Review*, 90: 60–74.

▶

▶

European Commission (2000) 'Employment Strategies in the Information Society' COM (2000) 48 final, 7 February.

Felstead, A., Gallie, D., Green, F. and Zhou, Y. (2007) *Skills at Work 1986–2006*, Oxford: SKOPE University of Oxford.

Ferner, A. (2000) 'The Embeddedness of US Multinational Companies in the US Business System: Implications for HR/IR', *Occasional Paper No 61*, Leicester: Leicester Business School.

Finegold, D. and Soskice, D. (1988) 'The Failure of Training in Britain: Analysis and Prescription', *Oxford Review of Economic Policy*, 4(3): 21–43.

Finegold, D., Wagner, K. and Mason, G. (2000) 'National Skill-Creation Systems and Career Paths for Service Workers: Hotels in the United States, Germany and the United Kingdom', *International Journal of Human Resource Management*, 11(3): 497–516.

Frean, A. (2007) 'A-level Reputation in Severe Decline…Now Even an Exam Board Chief Doubts Their Value', *The Times*, 10 November.

Friedman, A. L. (1977) *Industry and Labour: Class Struggle at Work and Monopoly Capitalism*, London: Macmillan.

Gallie, D. (1994) 'Patterns of Skill Change: Upskilling, Deskilling or Polarisation?' in Penn, R., Rose, M. and Rubery, J. (eds) *Skill and Occupational Change*, Oxford: Oxford University Press.

Gallie. D. and White, M. (1993) *Employee Commitment and the Skills Revolution: First Findings from the Employment in Britain Survey*, London: Policy Studies Institute.

Gautié, J. and Schmitt, J. (eds) (2009) *Low-Wage Work in the Wealthy World*, New York: Russell Sage Foundation.

Goos, M. and Manning, A. (2003) 'McJobs and MacJobs: The Growing Polarisation of Jobs in the UK', in Dickens, R., Gregg, P. and Wadsworth, J. (eds) *The Labour Market under New Labour*, Houndsmills: Palgrave Macmillan, 70–85.

Green, F. (2006) *Demanding Work: The Paradox of Job Quality in the Affluent Economy*, Princeton, NJ and Oxford: Princeton University Press.

Green, F. and Zhu, Y. (2008) 'Overqualification, Job Dissatisfaction and Increasing Dispersion in the Returns to Graduate Education', *Department of Economics Discussion Paper 03/08*, Canterbury: University of Kent.

Green, F., Felstead, A., Gaillie, D. and Zhou, Y. (2007) 'Computers and Pay', *National Institute Economic Review*, 201(1): 63–75.

Grugulis, I. (2007) *Skills, Training and Human Resource Development: A Critical Text*, Basingstoke: Palgrave Macmillan.

Grugulis, I. and Vincent, S. (2009) 'Whose Skill Is It Anyway? "Soft" Skills and Polarisation', *Work, Employment and Society*, 23(4).

Grugulis, I., Warhurst, C. and Keep, E. (2004) 'What's Happening to Skill', in Warhurst, C., Grugulis, I. and Keep, E. (eds) *The Skills That Matter*, Basingstoke: Palgrave Macmillan.

Hirst, P. and Thompson, G. (1999) *Globalization in Question*, Cambridge: Polity Press.

Hochschild, A. R. (1983) *The Managed Heart: Commercialization of Human Feeling*, Berkley: University of California Press.

▶

▶

House of Commons, Children, Schools and Families Committee (2009) 'National Curriculum, Fourth Report of Session 2008–09, Volume 1', HC344–1, London: Stationery Office.

Hurrell, S., Scholarios, D. and Thompson, P. (2009) 'More Than a "Humpty Dumpty Word": An Exploration of the Status of Soft Skills', *International Labour Process Conference*, Edinburgh.

Keep, E. (2001) 'If It Moves, It's a Skill', Presented at ESRC seminar on The Changing Nature of Skills and Knowledge, 3rd–4th September, Manchester.

Keep, E. (2006) 'State Control of the English VET System – Playing with the Biggest Trainset in the World', *Journal of Vocational Education and Training*, 58(1): 47–64.

Keep, E. and Mayhew, K. (2004) 'The Economic and Distributional Implications of Current Policies on Higher Education', *Oxford Review of Economic Policy*, 20(2): 298–314.

Keep, E. and Mayhew, K. (2009) 'Moving beyond Skills as a Social and Economic Panacea', *Work, Employment and Society*, 23(4).

Korczynski, M. (2001) 'The Contradictions of Service Work: Call Centre as Customer-Oriented Bureaucracy', in Sturdy, A., Grugulis, I. and Willmott, H. (eds) *Customer Service: Empowerment and Entrapment*, Basingstoke: Palgrave.

Lane, C. (1987) 'Capitalism or Culture? A Comparative Analysis of the Position in the Labour Process and Labour Market of Lower White-Collar Workers in the Financial Services Sector of Britain and the Federal Republic of Germany', *Work, Employment and Society*, 1(1): 57–83.

Lauder, H., Brown, P. and Ashton, D. (2008) 'Globalisation, Skill Formation and the Varieties of Capitalism Approach', *New Political Economy*, 13(1): 19–35.

Lawton, K. (2009) *Nice Work If You Can Get It*, London: IPPR.

Leadbeater, C. (2000) *Living on Thin Air*, London: Viking.

Leitch, S. (2006) 'Prosperity for All in the Global Economy – World Class Skills. Leitch Review of Skills, Final Report', London: The Stationery Office.

Littler, C. (1982) *The Development of the Labour Process in Capitalist Societies*, London: Heinemann.

Lloyd, C. and Payne, J. (2002) 'On the "Political Economy of Skill": Assessing the Possibilities for a Viable High Skills Project in the United Kingdom', *New Political Economy*, 7(3): 367–95.

Lloyd, C. and Payne, J. (2003) 'The Political Economy of Skill and the Limits of Educational Policy', *Journal of Education Policy*, 18(1): 85–107.

Lloyd, C. and Payne, J. (2005) 'A Vision too Far? Mapping the Space for a High Skills Project in the UK', *Journal of Education and Work*, 18(2): 165–85.

Lloyd, C. and Payne, J. (2009) ' "Full of Sound and Fury, Signifying Nothing": Interrogating New Skill Concepts in Service Work – the View from Two UK Call Centres', *Work, Employment and Society*, 23(4).

Lloyd, C., Mason, G. and Mayhew, K. (eds) (2008) *Low-Wage Work in the United Kingdom*, New York: Russell Sage Foundation.

▶

▶

Macdonald, C. L. (1996) 'Shadow Mothers: Nannies, au pairs, and Invisible Work', in Macdonald, C. L. and Sirianni, C. (eds) *Working in the Service Society,* Philadelphia, PA: Temple University Press.

Machin, S. and McNally, S. (2007) *Tertiary Education Systems and Labour Markets, Thematic Review of Tertiary Education,* Paris: OECD.

Mason, G., Osborne, M. and Voss-Dahm, D. (2007) 'Labour Market Outcomes in Different National Settings: UK German Comparisons in Retailing', *IWPLMS Conference,* Aix-en-Provence.

Nolan, P. and Wood, S. (2003) 'Mapping the Future of Work', *British Journal of Industrial Relations,* 41(2): 165–74.

Noon, M. and Blyton, P. (1997) *The Realities of Work,* Basingstoke: Palgrave.

OECD (1996) 'The Knowledge Based Economy', Paris: OECD.

OECD (2001) 'Education Policy Analysis 2001', Paris: OECD.

Paules, G. F. (1991) *Dishing It Out: Power and Resistance among Waitresses in a New Jersey Restaurant,* Philadelphia, PA: Temple University Press.

Payne, J. (2000) 'The Unbearable Lightness of Skill: The Changing Meaning of Skill in UK Policy Discourses and Some Implications for Education and Training', *Journal of Education Policy,* 15(3): 353–69.

Payne, J. (2006) 'What's Wrong with Emotional Labour?', *SKOPE Research Paper No 65,* Coventry: SKOPE, University of Warwick.

Payne, J. (2009) 'Emotional Labour and Skill: A Reappraisal', *Gender, Work and Organization,* 16(3): 348–67.

Pierce, J. L. (1995) *Gender Trials: Emotional Lives in Contemporary Law Firms,* Berkley: University of California Press.

Pierce, J. L. (1996) 'Reproducing Gender Relations in Large Law Firms: The Role of Emotional Labour in Paralegal Work', in Macdonald, C. L. and Sirianni, C. (eds) *Working in the Service Society,* Philadelphia, PA: Temple University Press.

Pollard, S. (1965) *The Genesis of Modern Management,* London: Edward Arnold.

Reich, R. (1991) *The Work of Nations: Preparing Ourselves for 21st Century Capitalism,* New York: Vintage Books.

Rolfe, H. (1990) 'In the Name of Progress? Skill and Attitudes towards Technological Change', *New Technology, Work and Employment,* 5(2): 107–21.

Rubery, J. and Grimshaw, D. (2003) *The Organization of Employment,* Basingstoke: Palgrave Macmillan.

Scottish Government (2007) 'Skills for Scotland: A Lifelong Skills Strategy', Edinburgh: The Scottish Government.

Sinclair, J., Ironside, M. and Seifert, R. (1996) 'Classroom Struggle? Market-Oriented Reforms and Their Impact on the Teacher Labour Process', *Work, Employment and Society,* 10(4): 641–61.

Skuratowicz, E. and Hunter, L. W. (2004) 'Where Do Women's Jobs Come From? Job Resegregation in an American Bank', *Work and Occupations,* 31(1): 73–110.

Streeck, W. (1992) *Social Institutions and Economic Performance: Studies of Industrial Relations in Advanced Capitalist Economies,* London: Sage.

▶

▶

Streeck, W. (1997) 'Beneficial Constraints: On the Economic Limits of Rational Voluntarism', in Rogers-Hollingworth, J. and Boyer, R. (eds) *Contemporary Capitalism*, New York: Cambridge University Press, 197–218.

Streeck, W. and Hassel, A. (2004) 'The Crumbling Pillars of Social Partnership', in Kitschelt, H. and Streeck, W. (eds) *Germany: Beyond the Stable State*, London: Frank Cass, 101–24.

Taylor, S. and Tyler, M. (2000) 'Emotional Labour and Sexual Difference in the Airline Industry', *Work, Employment and Society*, 14(1): 77–96.

Thelen, K. (2004) *How Institutions Evolve: The Political Economy of Skills in Germany, Britain the United States and Japan*, Cambridge: Cambridge University Press.

Thompson, P. (1983) *The Nature of Work: An Introduction to the Debates on the Labour Process*, London: Macmillan.

Thompson, P. (1990) 'Crawling from the Wreckage: The Labour Process and the Politics of Production', in Knights, D. and Willmott, H. (eds) *Labour Process Theory*, Houndsmills: Macmillan.

Thompson, P. (2004) *Skating on Thin Ice: The Knowledge Economy Myth*, Glasgow: University of Strathclyde/Big Thinking.

Thompson, P. (2007) 'Adler's Theory of the Capitalist Labour Process: A Pale(o) Imitation', *Organization Studies*, 28(9): 1359–68.

Thompson, P. and McHugh, D. (2009, 4th edition) *Work Organisations: A Critical Introduction*, Basingstoke: Palgrave.

Thompson, P. and Smith, C. (2009) 'Labour Power and Labour Process: Contesting the Marginality of the Sociology of Work', *Sociology*, 43(5): 913–30.

Tuselmann, H. and Heiss, A. (2000) 'The German Model of Industrial Relations at the Crossroads: Past, Present and Future', *Industrial Relations Journal*, 31(3): 162–76.

UKCES (2009) 'Ambition 2020: World Class Skills and Jobs for the UK', London: UK Commission for Employment and Skills.

Warhurst, C. and Thompson, P. (1998) 'Hands, Hearts and Minds: Changing Work and Workers at the End of the Century', in Thompson, P. and Warhurst, C. (eds) *Workplaces of the Future*, London: Macmillan.

Westergaard-Nielson, N. (ed.) (2008) *Low-Wage Work in Denmark*, New York: Russell Sage Foundation.

Wharton, A. S. (1996) 'Service with a Smile: Understanding the Consequences of Emotional Labour', in Macdonald, C. L. and Sirianni, C. (eds) *Working in the Service Society*, Philadelphia, PA: Temple University Press.

Whitley, R. (1999) *Divergent Capitalisms: The Social Structuring and Change of Business Systems*, Oxford: Oxford University Press.

Winch, G., Clarke, L. and Brockmann, M. (2009) 'Nuffield Study Crossnational Skills and Qualifications: Crossnational Synthesis', London: Nuffield.

Wood, S. (ed.) (1982) *The Degradation of Work? Skill, Deskilling and the Labour Process*, London: Hutchinson.

Normative Control and Beyond in Contemporary Capitalism[1]

6

Andrew Sturdy, Peter Fleming and Rick Delbridge

> In the longer run, the problem is to understand how, in a society that is increasingly pluralistic and thus goal in-congruent, in which interest groups become more distinct and in which a sense of community seems remote, the control of organizations can be achieved without recourse to an unthinking bureaucratization...
>
> (Ouchi, 1979: 846)

Introduction

Management control lies at the heart of labour process analysis (LPA). This is evident from its emergence with Braverman's (1974) deskilling thesis. This built on Marx's analysis of the capitalist labour process, most notably the challenge for capital of transforming labour power or potential into labour and the securing of surplus value to ensure profitable production. Braverman saw this as being achieved through management's control of labour and as inevitably leading to the degradation of work and decline in worker skill and autonomy as capitalists seek profits in increasingly competitive markets (cf. Adler, 2007). Early critiques of Braverman from within LPA challenged the determinism of his argument, advancing the conception of managers and workers as more active agents and extending his work to offer alternative strategies of management control, including 'responsible autonomy' (e.g. Friedman, 1977; see also Hyman, 1987). LPA in current forms thus recognizes the interrelationships between the positions and actions of actors ('owners', 'managers', 'workers' and even 'customers' and 'suppliers'), the nature and contexts of organizations, and the various material, social and economic outcomes of labour. However, it continues to be crucially concerned with the examination of fundamental tensions and contradictions within capitalism, what Edwards (1986) describes as the 'structured antagonism' of the capitalist labour process. The social structural characteristics of capitalism are thus understood to shape but not determine the negotiated outcomes at the level of the workplace. Within this framing then, management control is central to the concerns of labour process theorists.

Some early LPA was particularly concerned with mapping the historical development of the management of the labour process. There were numerous accounts charting the different combinations, conditions, contradictions, outcomes and dynamics to be found in approaches to controlling labour processes and a number of these studies form key reference points within the field (e.g. Edwards, 1979; Friedman, 1977; Littler, 1982; Ramsay, 1977). Some of these early accounts have been critiqued for assuming a linear or sequential trajectory of development of controls under which management develops ever more sophisticated and distinct approaches in response to worker resistance and prevalent market conditions (for an overview see Thompson and McHugh, 2009). These studies were augmented by work that emphasized the importance and persistence of worker resistance, the organization of consent and the incompleteness of attempts at management control (Burawoy, 1979; Edwards, 1986). Various empirical studies of workplace relations have shown the partial and negotiated nature of management control as well as its different forms in a given context (Delbridge, 1998; Edwards and Scullion, 1982; Sturdy, 1992; Wilkinson, 1983). Thus, personal, bureaucratic and cultural controls coexist and interact in sometimes complex combinations with uncertain outcomes. Acknowledgement of the contingent and combined or hybrid nature of management control in practice (Child, 1984) has thus become a dominant view. This has meant the early work outlining the historical evolution of distinct forms of managerial control has been moderated to show the hybrid nature of controls in practice. For example, Callaghan and Thompson (2001) show how Edwards' (1979) modes of control are 'blended' in the institutionalization of control in a particular workplace. Management control is thus understood to have different dimensions and combinations subject to varying strategies and conditions in specific organizations (see Hyman, 1987).

Some research has sought to tease out the precise nature of mixed or hybrid forms of control and to identify key novel characteristics of controls, especially those associated with the possibilities for surveillance in innovations in work organization and/or information technology (Barker, 1993; Sewell, 1998). Since context informs approaches to management control, various studies have also suggested that new (hybrid) forms of control have become more prevalent as capitalism develops. Reed (forthcoming) summarizes these developments in outlining a 'new control logic' which combines electronic surveillance, cultural engineering and political management. Key proponents such as Sewell (1998) have suggested this represents a fundamental break with the core features of established regimes, producing a new model of control. Others are more circumspect and recognize the continuities in contemporary developments, arguing that new forms of control rarely displace established ones (Thompson and Harley, 2007). In this chapter, we seek to walk that line in arguing that it is possible to identify an emerging form of managerial control regime, which we term neo-normative control, but acknowledging that it works in combination with other well-established forms of management control. In this, we see some resonance with others who have noted how the emphasis of control regimes shifts with changing patterns of capitalist economy and society (Ramsay, 1977; Barley and Kunda, 1992; cf. Guillen, 1993). Indeed, those with a broad view of LPA discuss some of the more macro aspects of control across workplaces, including the nature of financial markets and their implications for managers in securing workplace bargains (Thompson, 2003) and the prospects of technological developments heralding more 'efficient' control for dispersed or hollowed-out corporations (Ackroyd, 2002). Our primary focus in this chapter, however, is on the specifics of the labour process at the workplace level.

LPA represents a specific and, to many, sharply delineated view of control, but can also be seen as (a key) part of a broader critical approach to work and organizations. Here, a concern with management control is also evident and contributes to a long political tradition of revealing mechanisms of subordination from behind managerial masks of participation, autonomy and shared interests (Burawoy, 1985; Sewell, 2007: 274). Indeed, in the 20 years since the publication of *Labour Process Theory* (Knights and Willmott, 1990), the nature of management control and our theoretical resources to explicate its dynamics in capitalist contexts have undergone some change. The terrain remains contested, but the nature of these contests and the intellectual traditions drawn upon have shifted significantly. Recently, there have been a number of reviews of the ways in which control has been conceived and theories of control have developed, especially in relation to what might be seen as parallel concerns with discipline, surveillance and governmentality (see e.g. Barker, 1993; Delbridge and Ezzamel, 2005; Miller and Rose, 2008; Sewell, 2007). For example, Reed recognizes the areas where Foucauldian research has provided important insights into changing control relations and the tensions that are endemic. Nonetheless, he concludes that the emergent 'hybrid control' retains its neo-Weberian underpinnings and is best represented as 'a further elaboration, rather than reversal, of bureaucratization' in which there is both greater reliance on intra-organizational regimes based on the deployment of 'soft power' and inter-organizational governance structures that are more market-based and decentralized (Reed, forthcoming: 27–8; see also Thompson, 2003). We agree that LPA has been invigorated and revitalized in some ways by research from alternative ontological positions and that the prospects for further theoretical advance are increased by engagement and dialogue across these. Assessments of management control will be central in these debates.

In this chapter, we are not so much concerned with theoretical contests, but with exploring what we believe to be an increasingly evident approach to control in contemporary capitalist workplaces – neo-normative control. We attempt this through the use of a single case example. While we are aware that the case is an unusual one in a number of ways, it resonates clearly with regimes reported and promoted by various recent management writers and commentators of 'best places to work', but also with those identified in empirical academic studies (see Grugulis, Dundon and Wilkinson, 2000 and Kinnie, Hutchinson and Purcell, 2000 for example). The chapter is organized as follows. First, we outline our understanding of normative control. We then build on this to inform our discussion of the emergence of the neo-normative approach to managing employees where emphasis is placed on 'being yourself'. Next, we set out how such a seemingly liberal regime relates to other types of control and specifically, the key characteristics that mark neo-normative control as a particular form of control. Following a brief illustration of such a control regime in a call centre, we conclude by discussing what it means for our understanding of work and the capitalist labour process.

Beyond normative control

A prevalent concept used to understand contemporary variants of management domination is 'normative control' (Barley and Kunda, 1992; Kunda, 1992; Willmott, 1993). With special reference to corporate culture and its ideology of 'shared interests', normative control is said to help exploit workers not through traditional methods of direct coercion, but via the indoctrination of shared corporate beliefs, norms and values. In this sense, the very 'selves' of employees become a key mechanism of control, often expressed as a collective emotional attachment to the firm or, effectively, self-control (Casey, 1995). Building on this notion, our chapter is concerned with an empirical development in recent years of a seemingly benign and liberating approach to managing employees which in fact appears to us to mark both an extension of, and departure from, normative control, to what we term 'neo-normative control'. Our specific interest is to (re-)connect intra-organizational control regimes with their wider societal contexts to mark what we believe to be a number of significant developments that have been increasingly acknowledged empirically (e.g. Liu, 2004; Ross, 2004; Webb, 2004), but remain under-theorized. Our argument is both empirical and conceptual: neo-normative control works to create and sustain a corporate identity drawn from externally derived values and identities to which employees are expected to subscribe. In this sense, it is similar to normative control or corporate culture management which placed emphasis on instilling strong, common and organization-focused norms and values among employees in order to create a distinct, shared sense of identity and belonging. The key difference is that this 'corporate identity' draws upon, and harnesses, employees' values that are predominantly formed extra-organizationally. To deny one's alignment with the organization's corporate identity thus becomes to deny something of oneself.

As intimated in the opening quote by Ouchi, in the 1980s version of normative control, the corporation was thought to be displacing society as the fulcrum of values, beliefs and morality (e.g. Pascale and Athos, 1982). As many have argued since however, this was neither a legitimate nor effective way to cast the role of the firm in relation to employee identities (Scott, 1994). Workers resisted being completely defined by the organization through cynicism, resistance or other forms of non-compliance, often by protecting non-work selves as sites of authenticity. Indeed, with the corporation's inward-facing clan-like system of inculcation, the external and non-work realm was considered by management to be a potential source of impurity and dilution (see Hochschild, 1983; Kunda 1992; O'Reilly and Chatman, 1996). Pascale and Athos (1982) went so far as to advance the view that the modern corporation should occupy Durkheim's sacred realm, replacing organized religion as a source of morality and societal values (also see Ray, 1986).

We do not suggest that societal influences are necessarily greater now; rather that in some respects they are more likely to provide subordinating influences on employees and in other ways encourage behaviours that coincide with contemporary corporate objectives. With the subsequent rise of neoliberalism (or market rationality) and the growth of associated discourses of self-interest, diversity and enterprise in the US and UK (Webb, 2004), values inscribed by institutions outside of paid employment are now less easily considered 'dangerous' to the purposes and goals of the firm and are now of greater subordinating potential to corporations (Fleming, 2009). Discourses, laws and practices of inclusion act to formally embrace diversity and harness it to societal (and by extension, corporate capitalist) goals. Neo-normative control is therefore different. It sees the manager playing a mediating or channelling role in which already present values are 'liberated' or 'unleashed' to use the rather insipid language of pop-management commentators. We believe this is for the following reasons:

1. The tenacity of prior socialized values – even under normative control, it was difficult to proscribe societal identities in any complete manner.
2. It is no longer considered legitimate to bar the expression of the 'whole person' from the workplace, especially given the importance of liberalism and its emphasis of personal freedom, diversity and so forth.
3. The corporate recognition that outside or non-work norms and their 'free' and emotional expression can be a source of utility in relation to motivation, task execution (e.g. aesthetic labour) and 'totalizing' commitments to quality and 'doing a good job' and thus so-called flexibility.

The mechanisms of this control are similar to those used in normative control. Indeed, and as we shall see, there are parallels with other forms of control as well. However, the key difference is that the values are derived from what are traditionally (bureaucratically) considered non-work sources. Some of these are familiar such as family and community, but contemporary capitalism is marked by a wide variety of influences, including sexuality, consumerism, personal networks, partying and 'fun', lifestyle and even anti-work sentiments ('slacker cool'). The manager here is therefore not explicitly aiming to inculcate and socialize the worker to become a corporate clone, but to promote values from outside the firm in a manner that resonate with organizational objectives. Many conventional management writers herald this as a kind of freedom from control (e.g. Bains, 2007; Semler, 1993, 2004). However, following the political traditions mentioned earlier of seeking to unmask such managerialist claims, we view it as an insidious extension of value-based controls and one which may coexist with other, traditional forms of personal, bureaucratic and technological controls for example.

Market rationalism and the decline of corporate culture management

Numerous studies of normative control since the 1980s have shown how employees across a range of levels and sectors were exhorted to embrace a designed membership role as their own and become a 'company (wo) man' (e.g. Ray, 1986). But as noted above, many employees wanted to maintain a distance or private reserve that was truly theirs (Kunda, 1992). Indeed, it is unclear whether normative control was ever as successful as once claimed by both its champions and some of its critics (Jermier et al., 1991). Moreover, more prescriptive writers began to recognize the counterproductive elements that value conformity might have on innovation and initiative (e.g. Kanter, 1989). Such limitations were also echoed in broader shifts in the employment relationship. In particular, Kunda and Ailon-Souday (2005) argued that a new managerial paradigm – market rationality – associated with downsizing, outsourcing and distributed work emerged that undermined the normative control surge of the 1980s and 1990s. Of particular importance is the claim that 'market rationalists seem to have little patience for culture, no matter how strong' (203). There is, of course, a normative basis to market rationality. As opposed to the rhetoric of unitary values and extreme loyalty, we instead find individualism, entrepreneurial risk-taking and self-reliance as key themes (Webb, 2004).

Such developments allow for a certain degree of freedom in relation to the expression of 'non-organizational', diverse identities and lifestyles in the workplace. Indeed, to more optimistic commentators, workers are not only task empowered, but also 'existentially empowered' to bring different identities into the workplace (Bains, 2007; Peters, 2003; Pink, 2001). To others, such developments simply reflect organizational control assuming a traditional, laissez-faire, instrumental form (Kunda and Ailon-Souday, 2005). Here, employees are now expected (and expect) to receive little from the organization other than remuneration and the opportunity to develop their skills portfolios for subsequent use on competitive markets. Our argument, however, is that market rationalism not only trades in utilitarian contractual controls, but also allows for a certain type of identity management which has emerged out of normative control.

Be what you are! Identity freedom as control

Whereas normative controls were designed to instil a *shared* value orientation in the firm – love of the organization and/or the customer – *neo-normative control* entails an exhortation to *'be yourself'* or what you are outside of work. There is a growing wave of popular management rhetoric and associated practices that encourage diversity, dissent, idiosyncrasy and the expression of 'authentic' feelings in the work environment, especially those once explicitly barred from the bureaucratic or formal organization (see Fleming and Sturdy, 2009). Neo-normative control then involves the selective enlistment of the private dimensions of employee selves, usually under the rubric of individualism and free self-expression as a way extracting behaviour amendable to organizational objectives. As Bains puts it when describing South-West Airlines:

> Individuality is not just tolerated...but actively encouraged – particularly when it comes to employees expressing the fun side of their personalities...All

of this is based on the belief that when people are happy and have the freedom to be themselves, they are more productive and give more of themselves. (2007: 241)

Following Mirvis (1994), it is the complete person that is increasingly desired by the organization, with other extra-employment themes like sexuality, consumption and leisure especially salient. Control is extended when what was once protected from the organization via cynicism and psychological distancing is appropriated as a corporate resource to enhance output.

How does neo-normative control compare with other modes of control (see Table 6.1)? First, it clearly contrasts with bureaucratic control (Edwards, 1979) at least in the sense that fun, sexuality and consumption are not formally barred. Second, the human relations movement, with its emphasis on the informal organization and then, as 'neo-human relations', on

Table 6.1 Neo-normative control compared with other modes of control

Modes of Control	Neo-Normative Control
Bureaucratic Control (e.g. Edwards, 1979)	Does not bar the personal, emotional and unpredictable features of employees, but attempts to evoke and shape them as strategic resources. Difference and discretion rather than standardization of selves.
Human Relations (e.g. Ray, 1986)	Also seeks to appropriate the informal and emotional and to render routine work more palatable, but does not focus on norms developed in work groups but those prior to, and beyond, the organizational domain.
Neo-Human Relations (e.g. Johnson and Gill, 1993)	Similar in inviting the expression of authentic selves, but focused on social identities surrounding work more than self-actualization achieved through task-autonomy.
Normative Control (e.g. Kunda, 1992)	Similar elements and methods, but aim is normative diversity, not uniformity. Invites and supports the outside of work self ('warts and all') and not just the preferred 'front stage' corporate (specific) self.
Market Rationality (e.g. Kunda and Ailon-Souday, 2005)	Similar attention to the value of diversity and the constraints of homogeneity, but focuses on identity and values rather than market forces. Complements other (often unacknowledged) normative elements of market rationality (e.g. entrepreneurialism)

self-actualization, does have some parallels with neo-normative control. But rather than seeking to appropriate norms developed informally within work groups (Ray, 1986), the target of neo-normative control are those associated with non-working life. With regard to neo-human relations (Johnson and Gill, 1993), the similarities are perhaps even stronger. Here, managers were also invited to enhance the expression of 'authentic' selves among employees. The key difference, however, is in the way neo-normative control is concerned with social identities rather than the expression of creativity or 'self-actualization' through work tasks. In other words, *for the most part*, neo-normative control aims to enhance the enjoyment of the job via the freedom of identity and emotional expression *surrounding the work performance* rather than through it. Third, and as we have already suggested, neo-normative control is clearly linked to normative control. But the normative base is that of difference – the 'real lives' of employees are not externalized or engineered out in favour of a collective normative alignment (cf. Kunda, 1992). Fourth, the control regime of market rationalism associated with short-term contracts and portfolio careers is, as we have suggested, a major inspiration for neo-normative control, but the latter is more explicitly concerned with identity and its management (cf. Kunda and Ailon-Souday, 2005). This echoes historical accounts of forms of control in the emergent factory system of the industrial revolution where laissez-faire or what we might now call 'market rationalist' approaches existed alongside paternalist practices where employees' non-work values such as religious beliefs and teachings were drawn in to work and appropriated for productive ends (cf. Fleming, 2005).

It is important to point out that we approach neo-normative control as a new form of hybridity or combination of controls, rather than a replacement of normative, or other traditional, controls (also see Courpasson, 2006; Reed, forthcoming). For example, within the various forms and traditions of normative control, it is apparent how societal discourses promoting norms of quality, dependability, honesty and 'good work' contribute to values that are then readily harnessed in the workplace. We elaborate our arguments instead by reference to two key and interrelated elements of neo-normative control – the celebration of difference and workplace fun as expressions of societal identities – not so obviously consistent with corporate goals.

The celebration of difference

A growing body of guru and practitioner literature speaks of the dysfunctionality of the corporate cultures of the 1980s and 1990s. Tom Peters (2003) is a particularly strong critic, arguing that workers are *naturally* inclined to be innovative and exciting. But Peters is not simply calling for renewed emphasis on self-actualization through job discretion, but for a challenge to outdated management ideologies that desire conformity, rationality and unitary values. In direct contrast to his own earlier emphasis on culture management (Peters and Waterman, 1982), a laissez-faire approach to norms is the new imperative – a 'joyous anarchy' in which 'zanies' and mavericks are hired and celebrated. Because the market is based upon differentiation and variation, organizations should follow suit: 'pursue variation, not to manage (stifle) it' (Peters, 1994: 51; also Fierman, 1995). Clearly, there is a disjuncture between the world as imagined by Tom Peters and that experienced by most, if not all, workers. What is interesting, though, is the way Peters subverts previous dominant corporate managerial discourses.

Underlying this 'be yourself' ideology is the notion that employees are free agents, no longer objects of corporate control. In Semler's *Maverick!* (1993), which describes his own firm's practices and has sold over one million copies, workers are told: 'now control is passé and a badge of incompetence. Now, you are free' (xiii). The freedom to be yourself extends to expressing dissent towards management (Peters, 1992; Sutton, 2001). All the tropes of the free market are here and the conformity of previous cultural regimes is denigrated, associated with communism and the stifling of individual idiosyncrasies. This is why the ethos of the unruly youngster is often drawn upon – 'go for youth' (Peters, 1994: 204; see also Semler, 1993). Although not our focus here, the celebration of diversity has also absorbed liberalist motifs in relation to minority groups such as gays, ethnics and others often disenfranchised in traditional Western corporate settings (Florida, 2004; Janssens and Zanoni, 2005). Recent work advancing equality in the corporation has argued in favour of embracing diversity on the grounds of, for example, innovativeness and enhanced customer service, seeking to make a business case rather than the moral argument for eschewing discrimination (e.g. Maddock, 1995).

Fun as expressions of self

The other emerging way in which identity is managed under neo-normative control is to accentuate fun and playful dynamics of work. This has long been one element of conventional culture management regimes (Collinson, 2002), but has expanded significantly in some sectors as part of a reaction to the downsizing trend of the 1990s – the rise of the corporate 'play ethic' (Kane, 2004; also see *Employee Relations*, October, 2009). Employees are encouraged to express their fun and playful side, rather than suppressing it in the name of sober, bureaucratic productiveness and a 'bottom-line mentality' (Deal and Key, 1998: 6). Some surveyed 'best companies to work for' such as Kwik Fit, a car servicing chain in the UK, even had a full-time 'Minister of Fun' managerial position (*Sunday Times*, 2006).

As when interpreting Peters' calls for 'joyous anarchy', it is important to go beneath the froth and nonsense of such claims to examine the underlying dynamics and implications of what is actually happening in contemporary workplaces. Part of this drive to make work playful can still be framed in terms of normative, rather than neo-normative, regimes, in keeping with the view of controls as assuming multiple and hybrid forms. For example, while Deal and Key (1998: 25) argue that celebrations at work foster diversity and 'provide social support for being yourself', they also see them as generating a sense of belonging, shared camaraderie and loyalty (also see Hemsath and Sivasubramania, 2001).

Our focus is with the former whereby play and fun are a licence to be oneself in a way that leads workers to love being *in the* company rather than love *the* company itself. Indeed, such instrumentality is implied in managerial efforts to become an 'employer of choice' or 'best place to work', especially when tasks are predominantly routine and fun is primarily directed at compensating for limited job discretion rather than fostering innovation, such as in most call centres (Callaghan and Thompson, 2001). A key way in which this neo-normative feature of fun and playfulness is developed is through blurring the symbolic distinction that has traditionally separated home and the formal organization. The idea that employees must adopt an *organizational* persona at work is reversed – people can, and should, express their 'authentic' or 'full' selves at work rather than repress the intrinsic desire to be playful and curious (Bains, 2007: 219; Deal and Key, 1998; Peters, 2003; also Semler, 2004; Reeves, 2001).

Difference and fun as control

We have suggested that the market rationalism of contemporary capitalism allows for an approach to managing employees that aims for existential 'empowerment' – 'be yourself' – rather than the reshaping of selfhood into a uniform corporate identity. This clearly has potential to be liberating, especially for those whose identities have been hitherto silenced or stigmatized. However, we have argued that it also represents a new mode of control. How then are such seemingly liberal regimes controlling? First and most broadly, it is important to emphasize how management control commences long before individuals enter the workplace in that our values and lifestyles are schooled partly in accordance with the interests of employers from an early age (Illich, 1970). This is not a defining feature of neo-normative control. Indeed, this is one of the bases of normative control in terms of the value filtering of selection processes. Furthermore, recent times have seen management discourses and practices spread to almost all areas of human activity, to everyday life (Hancock and Tyler, 2009). Exploring these developments directly lies outside our concerns in this chapter other than to underscore our earlier contention that neo-normative control relies more directly on non-work identities being employer-friendly, or at least not 'dangerous'. Nonetheless, and second, we shall see how there are clear limits to the breadth and form of individuality that an organization might tolerate. In particular, managers act to harness norms that are founded extra-organizationally in shaping 'appropriate' corporate values. This is unsurprising since there are few social domains where value or identity freedom is unlimited. However, it is important to emphasize for it reveals the contradictory nature of managerial claims of freedom from control. More significantly and third, in attempting to draw more of the person into the employment situation, management practices utilize identity as a resource. Even the 'inner preserve' protected from normative control regimes, through cynicism for example, can now be used in an effort to enhance productivity. Moreover, and fourth, it is a self-disciplinary form of control. If an employee's performance is failing, this is seen to be a problem with her own values, personality or identity more than insufficient commitment to the corporate norm. Finally, and as the following illustrative case suggests, 'existential empowerment' can be seen as a form of control through the resistance it provokes, however bizarre the notion of resisting being what you are may initially seem.

An illustrative case: 'Outside-in'

We now present an illustrative case of a neo-normative control regime – *Sunray Customer Service* (a pseudonym), an American-owned call centre based in Australia. Given space limitations in this volume and the fact that the research methods used in the study of Sunray have been discussed elsewhere (Fleming, 2009), we set out only brief details here. Sunray was founded by James Carr (another pseudonym) in the early 1990s, who remains the CEO and cultural figurehead. It deals with outsourced communication functions for insurance firms, airlines and banks and thus, puts much emphasis on the customer service skills of its agents. Their work is demanding, mostly dealing with calls in eight-hour shifts. It is also largely routine and, in many respects, strictly controlled, through familiar call centre technology for example (e.g. Callaghan and Thompson, 2001). Indeed, aspects of each of technological, bureaucratic and cultural controls (combined with direct personal control from managers and supervisors) were clearly evident at Sunray. The most conspicuous form of control is that underpinned by the technology which provides for scripting calls through screen prompts, performance measurement systems and the surveillance of employee interaction. In addition, while management claimed the organization was non-hierarchical and non-authoritarian, various aspects of bureaucratic coordination including job descriptions and work rosters were enacted through a well-defined and traditional hierarchical structure. In all of these regards, this case has important similarities with other studies of call centres (see Russell, 2009).

However, we are concerned with the 'fun' side of what Kinnie, Hutchinson and Purcell (2000) describe from a similar context as a combination of 'fun and surveillance'. Sunray was selected for research because of its broader reputation as a 'best place to work' in a relatively tight labour market. The initial research aim was to understand experiences of *normative control*, but the data required an alternative conceptual framework to explain the emphasis on authenticity and individual diversity based on non-work values and identities.

The firm initially seems a classic example of normative control given the key role attributed to the founder and a culture programme entitled 'the 3Fs: Fun, Focus, Fulfilment'. Some employees were positive about this programme.

… it's like this: When you leave work you don't feel drained: 'Oh, I've just had another day at work' – the fun allows you to focus not only on your work but yourself as well – and at the end of the day you come out feeling fantastic and you like coming to work – you love coming here.

Nevertheless, prominent *neo-normative* control tendencies were also evident. Emphasizing freedoms around workplace norms, employees were invited to celebrate and display a commitment to *who they are* (rather than to the company itself). According to the CEO, Semler's (1993) *Maverick!* inspired this management style: 'the 3Fs philosophy delivers service excellence by simply allowing people to be themselves and communicate their uniqueness – we like different people here from all walks of life'. The discourse particularly trades on youthful anti-authoritarian chic, underground cool and designer subversion (a number of employees wore T-shirts with anti-corporate slogans). Janis, a team development manager avers:

Everyone is different and we make sure that people can express themselves and will be accepted for who they are. … It all comes down to our environment – the culture, the freedom to enjoy being themselves and to enjoy being at work.

The promotion of lifestyle, sexual and ethnic diversity is especially important. But the approach is not limited to 'diversity management' in the sense of encouraging/utilizing the visibility of various socio-demographically marginalized groups. It is also concerned with providing a space for authentic 'self-expression' which include prominent extra-employment themes. A selection of these practices is summarized below.

The expressive, playful, inner child

At Sunray, the recruitment strategy uses friendship networks to employ young and overtly youthful employees who have had little employment experience (also see Castilla, 2005). Aside from cost considerations, the employment of young people is typically associated with the relative ease with which an organizational culture can be inculcated. However, the rationale given reversed this logic in that 'young people find (the)...culture very, very attractive because they can be themselves and know how to have fun'. In other words, young people were seen as more likely to be expressive and playful, including with identities. For example, workers were required to bring to work an item that 'best explains who you are' – one agent responded by bringing a surfboard, and another a popular anti-capitalism book.

Organized events included a range of activities that were sometimes very characteristic of the schoolroom. While many of the interviewees found it fun, some were very cynical.

> Working at Sunray is like working for 'Playschool'. It's so much like a kindergarten...a plastic, fake kindergarten. The murals on the wall, the telling off if I'm late and the patronising tone in which I'm spoken to all give it a very childish flavour.

Partying and drinking

While such activities might be seen as infantilizing rather than empowering, practices also incorporated the expression of explicitly adult identities under the theme of partying. In particular, employees were openly encouraged to drink alcohol on Friday afternoons in the workplace and perpetuate a party-like atmosphere in the organization. Job advertisements were headed with the phrase 'do you know how to party?' and management often said that Sunray life is similar to a 'party' because of the energy and 'good times'. One training session, held in a nearby park, was analogous to an actual party with beer drinking and the open expression of sexuality and flirting.

Sexuality

The expression of sexuality and flirting among employees was not confined to parties nor simply a reflection of workplace life or, even, the demographics of the employees. Rather, according to some informants and confirmed by observations, it was openly accepted at Sunray. As already intimated and in keeping with the notion of 'being yourself', the sexual dimension of the Sunray culture had a strong gay focus (see also Clair, Beatty and MacLean,

2005). For example, one agent, Mary claimed that 'they (gays) like it because they can be themselves' and that 'Sunray definitely promote it [open homosexuality]...well, not promote it but, say, you are what you are and you are allowed to be that way'.

Dress code as identity

Part of the openly sexual culture at Sunray was its expression through clothing, encouraged through what some might see as a liberal dress code. This practice cut across others such as the organized parties and events (e.g. a 'fashion day', 'dress-up days' and 'pyjama days'). Once again, most employees seemed to enjoy these exercises by suggesting that it brought more fun to the work – 'treats me more as whole person...' While these events were clearly in a similar spirit to 'dressing up', another element was to express yourself through otherwise private clothing – as consumers – being centred on the latest fashion labels and promoted with the intention of creating a party-like atmosphere in the organization. Many of the employees interviewed relished this part of the 3Fs philosophy because they felt 'free to be who we are', as one agent put it, while others saw it as promoting a rather pretentious attitude.

Neo-normative control at Sunray

In many respects, the approach to managing Sunray employees matches the prescriptions of recent gurus and the publicized practices of 'leading' employers discussed earlier (see also Courpasson, 2006). Indeed, it was explicitly informed by such accounts. There is a strong emphasis on the expression – rather than suppression or transformation – of what hitherto might have been seen as non-work, individual and authentic identities, feelings and lifestyles and on the acceptance, and even celebration, of differences. We proposed earlier however, that such an apparently liberal approach to managing employees represents a form of control which is both distinct from and linked to other control typologies. In particular, we suggested that there were five related dimensions to neo-normative control, all of which we can observe at Sunray (see Table 6.2).

First, through both recruitment processes and the celebration of difference, Sunray reinforces broader societal constructions of identity. In this case, diversity is constructed as particular variants of sexuality, consumerism and playfulness rather than say, occupational skills, familial roles, politics and community (cf. Anteby, 2008). Second and most transparently, control is evident in the limits implicitly and explicitly imposed that contradict the

Table 6.2 Neo-normative control at Sunray

Dimensions of Neo-Normative Control	Expression at Sunray
Reinforces broader (e.g. late modern) societal constructions of identity.	Celebration of difference/variety with reference to youth, lifestyle, sexuality, consumption tastes and being yourself.
Limits to the expression of difference.	Fun activities were highly prescribed; intolerance of some expressions of difference (e.g. incident of conflict with family identity); anti-union policy.
Selective enlistment of private dimensions of self as a corporate resource.	Evocation of traditionally non-work motifs associated with fun, partying and sex in team exercises, social events etc. Discretion and authenticity in customer service function.
Individual responsibility and self-discipline.	Peer surveillance of attitudes in relation to 3Fs program and the counselling dynamic of the employment relationship.
Exhortation to 'be yourself' inspires resistance.	Recognition that be yourself ethos is contradictory. Challenging individualism through sentiments of solidarity and uniformity (e.g. 'we're all just pleb's').

rhetoric of a laissez-faire approach to self-expression. One manager revealed this contradiction:

> Every 3Fs activity we undertake is implemented in a controlled way and adherence is mandatory – although individualism and creativity are encouraged...we have one Sunray attitude, but people can still be themselves.

There was no room for the non-fun, non-'different' person in the organized events. As one agent recounted: 'A woman in my team was told that she had to go to the Away Day but she said she had family commitments, "I'm a mother." But she was told "no, we are all going"'. Likewise, in keeping with the policy of many other 'progressive' employers, there was considered 'no need' for a trade union presence (e.g. Semler, 2004).

The third way in which the regime served as a control was in the appropriation (and therefore, partial construction) of identities and other unrewarded characteristics for productive ends (also Janssens and Zanoni, 2005). This is particularly evident in the recruitment and production of youthfulness, sexuality and enthusiasm to facilitate, as well as compensate for, customer service – 'fun' as part of the job (Sturdy, Grugulis and Willmott, 2001). Also, up to a point, employees were encouraged or 'indulged' to challenge the way the organization operates, especially during new client projects and away days (cf. Gouldner, 1955). Furthermore, dissent as a lifestyle signifier relating to the 'slacker cool' and anti-establishment ethos of youth culture was a salient part of Sunray's corporate identity (also see Boltanski and Chiapello, 2005). There was, however, no place for a 'militant' self, 'fun as sabotage' or, as already noted, even a union identity. Furthermore, these indulgences were both made possible and effectively limited by other control mechanisms, notably the call centre technology and disciplinary performance assessment.

Fourth, the encouragement and colonization of identities and 'real' selves at Sunray served as a form of *self*-disciplinary control in that once 'private' identities were made more visible and accountable so that individual success and failure were attributed to the type of person the employee was (Miller and Rose, 2008). This was seen in judgemental comments made about fellow employees over the extent to which they embraced the 3Fs program as well as a more hierarchical counselling dynamic where team members were policed on their own personal mental state: 'I will first recognize a difference in their attitude...and I will say "What has happened? Is it the job or something at home? What can I do to help you with that?"'

Finally, the controlling elements of the 'be yourself' philosophy are evident in the resistance it inspires. As noted earlier, normative control engendered its own brand of resistance as employees hid their 'real' identities and feigned identification. But when the control function actually encourages workers to express these real identities, what form, if any, does resistance take? How might one resist being oneself? First, some employees displayed a brand of cynicism, also familiar under normative control regimes, which held the promise of achieving a different sense of authenticity:

I am empowered only in their terms, not mine...am I empowered to choose when to have my lunch break? No. Am I empowered to talk and have fun with my friends? [*Impersonates an angry supervisor*] 'SSHHHH!' – No.

The second or alternative step is to undermine the sentiment of diverse and individual authenticity by emphasizing solidarity, uniformity and collective subordination.

Well, to 'succeed' at Sunray you are basically gay, have to be really 'alternative' and Sunray likes people who have different coloured hair and who are into [*in a sarcastic tone*] 'being themselves'. Now I'm not too sure which one we fit into, but basically we are all plebs. Just plebs.

Conclusion

The Sunray example allows us to build on recent theorizing and the emerging empirical evidence on control in contemporary capitalism in advancing the concept of neo-normative control. We have suggested that following other recent research that reconnects organizational control regimes with their wider societal contexts (Elger and Smith, 2005; Thompson, 2003), it is possible to identify a new hybrid form of control. Neo-normative control is a hybridized extension of some other forms of control, whilst still operating alongside traditional mechanisms such as technical controls. It works most notably in inculcating a corporate identity that draws upon and harnesses the values and identities of employees that are formed and sustained beyond the workplace. In this sense, and in contradistinction to normative controls, the outside is brought in; rather than corporations seeking to develop and impose internally developed norms, corporate identity is constructed through reference to societal values as they are understood, enacted and embodied by the corporation's employees.

Whilst we accept that neo-normative control may not be generalizable across all conditions and contexts, we suggest that three aspects of contemporary capitalism have combined to facilitate such developments. First, the recognition on the part of managers of the tenacity of prior socialized values. The failure of corporate culture management programmes has brought an acknowledgement of the futility of proscribing values and identities. Second, societal norms of liberalism and personal freedom, allied with the discourses of equality, inclusivity and emotionality, mean it is no longer considered legitimate to bar the expression of the 'whole person' from the workplace. Third, managers have identified how outside norms and their 'free' expression can be a source of utility in relation to motivation, task execution and employee flexibility if managed within the boundaries of exploitation. It remains to be seen what the effect of the current economic recession will be on such regimes although it seems likely that fun will be increasingly substituted by 'dull compulsion' in all but the tightest of labour markets.

In relation to the illustrative example of Sunray, we believe that this new hybrid form of control represents an important extension of previous forms because it represents an attempt to *work through* some of the contradictions and tensions that undermined each of these various forms of control. Bureaucratic control mechanisms are undermined by the treatment of individual employees as anonymous 'cogs' of the bureaucratic machine rather than as knowledgeable sentient agents. Neo-normative control, in contrast, engages the personal and emotional nature of each employee and harnesses these attributes to action and organizational outcomes thus helping to address the disenchantment and depersonalization experienced under bureaucratic and technological controls. In contrast to the human relations and neo-human relations schools, neo-normative control reflects the extra-organizational norms and values of wider society and seeks to appropriate individuals' multiple identities in exhortations 'to be oneself' and act in accordance with personal and wider societal values to organizationally determined ends. Finally, we can recognize clear points of differentiation with previously described forms of normative control. In contrast to homogenizing pressures to conform to managerially constructed 'organizational' values that employees routinely recognized as 'false', contradictory or contrived, neo-normative control promotes diversity and individuality. To deny one's alignment with the organization's corporate identity, under neo-normative control, is to deny something of oneself. In this sense then, the task of management becomes the filtering and promotion of certain personal and societally derived norms and identities over others; the 'outside' is brought in and harnessed rather than ignored or contradicted as is the case in various ways with other forms of management control. However, in keeping with a now long tradition in LPA, we have pointed to how neo-normative control can also elicit forms of resistance, including those which draw attention to commonalities such as the shared experience of being subject to routine work and strict control.

Note

1   This chapter draws on the case study evidence, and extends the arguments, first reported in Fleming and Sturdy (2009) and Fleming (2009).

REFERENCES

Ackroyd, S. (2002) *The Organization of Business*, Oxford: Oxford University Press.

Adler, P. (2007) 'The Future of Critical Management Studies: A Paleo-Marxist Critique of Labour Process Theory', *Organization Studies*, 28: 1313–45.

Anteby, M. (2008) 'Identity Incentives as an Engaging Form of Control: Revisiting Leniencies in an Aeronautic Plant', *Organization Science*, 19(2): 202–22.

Bains, G. (2007) *Meaning Inc: The Blue Print for Business Success in the 21st Century*, London: Profile Books.

Barker, J. R. (1993) 'Tightening the Iron Cage: Concertive Control in Self-Managing Teams', *Administrative Science Quarterly*, 38(4): 408–37.

▶

▶

Barley, S. R. and Kunda, G. (1992) 'Design and Devotion: The Ebb and Flow of Rational and Normative Ideologies of Control in Managerial Discourse', *Administrative Science Quarterly*, 37: 1–30.

Boltanski, L. and Chiapello, E. (2005) *The New Spirit of Capitalism*, London: Verso.

Braverman, H. (1974) *Labor and Monopoly Capitalism*, New York: Monthly Review Press.

Burawoy, M. (1979) *Manufacturing Consent*, Chicago, IL: Chicago University Press.

Burawoy, M. (1985) *The Politics of Production*, London: Verso.

Callaghan, G. and Thompson, P. (2001) 'Edwards Re-visited: Technical Control and Call Centres', *Economic and Industrial Democracy*, 22(13): 13–36.

Casey, C. (1995) *Work, Self and Society: After Industrialism*, London: Sage.

Castilla, E. J. (2005) 'Social Networks and Employee Performance in a Call Center', *American Journal of Sociology*, 110: 1243–83.

Child, J. (1984) *Organization: A Guide to Problems and Practice*, London: Paul Chapman Publishing.

Clair, J. A., Beatty, J. E. and MacLean, T. (2005) 'Out of Sight but Not Out of Mind: Managing Invisible Social Identities in the Workplace', *Academy of Management Review*, 30(1): 78–95.

Collinson, D. (2002) 'Managing Humour', *Journal of Management Studies*, 39(3): 269–88.

Courpasson, D. (2006) *Soft Constraint: Liberal Organizations and Domination*, Copenhagen Business School Press/Liber.

Deal, T. and Key, M. (1998) *Celebration at Work: Play, Purpose and Profit at Work*, New York: Berrett-Koehler.

Delbridge, R. (1998) *Life on the Line in Contemporary Manufacturing*, Oxford: Oxford University Press.

Delbridge, R. and Ezzamel, M. (2005) 'The Strength of Difference: Contemporary Conceptions of Control', *Organization*, 12(5), 603–18.

Edwards, P. (1986) *Conflict at Work*, Oxford: Blackwell.

Edwards, P. and Scullion, H. (1982) *The Social Organization of Industrial Conflict*, Oxford: Blackwell.

Edwards, R. (1979) *Contested Terrain – the Transformation of the Workplace in the Twentieth Century*, New York: Basic Books.

Elger, T. and Smith, C. (2005) *Assembling Work: Remaking Factory Regimes in Japanese Multinationals in Britain*, Oxford: Oxford University Press.

Employee Relations, (2009) Special issue on 'Fun at Work', 31(6).

Fierman, J. (1995) 'Winning Ideas from Maverick Managers', *Fortune*, 6 February: 40–6.

Fleming, P. (2005) 'Kindergarten Cop: Paternalism and Resistance in a High-Commitment Workplace', *Journal of Management Studies*, 42(7): 1469–89.

Fleming, P. (2009) *Authenticity and the Cultural Politics of Work*, Oxford: Oxford University Press.

Fleming, P. and Sturdy, A. J. (2009) 'Just Be Yourself – Towards Neo-Normative Control in Organisations', *Employee Relations*, 31(6): 569–83.

Florida, R. (2004) *The Rise of the Creative Class*, North Melbourne: Pluto Press.

Foster, R. and Kaplan, S. (2001) *Creative Destruction: Why Companies That*

▶

▶

Are Built to Last Underperform the Market – and How to Successfully Transform Them, New York: Currency.

Friedman, A. (1977) *Industry and Labour: Class Struggle at Work and Monopoly Capitalism,* London: Macmillan.

Gouldner, A. (1955) *Wildcat Strike,* London: Routledge and Kegan Paul.

Grugulis, I., Dundon, T. and Wilkinson, A. 2000. 'Cultural Control and the "Culturemanager": Employment Practices in a Consultancy', *Work, Employment and Society,* 14(1): 97–116.

Guillen, M. (1993) *Models of Management,* Chicago, IL: University of Chicago Press.

Hancock, P. and Tyler, M. (eds) (2009) *The Management of Everyday Life,* London: Palgrave.

Hemsath, D. and Sivasubramania, J. (2001) *301 More Ways to Have Fun at Work,* San Francisco, CA: Berrett-Koehler Publishers.

Hochschild, A. R. (1983) *The Managed Heart: Commercialization of Human Feeling,* London: University of California Press.

Hyman, R. (1987) 'Strategy or Structure? Capital, Labour and Control', *Work, Employment and Society,* 1(1): 1–25.

Illich, I. (1970) *De-Schooling Society,* Harmondsworth: Penguin.

Janssens, M. and Zanoni, P. (2005) 'Many Diversities for Many Services: Theorizing Diversity (Management) in Service Companies', *Human Relations,* 58(3): 311–40.

Jermier, J. M., Slocum, J. W., Fry, L. W. and Gaines, J. (1991) 'Organizational Subcultures in a Soft Bureaucracy: Resistance behind the Myth and Facade of an Official Culture', *Organization Science,* 2(2): 170–94.

Johnson, P. and Gill, J. (1993) *Management Control and Organizational Behaviour,* London: Paul Chapman.

Kane, P. (2004) *The Play Ethic: A Manifesto for a Different Way of Living,* London: Macmillan.

Kanter, R. (1989) *When Giants Learn to Dance,* New York: Simon and Schuster.

Kinnie, N., Hutchinson, S. and Purcell, J. (2000) 'Fun and Surveillance: The Paradox of High Commitment Management in Call Centres', *International Journal of Human Resource Management,* 11(5): 967–85.

Knights, D. and Willmott, H. (eds) (1990) *Labour Process Theory,* Basingstoke: Macmillan.

Kunda, G. (1992) *Engineering Culture: Control and Commitment in a High-Tech Corporation,* Philadelphia, PA: Temple University Press.

Kunda, G. and Ailon-Souday, G. (2005) 'Managers, Markets and Ideologies – Design and Devotion Revisited', in Ackroyd, S., Batt, R., Thompson, P. and Tolbert, P. S. (eds) *Oxford Handbook of Work and Organization,* Oxford: Oxford University Press.

Littler, C. (1982) *The Development of the Capitalist Labour Process,* London: Heinemann.

Liu, A. (2004) *The Laws of Cool: Knowledge Work and the Culture of Information,* Chicago, IL: University of Chicago Press.

Maddock, S. (1995) 'Rhetoric and Reality: The Business Case for Equality and Why It Continues to Be Resisted', *Women in Management Review,* 10(1): 14–20.

▶

►

Miller, P. and Rose, N. (2008) *Governing the Present: Administering Economic, Social and Personal Life,* Cambridge: Polity Press.

Mirvis, P. H. (1994) 'Human Development or Depersonalization? The Company as Total Community', in Heuberger, F. W. and Nash, L. L. (eds) *A Fatal Embrace? Assessing Holistic Trends in Human Resources Programs,* New Brunswick, NJ: Transaction.

O'Reilly, C. A. and Chatman, J. A. (1996) 'Culture as Social Control: Corporation, Cults, and Commitment', in Staw, B. M. and Cummings, L. L. (eds) *Research in Organizational Behaviour,* Greenwich, CT: JAI Press, 8: 157–200.

Ouchi, W. G. (1979) 'A Conceptual Framework for the Design of Organizational Control Mechanisms', *Management Science* (September): 833–48.

Pascale, R. and Athos, A. (1982) *The Art of Japanese Management,* Harmondsworth: Penguin.

Peters, T. (1992) *Liberation Management: Necessary Disorganization for the Nanosecond Nineties,* London: Pan.

Peters, T. (1994) *The Tom Peters Seminar: Crazy Times Call for Crazy Organizations,* London: Macmillan.

Peters, T. (2003) *Re-Imagine! Business Excellence in a Disruptive Age,* London: Dorling Kindersley.

Peters, T. and Waterman, R. H. (1982) *In Search of Excellence,* New York: Harper and Row.

Pink, D. (2001) *Free Agent Nation: How America's New Independent Workers Are Transforming the Way We Live,* New York: Warner Business Books.

Ramsay, H. (1977) 'Cycles of Control', *Sociology,* 11(3): 481–506.

Ray, C. A. (1986) 'Corporate Culture: The Last Frontier of Control?', *Journal of Management Studies,* 23(3): 287–97.

Reed, M. (2010, forthcoming) 'Control in Contemporary Work Organizations', in Blyton, P., Heery, E. and Turnbull, P. (eds) *Reassessing the Employment Relationship,* Basingstoke: Palgrave Macmillan.

Reeves, R. (2001) *Happy Mondays: Putting Pleasure Back into Work,* London: Pearson Education.

Ross, A. (2004) *No-Collar: The Humane Workplace and Its Hidden Costs,* Philadelphia, PA: Temple University Press.

Russell, B. (2009) 'Call Centres: A Decade of Research', *International Journal of Management Reviews,* 10(3): 195–219.

Scott, A. (1994) *Willing Slaves? British Workers under Human Resource Management,* Cambridge: Cambridge University Press.

Semler, R. (1993) *Maverick! The Success Behind the World's Most Unusual Workplace,* London: Arrow.

Semler, R. (2004) *The Seven-Day Weekend,* New York: Penguin.

Sewell, G. (1998) 'The Discipline of Teams: The Control of Team-Based Industrial Work through Electronic and Peer Surveillance', *Administrative Science Quarterly,* 41: 397–429.

Sewell, G. (2007) 'Control', in Clegg, S. R. and Bailey, J. R. (eds) *International Encyclopaedia of Organization Studies,* New York: Sage.

►

Sturdy, A. J. (1992) 'Clerical Consent – "Shifting" Work in the Insurance Office', in Sturdy, A. J., Knights, D. and Willmott, H. (eds) *Skill and Consent in the Labour Process*, London: Routledge.

Sturdy, A. J., Grugulis, I. and Willmott, H. (2001) *Customer Service – Empowerment and Entrapment*, Basingstoke: Palgrave/Macmillan.

Sunday Times (2006) *100 Best Companies to Work For*, London: Sunday Times.

Sutton, R. (2001) *Weird Ideas That Work: 11 1/2 ways to Promote, Manage and Sustain Innovation*, New York: Penguin.

Thompson, P. (2003) 'Disconnected Capitalism: Or Why Employers Can't Keep Their Side of the Bargain', *Work, Employment & Society*, 17(2): 359–78.

Thompson, P. and Harley, B. (2007) 'HRM and the Worker: Labour Process Perspectives', in Boxall, P., Purcell, J. and Wright, P. (eds) *The Oxford Handbook of Human Resource Management*, Oxford: Oxford University Press.

Thompson, P. and McHugh, D. (2009) (4th edition). *Work Organizations*, London: Macmillan.

Webb, J. (2004) 'Organizations, Self-Identities and the New Economy', *Sociology*, 38(4): 719–38.

Wilkinson, B. (1983) *The Shopfloor Politics of New Technology*, London: Heinemann.

Willmott, H. (1993) 'Strength Is Ignorance; Slavery Is Freedom: Managing Culture in Modern Organisations', *Journal of Management Studies*, 30(4): 515–52.

The Repertoire of Employee Opposition

7

Jacques Bélanger and Christian Thuderoz

The thinking behind this paper was provoked by our scepticism and dissatisfaction with the arguments and assertions that are currently in vogue in social sciences regarding the inability of employees to offer opposition and resistance in the contemporary world of work. In both French and Anglo-American literature, it is often suggested and sometimes explicitly stated that faced with the inexorable forces driving and supporting management control, employees have no choice but to submit and comply. We seek to provide a counterweight to this interpretation.

Such assertions suggesting the 'end of resistance' obviously go against the classic foundations of industrial sociology. What about the autonomy, social cohesion and propensity to resist that were documented either in the French (Bernoux, Motte and Saglio, 1973; Dubois, 1977; Durand, 1978), American (from Donald Roy, 1952 and 1954, to Burawoy, 1979), or British (Beynon, 1973; Terry and Edwards, 1988) traditions? As we evolve towards a post-industrial society, the problem of compliance and opposition at work needs to be reconsidered.

Our starting point is that the process of struggle in the workplace is by no means on the verge of extinction, in spite of drastic changes in the worlds of employment and work. This is not a distinctive premise however, and recent sociological contributions have made progress in understanding current developments in workplace resistance (Ackroyd and Thompson, 1999; Fleming and Spicer, 2007). Indeed, a resurgence of interest for this area of study was recently observed in the sociological literature, particularly in Britain, where the labour process tradition remains very influential.

In 'All Quiet on the Workplace Front?', Thompson and Ackroyd issued a wake-up call denouncing 'the virtual removal of labour as an active agency of resistance in a considerable portion of theory and research' (1995: 615). They were particularly critical of the surging influence of Foucauldian perspectives in British workplace sociology. Their argument was then developed in a book entitled *Organizational Misbehaviour* (Ackroyd and Thompson, 1999). Reviewing a rich body of research, they highlight the multiple forms and modes of workplace resistance, which appear to have far from run out. 'The empirical evidence to show that old forms of misbehaviour are becoming relatively less important is not present. Neither is enough research being done which might show the way new forms of misbehaviour are being innovated' (Ackroyd and Thompson, 1999: 6). Besides establishing how various forms of resistance have been reinvented in the current world of work, this book provides an analytical framework for studying oppositional practices, conceived as 'dimensions of misbehaviour'. While the concept of 'misbehaviour' is not wholly adequate because it suggests an interpretation based on the intrinsic nature of behaviour,[1] it is actually constructed from the perspective of re-appropriation, which has the merit of putting individual or collective behaviour into the context of the employment relationship.[2]

This line of analysis, which is very much in continuity with the British labour process tradition in the way it pays attention to both structure and agency, was tested in field studies and had repercussions. In particular, empirical evidence on the opportunities for and realities of resistance were documented at some length in various studies on call centres, seen by many as epitomizing the 'factory' of the post-industrial landscape (for a useful review of research on call centres, see Russell, 2008). Labour process writers were influential in documenting at an early stage (e.g. Bain and Taylor, 2000) that most call centres remained contested terrains, and that the patterns of control and compliance were variable and in need of empirical study, there as elsewhere in the 'new economy'. Among their many contributions to the understanding of social relations in call centres, Bain and Taylor (2003) showed, for instance, how humour can, in particular contexts, have a subversive character in fostering countercultures and social cohesiveness. From their study of a Scottish call centre, Telebank, Callaghan and Thompson observed that technical control was high, but 'the space for worker resistance and misbehaviour remains even with a high surveillance context' (2001: 34). They also discussed how management sought to manage the 'attitudes' and emotions of customer service representatives (CSRs) but noted that 'far from being passive providers of emotional labour, employees are active and skilled emotion managers in their own right' (Callaghan and Thompson, 2002: 248). In short, observation at Telebank led them to conclude: 'The "electronic sweatshop" is good newspaper copy, but is a long way from the still contested reality of the contemporary call centre' (2001: 35).

In a recent book, Fleming and Spicer (2007) also underline the extent to which the world of work remains a contested territory, by considering not only the traditional forms of resistance but also its more subjective dimensions, such as cynicism and the stubborn refusal to internalize the conciliatory discourse put forward by management, which threatens identity. Whilst Ackroyd and Thompson's work is explicitly opposed to the postmodern thinking associated with Foucault, that of Fleming and Spicer is also highly critical of this thinking but uses it as a starting point for the study of domination and the construction of identity. Fleming and Spicer's project aims at transcending both the post-modern thinking, which they reproach for slipping towards the micro-political and identity-based dimensions at the expense of analyses of power and what structures it,[3] and analyses which deal with resistance in a way deemed too structural and too mechanistic. Fleming and Spicer thus distinguish themselves from analyses with a neo-Marxist influence (notably the focus on the labour process), which they consider to be mechanistic, dichotomic, and more deterministic than dynamic. Thus, 'the metaphor of "resistance" relies upon a Newtonian image of natural moving bodies. First there is action (power) followed by a reaction (resistance). The more closely we look at this relationship, however, the more *dynamic* and codependent it becomes' (Fleming and Spicer, 2007: 48; see also 183–5). Distinguishing themselves from the 'capital and labour' type of dichotomic analyses, they also write that, 'with the prima facie obliteration of class politics in many Western countries... the once black and white vista of the controlled and controllers is difficult to maintain' (49). They might, however, have considered the contribution of Edwards who explicitly sought to go beyond the limitations of a simplistic 'control versus resistance' framework (1986: 42–6, 52).

In concluding their review of research, Collinson and Ackroyd (2005: 318) point out that 'resistance, misbehaviour, and dissent have not gone away with the decline of trade unions or organized industrial action, or the introduction of new technologies and new working practices. Unlike strikes, which were concentrated in particular industries and geographical locations, misbehaviour continues to be ubiquitous and, in many circumstances, is more difficult to control.' But there is also the risk of falling into the trap of 'everything is resistance', by considering any pattern of behaviour that does not show total obedience and compliance as an instance of resistance (a point stressed by Thompson and Ackroyd, 2009). This would not only take the essence out of our object of study in this chapter, but it would also take our mind away from the structural foundations of the employment relationship under capitalism, a central focus of labour process theory (LPT). The conceptual model developed here seeks to overcome this difficulty.

This chapter aims at contributing to these debates in two complementary ways. As a first step, it outlines the underlying premises of the interpretation suggesting the 'end of resistance' and provides a critique of this view in the first section. As a second step, in the third and fourth sections, it formulates a conceptual model that goes beyond the study of the forms of opposition and helps uncover their underlying rationales and their likely evolution over time, as we evolve from an industrial to a post-industrial society. More than mapping the multiple forms of resistance, the object is to construct a conceptual model that helps uncover the possible meanings of employee opposition and considers the evolution of this repertoire[4] over time.

The vanishing of workplace opposition? A critique of received wisdom

The world of work is changing before our very eyes, but the problem of interpretation and theorization remains unsolved. As noted above, some alarming and somewhat impressionistic accounts of social domination at work have received much attention, not least because their straightforward and intuitive interpretations are appealing. It would appear that such narratives are underpinned by three related assertions concerning the overwhelming forces of globalization, management programs and information technology. At first sight, each of these assertions is seductive when considered separately. However, when examined more closely, uncertainties arise since the assertions cannot be said to be true or false, valid or invalid. And more crucially, the combined effect of these assertions leads to a deterministic perspective that misunderstands workplace relations. We will consider each of these briefly.

The inexorable nature of globalized capitalism

Depending on how globalization is viewed, either as inevitable and imposed by the markets or more as the result of a set of policies and decisions, analyses vary regarding the capacity of national and local actors to influence economic decisions within their territory or realm of activity. For some, financial globalization is perceived as such a 'disciplinary tool' that firms no longer have to 'manufacture consent'. According to such analysis, whereas there was a requirement to cooperate under the paternalistic and Fordist models, 'the neo-liberal firm seems to have dropped this obligation. It is closer to a despotic regime through the formidable coercion that employees are made to bear with the pressure from the financial markets, as well as mass unemployment and/or job insecurity' (Coutrot, 1999: 76; our translation). In a similar fashion, de Gaulejac presents constraint as being extreme, with the capacity for opposition atrophied in such a way that the employee is transformed into 'an agent in the service of production', and reduced to 'a freely consented submission', while 'the managerial power permanently neutralizes the violence of capitalism' (de Gaulejac, 2005: 56, 95–7, 112; our translation). Such statements are illustrative of very substantial and significant streams of analysis in French social sciences.[5]

This notion that globalization is socially constructed takes on even more significance when studying management control over work. In spite of the discourse on free markets and the internationalization of economic exchanges, the employment relationship remains, for the overwhelming majority of the working population, highly localized in a limited community or region and socially embedded in a specific local space. Of all the factors of production, and strikingly in comparison to financial capital and technology, labour power is always the one that is most likely to remain local. As noted by Coe, Dicken and Hess, 'a fundamental characteristic of labour is that it is "idiosyncratic and place-bound"' (2008: 284). Hence, to recall a central tenet of LPT, labour power has to be transformed in a given place and context, and the employee has to be convinced in some way, and to a relative extent, to do so. And at this level of action, either in a traditional workplace or in less standard forms of employment and organizations, as studied by the Manchester team (Marchington et al., 2005), the many contradictions of 'disconnected capitalism' (Thompson, 2003) are likely to be observed. In short, this contested terrain is always likely to lead to some form of social action and resistance.

A key analytical principle here is that globalization should also be approached with historical hindsight (Berger, 2003; Hirst and Thompson, 2001) in order to grasp its evolving nature and especially its limitations. Furthermore, a sociological perspective (Burawoy et al., 2000; Castells, 1998; Sassen, 2008) helps to consider how globalization is constructed and to study its implications for citizens and employees in action, in a given institutional and cultural environment.

Management programmes achieve their objectives

The second assertion that we wish to contest has to do with the actual effects of management programmes. A distinction should be made between two types of programmes that are often combined in different ways, depending mainly on the nature of production and technologies. On the one hand, the first type involves production management programmes that fit into the tradition of 'engineering rationality', as referred to by Daniel Bell in 1962. Nowadays, these rationalization and standardization mechanisms aim at coordinating increasingly complex processes. To this end, information technologies provide considerable support in the monitoring of processes such as supply management, throughput times and quality. On the other hand, a second type of management programme has to do with much 'softer' and subtler strategies that draw from the behavioural sciences rather than engineering. Here the employee is called upon to become an 'actor' within a team, a project, and so on, in the hope that the group members will associate themselves with production requirements.

The mechanisms and implications of this dynamic constituting an 'invisible chain' have been examined by Durand, who views lean production as the central mechanism. Thus, 'in implementing the principle of lean production, there is no longer any need for a disciplinary leader: the discipline is in the tight workflow itself. By accepting the principle of *lean production*, i.e. no stoppage in the flow of work, the employee is *enslaved* by the flow itself' (Durand, 2004: 78; our translation). This leads him to ask why employees have accepted such drastic rules (2004: 369, 371). Besides market constraint, Durand sees the main reason in the very structure of the productive system.

Here again, the extent to which management strategies are renewed should not be underestimated. However, the thesis that employees accept social domination brings scepticism on at least three counts. First, the suggestion that employees could be so naive in this respect, and thus be led to 'voluntary servitude' as they are 'blinded to their own situation' (Durand, 2004: 374), goes against the core of industrial sociology. Second, the overlooking of social relations leads to confusion between the real or declared goals of management programmes (and their related management rhetoric) and their effectiveness or actual results (Thompson and Ackroyd, 1995: 629). Third and last, the blind spot of those interpretations is the suggestion that employees might accept responsibilization and the internalization of production constraints without their consent being 'negotiated' in any way as part of a power relationship. Their consent is wrongly taken for granted; cooperation can never be effective without the conscious agreement of the 'dominated subject'.

Technology leads to panoptic surveillance

The third assertion underlying the narratives about the emaciation of employee resistance has to do with information technology being considered as a device for surveillance, a suggestion usually supported by Foucauldian influences. While this assertion is seductive, in that 'information systems...would have exceeded even Bentham's most outlandish fantasies' (Zuboff, 1988: 322), it is obviously problematic (Thompson and Ackroyd, 1995: 622–6), not least because it does not consider agency and workplace relations.

The proportion of employees whose work can be monitored through information collected throughout their daily routine is much higher than usually suggested. Although we are not aware of a sound measure of this, such a possibility does occur widely across sectors and professional frontiers. It is by no means specific to CSRs in call centres or routinized assembly work that have received so much attention; it also prevails broadly in continuous-process technology, among the huge majority of clerical workers, those working in design and engineering, and indeed most professional employees in the civil service, universities, and so on. Indeed, it is in the very nature of information technology that the operator often has much autonomy in the use of his or her working time; however, sooner rather than later, most operators inevitably have to connect their software to the mainframe technology of their employer. For most employees, being connected to the central information basis applies to every minute of work activity, although the impact of such a situation on patterns of control remains contingent.[6] So the relevant question is by no means technical, it is not the capacity for management to exert control over how the individual uses his or her working time; it is the relevance for management to do so and (if there is some relevance) the capacity to do so from a power or micropolitical perspective (Bélanger, 2006). Indeed, from a sociological rather than technological perspective, the relevant question is: to what extent are these information systems used as a surveillance tool for domination, and in what types of social relations is management allowed to proceed to such form of domination?

Considering the asymmetric and antagonistic nature of the employment relationship, information technology obviously creates considerable resources for management control, sometimes used in a repressive way. But to reify technology by dissociating it from the sphere of power relations (from its implementation to its use in day-to-day work) makes many commentators drift far beyond sociology. It also reflects a limitation of too many social scientists who see every new generation of technology as overwhelmingly sophisticated and reliable. Actually, such reliability occurs only in the most mature, standardized and stable production systems. As a general rule, the more work stations and human networks are integrated and interconnected, the more production systems are vulnerable and dependent upon employees' cooperation (de Terssac, 1992; Veltz, 2000). The search for technical systems that will free management from this dependence upon employee consent and know-how is part of managerial utopia.

Modes of control and opposition at work: A conceptual model

Before introducing our conceptual model, three key analytical points should be underlined. First, we need to develop conceptual tools that will be relevant for understanding the post-industrial era. History has to be taken into account in the study of the evolution of the rationalization and standardization of work over the long period (Bell, 1962; Marglin, 1973; Thompson, 1967), from Taylor to Deming and up to the most sophisticated approaches to process and quality management. Whilst it is important to acknowledge the extent and the significant implications of radical and ongoing changes in the world of employment and work (Bélanger and Thuderoz, 1998; Cohen, 2006; Veltz, 2000), a historical insight might indicate that employees adjust over time and find different ways to express opposition.

Second, the study of oppositional practices at work should be grounded in the structural foundations of the employment relationship. While our understanding of conflict at work is influenced by LPT, which rightly places the emphasis on the various patterns of control, coercion and consent by which management extracts labour in the production process, we take the employment relationship as the starting point. Capitalist employment relations set the foundations of a 'structured antagonism' between capital and labour and of a particular type of indeterminacy by which the agency that provides capital is led to organize production and to control the use of labour power (Edwards, 1986). These overall principles governing the employment relationship, and particularly its asymmetrical nature, have not lost their relevance, theoretically, as we move towards a post-industrial society. Nevertheless, this structured antagonism does not preclude cooperation or social compromise (Bélanger and Edwards, 2007; Edwards, Bélanger and Wright, 2006).

Third, it may be worth explaining briefly what we mean by employee *opposition*. It is widely acknowledged among sociologists that no concept is fully satisfactory to capture the various means by which employees express their discontent at work[7] and, in particular, to account for the evolution of such behaviour over time. Collinson and Ackroyd (2005: 320) observe that 'the field of employee resistance remains far from coherent. The fact that we have discussed the topic using the labels resistance, misbehaviour, and dissent itself suggests that there are differences of view about the relevant terminology and how the field should be defined'.[8] The reader will assess if the term opposition helps to step away from these difficulties. But we use it as an analytical device that covers the employees' rationales and broad range of behaviour associated with the antagonism that is built into the employment relationship, from the industrial to the post-industrial era.

The shape of Figure 7.1 is only hypothetical at this stage. As it stands, the diagram illustrates a work situation where management control is primarily characterized by responsibilization, commitment to work is rather weak and opposition more significant, although likely more covert than overt.

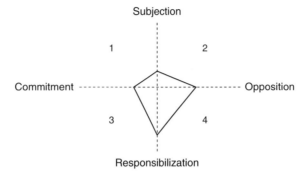

Figure 7.1 Modes of management control and employee behaviour

The axis of management control (subjection and responsibilization).
By his article on the conceptualization of domination, Danilo Martuccelli
(2004) makes a key contribution. First, he brings a distinction between 'the
two major dimensions of domination', that is, consent and constraint, stressing that the second dimension is currently getting stronger. He then adds
another axis, that of the 'subjective inscription of domination', that is a distinction between domination through subjection and domination through
responsibilization,[9] which is highly relevant to the world of work. This makes
it possible for him to identify four ideal types. As he observes, a movement
can be detected by which, 'next to the model of subjection and its multiple
variations, it is possible to trace the slow establishment of another mechanism of subjective inscription of domination. It assumes that the individual, at
all times and in all circumstances, feels responsible not only for everything
he or she has done (the notion of responsibility), but also for everything *that
happens to him or her* (the notion of responsibilization)' (Martuccelli, 2004:
479; our translation). Thus, 'through subjection, the actor is involved as a
subject (thus "subject to", in short, "subjected"). Through responsibilization,
the subject is asked to be an actor (in short, to "act", thus "responsibilized")'
(Martuccelli, 2004: 480).

We would add that this movement from subjection, by which the
employee is asked to conform to a set of detailed prescriptions, as with
Taylorism, to the forms of responsibilization observed in more recent management fashion has major implications. First, it changes the way the individual employee relates to the work group and to the organization as a whole.
While Taylorism started from the basis of an individual assignment, current
forms of work organization often mean working as part of a team, a service,
or a project, as in 'knowledge-based organizations'. Second and relatedly,
whilst the employee of the industrial era had to construct social organization
(often as part of a union) in parallel to his or her work activity, the discourse

underlying current modes of management suggests that a social dimension is encompassed into the employing organization. Often in a rhetorical way, and more significantly in organizations that find their competitive advantage in the exchange of formal and tacit knowledge, the idea of a work 'community' is now integrated into the construct of the organizational form.

It is ironic that this discourse of responsibilization that promotes a reinforcement of social ties in the 'work community' occurs in a period when the economic foundation of the employment relationship has often been weakened, in terms of duration, status of employment, and so on. In short, the demand for commitment and responsibilization gains pre-eminence at a time when the employment relationship is less insulated from market constraint and the standard employment relationship is less dominant than in the industrial era. This gap (or this contradiction) between discourse and reality may lead to new forms of opposition and is likely, over time, to affect the stability of current modes of management control.

This leads us to consider a second axis of analysis that takes these changes in managerial control strategies into account and helps explain the different forms of employee opposition to such strategies.

The axis of employee behaviour (commitment and opposition). It is standard knowledge in workplace sociology, in both the French and British traditions, that the same workers were often very proud of their craftsmanship and also very inventive in finding ways to resist management. Indeed, an underlying theme of the rich stream of workplace research in Britain was that shop-floor resistance was often fuelled by a deep frustration on the part of workers about the inability of management to organize operations efficiently (Hyman and Elger, 1981; Terry and Edwards, 1988). This productive ethos, and the fact that non-craft workers were also proud of their trade and skills (Bélanger and Evans, 1988; Bernoux, Motte and Saglio, 1973), was often existent but little solicited by management in the industrial era. The change is that management now often draws on this resource explicitly and openly. Similarly, it is also a classic principle of workplace union organization that leading and militant workers were often highly committed to their employment relationship in a given workplace. In contrast, low commitment to work would rather foster various forms of withdrawal or cynical behaviour. It is therefore surprising, and somewhat ironic, that both management discourse and academic accounts usually take commitment to work and employee resistance as two opposing principles in a binary mode of analysis.

It should be clear from the above that we are interested here in commitment to work, and not commitment to the organization or the company. It is peculiar that the managerialist literature often confounds the two, because these are quite different principles of action, at least from the employees' viewpoint. Commitment to work (the object of this axis of analysis) is associated with employees' attitudes and behaviour regarding their craft, their occupation or professional abilities, and the use of this set of knowledge and skills in productive activities. Such a productive ethos was observed broadly, in variable degrees, both among the traditional working-class and the currently emerging occupational communities. Inefficient work organization, outdated technology or product design, and the growing gap between management discourse and reality are among the factors that impede upon, and often alienate, the application of such commitment to work into production activities. In contrast, the rhetoric by which management implores employees to commit to the destiny of their organization or company originates from a completely different rationale. As noted by Van Maanen and Kunda in their classic paper on organizational culture, this has more to do with the ways by which 'organizational life can be structured to channel, mold, enhance, sustain, or otherwise influence the feelings organizational members assume toward the organization itself, others in the organization, customers of the organization, and, crucially, themselves' (1989: 58). This is actually a key dimension of the management strategy of responsibilization that we consider on the other axis. More to the point, management's earnest appeal for organizational commitment may actually foster cynicism and distance, hence being counterproductive by impeding upon commitment to work.

Instead, the horizontal axis on Figure 7.1 would rather introduce commitment and opposition as distinct poles on the same axis of analysis. As noted above, these two principles of behaviour are not mutually exclusive, and they often coexist. Indeed, it will become obvious in the third section of this chapter that our model seeks to account for various combinations of action and strategic behaviour. As hinted above, not only is it possible that some employees may be highly committed to work *and* prone to oppositional practices, whilst others may show low commitment *and* a tendency to withdraw from any open form of opposition, but such dynamics are likely to occur. These poles of commitment and opposition should not be understood as two digits on a binary scale, nor as a zero-sum game; they reflect the ambivalence on the part of labour as regards production, which is itself structured by the contradictory nature of the employment relationship (Cressey and MacInnes, 1980; Wright, 2000).

This point has major implications from our analytical perspective. First, it demands for a conceptual model that is not binary and that also considers more than one axis of analysis. Figure 7.1, which leads to Table 7.1, illustrates this by allowing for different scenarios on the axis of employee behaviour, these being related to different patterns of management control. Second, if this ambivalence is part of the very nature of the employment relationship, it should hold significance beyond a single historical phase (like the industrial

Table 7.1 Repertoire of employee opposition to management control

		Control by subjection		Control by responsibilization	
		Opposition		Opposition	
		Covert	*Overt*	*Covert*	*Overt*
Commitment	*Low*	Retreat	Recalcitrance	Cynicism	Rebellion
	High	Disrespect	Militancy	Distance	Repudiation

era) and beyond one dominant mode of management control (as with subjection or responsibilization).

The repertoire of employee opposition. As illustrated by Table 7.1, which remains a (somewhat complex) simplification of reality, the range of possible combinations defies any analytical model; this table should therefore be seen as a heuristic device. While we are careful not to make analytical propositions that could not be sustained by empirical studies here, an overall movement from management control by subjection (boxes 1 and 2 on Figure 7.1) to management control by responsibilization (boxes 3 and 4) is expected. Indeed, we suggest that this movement on the vertical axis could be fostered by a shift on the horizontal axis, in that employees' responses to direct control and subjection (either seen as a lack of commitment or, on the flip side, some form of opposition) may incite management to develop more subtle ways of soliciting employees' creativity through responsibilization.

This conceptual model aims at several complementary steps of analysis. First, it seeks to go beyond the binary types of analysis by which management is seen as following either a strategy of subjection or responsibilization, and employees are either committed or expressing opposition. To be clear, it does not suggest a drastic shift from one pole of the axis to the other (from subjection to responsibilization, or from commitment to opposition), but submits that some evolution is occurring over time, on each axis. Hence, the development of strategies of responsibilization does not eliminate control by subjection; rather, a given workplace comprises varying degrees of subjection and responsibilization. Second, it seeks to connect two axes of analysis that are usually considered separately, that is, management control and employee behaviour. Third, it seeks to go beyond the common pitfall consisting of taking the extremely various forms of employee opposition as 'resistance' without making analytical distinctions between them. In short, by helping uncover the possible meanings of employee behaviour, the model attempts to bring back some of the complexities of the real world into the analysis.

The Repertoire of employee opposition: Empirical illustrations

The notion of a repertoire of employee opposition does not focus on the *forms* of opposition, but rather on the *rationales* (or logics) underlying these. This was clearly the intent of Tilly in his original work on the 'repertoire of collective action' (1976, 1984). Hence, 'the classification as competitive, react- ive or proactive depends on the claims being asserted, not on the form of the action' (Tilly, 1976: 369). It is necessary to go beyond specific forms of action, not least because they are too multiple and varied to be ever accounted for, but also because any form of opposition (individual or collective) can have different meanings and be underpinned by different rationales, grievances or claims. In short, a given form of action (for instance a work-to-rule) may be organized for sustaining different sets of meanings, in different contexts. In the same way, a given rationale may translate into various forms of behaviour and oppositional practices, much depending upon resources and opportun- ities in a given work situation.

To illustrate the working of this conceptual model, we will not attempt to present each of the eight ideal types highlighted in Table 7.1, an exercise that would be cumbersome. Instead, we will provide sufficient information on two patterns of workplace relations that are distinct enough to show how the model works.

The first case, from a monograph conducted in a Coventry engineer- ing factory referred to as *Presswork* in earlier publications (Bélanger, 1987; Bélanger and Evans, 1988), is meant to illustrate a standard figure of indus- trial production. It is intended as a classic illustration of a breakdown of social regulation at plant level, a situation that was not uncommon in British engineering at the time of the Donovan Commission (1968), and beyond (for a critical analysis, see Goldthorpe, 1977; and Terry and Edwards, 1988). In-depth fieldwork, including observation at the shop floor, was conducted in 1979 and 1980. This manufacturer of components for the motor industry was at the lower end of the production chain in a declining industry, a market position that made management vulnerable. All manual workers were members of one of the five recognized unions, and the robust shop steward organization had plenty of opportunities for bargaining over production norms, hence further eroding management control. This pattern characterizes the type called *Recalcitrance* in Table 7.1, with low commitment to work and overt opposition to management, a situation where neither management nor labour could actually establish a sound strategy beyond the short-term because they had very little influence over what was happen- ing outside the gates of the factory. These were 'irreconcilable conditions' for capital and labour to develop a social compromise (Bélanger and Edwards, 2007: 720–2).

If we look at the vertical axis on Figure 7.2, the emphasis is obviously more on subjection than responsibilization. The managerial discourse of responsibilization by which employees are made accountable for the economic sustainability of the organization and led to internalize market pressure was not in the mood of the times. The rhetoric of production managers was that they were in command, and they only made appeals to workers' moderation by providing limited information on immediate market pressure, often invoking the risks of further redundancies. But while there is, therefore, much more subjection than responsibilization, the extent of subjection (or direct control) is not as high on the figure as some might expect. The point is that management was not in control of the situation on the shop floor. In reality, the extent of autonomy exerted by workers on the use of their labour power (our definition of job control) was high, even by the standard of this period. We documented traditional forms of craft control by the sheet metal workers and the toolmakers. But more attention was given to a large group of semi-skilled workers, the press operators, who had considerable control over work allocation, labour mobility, allocation of overtime, and the intensity and distribution of effort over the duration of every shift. Indeed, in many ways, 'management had capitulated' (Bélanger, 1987: 54–7). Hyman and Elger outlined the origin of such a pattern of workplace relations in British engineering:

> Facing managements which, both during and after the war, were preoccupied with output in a seller's market, stewards often found considerable scope for deals with particular foremen or for appropriation of decisions over overtime and manning, and were sometimes actively encouraged to take on tasks of self-supervision which afforded real opportunities for workers to regulate their own production. (Hyman and Elger, 1981: 134)

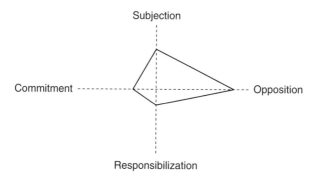

Figure 7.2 Pattern of management control and employee behaviour at Presswork

On the horizontal axis of Figure 7.2, the pattern of employee behaviour observed at Presswork is sharply tilted towards opposition. Over a long period, this Coventry factory was a classic case of overt resistance, in the most traditional sense, an illustration of the pattern of recalcitrance (on Table 7.1). For instance, a company dossier records in a systematic way that there were 99 stoppages in the press shops over the period of 10 months up to November 1969; 25 of them lasted less than 1 hour, but 45 lasted more than 4 hours, many of which stretching over more than one shift (Bélanger and Evans, 1988: 168–9). Most stoppages related to the effort bargain, and usually involved only one of the four press shops. The strife was by no means ended when we conducted observation ten years later. The problem for the company was that, by then, the press operators' overriding preoccupations had shifted from 'making it pay' to 'getting the day in', that is, managing their working time instead of boosting their piecework earnings, thus further affecting productivity. In a pattern that reflects the micro-social regulation famously analysed by Roy (1952 and 1954), but without the self-discipline by which operators often seek to protect production norms on 'gravy' jobs, press operators worked at high intensity and finished early, going 'upstairs' long before the end of the shift.

The workers we met at Presswork wished they could invest their tacit skill and know-how in smooth and efficient production; it is just that the social and technical conditions of production did not make it a possible course of action (Bélanger, 1994). There was no absence of productive ethos and commitment to work (see Figure 7.2), but these conditions did not allow them to apply these resources more willingly in the labour process. As it happened, the Donovan-type of voluntary reform of workplace bargaining that was initiated by management during the 1970s did not change significantly the pattern of relations, at least in the pre-Thatcher era. The foundations of this pattern of control and conflict were deeper, and its explanation required a close look at the technology in use and the ways the robust shop steward organization had developed along the lines of the technical division of labour (Bélanger, 1987).

The second case documented here, on the basis of Gideon Kunda's ethnography, illustrates the conceptual model by bringing us into the post-industrial era. In *Engineering Culture* (first published in 1991, with a revised edition in 2006; see also Van Maanen and Kunda, 1989), Kunda provides a sociological analysis of the social construction of an organizational culture at *Tech*, a pseudonym for the large American high-tech corporation where he conducted fieldwork in 1985.[10] This is a world of work that is obviously in sharp contrast with the previous case, and the pattern of relations observed there can be typified as *Distance* (in Table 7.1), which indicates high commitment and covert opposition.

Kunda's analysis is fine in explaining the processes by which organizational culture at Tech was much more than discourse, it was conceived as an ideology and then made operational through narratives and systematic rituals, such as training workshops often referred to as 'bootcamps', that aimed at shaping employees' thoughts and feelings. Management sought to establish the foundations of 'normative control...the attempt to elicit and direct the required efforts of members by controlling the underlying experiences, thoughts, and feelings that guide their actions' (Kunda, 2006: 11). By making more concrete 'the desire to bind employees' hearts and minds to the corporate interest' (ibid.: 218), normative control is a foremost manifestation of the principle of responsibilization, the high point on the vertical axis of the radial chart (Figure 7.3). Indeed, the engineers were made responsible for the success of Tech and, the author notes, the attempt to shape their feelings was also meant to blur the frontier between their self and the organization.

In their joint work (based on ethnographies at Tech and Disneyland), Van Maanen and Kunda are explicit in interpreting these 'conscious managerial attempts to build, sustain, and elaborate culture in organizations as a relatively subtle but powerful form of organizational control' (1989: 88; also 52). Control by culture is not presented as an alternative to other forms; it rather complements market control of labour, technical control and bureaucratic control, thus representing a fourfold scheme of management control (Van Maanen and Kunda, 1989: 88–92).

In Kunda's account, not so much attention is given to commitment to work, our focus on the horizontal axis. Clearly, the whole emphasis is given to their commitment to the company, which is conceptualized as 'role embracement' that 'means submitting to the company's definition of one's self' (2006: 173). However, one finds ample evidence of excessive work on the

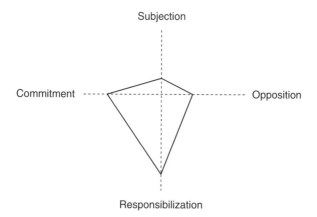

Figure 7.3   Pattern of management control and employee behaviour at Tech

part of many engineers and managers, and this appears to be one feature of professional identity in such high-tech firms. Indeed, the failure to keep a necessary distance between the self and the organization often led to burnouts, of which one reads alarming accounts (ibid.: 198–204).

But what were the engineers' responses to what is hence portrayed as 'subtle but powerful' managerial control? It is here that Kunda shows the best sociological insights. By all accounts, role embracement was by far the dominant pattern of behaviour. Clearly, the values of Tech were widely shared and highly internalized among professional and managerial employees. But the author offers a fine analysis of what is called (following Goffman) 'role distancing', which consists of ways by which employees succeed in establishing a frontier between the self and the company, hence protecting themselves by refusing to 'swallow' the managerial discourse and what comes out of the well-rehearsed narratives of normative control. The various forms of role distancing are analysed, with distinctions made between cognitive and emotional distancing. Kunda insists on what he sees as a 'potentially unstable balance between role embracement and role distancing' (159),[11] and a profound ambivalence on the part of employees between these two rationales. Hence, 'among full members, we find an ambivalent, fluctuating, ironic self, at war with itself and with its internalized images of self and other' (Kunda, 2006: 221; also 197, 214–15). However, on closer scrutiny, although the author provides much empirical evidence of humour, dissent and critical comments in day-to-day meetings and conversations, as well as manifestations of tensions and conflicting views between participants, normative control worked efficiently enough to keep opposition within limits. Hence, 'real dissent is preempted' and criticisms were better received when they were subtle and constructive in tone (ibid.: 158, 196). As pointed out by Van Maanen and Kunda (1989: 83), 'there are boundaries beyond which negative displays and signs of detachment are not tolerated by many organizational members'. Furthermore, and this represents a limit of this ethnographic study, these covert forms of opposition were apparently only observed at the level of the individuals, who were seeking to protect their self. The reader does not find evidence of any attempt among participants to build upon social cohesiveness (not to mention social organization, which does not seem possible at all in this context) in their search for preserving a healthy basis of social distance from the company.

Conclusion

The starting point of this chapter was to formulate a critique of various streams of 'critical' sociology and management studies that suggest that resistance at work is vanishing. In their 1995 article, Thompson and Ackroyd already noted that there is a recurrent tendency for such claims to reappear, more or less in a cyclical way. We noted that such assertions were highly noticeable in France recently, although the influence of Foucauldian perspectives was much more sustained and pervasive in Britain, at least in workplace sociology. However, the research literature rather indicates that evolving patterns of management control actually lead to more 'ingenuity' on the part of employees. Many forms of oppositional practices and behaviour have been documented in recent studies in services settings, and significant attention is now given to oppositional practices such a cynicism, dissent and disengagement. What is needed though is an integrated model that takes us beyond the description and mapping of these oppositional practices.

Social scientists should not look at employee resistance through the lenses used for studying the industrial era. There is a need to be sensitive to the likely shifts in the repertoire of employee opposition, and to develop conceptual tools for understanding these developments. Such analytical tools should capture not only the forms of employee opposition associated with the industrial era (which are not meant to disappear) but also those that are more likely to be observed under current technologies and modes of management control.

This chapter introduces such a conceptual model and it is worth highlighting some of its key objectives and features. There is much agreement among readers familiar with LPT not to consider seriously any suggestion of an 'end of resistance', and this was our starting point. But we seek to go beyond other analytical limitations that are still pervasive. Indeed, there is sometimes a tendency to consider any instance of non-compliance as a form of 'resistance' and, more commonly and more challenging, there is a persistent difficulty among sociologists to make analytical distinctions between the highly varied forms of behaviour that might be considered as 'resistance'. Making this step forward is only possible, as suggested in the second section of this chapter, by looking beyond the *forms of action* and by considering the *distinct rationales* underlying these, seeking to uncover their meanings. These rationales can be uncovered by connecting two axes of analysis that are usually analysed separately, that is, management control and employee behaviour. This opens the opportunity for going beyond binary types of analysis that would take commitment and opposition, or subjection and responsibilization, as mutually exclusive. The conceptual model developed here aims at going deeper in understanding such social dynamics that only reflect the contradictory nature of the employment relationship. In short, it attempts to bring back some of the complexities of the real world into the analysis and suggests a way to comprehend the evolution of this repertoire of opposition over time.

The contrasting cases documented in some detail in the third section of this chapter illustrate how the model works. They help understand very distinct analytical configurations as regards the range of strategies and behaviour on the part of management and labour, in a very traditional industrial setting and then in a high-tech environment. Testing the model by considering other patterns of control and opposition in both industrial and post-industrial settings opens much opportunity for further research.

Notes

1 Hence, breaking the rules or rebalancing the use of working time when the strain of work is excessive could not be seen as 'good' or 'bad' in itself, it can only be understood in a specific context, in a given social structure. Actually, Ackroyd and Thompson might agree with this point that seems compatible with their analysis.

2 'Broadly speaking, we contend that there are four directions that misbehaviour can take... We envisage the possibility of: 1, disagreement over the appropriation of work; 2, over the appropriation of the materials used in work; 3, over the appropriation of the time spent on work; and 4, over the extent to which employees identify with their work activity and employers, or more simply, the appropriation of employee identity' (Ackroyd and Thompson, 1999: 25).

3 'Another objective of this book has been to regenerate interest in modalities of resistance that may not exactly be de rigueur in the current academic climate of postmodernist celebrations of micro-political and identity-based subversions' (Fleming and Spicer, 2007: 185; see pages 7 and 185–8).

4 This notion of the evolution and transformation of the repertoire of opposition over the long period is induced from Charles Tilly (1976 and 1984). The concept of repertoire was applied as a central analytical device in his later work, as a way to 'circumscribe the means by which people engage in contentious politics' (Tilly, 2006: vii).

5 Bouquin also observes this major trend in sociology in France, by which 'most of critical sociologists have presented management as hegemonic, class domination as absolute (through symbolic violence) and the labour process as mastered and controlled by management' (2009: 5). He outlines a contrasting interpretation, as a counterpoint.

6 Being connected to the central information basis often leads to excessive management control, but this need not necessarily be the case. For many, particularly among technicians and professional employees whose work requires considerable autonomy in order to be efficient, free access to internet and to electronic mail also opens opportunities for significant

spells of re-appropriation of working time, for surfing on the web, planning and settling personal matters, and so on. This brings us back to some classic themes among sociologists of the industrial era, from Donald Roy onwards, and also illustrates that the 'problem of management control' remains enduring and pervasive.

7 In the words of an industrial relations classic, the forms of employee resistance, or the means by which they can express discontent and opposition is 'as unlimited as the ingenuity of [*sic*] man' (Kerr, 1964: 171).

8 Besides the 'important theoretical differences and disagreements between the various frameworks used to interpret employee practices', Collinson and Ackroyd stress that 'while the terms "resistance", "misbehaviour", and/or "dissent" have informed our discussion, we also acknowledge their inadequacy as descriptors of employee practices' (2005: 320).

9 When working at the conceptual level, the problem of translation is much more than technical, it has to do with meanings in different intellectual traditions. Subjection ('assujettissement' in French) and responsibilization ('responsabilisation' in French) are very unusual in English. But responsibilization is taken to mean not only accountability (being responsible for one's actions) but also the internalization of the risks associated with the work situation. And responsibilization is less fraught with ambiguity than the more usual notion of 'empowerment', which is far from a trouble-free concept (Denham Lincoln et al., 2002).

10 Kunda's work focused on the engineering division of this company, and much of the observation was conducted at an engineering facility located along Route 61, also referred to as the 'Technology Region'. Most of the analysis has to do with professional engineers and the management personnel associated with their work (see Kunda, 2006: chapter 2; also Van Maanen and Kunda, 1989: 97, note 24).

11 Indeed, 'successful organizational selves are founded on control of the balance of role embracement and role distancing and the ability to maintain and display an air of ambiguity that allows multiple, occasionally contradictory, interpretations of one's stance' (Kunda, 2006: 198).

REFERENCES

Ackroyd, S. and Thompson, P. (1999) *Organizational Misbehaviour*, London: Sage.

Bain, P. and Taylor, P. (2000) 'Entrapped by the "Electronic Panopticon"? Worker Resistance in the Call Centre', *New Technology, Work and Employment*, 15(1): 2–18.

▶

▶

Bain, P. and Taylor, P. (2003) '"Subterranean Worksick Blues": Humour as Subversion in Two Call Centres', *Organization Studies*, 24(9): 1487–509.

Bélanger, J. (1987) 'Job Control after Reform: A Case Study in British Engineering', *Industrial Relations Journal*, 18(1): 50–62.

Bélanger, J. (1994) 'Job Control under Different Labor Relations Regimes: A Comparison of Canada and Great Britain', in Bélanger, J., Edwards, P. and Haiven, L. (eds) *Workplace Industrial Relations and the Global Challenge*, Ithaca, NY: ILR Press, 43–69.

Bélanger, J. (2006) 'Technology and Work', in Korczynski, M., Hodson, R. and Edwards, P. (eds) *Social Theory at Work*, Oxford: Oxford University Press, 325–55.

Bélanger, J. and Edwards, P. (2007) 'The Conditions Promoting Compromise in the Workplace', *British Journal of Industrial Relations*, 45(4): 713–34.

Bélanger, J. and Evans, S. (1988) 'Job Controls and Shop Steward Leadership among Semiskilled Engineering Workers', in Terry, M. and Edwards, P. K. (eds) *Shopfloor Politics and Job Controls*, Oxford: Blackwell, 150–84.

Bélanger, J. and Thuderoz, C. (1998) 'La recodification de la relation d'emploi', *Revue française de sociologie*, 39(3): 469–94.

Bell, D. (1962) 'Work and Its Discontents: The Cult of Efficiency in America', *The End of Ideology*. Revised edition, New York: The Free Press, 227–72.

Berger, S. (2003) *Notre première mondialisation: leçons d'un échec oublié*, Paris: Seuil.

Bernoux, P., Motte, D. and Saglio, J. (1973) *Trois ateliers d'O.S*, Paris: Économie et humanisme.

Beynon, H. (1973) *Working for Ford,* Harmondsworth: Penguin.

Bouquin, S. (2009) 'Resistance to Work and at the Workplace: A Blind Spot for French Sociology of Work?', Paper presented at the International Labour Process Conference. Edinburgh, 6–8 April.

Burawoy, M. (1979) *Manufacturing Consent: Changes in the Labor Process under Monopoly Capitalism*, Chicago, IL: University of Chicago Press.

Burawoy, M., Blum, J. A., George, S., Gille, Z., Gowan, T., Haney, L., Klawiter, M., Lopez, S. H., O Riain, S. and Thayer, M. (2000) *Global Ethnography*, Berkeley: University of California Press.

Callaghan, G. and Thompson, P. (2001) 'Edwards Revisited: Technical Control and Call Centres', *Economic and Industrial Democracy*, 22(1): 13–37.

Callaghan, G. and Thompson, P. (2002) '"We Recruit Attitude": The Selection and Shaping of Routine Call Centre Labour', *Journal of Management Studies*, 39(2): 233–54.

Castells, M. (1998) *La société en réseaux*, Paris: Fayard.

Coe, N. M., Dicken, P. and Hess, M. (2008) "Global Production Networks: Realizing the Potential", *Journal of Economic Geography*, 8(3): 271–95.

Cohen, D. (2006) *Trois leçons sur la société post-industrielle,* Paris: Seuil.

Collinson, D. and Ackroyd, S. (2005) 'Resistance, Misbehaviour, and Dissent', in Ackroyd, S., Batt, R., Thompson, P. and Tolbert, P. S. (eds) *The Oxford Handbook of Work and Organization*, Oxford: Oxford University Press, 305–26.

▶

▶

Coutrot, T. (1999) *Critique de l'organisation du travail*, Paris: La Découverte.

Cressey, P. and MacInnes, J. (1980) 'Voting for Ford: Industrial Democracy and the Control of Labour', *Capital and Class*, 11: 5–33.

Denham Lincoln, N., Travers, C., Ackers, P. and Wilkinson, A. (2002) 'The Meaning of Empowerment: The Interdisciplinary Etymology of a New Management Concept', *International Journal of Management Reviews*, 4(3): 271–90.

Dubois, P. (1977) *Sabotage in Industry*, Harmondsworth: Penguin.

Durand, C. (1978) *Le travail enchaîné: organisation du travail et domination sociale*, Paris: Seuil.

Durand, J. P. (2004) *La chaîne invisible. Travailler aujourd'hui: flux tendu et servitude volontaire*, Paris: Seuil.

Edwards, P. (1986) *Conflict at Work: A Materialist Analysis of Workplace Relations*, Oxford: Blackwell.

Edwards, P., Bélanger, J. and Wright, M. (2006) 'The Bases of Compromise in the Workplace: A Theoretical Framework', *British Journal of Industrial Relations*, 44(1): 125–46.

Fleming, P. and Spicer, A. (2007) *Contesting the Corporation: Struggle, Power and Resistance in Organizations*, Cambridge: Cambridge University Press.

Gaulejac, V. de (2005) *La société malade de la gestion: idéologie gestionnaire, pouvoir managérial et harcèlement social*, Paris: Seuil.

Goldthorpe, J. H. (1977) 'Industrial Relations in Britain: A Critique of Reformism', in Clarke, T. and Clements, L. (eds) *Trade Unions under Capitalism*, London: Fontana, 184–224.

Hirst, P. and Thompson, G. (2001) *Globalization in Question*, 2nd edn, London: Polity.

Hyman, R. and Elger, T. (1981) 'Job Controls, the Employers' Offensive and Alternative Strategies', *Capital and Class*, 15: 115–49.

Kerr, C. (1964) *Labor and Management in Industrial Society*, Garden City, NY: Anchor Books.

Kunda, G. (2006) *Engineering Culture: Control and Commitment in a High-Tech Corporation*, Philadelphia, PA: Temple University Press (First published in 1991).

Marchington, M., Grimshaw, D., Rubery, J. and Willmott, H. (eds) (2005) *Fragmenting Work: Blurring Organizational Boundaries and Disordering Hierarchies*, Oxford: Oxford University Press.

Marglin, S. (1973) 'Origines et fonctions de la parcellisation des tâches', in Gorz, A. (ed.) *Critique de la division du travail*, Paris: Seuil, 41–89.

Martuccelli, D. (2004) 'Figures de la domination', *Revue française de sociologie*, 45(3): 469–97.

Roy, D. (1952) 'Quota Restriction and Goldbricking in a Machine Shop', *American Journal of Sociology*, 57(5): 427–42.

Roy, D. (1954) 'Efficiency and the "Fix": Informal Intergroup Relations in a Piecework Machine Shop', *American Journal of Sociology*, 60(3): 255–66.

Russell, B. (2008) 'Call Centres: A Decade of Research', *International Journal of Management Reviews*, 10(3): 195–219.

▶

▶

Sassen, S. (2008) *A Sociology of Globalization*, New York: W.W. Norton.

Terry, M. and Edwards, P. (eds) (1988) *Shopfloor Politics and Job Controls: The Post-War Engineering Industry*, Oxford: Blackwell.

Terssac, G. (de) (1992) *Autonomie dans le travail*, Paris: PUF.

Thompson, E. P. (1967) 'Time, Work-Discipline, and Industrial Capitalism', *Past & Present*, Number 38, (Dec. 1967), 56–97.

Thompson, P. (2003) 'Disconnected Capitalism: Or Why Employers Can't Keep Their Side of the Bargain', *Work, Employment and Society*, 17(2): 359–78.

Thompson, P. and Ackroyd, S. (1995) 'All Quiet on the Workplace Front? A Critique of Recent Trends in British Industrial Sociology', *Sociology*, 29(4): 615–33.

Thompson, P. and Ackroyd, S. (2009) 'Resisting Resistance: Moving the Debate On', Paper presented at the International Labour Process Conference, Edinburgh, 6–8 April.

Tilly, C. (1976) 'Major Forms of Collective Action in Western Europe 1500–1975', *Theory and Society*, 3(3): 365–75.

Tilly, C. (1984) 'Les origines du répertoire de l'action collective contemporaine en France et en Grande-Bretagne', *Vingtième siècle. Revue d'histoire* (4): 89–108.

Tilly, C. (2006) *Regimes and Repertoires,* Chicago, IL: The University of Chicago Press.

Van Maanen, J. and Kunda, G. (1989) ' "Real Feelings": Emotional Expression and Organizational Culture', in Cummings, L. L. and Staw, B. M. (eds) *Research in Organizational Behaviour*, vol. 11, Greenwich, CT: JAI Press, 43–103.

Veltz, P. (2000) *Le nouveau monde industriel*, Paris: Gallimard.

Wright, E. O. (2000) 'Working-Class Power, Capitalist-Class Interests, and Class Compromise', *American Journal of Sociology*, 105(4): 957–1002.

Zuboff, S. (1988) *In the Age of the Smart Machine: The Future of Work and Power*, New York: Basic Books.

Renewing and Revising the Engagement between Labour Process Theory and Technology

8

Richard Hall

From a critical perspective, the social study of technology at work is fragmented and at something of a theoretical dead end. The field is currently fragmented along three general lines: a distinctly managerialist, 'management of technology' perspective that has come to dominate the burgeoning area of information systems research; a political-materialist tradition, strongly associated with Labour Process Theory (LPT) which has lost its way and retreated to offering empirically rich but theoretically modest studies of technology at specific worksites and particular industrial settings; and a social constructivist perspective which has become increasingly theoretically arcane and empirically focused on the particularistic processes of social construction of technologies in specific settings. For critical social scientists seeking to promote progress in the understanding of contemporary technology at work, the 'management of technology' perspective has little to offer, concentrating, as it does, on the development of best practice management approaches to technology implementations. Recent contributions in the political-materialist and social constructivist traditions, while offering many interesting and compelling accounts of the ways in which technologies are interpreted, deployed, enacted and constructed, have left us with a relatively modest set of general propositions that might provide the makings for a theory of technology at work.

This chapter provides an account of LPT's engagement with technology at work and, in the process, critically considers the contribution of other perspectives from both political-materialist and social constructivist traditions. It argues that LPT has much to offer a reinvigoration of the social study of technology at work. In particular, it argues that understanding technology at work in terms of the control-resistance paradigm represents a promising way forward. However, it is claimed that LPT can be usefully informed by some of the insights from the social constructivist perspective that it has traditionally dismissed. In particular, LPT can use these approaches to strengthen its analysis of worker agency and deepen its account of the ongoing and contingent character of the struggles between labour and capital over the nature, use and implications of technology at work.

The first section attempts to characterize the LPT approach to technology at work. In doing so debates around core LPT are considered and their implications for a contemporary LPT of technology are identified. The section concludes with a set of propositions that might constitute an LPT of technology. In the second section the potential application of a renewed LPT of technology is illustrated through the analysis of one significant example of contemporary technology at work – Enterprise Resource Planning systems (ERPs).

Labour Process Theory and the social study of technology

Core LPT (Jaros, 2005; Thompson, 1990; Thompson and Harley, 2007; Thompson and Smith, 2001) is not, of course, a theory of technology, but a theory of the labour process in capitalism. Nevertheless, LPT has made a significant contribution to the study of technology at work and overviews of theories of technology at work typically assign LPT a prominent place. The role of science and technology in shaping and being shaped by work relations was very prominent in early writings and research. Some of that work was theoretical (Slater, 1980); others historical (Berg, 1979; Noble 1979, 1984) and contemporary. Amongst the latter were two volumes on *Science, Technology and the Labour Process* (Levidow and Young, 1981, 1985), reflecting, in part, strong connections between labour process debates, the *Radical Science Journal* and the Conference of Socialist Economists. There were some useful policy spin-offs to union and local government policies towards the 'new' microprocessor-based technologies.

What was distinctive about this body of work? Schemas of theories of technology at work often highlight LPT as distinctive because it emphasizes the political character of technological implementations and effects. Liker, Haddad and Karlin (1999) place LPT approaches within a broader *political interests* paradigm in which the effects of technology are seen to be decisively influenced (if not determined) by the 'static, predictable' interests of the key actors ('labour' and 'management'). According to this interpretation, management introduces new technology in order to increase its control over the labour process and this control imperative takes many forms: using technology to replace labour (Marx, 1976), to separate conception from execution

(Braverman, 1974), to deskill labour (Noble, 1979; Wood, 1987), to monitor worker performance more closely (Shaiken, 1985) and to marginalize unions. Technology is therefore viewed as a 'control system' (Liker, Haddad and Karlin, 2001: 585). While this interpretation portrays the interests of management and labour as relatively fixed and deterministic, the outcomes of struggles between labour and management at the workplace are contingent. Technology choice, for example, is seen to be the result of the relative bargaining power of labour and management (ibid.: 585).

A second wave of LPT emerges in the wake of the criticisms of Braverman. Whilst not denying that technology was used by capital to enhance its control over the labour process, writers such as Friedman (1977), Edwards (1979) and Burawoy (1979) pointed to other mechanisms of control and to various forms of worker agency, from resistance to consent. Even the central deskilling thesis was being revised: while Thompson (1989: 118) maintained that deskilling was 'the major *tendential* presence within the development of the capitalist labour process' he conceded that there were limits on capital's capacity to use technology to deskill as a result of worker resistance and labour market conditions.

In the wake of second wave LPT contributions, Thompson and others (Thompson, 1989; Thompson and Smith, 2000–1) attempted to map the 'core theory of the labour process' by identifying a number of key elements (Thompson and Smith, 2000–1: 56–7). The second, third and fourth are the relevant concerns here (for a full list see Thompson and Vincent, this volume).

1. The necessity for constant renewal and change in the forces of production and the skills of labour due to the discipline of the profit rate and competitive accumulation of capital. This impacts on the composition of skills, both cheapening labour costs and creating a complex structure to the workforce.

This element might be termed *the imperative to constantly renew production*.

2. The necessity for a control imperative in the labour process in order for capital to secure profitable production and translate its legal purchase of labour power into actual labour and a surplus.

This is the traditional starting point for LPT: the indeterminacy of labour and the attendant conversion problem. This might be termed *the control imperative*.

3. Given the dynamics of exploitation and control, the social relations between capital and labour in the workplace are of 'structured antagonism'.

At the same time, capital, in order to constantly revolutionize the production process, must seek some level of creativity and cooperation from labour. The result is a continuum of possible, situationally driven and overlapping worker responses – from resistance to accommodation, compliance and consent.

This element appears to accommodate much of the revision of Braverman's original formulation in second wave research. While labour process struggles might be structurally conditioned, their outcomes reflect the relative autonomy of the labour process within the broader capitalist political economy. This element might best be termed *the structured antagonism/relative autonomy principle*.

'Technology' per se does not feature explicitly in the core theory. An account of technology can, however, be derived from this core theory and the research on technology influenced by it.

The imperative to constantly renew production

Technology is a vital element of the forces of production that characterize the labour process. Therefore, LPT approaches to technology would be expected to highlight not just the significance of technologies in shaping the organization of work, but that its renewal is connected to sustaining capital accumulation in the context of competition. Therefore, technology is not seen as something that lies 'outside' the labour process. As with the forces of production more generally, it is 'imprinted with the social relations of ownership and control in the capitalist labour process' (Boreham et al., 2008: 3). So, from this perspective, theories of the information economy which see the rise of information technology (IT) and the internet and the alleged growth in the information economy as leading to the democratization of work, the transformation of market capitalism and the reconfiguration of class society (e.g. Rifkin, 2000) are naïve and misconceived. Because an LPT of technology sees technology at work as inevitably created, deployed and exploited in the context of the capitalist labour process, it will tend to emphasize capitalist continuity rather than post-capitalist transformation.

It follows from this that technological innovation should not be seen as an autonomous process of scientific progress but as part of the process of 'constant renewal and change in the forces of production' that is central to capital accumulation. 'In contrast to the conventional wisdom of a neutral technology determining the nature of production, its social construction is located inside class relations and their antagonisms' (Thompson, 1989: 57). In addition to distinguishing an LPT of technology from that offered by the information economy approach, this position also differentiates the theory of technology from that suggested by Adler's 'paleo-Marxist' theory (Adler, 2007). Adler, claiming a more traditional reading of Marx, argues that technology ('in the form of instruments' (2007: 1319)) is simply one of the forces of production, and that it is separate from the 'relations of production', which is the sphere in which capital achieves its control over technology. As Thompson (2007), in his debate with Adler, has argued, this implies that technology is essentially 'neutral and determinate' and that the forces of production are 'good' while the relations of production are 'bad'. He argues that this has led Adler to see a 'long-run technology-led upskilling trajectory' in which 'Taylorism and lean production are mainly positive reflections of a progressive socialization of the productive forces' (ibid.: 1360).

While an LPT of technology in general rejects a view of technology as benign or neutral, and instead asserts an admittedly pessimistic 'capitalist continuity scenario', it must be emphasized that it also rejects a deterministic view of technology as sinister or malignant. As will be seen below, the key lesson from LPT and studies of technology in the labour process is that the effects of technology are various and depend on struggle and contestation at different levels: workplace, enterprise, organization, sector, economy and society. However, after second wave research and the important contributions from the radical science movement, LPT has somewhat lost its way in analysis of the origins and applications of technology. Indeed, the task of developing a critical and non-deterministic theory of the emergence of new technology has largely been taken up by scholars from rather different theoretical perspectives: the Social Construction of Technology (SCOT) perspective and the Social Shaping of Technology approach.

SCOT perspectives have argued that particular forms of technology are the result of the social claims of specific groups ('relevant social groups') whose 'constructions' of a technology become dominant at a decisive moment in the development of the technology. Over time, the 'interpretive flexibility' of the technology becomes 'closed' or 'stabilized' and a generally accepted form and meaning of the technology becomes dominant (Bijker, Hughes and Pinch, 1987; Pinch and Bijker, 1984). In a similar fashion the Social Shaping of Technology theorists emphasize the social, institutional, economic and cultural factors that shape the form of technologies over time (MacKenzie and Wajcman, 1999). Labour process theorists would take issue with both SCOT and the Social Shaping perspective on various points: the SCOT notion that technologies are actually constituted by the constructions of actors and are open to interpretive flexibility sits uneasily with the materialist and realist tenets of LPT; and, from an LPT perspective, the Social Shaping approach of seeing a wide range of forces and factors as potentially shaping the form and nature of technology fails to accord due significance to the power of capital in shaping and exploiting technology. Nevertheless, the general claim of both SCOT and Social Shaping – that technology is decisively shaped by particular actors, forces and social factors – is consistent with an LPT of the origins and use of technology. The key distinctiveness of an LPT approach, however, is that technology is seen as part of the labour process, appropriated, deployed, designed, implemented, even 'invented' by management in the interests of capital accumulation and with the purpose of organizing work.

Perhaps the classic labour process analysis of technology is provided by Noble (1979, 1984) whose interpretation of the use of numerical control (NC) machines is sensitive to both the characteristics of the technology and the management strategies (contested by labour) that determined the way in which that technology was deployed. In many ways Noble's work is an exemplar of LPT analysis of technology, and it underlines two key features of the LPT approach to technology that derive from this second core element: the materialism of the artefact and the materialism of its consequences.

First, the technological artefact is recognized to have an objective material reality. That is, particular technological artefacts have observable characteristics and qualities that are capable of having an effect. However, LPT analyses do not subscribe to a thoroughgoing technological determinism, in the sense that while technological artefacts have objective characteristics these are not seen to be deterministic in character. As Noble's own analysis demonstrates, the objective characteristics of NC machines do not mean that NC machines determine the labour process. Rather the way in which NC machines are configured, deployed and used varies according to decisions taken by management, and as a result of conflicts and accommodations between labour and management, concerning the implementation of NC machines in any given workplace.

Second, technological artefacts deployed at work are seen to have material consequences. That is, the deployment of any given artefact can have an effect on the objective conditions and circumstances of work, the division of labour, the distribution of rewards and labour market outcomes. This second dimension of materialism is more closely related to the fourth element of the core theory and will therefore be discussed more fully below.

The imperative to constantly renew production has implications for LPT's understanding of technology's impact on skills as well as the nature of technological innovation more generally. On the basis of their own and others' empirical investigations, researchers in the LPT tradition came to conclude that deskilling was not the inevitable consequence of technological change for all workers all of the time. Over time, LPT researchers became more sensitive to a broader range of labour process outcomes beyond a simplistic upskilling/deskilling dualism – work intensification, multitasking, flexibility, autonomy and discretion proved to be some of the more popular categories; however, these studies sought to make a contribution to the third element of the core theory rather than the second.

Reference was made earlier to Thompson's claim that deskilling remained the major empirical tendency (1989: 118). However, it is notable that even such a *tendency* is not present in the LPT core. Rather the claim is that capital's constant search for renewal in the labour process implies constant changes to skill demands and technology. The outcomes of any new technology might include deskilling, upskilling, the division and recombination of tasks leading to both upskilling and deskilling of different aspects of individual jobs (Greenbaum, 1998), or different jobs in the same workplace ('skill polarisation'; Milkman, 1997). In fairness, all of these potential outcomes were recognized by Thompson (1989) in his review of LPT studies of technological change and skills.

Subsequent research has tended to confirm this picture of complexity and contingency when it comes to the question of the impact of technology on skills. This research programme has succeeded in moving beyond earlier formulations of technology as automation, common in earlier studies of new technology in manufacturing. The shift from a relatively simple story of 'technology-as-deskilling' to a more complicated story of diverse skill implications mirrors the increasing complexity of technologies at work, and, in particular, the rise of information and communication technologies (ICTs) at work. The automation of manufacturing processes and the emerging use of microprocessor technologies to facilitate data processing in the office were the big technological stories of Braverman's time. At that time, it was easy to see the deskilling of craft and clerical workers (Baldry and Connelly, 1986; Buchanan and Boddy, 1983; Crompton and Jones, 1984), although some studies found mixed results (Clark et al., 1988). However, increasingly sophisticated and invasive ICTs were to more broadly revolutionize and recast work, especially the rapidly expanding range of service work. As the focus of empirical study shifted to these new technologies, the findings became more complicated and diverse. In general, while ICTs have typically had the effect of routinizing back-office processing work (Korczynski, 2004), they have opened up the space for more interactive service work in which workers are required to utilize a broader range of skills, including emotional labour, communication and teamwork skills (Boreham et al., 2008: chapter 4; see also Zuboff, 1988).

LPT's considerable contribution to studies of call centre work nicely illustrates the complexity of more recent accounts of technology and skills. Call centre work relies on Automatic Call Distribution (ACD) systems to allocate incoming calls to customer service representatives (CSRs). Similar systems automate outbound calling. CSRs in both contexts often work with online scripts and routinely access online databases for information and transaction tasks (Taylor and Bain, 1999). On the one hand, there is a relatively broad range of skills required in call centre work: keyboard and database skills, knowledge of procedures, products and services and interactive service skills (Batt, 1999). On the other hand, the skills are not especially deep or difficult to acquire. Most studies of skills in call centre work confirm that the key skills are social rather than technical, and that employers look to recruit the right personality or 'attitude' (Callaghan and Thompson, 2002). The (somewhat ironic) rise in the importance of 'generic' social skills facilitated by ICTs and the growth of interactive service work also prompted increasing attention from LPT perspectives to the significance of, and the skills associated with, emotional labour (Bolton, 2005: 32; Taylor and Bain, 1999).

While call centre work is illustrative of the variegated impact of contemporary ICTs (and indeed other forces) on work and skills, similar trends can be observed in other service work: the transformation of bank teller work to customer service and sales work in retail banking (Regini, Kitay and Baethge, 1999); the expansion of tasks and skills required in many administrative and clerical roles (Baran, 1988); and, in contrast, the partial clericalization of professional work (Greenbaum, 1995). While generalizations are difficult in all of this, the best conclusion might be that LPT studies have typically seen ICTs in service work as having led, in conjunction with other changes to work organization, to an expansion, but not deepening of skills (Thompson and Smith, 2009: 7–8).

The control imperative

Whereas the deskilling thesis, at least in its original formulation, proved to be unsustainable, the control imperative has been a durable LPT contribution. In the first wave of LPT, technology was seen to have a major role in enabling capital to secure control through the separation of conception and execution and subsequent deskilling. The strategy of using new technology to automate parts of the production process was seen to facilitate the extraction of conception and control over work methods to the management level leaving a residue of deskilled work for production workers.

The study of manufacturing technologies and mechanization in particular led to the identification of 'technical control' (Edwards, 1979) as a critical means through which technology was used to control the labour process – the assembly line providing the classic example. While Edwards suggested that technical control was being superseded by bureaucratic control, Thompson (1989: 112) asserted that computer technologies offered the prospect of significantly extending technical control resulting in more sophisticated technological controls beyond the machine (or computer mediated) pacing of work. Sophisticated technological controls were combined with increasingly sophisticated bureaucratic controls, together regulating and coordinating the division or recombination of tasks and jobs.

Thompson's (1989: 152) observation that it was the task of LPT to untangle and interpret the precise ways in which different dimensions of control were used in combination in the contemporary workplace was prescient. His notion of more sophisticated forms of technical control pointed to the recognition that contemporary technologies shaping the labour process were now ICTs rather than production technologies like the assembly line and the NC machine. Indeed, it was control of information that was to prove critical in manufacturing, but also, and increasingly, in the services sectors.

The recognition that new forms of technology were centred on enhancing management's control over information was consistent with greater attention to the ways in which technology enhanced surveillance and thus had the capacity to revolutionize traditional direct control strategies. Relying on metaphors such as the 'electronic panopticon', a series of researchers (Fernie and Metcalf, 1998; McKinlay and Taylor, 1998; Sewell, 1998; Sewell and Wilkinson, 1992) with varying degrees of affinity to the LPT tradition have identified the role of IT in increasing the direct surveillance of work, the measurement of productivity and performance and adherence to standard operating procedures and protocols. When combined with the kinds of bureaucratic and cultural controls identified by others, this led to the proposal of ideas such as info-normative control (Frenkel et al., 1999).

In a recent reconsideration of LPT, Thompson and Harley (2007) focus on the derivation of some key propositions on control. What do these propositions imply for the relationship between contemporary control and technology? First, Thompson and Harley identify the *persistence of resistance*. Given the contested nature of the 'conversion problem', control inevitably begets resistance. Forms are diverse, complex, emergent, contingent and characterized by a range of combinations and blends of overt and covert resistance and misbehaviour (Ackroyd and Thompson, 1999). However, for present purposes, their account is lacking in two respects: it does not provide much insight into the role of technology and the question of distinctive patterns of resistance to technologically facilitated forms of control; and it does not present a clear picture of the role of the labour subject – the ways in which individual workers and workers acting collectively might seek to resist, shape, construct, exploit, avoid, comply with or actively support contemporary forms of control. While they certainly anticipate the range of possible responses, the subject is still largely cast as a 'resistive subject', and their account downplays the proactive role of the subject in constitution of contemporary regimes of control. This might suggest that LPT has yet to fully overcome its lack of a thorough account of subjectivity.

Thompson and Harley's second claim is that control regimes are not successively superseded and displaced, but that there is rather *continuity, in combination*: different control strategies (direct, technical, bureaucratic, cultural, etc.) are used in combination by contemporary management. They point to a number of examples from lean production in manufacturing to surveillance and monitoring in call centres in support. Evidently, a range of technologies – production, logistics, information and communication technologies – could be used by management to sustain and facilitate various mixes of control strategies. We would not, therefore, expect to see a single technology control strategy displacing earlier or other forms of control.

The third claim made by Thompson and Harley is the most important: the *extension of controls* into new territories. Here the authors point to two examples: the use of scripting to control service encounters and regulate the deployment of emotional labour and the use of knowledge management systems to capture and codify the tacit knowledge of workers. Again, technology seems to be heavily implicated in these kinds of examples. In scripting service encounters in call centres, for example, computer software prompts CSRs and computer-based monitoring helps enforce compliance. Knowledge Management systems are typically coordinated through computer-based systems of knowledge databases, repositories for past project experiences and CRM systems that all help organizations extract tacit knowledge from workers in forms amenable to future reuse. These examples suggest that IT has played a major role in facilitating the extension of contemporary control strategies.

Thompson and Harley's fourth claim is that contemporary control regimes are marked by *increased hybridity*: a variety of control strategies are used in combination in a highly integrated fashion. They note that particular hybrids appear to be characteristic of particular industries, but that they commonly involve a range of integrated technical, bureaucratic and normative controls. This claim raises the possibility that particular IT artefacts may in fact be playing a role in integrating various control strategies into coherent industry-specific systems that have distinctive characteristics.

The structured antagonism/relative autonomy principle

This principle suggests that the relations between management and workers will tend to be characterized by a structurally based opposition of interests, but that within this framework there is considerable scope for a variety of relations and dynamics such that labour might be expected to manifest the range of behaviours envisaged by Thompson and Harley (2007) above.

When considered from the perspective of the role of technology, two features can be highlighted. First, it confirms the earlier observation that LPT is not proposing a thoroughgoing technological determinism. If labour-capital struggles are afforded a degree of autonomy from the structural forces that

frame the antagonism of fundamental interests, then the form and implications of technological artefacts will not be simply determined by those
fundamental interests. Therefore, new technologies will not always and
simply be introduced by management with the intention or effect of extending control at the expense of workers, and workers will not always and simply
resist and frustrate those technological changes. Technologies, therefore, are
not structurally determined.

Second, the effects of technologies are not determined either. Given the
relative autonomy of labour-capital struggles we would expect the form,
implementation and consequences of technological artefacts to be contested,
within certain structural constraints or limits. Those structural limits or constraints can be traced to two sources: the structured antagonism of interests
(the political structure) and the materiality of the technological artefact (the
technological artefact). Here, the two senses in which the LPT approach is
materialist are highlighted. The claim that the technological artefact will
have certain objective characteristics that limit or structure its potential use
and implications is characteristic of LPT approaches. LPT studies of technology have always taken technological artefacts as serious objects of study in
their own right and tried to identify and generalize the impacts of those
technologies, in the context of labour-capital struggles and other exigencies.
The second sense in which LPT approaches to technology are materialist
relates to the political structure recognized by LPT. The implementation of
technological artefacts will have (contested) consequences for the labour
process and this matters, in a political sense, because those consequences can
have material implications for workers. The kinds of outcomes emphasized
by LPT have typically been conceptualized in the terms of skills, control-
autonomy, work intensification, job security and wages.

In order to respond to critics and develop an account of what happens
in this sphere of relative autonomy, LPT became particularly concerned in
the 1990s with 'bringing the subject back in'. Within mainstream labour
process thinking, the emphasis was on recognizing the resistive subject,
the necessary creativity of the worker, and the reality of consent (as well
as resistance). This gives us useful categories for analysis and signals some
phenomena to be sensitive to, but it might not deepen our understanding
of the role of worker agency or strengthen the power of our explanations of
worker and workplace behaviour in the context of technology. In particular, LPT approaches to technology at work continue to be constrained by a
tendency to see workers as 'subject to' technology, and to analyse worker
behaviour within the 'traditional' LPT categories of 'control', 'resistance',
'work intensity' and 'skills'.

LPT's engagement with subjectivity only took us so far before the post-
structuralists and the political-materialists parted ways and got back to their
own business (Thompson and Smith, 2000–1: 52–4). I would argue that

insights gleaned from post-structuralist and related approaches such as social constructivism, can be used to progress LPT analyses. (The controversial point here is that processes of social construction can be admitted into an LPT analysis without accepting the post-modernist ontology that is associated with social constructivism). The reticence of LPT analysts to push on with 'bringing the subject back in' has been to its detriment. They have had relatively little to say about the ways in which workers might individually and collectively shape and construct technologies. In other words, workers may well exercise considerable agency in their interactions with technology beyond resistance, misbehaviour, accommodation and consent.

From this perspective, it might be useful for LPT to reconsider social constructivist approaches to technology (broadly defined) as a means of developing stronger accounts of worker subjectivity and agency in relation to technology at work. What these social constructivist approaches have demonstrated, albeit working with different ontological assumptions and using different terminology, is that workers often engage with and 'enact' technologies in ways that influence their function and shape their impact in, and on, organizations. For example, Orlikowski's (2000) study of the use of Lotus Notes software shows how different groups of users adopt different 'technologies-in-practice' resulting in very different applications and implications of the same technology in different organizational settings. Barley's (1986) earlier study of the introduction of CT scanners at two hospitals shows how the use of the technology and its impact on each organization was decisively shaped by the interaction and power dynamics between (more or less experienced) technologists and radiologists. More recently, Mazmanian, Yates and Orlikowski's (2006) study of the use of BlackBerrys at a private equity firm illustrates the way in which the everyday practice of workers deciding to access and use their email at all hours of the day and night generates, over time, an organization-wide set of expectations of constantly being available. While these studies are only indicative, they do suggest that the way workers interact with, and enact, technologies can have decisive consequences for the very nature and material character of the technology itself, as well as its effects on the experience and organization of work.

A renewed LPT of technology might benefit from more explicitly considering these dimensions of individual and collective worker agency: accepting that workers can actively shape technology in practice in decisive ways while retaining LPT's distinctive insistence on understanding worker agency in the context of labour-capital struggles at work. Technology would continue to be seen as a focus of contestation, but one in which the range of possibilities for workers, as users of technology at work, was significantly broadened. In the next section, some recent empirical research into the implementation and application of an important contemporary form of ICT is reviewed as a means of illustrating the potential for this kind of renewed LPT of technology. First, however, by way of summarizing the foregoing review of LPT's engagement with technology at work, a core LPT of technology is sketched.

A core LPT of technology might be defined by the following propositions:

1. Technology is central to the labour process and is appropriated, deployed and developed by management in the furtherance of capital accumulation and with the purpose of organizing work.
2. Technological artefacts have a material reality and material consequences for workers; however, technology does not have deterministic consequences, because the impact of any given technological artefact will be shaped by labour-capital struggles over the way in which the technology is implemented and utilized.
3. Technology facilitates the extension of control into new territories and integrates a range of control strategies (technical, bureaucratic and normative).
4. Technological change in the context of labour-capital struggles has political-materialist consequences in the sense that it can affect the material outcomes for workers in terms of their skills, experience of work, labour market outcomes and power.
5. Technological change will tend to generate worker resistance, although worker agency is characterized by a diverse range of behaviours: resistance, misbehaviour, consent and compliance.

Propositions 1 and 2 can be derived from LPT's history of engagement with technology and they remain central claims. Proposition 3 is derived from Thompson and Harley (2007) but hypothesizes that the role of technology is central to these two key trends. Proposition 4 reaffirms the political-materialism of LPT approaches to technology. Proposition 5 represents the tentative conclusions reached by LPT relating to worker subjectivity and agency. As noted above, this account is less than complete.

The next section seeks to illustrate the way in which a renewed LPT of technology, based on the propositions above, might be applied to the example of a contemporary form of technology at work: Enterprise Resource Planning (ERP) systems.

The LPT of technology and the example of Enterprise Resource Planning (ERP) systems

ERPs are IT systems designed to help manage company-wide business processes, using a common database and shared reporting tools. Sometimes referred to as 'enterprise systems' (Davenport, 2000), these large and complex IT arrangements purport to integrate all the functional areas of organizations into one integrated information system (Monk and Wagner, 2006). The key features of these enterprise systems (in addition to their comprehensiveness) is their use of shared data (implying that the inclusion or updating of data at any point in the system will automatically update all modules in the system) and real-time information (implying that reports reflect real-time data).

The empirical evidence drawn on here derives from the research of a team of researchers, including the current author, involved in a study of the implementation and impact of ERPs across six large Australian organizations (Grant et al., 2006). The research method was based on site visits, document analysis and semi-structured interviews with between 8 and 15 respondents at each organization drawn from senior management, implementation team members, middle managers and users. The primary focus of the research was the impact of the ERPs on work organization, business processes and organizational performance.

The material reality and material consequences of ERPs as technological artefacts

On the basis of earlier research and analysis of ERP systems, it was hypothesized that the distinctive features of ERPs would be likely to have a series of distinctive consequences for work organization and the labour process. In particular it was argued that ERPs would lead to downsizing and delayering associated with the automation of some processes, the decentralization of responsibility and the concentration of control in the hands of management, some deskilling of front-line work and the intensification of work in some jobs (Hall, 2002). The research revealed that ERP implementations were associated with some downsizing in most of the organizations studied, particularly in areas of data processing, reporting and support functions, although aggregate level headcount reductions were often offset by increased staffing in other areas as a consequence of the ERP. It was concluded that management decisions decisively mediated the relationship between the ERP and downsizing in most cases (Hall, 2005).

It was also found that ERPs facilitated an increase in management control over the labour process, but not necessarily through any one control strategy such as enhancing direct control, deskilling, technical control or increased management surveillance (although each of these trends were apparent in one or more of the case studies). The principal means through which ERPs facilitate control is associated with their integration imperative – ERPs integrate business processes by compelling users to enter and extract data and complete business processes according to preset conventions and formats. Indeed, so-called best practice business processes are embedded in the routines prescribed by ERP modules that govern business processes in various functional areas (financial accounting, workflow, sales and distribution, materials management and so forth) (Davenport, 2000: chapter 5). In this way, ERPs enforce standard business processes on users thereby directly affecting the labour process. For example, at the Fast Moving Consumer Goods (FMCG) case-study site, workers in a distribution centre reported that they could no longer purchase raw materials from suppliers of their choice but were now forced by the ERP Materials Management module to use designated, preset suppliers according to a specific business process for procurement (Hall, 2005: 249).

Both deskilling and upskilling was evident in the case studies. Some front-line work was deskilled as the reliance on tacit knowledge and experience was replaced by set routines and processes for the completion of work tasks as dictated by the ERP. In other cases, there was evidence of upskilling (or at least new skill demands), particularly where new business processes introduced the need for workers to adopt new techniques, for example, as in the case of OzUni where accrual accounting methods were introduced as part of the implementation of the Financial Accounting module (ibid.: 250). Finally, widespread work intensification, directly attributable to the introduction of the ERP was reported. This appeared to be most prevalent at the supervisor/operational manager level (Harley et al., 2006: 11).

ERPs as non-deterministic technological artefacts

Despite their characteristic capacity to integrate and standardize business processes as a means of increasing management control, the effect of ERPs at the case studies was far from uniform. The impact of ERPs on work organization was inevitably mediated by management choice and often quite intense struggles between and amongst various factions of management and groups of workers. Typically these struggles concerned the extent to which the ERP modules should be 'customized' or left as 'vanilla'. In BankCo for example, despite an initial management determination to implement a strictly vanilla version of the ERP, persistent worker resistance to the implementation of a vanilla HR module led to the gradual customization of numerous processes (Grant et al., 2006: 9–10).

ERPs extending management control into new territories

The implementation of the ERPs at the sites studied typically extended the range, depth and the effectiveness of management control over the labour process. First, the *range* of business divisions and functions governed by ERP routines was extended in the sense that virtually all business functions were coordinated through the ERP: financial accounting, sales and distribution, materials management, production planning, quality management, plant maintenance, asset management and human resources. As noted above, each of these functional areas was compelled to follow standardized business processes consistent with ERP routines. Second, the *depth* of control was extended as an increased number of tasks and decisions were regulated by the ERP routines. The case of procurement decisions at the FMCG site noted above provides one example. Third, the *effectiveness* of management control was enhanced through a superior capacity to monitor both performance and compliance with ERP routines. The ERPs could produce reports based on real-time data and workers (or their supervisors) were required to enter data according to standardized fields and formats thereby allowing management to quickly identify the extent of compliance with business processes and monitor performance more generally (Hall, 2005: 248).

ERPs' capacity to integrate control strategies

ERPs have the capacity to integrate technical, bureaucratic and normative control strategies by providing a single, overarching, enterprise-wide information system. ERPs as implemented in the study sites, exemplified a contemporary systemic control strategy. Rather than directly regulating the pacing of work, in the way of earlier technical control methods (e.g. the assembly line), ERPs impose relatively rigid business processes on workers and supervisors such that data need to be entered into the system in a particular form before business process steps can be triggered. When combined with an enhanced capacity for management to monitor compliance and performance, this generates a powerful incentive for workers and teams to conform to set business processes. This feature of the technology also facilitates the establishment of discrete functions, divisions or teams as business units or cost centres within the larger organization and allows management to more effectively evaluate performance and productivity against benchmarked targets and key performance indicators (KPIs). In this sense, ERPs cannot be thought of as just technical control systems. When combined with other organizational practices (such as teams, business units and performance management systems), they represent a new control strategy that is fundamentally *systemic* combining technical, bureaucratic and normative dimensions.

ERPs, worker resistance and agency

As noted above, one of the distinctive features of ERPs is that they concentrate control (over business processes and the general organization of work) while decentralizing responsibility (for the completion of particular work tasks and business processes). This decentralization of responsibility provides workers leverage to exercise resistance. Thus, in most of the case studies we discovered the emergence of 'shadow systems' and 'workarounds' that enabled workers and their supervisors to maintain control over business processes by maintaining their own systems and practices 'under the radar' of the ERP. However, as predicted from a contemporary LPT perspective, workers exhibited a range of responses including accommodation, compliance and even consent.

It has also been argued in this chapter, however, that a renewed LPT approach to technology needs to develop a stronger account of worker agency and more explicitly investigate the ways in which worker enactments of technology actually shape the application and implications of technology. The illustrative ERP case studies discussed in this section revealed two different ways in which worker agency decisively affected the implementation and implications of the technology in question: one provides an example of collective action, the other an example of individual agency.

From an LPT perspective we anticipated that ERP implementations would be a site of contestation and struggle between management and workers. While this was indeed the case, the study of the implementation processes at the case-study sites over time suggested the critical significance of discursive practices as the means through which management power was deployed and contested by workers (Grant and Hall, 2005). Thus we found that in each case-study site, ERP implementations tended be supported by an 'original sponsoring discourse' authored by management that portrayed ERPs as beneficial for the organization. Typically this discourse was then countered by a 'user discourse', authored by workers who used the ERP, which portrayed ERPs as flawed and inefficient. In response to that counter discourse, management then developed a 'revised sponsoring discourse' which made certain concessions to workers and reframed the purpose and impact of the ERP. Through this process of discursive contestation, the implementation of the ERP was often decisively shaped, often through various customizations to the technology. Discursive power is evidently not the only power resource used by labour and capital in workplace struggles over ERP implementations; nevertheless, it appears that in many cases it proved to be a decisive medium through which workers not only mobilized their resistance to management plans for ERP implementations, but were also able to affect the configuration of the systems as ultimately implemented.

While the example of workers deploying a user discourse of ERPs suggests the efficacy of collective worker action, another study suggested the efficacy of individual worker agency in the construction of the ERP technology. In an attempt to develop a better understanding of diverse user responses to

ERPs, we studied the responses of five different branch managers to the introduction of ERP at one of the case-study organizations, BankCo (Dery, Hall and Wailes, 2006). In taking a social constructivist approach, we adopted a 'situated practice perspective' (Orlikowski, 2000) that focused on the ways in which individual managers 'enacted' the technology by observing how they interpreted and used the ERP system at each branch. A traditional LPT perspective might predict that the ways in which a given technological artefact will be used will depend upon the characteristics of the technology as implemented, with the important proviso that that implementation will be shaped by labour-capital struggles. In this case however, workers in very similar roles (branch managers) using identical technological artefacts (the same ERP identically configured) did not respond in a uniform way suggestive of a simple unity of structural interests. On the contrary, some managers adopted a 'limited use practice' in which the ERP was avoided, shadow systems and workarounds were used and minimal, superficial compliance was the order of the day. Other managers were much more proactive and exhibited an 'individual productivity practice' whereby they used the ERP to enhance their strategic decision-making and capacity to manage the branch. The key difference that appeared to explain these different practices was not the history of labour-capital contestation over the ERP but a range of organizational factors associated with the nature of the demands at each branch. Again, the agency of workers in these cases seemed to go beyond resistance, and involved decisive and variable enactments of the technology.

These illustrations of collective and individual worker agency in the context of technology at work suggest that, on occasion, workers might do more than simply resist or accommodate technology; they might actually play an active role in the social construction of those technologies (see also Boudreau and Robey, 2005 for a human agency perspective on ERPs). To reiterate the argument above, this kind of comprehension of agency as social construction might make a valuable contribution to a renewed LPT of contemporary technologies at work.

Conclusions

Core-LPT theory has much to offer a reinvigorated theory of technology at work. While it is possible to develop an LPT of technology, this chapter has argued that a number of revisions and extensions to the existing LPT account are warranted.

Labour process theories of technology need to retain their political-materialist character by continuing to examine the material characteristics of technological artefacts and continuing to insist on investigating the material implications of technological change in the contemporary workplace in the context of capital accumulation. LPT has moved beyond grounding explanations of worker behaviour in a set of 'static and predictable' interests (Liker, Haddad and Karlin, 1999) and it has achieved this by recognizing the relative autonomy of labour-capital struggles in the context of overarching relations of structured antagonism. However, LPT has made only modest progress in developing an account of worker agency in this realm of relative autonomy. The behaviour of workers, considered as resistive subjects, is shaped by their labour interests, but it is also shaped by their interests as organizational members. Second, their behaviour and agency needs to be registered beyond the categories of resistance, creativity and consent. Workers also interpret, engage with and enact technologies through processes of social construction – not simply by resisting technologies, but also by actively using technologies and thereby constituting technologies in forms different from those intended by management. Third, the analysis here also suggests that workers use discourse as a key medium for political mobilization. In the sites studied, workers developed technology discourses counter to prevailing management discourses as a means of effecting material changes to the technology and justifying and sustaining different practices with respect to the use of the technology. These examples suggest that this terrain of discourse and practice can be usefully investigated by LPT approaches as a means of deepening our accounts of worker action.

A revised LPT of technology might also usefully extend its tradition of taking technological artefacts seriously by engaging more directly with one of the most important technologies characteristic of contemporary organizations – enterprise systems. Enterprise systems are especially important because of their role in facilitating the extension and coordination of managerial control. ERPs, to take the most common form of enterprise system, extend control by enhancing the range, depth and effectiveness of managerial control. ERPs integrate technical, bureaucratic and normative dimensions of control through their capacity to impose standardized business processes on workers and the labour process. By imposing standardized business processes, and by facilitating the decentralization of responsibility for performance to teams and the front line, ERPs facilitate a form of systemic control. However, ERPs as example of contemporary organizational ICTs are also especially important given their capacity to extend control over relatively dispersed, multi-unit organizational forms. LPT has traditionally focused on the control of labour at the site of production; however, the contemporary labour process must be understood as involving a wider range of control relations that attempt to control and coordinate the activities of organizations across teams, business units, divisions, sites, regions and countries, not to mention supply chains and networks of various kinds.

These broader and more complex control and coordination processes have significant implications for labour, but implicate supervisors, managers and contractors as well. And technologies, especially technologies such as ERPs, are critical to these control regimes.

Nevertheless, as LPT has long recognized, control, no matter how sophisticated, is never perfect or total. Renewed attention to the agency and actions of workers reveals new opportunities for proactive action in the constitution of these technologies in addition to more traditional patterns of resistance. Recognizing and theorizing these practices may well be essential if LPT is to survive and prosper for another 25 years.

REFERENCES

Ackroyd, S. and Thompson, P. (1999) *Organisational Misbehaviour,* Thousand Oaks, CA: Sage.

Adler, P. S. (2007) 'The Future of Critical Management Studies: A Paleo-Marxist Critique of Labour Process Theory', *Organization Studies,* 28(9): 1313–45.

Baldry, C. and Connelly, A. (1986) 'Drawing the Line: Computer Aided Design and the Organisation of the Drawing Office', *New Technology, Work and Employment,* 1(1): 59–66.

Baran, B. (1988) 'Office Automation and Women's Work: The Technological Transformation of the Insurance Industry', in Pahl, R. H. (ed.) *On Work,* Oxford: Basil Blackwell.

Barley, S. R. (1986) 'Technology as an Occasion for Structuring: Evidence from Observations of CT Scanners and the Social Order of Radiology Departments', *Administrative Science Quarterly,* 31: 78–108.

Batt, R. (1999) 'Work Organization, Technology and Performance in Customer Service and Sales', *Industrial and Labour Relations Review,* 52(4): 539–64.

Berg, M. (ed.) (1979) *Technology and Toil in Nineteenth Century Britain,* London: CSE Books.

Bijker, W. E., Hughes, T. P. and Pinch, T. J. (eds) (1987) *The Social Construction of Technological Systems: New Directions in the Sociology and History of Technology,* Cambridge, MA: MIT Press.

Bolton, S. C. (2005) *Emotion Management in the Workplace,* Houndmills: Palgrave Macmillan.

Boreham, P., Parker, R., Thompson, P. and Hall, R. (2008) *New Technology @ Work,* London: Routledge.

Boudreau, M-C. and Robey, D. (2005) 'Enacting Integrated Information Technology: A Human Agency Perspective', *Organization Science,* 16(1): 3–18.

Braverman, H. (1974) *Labor and Monopoly Capital: The Degradation of Work in the Twentieth Century,* New York: Monthly Review Press.

Buchanan, D. and Boddy, D. (1983) *Organisations in the Computer Age: Technological Imperatives and Strategic Choice,* Aldershot: Gower.

▶

▶

Burawoy, M. (1979) *Manufacturing Consent: Changes in the Labor Process under Monopoly Capitalism,* Chicago, IL: University of Chicago Press.

Callaghan, G. and Thompson, P. (2002) 'We Recruit Attitude: The Selection and Shaping of Call Centre Labour', *Journal of Management Studies,* 39(2): 233–54.

Clark, J., McLoughlin, I., Rose, H. and King, R. (1988) *The Process of Technological Change: New Technology and Social Choice in the Workplace,* Cambridge: Cambridge University Press.

Crompton, R. and Jones, G. (1984) *White Collar Proletariat, Deskilling and Gender,* London: Macmillan.

Davenport, T. (2000) *Mission Critical: Realising the Promise of Enterprise Systems,* Boston, MA: HBS Press.

Dery, K., Hall, R. and Wailes, N. (2006) 'ERPs as "Technologies-in-Practice": Social Construction, Materiality and the Role of Organisational Factors', *New Technology, Work and Employment,* 21(3): 229–41.

Edwards, R. (1979) *Contested Terrain: The Transformation of the Workplace in the Twentieth Century,* London: Heinemann.

Fernie, S. and Metcalf, D. (1998) '(Not) Hanging on the Telephone: Payment Systems in the New Sweatshops', *Discussion Paper 390,* Centre for Economic Performance, London School of Economics and Political Science.

Frenkel, S., Korczynski, M., Shire, K. and Tam, M. (1999) *On the Front Line: Organization of Work in the Information Economy,* Ithaca, NY: Cornell University Press.

Friedman, A. (1977) 'Responsible Autonomy versus Direct Control over the Labour Process', *Capital and Class,* 1.

Grant, D. and Hall, R. (2005) *Power and Discourse in the Management and Organization of ERPs.* Proceedings of the 4th Critical Management Studies Conference, Judge Institute of Management, University of Cambridge, 4–6 July 2005.

Grant, D., Hall, R., Wailes, N. and Wright, C. (2006) 'The False Promise of Technological Determinism: The Case of Enterprise Resource Planning Systems', *New Technology, Work and Employment,* 20(1): 2–24.

Greenbaum, J. (1995) *Windows on the Workplace – Computers, Jobs and the Organization of Office Work in the Late Twentieth Century,* New York: Monthly Review Press.

Greenbaum, J. (1998) 'The Times They Are A'Changing: Dividing and Recombining Labour through Computer Systems', in Thompson, P. and Warhurst, C. (eds) *Workplaces of the Future,* Houndmills, Basingstoke: Macmillan.

Hall, R. (2002) 'Enterprise Resource Planning Systems and Organisational Change: Transforming Work Organisation?', *Strategic Change,* 11(5): 263–70.

Hall, R. (2005) 'The Integrating and Disciplining Tendencies of ERPs: Evidence from Australian Organisations', *Strategic Change,* 14(5): 245–54.

Harley, B., Wright, C., Hall, R. and Dery, K. (2006) 'Management Reactions to Technological Change: The Example of Enterprise Resource Planning', *Journal of Applied Behavioral Science,* 42(3): 58–75.

▶

Jaros, S. (2005) 'Marxian Critiques of Thompson's (1990) Core Labour Process Theory: An Evaluation and Extension', *Ephemera*, 5(1): 5–25.

Korczynski, M. (2004) 'Back-Office Service Work: Bureaucracy Challenged?', *Work, Employment and Society*, 18(1): 97–114.

Levidow, L. and Young, B. (eds) (1981) *Science, Technology and the Labour Process* Vol. 1, London: CSE Books.

Levidow, L. and Young, B. (eds) (1985) *Science, Technology and the Labour Process* Vol. 2, London: CSE Books.

Liker, J. K., Haddad, C. J. and Karlin, J. (1999) 'Perspectives on Technology and Work Organization', *Annual Review of Sociology*, 25: 575–96.

MacKenzie, D. and Wajcman, J. (eds) (1999) *The Social Shaping of Technology*, 2nd edition, Maidenhead: Open University Press.

McKinlay, A. and Taylor, P. (1998) 'Foucault and the Politics of Production', in McKinlay, A. and Starkey, K. (eds) *Foucault, Management and Organization*, London: Sage.

Marx, K. (1976) *Capital Volume 1*, Harmondsworth: Penguin.

Mazmanian, M., Yates, J. and Orlikowski, W. (2006) 'Ubiquitous Email: Individual Experiences and Organizational Consequences of BlackBerry Use', *Proceedings of the 65th Annual Meeting of the Academy of Management*, Atlanta, GA: August.

Milkman, R. (1997) *Farewell to the Factory: Auto Workers in the Late Twentieth Century*, Berkeley: University of California Press.

Monk, E. and Wagner, B. (2006) *Concepts in Enterprise Resource Planning*, 2nd edition, Boston, MA: Thomson.

Noble, D. (1979) 'Social Choice in Machine Design', in Zimbalist, A. (ed.) *Case Studies in the Labour Process*, London: Monthly Review Press.

Noble, D. (1984) *Forces of Production: A Social History of Industrial Automation*, New York: Knopf.

Orlikowski, W. (2000) 'Using Technology and Constituting Structures: A Practice Lens for Studying Technology in Organisations', *Organisation Science*, 11(4): 404–28.

Pinch, T. J. and Bijker, W. E. (1984) 'The Social Construction of Facts and Artefacts: Or How the Sociology of Science and the Sociology of Technology Might Benefit Each Other', *Social Studies of Science*, 14(3): 399–441.

Regini, M., Kitay, J. and Baethge, M. (1999) *From Tellers to Sellers: Changing Employment Relations in Banks*, Cambridge, MA: The MIT Press.

Rifkin, J. (2000) *The Age of Access: How the Shift from Ownership to Access Is Transforming Capitalism*, Harmondsworth: Penguin.

Sewell, G. (1998) 'The Discipline of Teams: The Control of Team-Based Industrial Work through Electronic and Peer Surveillance', *Administrative Science Quarterly*, 43: 406–69.

Sewell, G. and Wilkinson, B. (1992) 'Someone to Watch Over Me: Surveillance, Discipline and the Just-in-time Labour Process', *Sociology*, 26(2): 271–89.

Shaiken, H. (1985) *Work Transformed: Automation and Labor in the Computer Age*, New York: Holt, Rinehart and Winston.

Slater, P. (ed.) (1980) Outlines of a Critique of Technology, London: Ink Links.

▶

Taylor, P. and Bain, P. (1999) ' "An Assembly Line in the Head" Work and Employee Relations in the Call Centre', *Industrial Relations Journal*, 30(2): 101–17.

Thompson, P. (1989) *The Nature of Work*, London: Macmillan.

Thompson, P. (1990) 'Crawling from the Wreckage', in Knights, D. and Willmott, H. (eds) *Labour Process Theory*, London: Macmillan.

Thompson, P. (2007) 'Adler's Theory of the Capitalist Labour Process: A Pale(o) Imitation', *Organization Studies*, 28(9): 1359–68.

Thompson, P. and Harley, B. (2007) 'HRM and the Worker: Labor Process Perspectives', in Boxall, P., Purcell, J. and Wright, P. (eds) *The Oxford Handbook of Human Resource Management*, Oxford: Oxford University Press, 147–65.

Thompson, P. and Smith, C. (2000–2001) 'Follow the Red Brick Road', *International Studies in Management and Organization*, 30(4): 40–67.

Thompson, P. and Smith, C. (2009) 'Labour Power and Labour Process: Contesting the Marginality of the Sociology of Work', *Sociology*, 43(5): 913–30.

Wood, S. (1987) 'The Deskilling Debate: New Technology and Work Organization', *Acta Sociologica*, 30(1): 3–24.

Zuboff, S. (1988) *In the Age of the Smart Machine: The Future of Work and Power*, Oxford: Heinemann.

Gender, Labour Process Theory and Intersectionality: *Une Liaison Dangereuse?*

9

Susan Durbin and Hazel Conley

Given that one of the aims of this edited collection is to follow on in the tradition of the *Labour Process Theory* published in 1990, our starting point was to revisit the chapter in that volume written by Jackie West, entitled, 'Gender and the Labour Process: A Reassessment'. Rereading this chapter was a useful and interesting exercise as it emphasized how much and how little has changed in the intervening 20 years. Our intention in this chapter is to revisit some of the key intersecting themes in relation to feminist and labour process theories to assess both continuity and change. As one might expect there are some important shifts in how we think about work, especially in relation to gender. We have chosen to focus on emotional labour and inter-sectionality, which we believe have had particular impact at different levels of a gendered labour process analysis (LPA). Whilst undoubtedly adding to our understanding, we argue that unpacking these concepts reveals that some familiar problems, notably in relation to skill and class, continue to surface.

To set the scene for these conceptual and theoretical developments, we begin by examining the current labour market and regulatory context of women's and men's work. For reasons of space, our focus here is largely the UK. Continuing labour market trends, notably the growth in service sector employment, are gendered and have influenced labour process theory (LPT). However, our analysis highlights that it is no longer sufficient simply to talk of gendered labour markets as it is increasingly clear that women and men of different ethnic groups have different labour market outcomes. Whilst we recognize that other strands such as disability, sexuality and age are also important, again for reasons of space, our focus is largely on the intersections between gender, ethnicity and class.

The second part of the chapter examines critical debates on emotional labour, a key area of conceptual development in relation to gender, skill and service sector employment. Here we highlight that whilst gender has been a key part of this debate, class has often been misunderstood and ethnicity almost completely ignored. The third section moves up a level of analysis to examine developments in feminist theory in relation to intersectionality and social structures, particularly in relation to gender, ethnicity and class. Here we specifically examine debates on gender regimes and regimes of complex inequalities (Walby, 1990, 1997, 2004, 2007, 2009), inequality regimes, class and intersectionality (Acker, 1990, 1998, 2006) and black feminist theory (Collins, 1986, 1998, 2000; Crenshaw, 1989, 1991).

Gender, inequality and the UK labour market in the twenty-first century

In 1985, men held 2 million more jobs than women. By 2008, women and men held the same amount of jobs (approximately 13.6 million each) but their position within the labour market continues to be influenced largely by what they do outside of it, albeit in different ways. Having children, particularly young children, continues to determine whether or not women work and, if they do, for how many hours. In 2008, 68 per cent of working aged women with dependent children worked compared with 73 per cent of working aged women without children. The reverse pattern is observed for men, that is, working aged men with children of any age are more likely to work (90 per cent) than working aged men without children (73 per cent) (ONS, 2008). To accommodate their caring responsibilities, women continue to be employed in part-time work to a far greater extent than men – 5.65 million compared with 1.88 million (ONS, 2009).

The above are aggregate figures and do not capture the heterogeneity that Bottero (2000) argues is characteristic of the labour market at the turn of the new century. Aggregate figures more closely reflect the labour market positions of the white majority. Bradley and Healy (2008) highlight that labour market participation rates vary widely between women and men of different ethnic groups. The same holds true for part-time working. White women are more likely to work part-time than women from any other ethnic group, whilst men from all other ethnic groups, apart from Chinese, are more likely to work part-time than white men (ibid.: 20).

One issue that holds constant for women of all ethnic groups, including white, is the importance of the service sector, public and private, as a source of paid work. In 2008, the service sector provided 74 per cent of men's jobs and 92 per cent of women's jobs. However, as Figure 9.1 shows, occupational segregation is still prevalent, particularly in relation to service sector jobs.

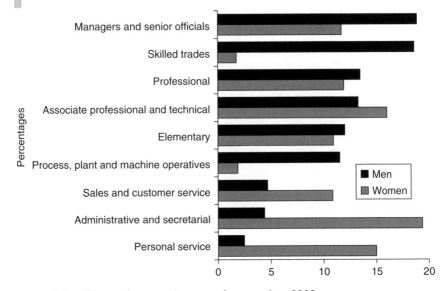

Figure 9.1 All in employment: By sex and occupation, 2008
Source: ONS, 2008.

Although the occupations that comprise the service sector are extremely heterogeneous, a number of studies have noted that the majority of jobs newly created in the sector are amongst low-paid, low-skilled work in sales and personal services and therefore likely to be filled by women workers, usually working part time (e.g. Fagan, O'Reilly and Halpin, 2005; Nolan, 2001; Nolan and Wood, 2003). The type and quality of these jobs have also prompted a great deal of research around 'non-standard' forms of employment, including part-time and temporary jobs. Some of this research has focused on the numerical extent of these forms of work and how far they have led to labour market insecurity (e.g. Doogan, 2001; Fevre, 2007; Forde and Slater, 2005) rather than on their gendered nature. Others have put gender at the centre of their analysis (Casey and Alach, 2004; Charles and James, 2003; Standing, 1999; Tailby, 2005) but again the experience of temporary work is often racialized as well as gendered (Conley, 2002, 2003, 2006). In the UK the highest percentages of temporary jobs are found amongst women in the 'Black and Other group' and women from ethnic minority groups are more likely than white women to hold full-time temporary as opposed to part-time jobs (Dex and McCulloch, 1997). Similar findings have been reported in the US (Cassirer, 2003). These studies cover a wide spectrum of women's work and experiences. What draws them together is women's position, actual or presumed, between public and private spheres that has allowed capital and often the State to exploit their labour.

The most concrete and persistent manifestation of the exploitation of women's labour is the gender pay gap which can be measured in a variety of ways but is usually illustrated as the percentage difference between men's and women's pay.[1] Using a calculation based on mean full-time hourly rates, the gender pay gap in 2008 stood at approximately 17 per cent. The gap between mean hourly rates of full-time men and part-time women is much wider at approximately 36 per cent. These figures vary based on ethnicity. As Table 9.1 shows, black women have a higher hourly rate than any ethnic group – male or female, but these figures need to be considered within the broader social context where black women are concentrated in full-time work in urban areas (Bradley and Healy, 2008).

Within these broad ethnic groups there is variation. For example, the category 'Asian/Asian British' in Table 9.1 combines employees of Indian, Pakistani and Bangladeshi origin. These groups have widely different labour market outcomes with Indian men and women more likely to be located in professional work and Pakistani and Bangladeshi men and women more likely to work in lower-paid manual service work (Bradley and Healy, 2008). Aggregate figures therefore disguise the lowest-paid women and the largest gender pay gap.

Like labour market participation, the factor which has the biggest impact on the gender pay gap is the number of dependent children that employees have. As Table 9.2 shows, men with dependent children earn more than men with no children. Women, on the other hand, earn less when they have more than two dependent children.

The new century has not seen progress in the closure of the gender pay gap in the UK. In 2001, the gap increased for the first time since the introduction of the Equal Pay Act in 1970. It has fluctuated up and down by a couple of percentage points since.

Table 9.1   Median hourly earnings (full time) by gender and ethnicity

Ethnicity	Male	Female	Gender pay gap (%)
White	10.73	9.40	12.4
Mixed	10.69	9.71	9.2
Asian/Asian British	10.13	8.85	12.6
Black/Black British	10.74	11.43	−6.4
Other including Chinese	11.05	10.00	9.5

Source: Leaker, 2008.

Table 9.2 Median hourly earnings (full time) by gender and number of dependent children

No. Dependent Children	Male	Female	Gender pay gap (%)
0	10.23	9.41	8.0
1	10.63	9.32	12.3
2	12.49	10.63	14.9
3	11.54	9.35	19.0
4 or more	11.22	7.24	35.5

Source: Leaker, 2008.

The State and the gendered labour process – legislating for change?

Labour process theory has not generally prioritized analysing the role of the State (Thompson, 2007). Because the State employs mostly women and improvements in pay and conditions of work for women are usually pursued by legislative reform rather than collective bargaining, more effort is required in this direction if LPT is to develop a comprehensive gendered analysis. For example, the persistence of the gender pay gap has been attributed to the inadequacy of equal pay legislation (Dickens, 2007; EOC, 2007; Leaker 2008). Whilst legislation is only one of a number of social influences on the gender pay gap and other forms of inequality (e.g. see Women and Work Commission, 2006), legislative reform has been a central element of the New Labour government's social policy. Shortly after taking office in 1997, the government signed the Social Chapter of the 1992 Maastricht Treaty, meaning that the UK would be required to transpose a number of European legal regulations into domestic law. Some of these, such as the Part-Time Workers (Prevention of Less Favourable Treatment Regulations 2000) the Fixed-Term Employees (Prevention of Less Favourable Treatment) Regulations and the still awaited implementation of the Agency Workers Directive should have a direct effect in the workplace because they strengthen the position of vulnerable workers. There have also been legislative steps beyond the requirements of the Social Chapter, such as the introduction of a National Minimum Wage (NMW) the Public Sector Equality Duties on race, disability and gender and the proposed overhaul of the other equality legislation in the impending Equality Bill that provide the potential to challenge the discriminatory behaviour of employers. How far these measures have or will impact on gendered labour processes is subject to debate.

The introduction of the NMW in 1999 was expected to have an impact on the gender pay gap because it would raise the pay of largely low-paid women workers (Edwards and Gilman, 1999). Others argued that the rate at which it was set would very much reduce its impact (Thornley and Coffey, 1999). Research following the implementation indicates that scepticism was probably well placed, in that whilst there may have been some small initial impact, there has been little lasting effect on the gender pay gap (Dex, Sutherland and Joshi, 2000; Robinson, 2005). Similarly, given the impact of part-time working on the gender pay gap, the Part-Time Worker Regulations, because they made differential pay rates for part-time workers doing the same job unlawful, should have had a positive impact on the gender pay gap. However, the gender pay gap for part-time workers has proved stubbornly resistant to any closure despite the legislation (Manning and Petrongolo, 2005). In relation to temporary workers, the Fixed-Term Employee Regulations did not come into full effect until 2006 but early indications are that it has had only a muted impact on the most affected sectors (Conley, 2008). In addition, the Agency Workers' Directive has been strongly contested by employers' bodies and, at the time of writing, is still under consultation.

Perhaps the greatest hope for legislative improvements for equality at work in the UK has been pinned on the impending Single Equality Act (Dickens, 2007). Calls for a review of the anti-discrimination legislation began to gain momentum following the change of government in 1997. The move to formalize significant changes to the equality legislation appeared on the last page of the 2005 Labour Party Manifesto where the government included a pledge to introduce a Single Equality Act, to 'simplify' and 'modernise' 40 years of complex equality legislation, during the 2005–10 parliament. The Discrimination Law Review (DLR) was established in 2005 to work towards this goal. In addition, the Equalities Review was commissioned by the government to provide an independent assessment.

Despite the resources that have been allocated to the project, the road to reforming the equality legislation has proved to be extremely rocky, with both employers and trade unions recognizing the potential for change. However, one of the key issues is conceptual – how to move from legislation and institutions originally designed to address separate equality strands towards a more holistic, or intersectional, approach to dealing with disadvantage and discrimination? The method adopted has been largely one of integration. First, the new legislation was preceded by the merger of the three existing equality bodies[2] in 2007 to create the Equalities and Human Rights Commission (EHRC) which has experienced the usual problems and power struggles associated with a merger. Similarly, although two years in the making, the Green Paper produced by the DLR was met by disappointment at its lack of ambition and vision for dealing with multiple forms of discrimination. There were some improvements to the Bill following the disappointment of the Green Paper; however, the proposed legislation has met with rather muted support from the TUC and the EHRC.

From the late 1960s to the present, deference of various governments to the interests of capital has prevented the formulation of equality legislation that effectively improves labour market outcomes. As Bradley and Healy argue, '... governments may espouse an egalitarian stance, but only as long as it doesn't interfere too greatly with profits or markets' (2008: 71). The result is that because of the historic division of labour in the public and private spheres, coupled with intersecting forms of discrimination and prejudice, women are still an easy target for exploitation in the twenty-first century.

Gender, skill and the discovery of emotional labour

In West's (1990) chapter on gender and the labour process, her aim was to move away from the structural dualisms, notably between patriarchy and capital, which have dominated theoretical thinking. Important ethnographic research had already begun to gender LPT through close analysis of female waged labour (e.g. Cavendish, 1982; Pollert, 1981; Westwood, 1984). Following this earlier work, West argues for a level of analysis that hones in on gender and class relations at the point of production by reviewing the work of Phillips and Taylor (1980) and Cockburn (1983, 1985). The major contribution of the former was to highlight that skill is itself a socially constructed concept that is heavily influenced by gendered relations both in and outside of the labour process. West argues that whilst this was a major leap forward for a gendered understanding of LPT, there is a tendency to focus on the undervaluation of women's work and to underplay the differences between what women and men do. Cockburn's work, on the other hand, stressed the way in which women were excluded by capital (class relations) men and trade unions (gendered social relations) from high-skill jobs. West again acknowledges the very great and lasting contribution Cockburn's work has made whilst contending that her argument sometimes underplays the differences between men's jobs and the class relations between men.

Although the preceding is only a very brief analysis of what are complex issues, one thing is clear: in West's (1990) chapter the focus is on the physical and technological aspects of what women and men (as homogeneous groups) do at work rather than how they are expected to look and behave. It could be argued that such a conceptualization of skill allowed an essentially masculine agenda to continue to lead the debate. There were some glimpses that alternative facets of the labour process were important for developing a gendered understanding. For example, an analysis of Game and Pringle (1984) identifies capital's exploitation of gendered skills developed in the private sphere and there is an acknowledgement that in Cockburn's work an exploration of attributes such as diligence and 'public relations' work tapped into what might now be referred to as soft skills.

Unfortunately, there have been no similar detailed ethnographic studies in the service sector that have been as influential in shaping LPT as the 1980s work of Pollert, Cavendish, Westwood and Cockburn, which focused on female work in mainly manufacturing contexts. However, the most substantial body of work on an alternative view of the gendered labour process, starting with Arlie Hochschild's (1983) theorization of emotional labour, had not in 1990 made an impression on UK labour process debates. Hochschild's classic work, *The Managed Heart: Commercialization of Human Feeling,* theorizes how some work is predicated on the exploitation of a type of labour, emotional labour, that hitherto had largely gone unexamined in the sociology of work. Hochschild adds emotional labour into a Marxist framework whereby some emotions become commodified, constitute an aspect of labour power and are sold for a wage in the public sphere. Emotions thereby come under the control of the purchaser, ultimately leading to the 'transmutation', of workers from the emotional product of their labour. Although the gendered nature of emotional labour is still not explicit in this Marxist framework, emotional labour is most clearly tangible in caring and serving work, making it essentially gendered. As James (1998: 219–20) argues, 'its value lies in its contribution to the social reproduction of labour power and the social relations of production, with the divide between home and work and the gender division of labour influencing the forms in which it is carried out'. In this way, emotional labour theories have undoubtedly enhanced our understanding of the gendered labour process.

There has been a colossal amount of literature on emotional labour since *The Managed Heart,* most of it implicitly, if not always explicitly, gendered and much of it critical of Hochschild's theoretical framework. In relation to LPT the debates have taken two major lines. The first of these has questioned how far emotional labour can be considered as skilled. The second has problematized emotions as labour within a Marxist framework, even when performed for the benefit of a paying customer. In some ways these arguments have continuity with the debates analysed in West's 1990 chapter and are reviewed briefly below.

Is emotional labour skilled?

Bolton (2000a,b, 2004; Bolton and Boyd, 2003) has led the emotional labour debate in the UK and has sought to develop a reading informed by LPA (see her chapter in this volume). In relation to skill, Bolton (2004) uses Littler's

(1982) typology to argue that emotional labour is indeed skilled work. The thrust of the argument is that service workers who engage with customers have to become extremely skilled in gauging the emotional context of their work and at tailoring their behaviour accordingly. For example, dealing with angry or lonely customers or simply those who are in a rush requires different levels of interaction. Furthermore, workers have discretion over not only the type of emotional labour they use in a particular situation, but also whether they will withhold or dilute it.

The battle for the recognition of emotional labour as skilled work has a strong gendered dimension. James (1998) and Korczynski (2005) have argued that the skills involved in emotional labour are not recognized as such because it is often women who undertake the forms of work in which emotional labour is embedded. Furthermore, emotional labour is undervalued because of gendered reasoning that it simply harnesses dispositional attributes rather than acquired skills. These arguments are clearly resonant with the earlier work of Phillips and Taylor (1980). However, Payne (2006) has cautioned against a blanket approach to considering all emotional labour as skilled. Drawing on Attewell (1990), Payne argues that a distinction has to be drawn between those complex physical, mental and moral actions that make us human and those that have to be learned as part of the labour process. Payne asks the question '... where does the basic requirement for politeness in the service work of an advanced western society *end* and skilled emotion work *begin?*' (2006: 17, emphasis in original). Payne acknowledges the argument to recognize all emotional labour as skilled is an attempt to increase the value of low-paid service work mostly undertaken by women. However, he notes that implicit in the concept of skill is the notion of rarity:

> One of the problems with trying to win improved pay rewards by re-labelling emotion work as skill is that there may be no real shortage of those able to perform the kind of 'skilled' emotion work required in the bulk of low-end service jobs... (2006: 22)

The need to retain an element of scarcity is why powerful groups have sought to control the numbers of workers who can claim to be skilled. In this way, Payne is invoking the arguments of Cockburn discussed earlier in relation to the exclusion of women by men and trade unions from skilled work. Payne also notes that relying on emotional labour as a lever to increase the pay of low-paid women is only a partial response because it does nothing to help the low-paid 'backroom' workers, such as cleaners and packers and, if it eclipses social justice arguments for fair pay, it may even be detrimental.

When are emotions at work labour and when are they not?

Payne's argument that a separation needs to be drawn between emotions that are skilled and emotions that are not can be taken further. If not all emotions at work are skilled it could also be argued that not all emotions at work are labour. A more recent debate along these lines has emerged in relation to how far Hochschild's framework captures the entirety of emotion work.[3] Bolton and Boyd (2003) argue that Hochschild presents an absolutist analysis, whereby all emotions in the workplace are captured for commercial purposes. This is largely because, they argue, Hochschild conflates emotional labour with physical labour and fails to recognize that workers retain the means of producing emotional labour. Bolton and Boyd propose an alternative framework whereby emotional management (as opposed to emotional labour) can take four forms: pecuniary, prescriptive, presentational and philanthropic. Only the first two of these forms provides emotional labour which is appropriated by employers for profit. The other two remain within the control and 'gift' of workers.

Brook (2009a and 2009b) challenges Bolton's critique of Hochschild on a number of levels by arguing that Bolton misunderstands what constitutes the means of production in line with a LPA and overplays Hochschild's theory of transmutation. Most importantly he contends that by moving away from Hochschild's (albeit inadequate in places) Marxist framework, Bolton has de-politicized the concept of emotional labour and moves it away from a LPA. Bolton (2009) offers a vigorous defence of her position, arguing that Brook exaggerates the Marxist content of Hochschild's work and demonstrates only a selective reading of her work.

LPA has, since the 1980s, become a 'broad church' including Marxist and non-Marxist theorists. The crux of Brook's critique revolves around different interpretations of what is meant by LPA and whether and how far it should adhere to its Marxist origins – how far can Marxist concepts such as 'labour power', 'means of production' and 'surplus value' be stretched and mean the same thing? What Brook does not do is consider the gendered implications of either Marxist or non-Marxist interpretations of emotional labour. Marxist analyses of the labour process have historically struggled to provide a coherent gendered interpretation because the work often undertaken by women, sometimes in the form of emotional labour, is concerned with the reproduction of labour power rather than the production of labour. Even when emotional labour is undertaken in the public sphere for a wage, the production of surplus value, and therefore the source of exploitation, is often indirect, for example, when it takes the form of State funded public services or paid work in the voluntary sector. If, on the other hand, one moves beyond this framework in the way that Bolton has, there is a danger that the political and material focus of a LPA is lost. Lewis (2005: 578) touches upon this when, in relation to nurses, she argues, 'the conflation of gender with the requirements of emotional labour, particularly philanthropic emotion management work, causes the work skills necessary for this job to be taken for granted and not listed as bone fide requirements. Such work is not valued and is not viewed as an occupational resource of benefit to the workplace.' In addition to leading to an undervaluing of emotion skills, the conceptualization of emotion work as a gift reinforces the public image of some women's occupations, such as nursing, as largely vocational and women employed in care work as 'ministering angels' rather than workers who have no other means of subsistence. While a concept of 'gifting' aspects of emotional labour might seem like a positive image of women's work, it misreads class as an analytical concept and backfires when women, as workers, need to take collective action to improve their terms and conditions of work. The 'gift' might be viewed as angelic, but withdrawing it is seen as inhuman.

From the above analysis it is clear that emotional labour is an important aspect of the gendered labour process but, as the labour market data indicate, gender is mediated by other demographic characteristics. Service work has historically been ethnicized as well as gendered. It is therefore surprising that very few empirical studies on emotional labour have researched intersectionality. Zhao (2002) is one of the few who have identified that ethnicity impacts on emotional labour, particularly in the globalized tourism and leisure industry. Public sector work is also ethnicized as well as gendered and there is great scope to develop research in this direction.

Looking back, the relatively late appreciation of Hochschild's work within LPA now seems odd, given that her theories adapted some Marxist concepts. It is perhaps even odder that since emotional labour has become a key component of gender and LPA, it has become largely separated from Hochschild's work and from labour as the focus of the analysis. This might indicate two things. First, the complexity of theorizing a gendered *and* ethnicized labour process that requires an integration of the production of surplus value in the public sphere with the reproduction of labour power within both the public and private spheres. Second, it illustrates the detachment of LPA from its Marxist roots and the dangers of viewing work, particularly gendered and ethnicized forms of work, outside of a class analysis.

Intersectionality, feminist theory and the labour process

So far our analysis has identified that, although gender, ethnicity and class are key to understanding the labour market outcomes and experiences of women and men, the combination has often evaded new developments in LPT. Therefore, in this section, we focus upon an important and increasingly utilized concept in feminist theory, that of intersectionality which, although not new, has developed and become increasingly popular since the 1990s (e.g. Acker, 2006; Bradley, 2007; Bradley and Healy, 2008; Walby, 2007, 2009) especially through the work of black feminists (e.g. Collins, 1986, 1998, 2000; Crenshaw, 1989, 1991). In essence, 'intersectionality is a relatively new term to describe an old question in theorization of the relationship between different forms of social inequality' (Walby, 2007: 450).

Following in the Marxist labour process tradition, some maintain that class remains central to gender analysis (Acker, 1988, 2006), but not in the 'traditional' Marxist form (Bradley, 2007). Intersectionality is seen by some as a means to develop the analytical links between different forms of inequality further, for example, through the work of feminists who draw attention to how gender, class, race/ethnicity, sexual orientation, age and disability interrelate to produce multiple inequalities, for example, black women experience discrimination based on both their ethnicity and gender, although intersectionality is acknowledged by some to be both an important but 'contested contribution' to sociological analysis (Denis, 2008). Nevertheless, interest in debates on intersectionality as a key concept in feminist enquiry has remained (Lewis, 2009).

Bradley (2007) cautions against returning to the 'older forms of Marxism' and its tendency to not only reduce everything to the 'economic' but also to see gender as a second-order phenomenon. She recognizes what she describes as, 'the currently fashionable idea of intersectionality' or what she refers to as 'multiple positioning' and 'multiple disadvantage'. Different authors see intersectionality in different ways (Acker, 2006; Collins, 1986, 1998, 2000; Crenshaw, 1989, 1991; Walby, 2007, 2009) approaching it from empirical and theoretical perspectives and often prioritizing one form of inequality over another. Denis (2008: 677) defines intersectional analysis as, '...the concurrent analyses of multiple, intersecting sources of subordination/oppression [that is] based on the premise that the impact of a particular source of subordination may vary, depending on its combination with other potential sources of subordination (or relative privilege)'. This section will review both established and emerging work on intersectionality and consider what this means for LPT in the twenty-first century.

Crenshaw (1989, 1991) and Collins (1986, 1998, 2000) were amongst the first to establish the concept of intersectionality, Crenshaw being attributed as the first to use the term itself (Denis, 2008; Walby, 2007). In her 1991 article, Crenshaw explored the race and gender dimensions of violence against women of colour and how their experiences are the product of intersecting patterns of racism and sexism. Crenshaw creates a framework of three forms of intersectionality: structural intersectionality[4] (the location of women of colour at the intersection of race and gender and how this makes their actual experience of violence qualitatively different than that of white women); political intersectionality[5] (how feminist and antiracist politics have often helped to marginalize the issue of violence against women of colour); and representational intersectionality[6] (the cultural construction of women of colour).

Collins' (1986, 1998) focus is also on violence. She explores African American women's experiences of violence as a site of intersectionality, linking hierarchical power relations of race and gender and arguing that the same violent act will have different outcomes dependent upon the victim's race and gender. Collins (2000) also explores black women's position *vis-à-vis* the work/family nexus arguing that paid work and work inside the home is difficult to separate for black women and challenges work as a public, male domain and the family as a private, female haven (ibid.). The family for black women is also considered via gender, sexuality, race, class and nation. Collins defines intersectionality as, 'opposed to examining gender, sexuality, race, class and nation as separate systems of oppression, the construct of intersectionality references how these systems mutually construct one another' (2000: 4). The work of black feminists has been pivotal in analysing multiple inequalities and in shifting the focus away from white, middle-class feminism with its tendency to homogenize all women.

The labour market has also become a key focus for intersectionality, perhaps most notably through the work of Joan Acker (2006) whose early and later work focus upon class relations as always gendered.[7] Writing at a time when the inclusion of women and gender in organization theory was still 'cursory', Acker's (1990) work focused predominantly on the gendering of organizations and how this contributes to gender segregation. In her 1998 reassessment of the future of gender and organizations, 'race' slips into her analysis, a theme she revisits in more depth in her later work (2006) on intersectionality and inequality regimes. In the labour process tradition, the focus of Acker's (2006) work is class as a central concept and how organizations produce and reproduce gendered and racialized class relations through 'inequality regimes'. This approach is what Collins (1986) describes as the prioritization of one form of primary oppression with remaining types of oppression acting as variables within what is seen as the most important system, for example, inserting race and gender into Marxist theory (Collins, 1986: S20).

Acker argues that the old notions of class, implicitly based on images of male lives, should be abandoned. By doing this, Acker extends LPT by focusing on the intersectionality of class, gender and race but at the same time, retaining class as the inequality that is 'more legitimate' than racial and gender inequality in the US. She argues that pursuing an approach to class displaces the white male model because class and capitalism are gendered and racialized. This is a different approach from arguing for intersections between systems or structures with their own pre-existing internal elements and dynamics: 'rather than existing, distinct systems, I see ongoing processes and practices in which gendering and racialisation are integral to the creation and recreation of class inequalities and class divisions, emerging in complex, multifaceted boundary-spanning capitalist activities' (2006: 45). Furthermore, to bring women of all races into class analysis, she argues that the idea of what counts as 'economic' should be expanded to include unpaid work.

From this perspective, class 'uses' gender and race to create and sustain inequalities in capitalist organizations, adopting the term 'inequality regimes' to demonstrate how this operates in the organization context. Acker defines inequality regimes as, '... the configuration of inequality-producing practices and processes within particular organisations at particular times' (2006: 10) that produce and maintain racialized and gendered class relations. Within inequality regimes, class is the most 'legitimate' but the least visible inequality; there are different bases of inequality; organizing practices maintain inequalities, such as job design and job segregation by gender and race; there are methods of control, such as bureaucratic rules; and there are competing interests. Acker argues that every large, capitalist organization has an inequality regime. She also acknowledges that putting gender, race and class together is conceptually difficult, even when the focus is primarily on class.

Acker's work comprises a class base that is both gendered and racialized and renders visible the previously invisible 'other' under class analysis. Her utilization of 'inequality regimes' is useful for understanding how multiple inequalities manifest in organizations. Walby (1990, 1997, 2004) also adopts the concept of 'regime' in the form of 'gender regimes', placing a much tighter focus around gender and shifting from her original usage of the term 'patriarchal structures' (1990) although this focus shifts again in her later work to 'complex multiple social inequalities' (2007, 2009). Through her earlier work, Walby combined a class analysis and theorization of patriarchy through 'dual systems theory', arguing that both patriarchy and capitalism were 'analytically necessary' to understand gender relations. Avoiding a base-superstructure model, Walby identified six causal bases of women's oppression[8] and argued that we have witnessed a shift from private to public forms of patriarchy.

The conceptual difficulties surrounding intersectionality highlighted by Acker are further addressed by Walby (2007, 2009). In contrast to Acker, Walby retains gender as the central concept in her analysis in terms of the patriarchal domination of women by men, although she does broaden this in her later work (1997) by acknowledging the complex relations between gender, class and ethnicity. She argues that these new patterns of gender transformations, based on, for example, women's achievements in education, are intertwined with diversities and inequalities generated by social divisions, including class, ethnicity and (geographical) region. For Walby, 'the divisions in society caused by gender lead to the intensification of other forms of inequality' (1997: 13). Thus, gender relations impact on the economy as a whole, and on the class structure. This ongoing transformation of the gender regime from a domestic to a public form is further expanded at the EU level (2004) at a quite complex level of abstraction, a complexity that reaches a higher level of theoretical abstraction in Walby's more recent work on the intersection of multiple complex inequalities and complexity theory (Walby, 2007, 2009), which remains 'difficult and contested' (Walby, 2007). Walby argues that, 'social theory is challenged to take account of complex inequalities beyond class' (2009: 1) as it is difficult to take account of the presence and mutual constitution of multiple social inequalities (gender, ethnicity, age, religion, nation, sexual orientation and disability) and 'difference'. Walby's aim is to include these intersecting complex inequalities within the core of social theory, an aim echoed by Denis (2008) who states that intersectional analysis is, 'an emerging, important theoretical contribution by feminism to sociology' (Denis, 2008).

Walby argues that simply 'adding up' multiple complex inequalities is not sufficient as they can change each other. Again, Walby dismisses a base/superstructure model, opting instead for a range of domains (economy, polity, violence nexus and civil society) and within each domain, multiple sets of social relations (e.g. gender, class, ethnicity). Importantly, each institutionalized domain and each set of social relations are conceptualized as systems,[9] rather than parts of systems, that can be overlapping and non-nested. This 'system' allows for more than one set of social relations, without a hierarchy that is not theoretically subordinated to class. Rather, it allows class and gender to have ontological depth, each constituted in all the domains.

Under this complexity theory umbrella, each system takes all other systems as its environment, going beyond the idea that parts of a system make up the whole. 'System' thus becomes more fluid. Each set of social relations is a social system; gender, ethnic and class relations are constituted in the economy, polity, violence and civil society. These systems of social relations are constituted at different levels of abstraction with one level emerging from another. These are overlapping, non-saturating and non-nested systems of social relations. Gender is not contained within class relations; they are not nested. Gender relations are a separate system; they overlap with class, but neither gender nor class fully saturate the institutional domains. Importantly, because there is a lack of saturation, it is possible to conceptualize simultaneous multiple forms of inequality. Walby claims: 'the lack of saturation of any field by a single set of social relations or a single social institution opens the theoretical agenda that was prematurely closed by traditional systems thinking. It allows the possibility of analysis of multiple simultaneous complex inequalities, while retaining concepts of social structure and system' (2007: 460).

These are interesting developments in the debate on 'intersectionality'. While Walby's perspective challenges how we think about the theorization of multiple intersecting social inequalities via complexity theory, Acker's more empirical 'inequality regimes' help us to see how class is both gendered and racialized and needs to be revised from the traditional Marxist theorization of class inequalities. This challenge of implementing the concept of intersectionality into empirical analysis whilst taking account of three or more variables concurrently is noted by Denis (2008) although she cites McCall's (2005) continuum as a useful tool.[10] Walby and Acker both agree that we must move away from the 'older forms' of Marxist analysis of class and at the same time, acknowledge the conceptual difficulties in theoretically linking multiple social inequalities. However, it should be remembered that labour process and intersectionality are still played out within capitalist States and economies. Therefore, Marxist theories of class should still be relevant at some levels of analysis. After two decades, finding the path between these different routes is still the challenge for LPT.

Conclusions

Whilst the focus of gender and the labour process in West's (1990) chapter was still on the physical and technological aspects of work, there has been a seismic shift in thinking around what we mean by 'work' and who participates in it. Emotional labour theories have stretched the former whilst researchers seeking an intersectional approach have expanded the latter. Feminist theorists have made attempts to shift from traditional Marxist approaches whilst at the same time retaining class as a key social inequality.

The importance of including gender, class and ethnicity in LPT is illustrated in ours and others' critique of the development of emotional labour as a labour process concept. Similarly, intersectionality raises important theoretical questions as to whether we see multiple inequalities as separate systems, or regimes that intersect and mutually adapt (Walby, 2007, 2009) as mutually constructing one another (Collins, 1986, 1998, 2000) or as some inequalities being integral to others (Acker, 2006). These are big theoretical challenges not only for feminist theory and LPT as our critique of current emotional labour theories suggest, but also for social policy.

As the workforce becomes more feminized, older and diverse, we have to think of innovative ways to both theoretically and empirically investigate multiple inequalities and how these impact upon diverse groups within and outside of the paid labour market. In order to do this a better theorization of the role of the State is required within LPT. We have identified developments in legislation and social policy that interpret intersectionality as integration. However, in empirical terms, labour markets remain segregated on the grounds of gender, ethnicity, class, age, disability, as well as other forms of inequality that are, as yet, less easily measured. In theoretical terms there is still a tendency for hierarchies of inequality, the prioritization of one form of social inequality over another, to emerge within models of intersectionality. For Acker, this is class and for Collins, race. In her later work (2007, 2009) Walby acknowledges that regimes of complex inequalities are rarely coequal and that one regime may be more significant than another, although 'this is rarely overwhelming' due to non-saturation and non-nesting. Importantly, each regime takes all others as its environment. Others (e.g. Bradley and Healy, 2008) claim not to prioritize any particular social inequality but rather to, 'situate women in their context' and attempt to understand different social inequalities at different times. However, in this view, hierarchies of inequality are not dispelled; they become temporally contingent. Perhaps intersectionality, as it is currently conceptualized, is not the panacea some thought it might be, but it does represent a key departure from analyses based solely on gender *or* class. We suggest that this is an important shift for LPT and the study of labour markets.

Notes

1 For a detailed account see ONS (2008).
2 Equal Opportunities Commission (EOC), Commission for Racial Equality (CRE) and Disability Rights Commission (DRC).
3 For a detailed analysis see Brook (2009a,b).
4 For example, non-English speaking women often experience language barriers that may prevent them from taking up support services, such as information about shelters.
5 For example, the failure of feminism to interrogate race means that the resistance strategies of feminism will often replicate and reinforce the subordination of people of colour (1991: 1241).
6 For example, how women of colour are represented in cultural imagery.
7 For example, the structure of the labour market and relations in the workplace are always affected by symbols of gender, processes of gender identity and material inequalities between men and women. These processes

are completely related to and powerfully support the reproduction of the class structure (Acker, 1990).

8 Paid work, housework, sexuality, culture, violence and the State.

9 Although Walby recognizes that these domains are not the only social systems as there are others at different levels of abstraction.

10 McCall's continuum is based upon three approaches to the study of complex social relations: anti-categorical complexity, intracategorical complexity and intercategorical complexity. See McCall (2005) for a full discussion of this framework.

REFERENCES

Acker, J. (1988) 'Class, Gender and the Relations of Distribution', *Signs*, 13: 473–97.

Acker, J. (1990) 'Hierarchies, Jobs, Bodies: A Theory of Gendered Organisations', *Gender and Society*, 4(2): 139–58.

Acker, J. (1998) 'The Future of "Gender and Organisations": Connections and Boundaries', *Gender, Work and Organisation*, 5(4): 195–206.

Acker, J. (2006) *Class Questions, Feminist Answers*, Maryland, USA: Rowman and Littlefield Publishers.

Attewell, P. (1990) 'What Is Skill?' *Work and Occupations,* 14(4): 442–8.

Bolton, S. C. (2000a) 'Emotion Here, Emotion There, Emotional Organisations Everywhere', *Critical Perspectives on Accounting*, 11(2): 155–71.

Bolton, S. C. (2000b) 'Who Cares? Offering Emotion as a Gift in the Nursing Labour Process', *Journal of Advanced Nursing*, 32(3): 580–86.

Bolton, S. C. (2004) 'Conceptual Confusions: Emotion Work as Skilled Work', in Warhurst, C., Grugulis, I. and Keep, E. (eds) *The Skills That Matter*, London: Palgrave.

Bolton, S. C. (2009) 'Getting to the Heart of the Emotional Labour Process: A Reply to Brook', *Work, Employment and Society*, 23(3): 549–60.

Bolton, S. C. and Boyd, C. (2003) 'Trolly Dolly or Skilled Emotion Manager? Moving on from Hochschild's Managed Heart', *Work, Employment and Society*, 17(2): 289–308.

Bottero, W. (2000) 'Gender and the Labour Market at the Turn of the Century: Complexity, Ambiguity and Change', *Work Employment and Society*, 14(4): 781–91.

Bradley, H. (2007) *Gender*, Cambridge: Polity Press.

Bradley, H. and Healy, G. (2008) *Ethnicity and Gender at Work: Inequalities, Careers and Employment Relations*, Hants: Palgrave Macmillan.

Brook, P. (2009a) 'The Alienated Heart: Hochschild's Emotional Labour Thesis and the Anti-Capitalist Politics of Alienation', *Capital and Class*, 98: 3–27.

Brook, P. (2009b) 'In Critical Defence of "Emotional Labour": Refuting Bolton's Critique of Hochschild's Concept', *Work, Employment and Society*, 23(3): 531–48.

▶

▶

Casey, C. and Alach, P. (2004) 'Just a Temp? Women, Temporary Employment and Lifestyle', *Work, Employment and Society,* 18(3): 459–80.

Cassirer, N. (2003) 'Work Arrangements among Women in the United States', in Houseman, S. and Machiko, O. (eds) *Non-Standard Work in Developed Economies. Causes and Consequences,* Kalamazoo, MI: Upjohn Institute.

Cavendish, R. (1982) *Women on the Line,* London: Routledge and Kegan Paul.

Charles, N. and James, E. (2003) 'The Gendered Dimensions of Job Insecurity in a Local Labour Market', *Work, Employment and Society,* 17(3): 531–52.

Cockburn, C. (1983) *Brothers: Male Dominance and Technological Change,* London: Pluto.

Cockburn, C. (1985) *Machinery of Dominance: Women, Men and Technical Knowhow,* London: Pluto.

Collins, P. H. (1986) 'Learning from the Outsider Within: The Sociological Significance of Black Feminist Thought', *Social Problems,* 33(6): S14–S32.

Collins, P. H. (1998) 'The Tie That Binds: Race, Gender and US Violence', *Ethnic and Racial Studies,* 21(5): 917–38.

Collins, P. H. (2000) 'Gender, Black Feminism and Black Political Economy', *The Annals of the American Academy of Political and Social Science,* 568 Annals 41.

Conley, H. (2002) 'A State of Insecurity: Temporary Work in the Public Services', *Work, Employment and Society,* 16(4): 725–37.

Conley, H. (2003) 'Temporary Work in the Public Services: Implications for Equal Opportunities', *Gender, Work and Organization,* 10(4): 455–77.

Conley, H. (2006) 'Modernisation or Casualisation? Numerical Flexibility in the Public Services', *Capital & Class* 89, Summer: 31–57.

Conley, H. (2008) 'The Nightmare of Temporary Work: A Comment on Fevre', *Work, Employment and Society,* 22(4): 731–36.

Crenshaw, K. (1989) 'Demarginalising the Intersection of Race and Sex: A Black Feminist Critique of Antidiscrimination Doctrine', *Feminist Theory and Antiracist Politics, University of Chicago Legal Forum,* 138–67.

Crenshaw, K. (1991) 'Mapping the Margins: Intersectionality, Identity Politics and Violence against Women of Colour', *Stanford Law Review,* 43(6): 1241–99.

Denis, A. (2008) 'Intersectional Analysis: A Contribution of Feminism to Sociology', *International Sociology,* 23(5): 677–94.

Dex, S. and McCulloch, A. (1997) *Flexible Employment: The Future of Britain's Jobs,* Basingstoke: Macmillan.

Dex, S., Sutherland, H. and Joshi, H. (2000) 'Effects of Minimum Wages on the Gender Pay Gap', *National Institute Economic Review,* 173, 80–8.

Dickens, L. (2007) 'The Road Is Long – Thirty Years of Equality Legislation in Britain', *British Journal of Industrial Relations,* 45(3): 463–94.

Doogan, K. (2001) 'Insecurity and Long-Term Employment', *Work, Employment and Society,* 15(3): 419–41.

Edwards, P. and Gilman, M. (1999) 'Pay Equity and the National Minimum Wage: What Can Theories Tell Us?', *Human Resource Management Journal,* 9(1): 20–38.

EOC (2007) Gender Equality Duty Code of Practice England and Wales Manchester: EOC.

▶

▶

Fagan, C., O'Reilly, J. and Halpin, B. (2005) *Job Opportunities for Whom? Labour Market Dynamics and Service-Sector Growth in Germany and Britain,* London: Anglo-German Foundation.

Fevre, R. (2007) 'Employment Insecurity and Social Theory: The Power of Nightmares', *Work, Employment and Society,* 21(3): 517–35.

Forde, C. and Slater, G. (2005) 'Agency Working in Britain: Character, Consequences and Regulation', *British Journal of Industrial Relations,* 43(2): 249–71.

Game, A. and Pringle, R. (1984) *Gender at Work,* London: Pluto.

Hochschild, A. R. (1983) *The Managed Heart: Commercialisation of Human Feeling,* Berkeley: University of California Press.

James, N. (1998) 'Emotional Labour: Skill and Work in the Social Regulation of Feelings', in Mackay, L., Soothill, K., Melia, K. (eds) *Classic Texts in Healthcare,* Oxford: Butterworth-Heinemann.

Korczynski, M. (2005) 'Skills in Service Work: An Overview', *Human Resource Management Journal,* 15(2): 3–14.

Leaker, D. (2008) 'The Gender Pay Gap in the UK', *Economic and Labour Market Review,* 2(4): 19–24.

Lewis, G. (2009) 'Celebrating Intersectionality? Debates on a Multi-faceted Concept in Gender Studies: Themes from a Conference', *European Journal of Women's Studies,* 16: 203–10.

Lewis, P. (2005) 'Suppression or Expression: An Exploration of Emotion Management in a Special Care Baby Unit', *Work, Employment and Society,* 19(3): 565–81.

Littler, C. (1982) *The Development of the Labour Process in Capitalist Societies,* London Heinemann.

Manning, A. and Petrongolo, B. (2005) *The Part-Time Pay Penalty,* Centre for Economic Performance Discussion Paper 679, London: CEP.

McCall, L. (2005) 'The Complexity of Intersectionality', *Signs,* 30(3): 1771–800.

Nolan, P. (2001) 'Shaping Things to Come', *People Management,* London: CIPD.

Nolan, P. and Wood, S. (2003) 'Mapping the Future of Work', *British Journal of Industrial Relations,* 41(2): 165–74.

ONS (2008) Focus on Gender: http://www.statistics.gov.uk/cci/nugget.asp?id=1654.

ONS (2009) 'Labour Market Statistics', *Statistical Bulletin,* July, Newport: ONS.

Payne, J. (2006) 'What's Wrong with Emotional Labour', SKOPE Research Paper 65: University of Warwick.

Phillips, A. and Taylor, B. (1980) 'Sex and Skill: Notes towards a Feminist Economics', *Feminist Review,* 6: 79–88.

Pollert, A. (1981) *Girls, Wives, Factory Lives,* London: Macmillan.

Robinson, H. (2005) 'Regional Evidence of the Effect of the National Minimum Wage on the Gender Pay Gap', *Regional Studies,* 39(7): 855–72.

Standing, G. (1999) Global Feminization through Flexible Labour: A Theme Revisited World Development, 27(3): 583–602.

Tailby, S. (2005) 'Agency and Bank Nursing in the UK National Health Service', *Work, Employment and Society,* 9(2): 369–89.

▶

▶

Thompson, P. (2007) 'Adler's Theory of the Capitalist Labour Process: A Pale(o) Imitation', *Organization Studies,* 28(9): 1359–68.

Thornley, C. and Coffey, D. (1999) 'The Low Pay Commission in Context', *Work, Employment and Society,* 13(3): 525–38.

Walby, S. (1990) *Theorising Patriarchy,* Cambridge: Basil Blackwell.

Walby, S. (1997) *Gender Transformations,* London: Routledge.

Walby, S. (2004) 'The European Union and Gender Equality: Emergent Varieties of Gender Regime', *Social Politics,* 11(1): 4–29.

Walby, S. (2007) 'Complexity Theory, Systems Theory and Multiple Intersecting Social Inequalities', *Philosophy of the Social Sciences,* 37(4): 449–70.

Walby, S. (2009) *Globalisation and Inequalities: Complexity and Contested Modernities,* London: Sage.

West, J. (1990) 'Gender and the Labour Process: A Reassessment', in Knights, D. and Willmott, H. (eds) *Labour Process Theory,* London; Macmillan.

Westwood, S. (1984) *All Day, Every Day: Factory and Family in the Making of Women's Lives,* London: Pluto.

Women and Work Commission (2006) *Shaping a Fairer Future,* London: Government Equalities Office.

Zhao. M. (2002) 'Emotional Labour in a Globalised Labour Market. Seafarers on Cruise Ships', School of Social Sciences Working Paper 27 Cardiff University.

New Concepts, New Realities

Old Ambiguities and New Developments: Exploring the Emotional Labour Process

10

Sharon C. Bolton

The subject of emotion in organizations is now well established and widely debated, with terms such as *emotional labour* becoming common parlance in academic and practitioner literatures and being empirically applied to a range of sectors and occupations. There is enormous interest in the role of emotion in organizational life; different conceptualizations are applied to a diverse range of occupational groups, from care workers to lawyers; and a range of concerns are expressed, from interactional efficiency to emotional burnout. Though not claiming to explore all of the available literature on emotions and work, it is relatively safe to say that such an array of interests offers complexity, but little clarity on how we might think about different facets of emotion in organizations. Nevertheless, some key themes do emerge concerning what is or is not emotional labour, who are and who are not emotional labourers and, by association, how organizations attempt to control our feelings, and the potential impact this has on our fragile identities. The net effect is that conceptual devices such as emotional labour, that should help us to understand the role of emotion within changing forms of work, have been stretched beyond recognition and now serve to confuse, rather than clarify, important issues. How do we work our way through this labyrinth of literatures and get back to our original concern with the rigours involved in, and the exploitation of, the actual labour involved in the exercise of emotion work and labour?

This chapter will argue that we require an analysis, notably Labour Process Theory (LPT), that highlights the context of a capitalist economy, the tensions and contradictions inherent in the emotional labour process, along with the realities of it as hard and productive work. The argument presented suggests that, if we are to ever understand the daily lived reality of many contemporary forms of work, we need to get back to basics and redefine what is emotional labour (i.e. activity directly involved in the accumulation of capital), and what is not (i.e. emotion work). LPT is proposed as a vehicle that offers us a way out of the now static emotional labour debate by creating possibilities for important analytical distinctions. It does this in three ways: it deals in the material realities of work; it recognizes the tensions inherent in capital's attempt to transform labour power into a commodity form; and it views (and celebrates) agency as a creative force. The chapter will review existing ambiguities in the debate on emotional labour and, in so doing, highlight how LPT offers the potential for new developments by placing analytical and context-specific boundaries around our understanding of the emotional labour process.

Discovering the managed heart

Emotion has long been recognized as making important contributions to organizational life. For example, the enactment of 'display rules' in service industries has never ceased to be a focus of analysis (Fine, 1988; Goffman, 1967; Whyte, 1948), and prescriptions for managing and shaping employee emotion into a positive form continue to reappear in a variety of guises within a broad range of management literature (Ashkanasy, Zerbe and Hartel, 2002; Dutton et al., 2006; Fredrickson, 2003; Frost, 2004). However, there is little doubt that there are changes in the emotional demands made of employees in the contemporary organization (Fineman and Sturdy, 1999; Hochschild, 1983; Sturdy, 1998). Emotion is no longer seen as a by-product of organizational life, but as a resource to be harnessed by the organization. This development is said to be due to the movement towards a post-industrial era where knowledge workers are the key to competitive advantage. Post-bureaucratic organizations operate through networks and cultures, rather than rules and structures, and engage with 'hearts and minds' (Warhurst and Thompson, 1998) as a means of harnessing the commitment and talents of its employees. The rising service sector is particularly reliant on the 'soft skills' of its employees. For example, workers in the entertainment industry must produce 'laughter and well-being' (Van Maanen, 1991), in other service industries the sale of a product depends upon employees' interaction with potential customers (Sutton, 1991; Taylor, 1998) and the survival of a company in a competitive market relies on employees' ability to deliver a quality service to customers (Bolton and Boyd, 2003; Hochschild, 1983). Whereas the 'smile factories' (Van Maanen, 1991; The Project on Disney, 1995) such as Walt Disney were once seen as the extreme, they have now become the normative model which service sector organizations wish to achieve. Little wonder that our capacities to interact with others and foster and create emotional experiences and ecologies have become valuable commodities.

Amongst contemporary literature, perhaps the greatest contribution to advance an understanding of emotion in organizations is Hochschild's (1979, 1983) work concerning the 'Managed Heart'. Hochschild successfully links the ideas of work and emotion, thereby recognizing that social actors are able to carry out emotion work which can be used as a vital part of the capitalist labour process – in what has now become commonly known as emotional labour (Hochschild, 1983). Hochschild states quite clearly that jobs requiring emotional labour have three distinct characteristics in common:

> First, they require face-to-face or voice-to-voice contact with the public. Second, they require the worker to produce an emotional state in another person – gratitude or fear for example. Third, they allow the employer, through training and supervision, to exercise a degree of control over the emotional activities of employees. (1983: 147)

Moreover, in the case of Hochschild's air cabin crew and debt collectors ('The toe and heel' (1983) of emotional labour), there is a fourth criterion which needs to be fulfilled before the term emotional labour can be applied: the creation of a profitable product with the use of emotional labour as a major factor in its production. For Hochschild, there are personal costs associated with the performance of emotional labour. Offering emotional labour that is not invested with feeling, what she describes as 'surface acting', results in ultimate alienation from one's 'true self', and deep acting, that is efforts to ensure, for instance, that our smiles are sincere, results in 'altering' one's self (Hochschild, 1983: 186–8). Either way, feelings become 'transmutated' by the organization and the 'smile', 'mood', 'feeling', or 'relationship', 'comes to belong more to the organization and less to the self' (ibid.: 198). In this way, Hochschild firmly places emotion within the public realm of work, highlighting its commodification and, hence, its exchange value (Fineman, 2005; Steinberg and Figart, 1999). Hochschild's contribution remains seminal and the contours of the emotional labour debate over the past 30 years can be traced back to her original work (Hochschild, 1979, 1983). Such is the popularity of the term 'emotional labour' that it serves as an anchor in most contemporary studies of emotion in work and is utilized in a myriad of ways.

Originating in the North American management literature, and utilizing a psychological perspective, core contributors to the debate direct attention to an employee's tendency to experience emotional burnout, dissonance and low job satisfaction (Morris and Feldman, 1996; Wharton, 1996; Zapf, 2002). The origins of this are attributed to a variety of organizational factors: role ambiguity, role conflict, poorly defined control systems, constraining work arrangement and, most importantly, poor employee-job fit (Ashforth and Humphrey, 1993, 1995; Ashkanasy, Zerbe and Hartel, 2002; Brotheridge and Lee, 2003; Holman, Chissick and Totterdell, 2002; Morris and Feldman, 1996; Shuler and Davenport, 2000; Weatherly and Tansik, 1992; Wharton and Erickson, 1993). With few exceptions (Ashforth and Humphrey, 1995; Fine, 1988), these accounts share some of Hochschild's concerns about the negative consequences of organizations' attempts to shape and control employees' feelings – though the emphasis lies in ineffective management rather than the forces of capitalism, with frustrated managers, emotionally exhausted workers and dissatisfied customers becoming the central focus of analysis. A major element of this approach is the inclusion of therapies that serve to mediate negative effects of the emotional labour process (Ashkanasy, Zerbe and Hartel, 2002; Holman, Chissick and Totterdell, 2002). Its raison d'etre is to invent ever more management prescription as a means of creating efficient emotion transactions with colleagues and customers.

Other developments in the debate on emotional labour build on an exploration of the labour of emotional labour. These developments progress Hochschild's valuable work concerning the gendered nature of emotional labour and its devaluation as a skill (Bolton, 2004, 2009a; Junor, Hampson and Ogle, 2009; Lewis, 2005; Sharma and Black, 2001; Steinberg and Figart, 1999; Tyler and Taylor, 1998, Wellington and Bryson, 2001; Williams, 2003); broaden its empirical and conceptual focus and highlight its exploitative potential (Bolton and Boyd, 2003; Callaghan and Thompson, 2002; Fineman and Sturdy, 1999; Taylor, 1998) and emphasize how organizations seek to regulate an employee's emotion work as part of the labour process (Bolton, 2005, 2009b; Gatta, 2009; Sosteric, 1996; Sturdy and Fineman, 2001; Taylor, 1998). These studies tend to be empirically grounded and highlight the workplace experience from an employee's perspective, offering insights into the gruelling nature of emotional labour and its status as hard and demanding work, yet also the capacity of emotion workers to step beyond managerially prescribed feeling rules in order to offer care and concern to colleagues, clients and customers. In sum, this approach utilizes Hochschild's concept of the commodification of feeling in order to capture both the pains and pleasures of contemporary service work through an examination of its emotional content.

However, despite emotional labour becoming a (if not *the*) central vehicle for analysing workplace emotion, the concept is not without critique. Concern is expressed regarding Hochschild's one-dimensional approach, her potentially absolutist understanding of the colonization of workers' capacity to manage their emotions, and her ambiguity regarding the application of the concept (Ashforth and Humphrey, 1995; Bolton, 2005; Bolton and Boyd, 2003; Korczynski, 2002; Lewis, 2005). Indeed, ambiguity in the way the term emotional labour is defined and applied is the key to how the debate has evolved. Many writers, for instance, consider that the purchase of emotional labour power and its transformation into a commodity, as it is exchanged for a wage, is not confined to front-line service workers, or necessarily, the service sector itself and that certainly it need not be driven by profit (Brook, 2009; Harriss, 2002; Hearn, 1993; James, 1989; Smith, 1992; Taylor, 1998). In other words, we do not need to treat the emotion work of a public sector nurse any differently to that of a telesales operator working for a for-profit organization. These ambiguities are magnified when attempting to delineate what emotion can be regarded as a distinctive part of the labour process and what emotion is, and always has been, part of organizational life. The term emotional labour has been applied to any sort of workplace relations, those of manager and subordinate, or group membership, for instance – in effect, any and every type of emotion in organizations. It is difficult to know how we can expect one concept to do so much and yet retain any form of analytical rigour.

These ambiguities are also represented in the most recent subplot to emotional labour. What has become known as 'affective labour' (Hardt and Negri, 2000, 2005), repeats and embellishes Hochschild's concerns with management attempts to seduce employees into committing all to the company, its product and its customers (Carls, 2007; Harriss, 2002; Hopfl, 2002; Hughes, 2003). This increasingly popular analytical trend, though rarely empirically supported, does not recognize a distinct emotional labour process – labour power is situated in a 'non-place', as production and consumption blends together into 'immaterial labour' (Carls, 2007; Hardt and Negri, 2000; Lazzarato, 2004; O'Doherty and Willmott, 2001). As a result, affective labourers are seen as mere simulacrums, empty shells of humanity who produce nothing but a marketable self: self-monitored, self-controlled within a totalizing discourse of global capitalism (Cremin, 2003; Hopfl, 2002; Hughes, 2003; Lazzarato, 2004; Ritzer, 1999). Such an emphasis on immateriality, from various quarters, but representing the same retreat from a 'politics of civil society' (Thompson, 2005), has lead to claims that we live in a postemotional (Meštrović, 1997), sentimentalized (Anderson and Mullen, 1998), McDonaldized (Ritzer, 1996), Disneyized (Bryman, 1999), even 'post-ironic' (Cremin, 2003), society and some wait with excited anticipation for the 'posthuman' body to emerge (Hardt and Negri, 2000). In what can only be described as a 'discourse of despair' (Thompson and Smith, 2001), a materialist analysis of emotion at work has been selectively misshapen into an immaterial form and it becomes impossible to identify what is emotional labour and what is not.

What this condensed review tells us is that the debate on emotional labour covers a broad terrain, with a range of conceptual and empirical foci offering different insights and perspectives on the nature of the emotional labour process. However, what it also tells us is that having spent 30 years debating the concept of emotion as a commodity in the shape of emotional labour, and despite many studies interested in the lived reality of the day-to-day experiences of those involved in various emotional labour processes, we are left with a dominant focus on identity rather than labour (ibid.). The inherent ambiguities in the use of the term emotional labour (and, more recently, affective labour) have contributed greatly to the lack of clarity in contemporary approaches to understanding new forms of work. These ambiguities are fundamentally problematic in that they undermine the agency and indeterminacy involved in the emotional labour process in two ways: first, they devalue the work involved in emotional labour by not carefully defining what it is and what it does and, second, they have muddied the conceptual waters by confusing appropriation of potential labour power with an appropriation of identity. LPT can help to introduce conceptual clarity by placing analytical boundaries around the emotional labour process. These boundaries emphasize emotion work and emotional labour as hard and productive work, with irregular and often unintended consequences. They define the motivations and outcomes of different labour processes in different contexts. They also highlight that offering emotion work as productive labour does not negate our capacity to offer emotion work to friends, family and colleagues.

The emotional labour process

Whilst staying loyal to its critical materialist roots, LPT has continually evolved and has proved adept at capturing the changing nature of work, workers and workplaces. It is its ability to ride various 'waves' of organizational analysis (Thompson and Newsome, 2004) that enables LPT to introduce some clarity into the ongoing debate on emotions at work and resolve the ambiguities of what is or is not emotional labour (Bolton, 2005). The term *emotional labour process* is used as a descriptive device to denote the distinctive qualities of labour processes where a core function is emotion work – rather than those that mainly consist of physical and/or mental labour. Moreover, such an analytical distinction does not attempt to separate the physical and emotional elements of work into the material and immaterial; they are integral to each other: we buy an insurance policy over the telephone or a dress over the shop counter and we expect the transaction to be fuelled by friendly exchange: the ubiquitous 'service with a smile'; we need intimate bodily care at vulnerable points in our lives and we expect, and hope, that this 'service' will be delivered with good humour and respect for our humanity (Bolton,

2007; Lawler, 1991; Lee-Treweek, 1997; Toynbee, 2007). Ask both the deliverers and receivers of such services and you will receive clear answers concerning the very real nature and affect of the physical and, most especially, the emotion work involved in the final product (Bolton, 2002, 2007; Bolton and Houlihan, 2005; Callaghan and Thompson, 2002; Gatta, 2009). However, what appears not to be recognized in the wide use of the term emotional labour is that these emotional labour processes take place within different occupations and within different sectors. There are two key issues: Is every worker an emotional labourer? And is every workplace emotion emotional labour? To address these I will exemplify how analytical boundaries can be drawn around the emotional labour process.

Who are emotional labourers?

LPT refers to theories of the labour process and draws important distinctions between a labour process whose activity is aimed at increasing capital through the creation of surplus value (emotional labour) and a labour process involving purposive activity that prioritizes the meeting of human needs rather than profit (emotion work) (Bolton, 2009b; Marx, 1976; Thompson, 1989). Such a distinction can be further elaborated to highlight the control and deskilling tendencies inherent in different ways in different labour processes, and displays how some occupations are able to exert greater discretion in their work than others (Braverman, 1974; Edwards, 1979). And, finally, a focus on the actual demands of different emotional labour processes shows us how care, concern, the production of smiles, or certain modes of presentation of self are an essential and explicit demand from employers in some occupations (i.e. front-line service sector jobs = emotional labour), whereas for others they are an implicit part of what it is to be a professional (i.e. doctors, nurses = emotion work): an (often) unwritten, and unrewarded, expectation (i.e. care work = emotion work), or not actually critical to getting the job done (i.e. lawyer, manager = emotion work). Elsewhere I have referred to *presentational, prescriptive, pecuniary* and *philanthropic* as different forms of emotion management which serves to highlight that there are many labour processes involving the exchange of labour for a wage that requires some form of emotion work, but with very different motivations, processes and outcomes (Bolton, 2005). For instance, by enabling analytical distinction between emotion work and emotional labour, LPT is able to capture the nuances of the full spectrum of emotional labour processes – those of a nurse and retail assistant, for example, or those of a lawyer and telesales agent.

Emotional labour remains a useful description for a capitalist labour process that relies heavily on emotion work. It emphasizes how emotion is utilized as a resource for capital and thus brings attention to attempts to harness its potential through the division of labour and the application of new technologies. In addition, it highlights how imposed scripts and impossible targets, in addition to the unequal social exchange of a service encounter, create a distorted relationship between customer and service provider. For a detailed example of how this is played out in action we can return to Hochschild, who questions what happens 'when deep gestures of exchange enter the market sector' (1983: 86) and goes on to argue that when emotion work becomes another aspect of saleable labour power, then feelings become 'commoditized'. Indeed, let us return to her original conception of emotional labour and its distinct qualities: control over employees' emotional activities, face-to-face contact with customers, and the production of an emotional state desired by the organization; all underpinned by a profit motive (ibid.: 147). Using air cabin crew as an example, Hochschild shows how feelings are induced or suppressed so that they match the airline's advertised image, thus giving the company a competitive edge and selling to customers on the strength of the quality of service they deliver. It could be said that the profitable product manufactured by cabin crew is 'passenger contentment' (Bolton and Boyd, 2003; Hochschild, 1983).[1]

Much in the same way as the cabin crew, Gatta's vivid description of the work of waiting staff exemplifies the multifaceted nature of work that involves emotional labour, along with clear statements regarding the restaurant server's recognition of it as hard and demanding physical, mental and emotional work – as Gatta states, it involves a balancing of trays and smiles:

> It is 8.30 on a Saturday night. The restaurant is on a 20 minute wait and you are 'in the weeds'; all your tables need something and you have to determine how to get everything done. Table number 601 needs a beer; 602 asked for their check five minutes ago; you still have to put 603's order into the micro-computers. ... Finally, table 605 has been waiting 33 minutes for their meal. You have been working since noon without a formal break. ... You go over to 605 to apologise for their meal delay and tell them the manager will buy them a round of drinks for their inconvenience. However, the free drinks do not make things better and instead the customer starts yelling at you. ... This makes you angry, but you have to maintain your composure. You still have to bring their food out; put other tables' orders in; and, of course, you can't forget to fill the ice ... (Gatta, 2009: 114)

Turning to a very different occupation within a very different sector (though both described as front-line service sector work), in her experiences of work in 'low paid Britain', Polly Toynbee worked as a care assistant in a care home for the elderly. Her experience of working as a care assistant was of 'demanding' and 'exhausting' work which was a complex combination of physical and emotional work. Toynbee (2007: 239) reflects on her time as a care assistant:

> It was emotionally draining work, hurrying from drama to drama, from one suffering and demanding person to another, torn between pity, anxiety and irritation. It had its rewards when a resident smiled and expressed pleasure or gratitude, when you had the time to do something extra, to listen to them and talk for a while. ... But I doubt this is work many would choose if they had real choice. ... I left Margaret, Minnie, Paula, Mrs Knightsbridge and all the rest, but they haunted me for weeks, daytime ghosts. It was more demanding work than the school kitchen, since the scrubbing of inanimate pots and pans was nothing compared to the washing of fragile old people with raw sores on their legs, who winced at the pain. The strain of engaging emotionally with all that misery was exhausting. The kindness and hard work of the care assistants here was worth far more than they were paid. But this is unseen, unmentionable labour, hidden away in these human oubliettes we would rather not think about.

Toynbee's vivid description highlights the rigours of this particular emotional labour process and its productive potential: clean, pain-free bodies, contentment and well-being. Much of the emotion work delivered as part of this labour process is not normally explicitly demanded in the job description, but is a taken-for-granted aspect of care work that represents the demands of society rather than demands of capital. As emotions in the labour process are part of the previously described spectrum, that may change according to new conditions or actors' strategies.

Is every workplace emotion emotional labour?

What of defining emotion in and out of the emotional labour process? Emotion work creates the social relations necessary for production and should be analysed and valued as such, but that does not necessarily mean it is part of every labour process in the same way or, indeed, as part of the labour process at all. LPT explores the analytical boundaries of the emotional labour process in its understanding of how labour is not just an instrumental activity but a social one, as it involves and sustains relations with others. The labour process is mediated through human action. Hence, our friendships at work, and our interactions with colleagues and managers, may act to support the emotional labour process but are not part of it and are not emotional labour.

That is not to say that what is classified as part of the emotional labour process has been entirely captured. Through what has become known as the 'indeterminacy of labour', LPT examines the very human struggles within the employment relationship (Ackroyd and Thompson, 1999; Thompson and Smith, 2001, 2009). Struggles that centre on labour power as a capacity to labour that is only ever partially realized. Emotional labour, unlike many labour processes, involves the direct transformation of the object by the worker, that is, a feeling, a mood, an atmosphere. Of course, there is a control imperative implicit in the emotional labour process and there are processes of routinization at play, and efforts made to tightly control emotion work and render it predictable, but this simply cannot have the same consequences as a factory model of production. Emotional labourers possess the ability to offer empty performances or to invest interaction with feeling; the capacity to care and yet to shape that into the labour process; the potential to deeply affect the 'product', that is, customers, clients, and so on, and be affected by it (Bolton, 2005, 2009b). And the interesting thing, and what is most neglected in much of the literature on emotional labour, is that workers are fully aware of this and recognize the productive potential of their own emotional labour power – they state that they 'work hard' (physically and emotionally); that it takes 'effort' to smile at customers and/or to mask repugnance or disdain; that they exercise 'skill and discretion' in the management of feeling; that they find their work 'rewarding' or 'exhausting' or 'demanding', or all of these in combination (Bolton and Boyd, 2003; Bolton and Houlihan, 2005; Hochschild, 1983; Paules, 1996; Seymour and Sandiford, 2005; Toynbee, 2007). In other words, they recognize emotion work as *work* and are fully aware of the effort involved to create the affect desired by the organization.

LPT is well placed to shed light on the peculiarities of what has become known as the 'emotional effort bargain' (Bolton and Boyd, 2003; Callaghan and Thompson, 2002; Sharma and Black, 2001; Taylor, 1998). It accepts conflict as an inherent part of the employment relationship and recognizes that management control regimes are unlikely ever to be completely successful in securing the full compliance of labour; an approach that is particularly useful when considering the emotional labour process. If management in the past have experienced difficulty in fully utilizing the physical labour of employees, how much more onerous is their task of controlling emotional labour? The realization that organizational emotion is not a space empty of humanity means that we can think about the emotional labour process in new ways. We frequently hear of call centre workers, waitresses and fast-food workers resisting the strictures of enforced customer interaction in a myriad of ways. They may set out to deliberately disrupt the carefully preserved emotional climate of servitude, as highlighted by Paules' waitresses who refuse to be denied 'the courtesies of personhood' (Paules, 1996: 266). Or there are those who, more subtly, withdraw their emotion work and only ever present a hollow smile, if a smile at all; as a sample of trainee hairdressers state 'you plaster a false smile on your face, grin and bear it' (Parkinson, 1991: 430), and similarly a Delta Airline stewardess describes her job as being an 'illusion maker' (Hochschild, 1983: 127). Or for many service workers, rather than withdrawal, they actually offer more than scripted interaction would normally allow. For instance, a debt collector may show a sympathetic face to a client rather than the prescribed aggressive one (Bolton and Houlihan, 2005; Sutton, 1991); an air stewardess may retain some autonomy in how she/he provides customer contentment and gains satisfaction from providing that 'little extra' (Bolton and Boyd, 2003; Hochschild, 1983; Tyler and Taylor, 1998), and a call centre worker, whilst aware of the pressure of performance targets, maintains the social elements of customer interaction (Callaghan and Thompson, 2002).

All of these twists and turns within the emotional labour process represent a form of systematic soldiering, or 'micro-emancipation' (Sotirin and Gottfried, 1999), but in terms of what we offer emotionally rather than physically. And what is also notable in these accounts is the constant referral to the nature and demands of the work involved, indicating that the 'struggles' involved in the emotional effort bargain may involve questions of identity but they also represent a measured approach to just how much of our labour power we are prepared to invest in the emotional labour process. The customer service representative cited below displays this very well as she negotiates her own effort bargain:

> A big thing is, in the job that we do, you're there for two reasons – you're there because you want to give people a service and you're there because you want to earn money. I used to like my job, when it was a slower pace, letting them lose the calls rather than rush, doing it properly. At the end of the day, they are such a big company they should have extra staff in to deal with the queues. But they don't, and the game is to get through it quickly. And now they've changed the bonus structure so it's how many calls in an hour you can get a sale out of. And when it's so many an hour, I have to think 'one for them, one for me'. And quality goes out the window. I think people like me are finding it very difficult, because you *do* care about the person on the other end of the phone. ... But now I have to just sit there and think, 'I need the money'. (Diane, CSR – Quotes Direct, in Bolton and Houlihan, 2005)

What also needs to be questioned is just how much effort is actually being demanded of employees in the emotional effort bargain. Despite talk of either the colonization of our emotions by organizations or the emancipation of emotional withdrawal, when discussing the emotional investment required of service work (and that which is delivered) we must question just how much sincerity is actually required or indeed invited. Interaction with customers is so brief and the business at hand so tedious that investment in the performance is hardly necessary. A perfunctory politeness will fuel such brief interludes towards successful completion. Customers neither want nor expect to enter into the game of social interaction and organizations show a larger regard for quantity of sales interactions rather than quality of emotional encounters (Korczynski et al., 2000). Hence front-line service workers draw on scripts and routines and answer telephone queries about bank balances whilst also thinking about calling in at the supermarket on the way home, and they serve children their 'happy meals' with a smiling face but are all the while planning their own happy pursuits later in the day.

Clearly, service workers, though aware of the material demands made of them by the emotional labour process, reinterpret encounters with customers and clients depending upon context and different motivations. Just as in physical labour, there is a large element of indeterminacy in how their labour power will be realized. Whilst they may have little influence over the setting of the stage on which they must carry out their work role, service workers are, nevertheless, an active and controlling force in the service encounter (Paules, 1996) and, as a result, the emotional labour process remains a contested terrain (Callaghan and Thompson, 2002; Edwards, 1979).

Old ambiguities, new developments

The aim of this chapter has been to offer some much needed conceptual clarity to the ongoing emotional labour debate. It has attempted to do this by utilizing LPT to emphasize emotion work as hard and productive *work* that involves an emotional labour process which relies on the realization of our labour power. It has also offered a context-specific understanding by drawing on theories of the labour process and emphasizing the differences between the performance of emotional labour that contributes directly to the accumulation of capital, and emotion work that does not – an important distinction if we are to understand the motivations, pressures and outcomes of the full spectrum of different emotional labour processes. How can we possibly analyse the emotional labour processes of lawyers, senior managers, telesales agent or care workers in the same way?

Nevertheless, regardless of whether we are a waitress or a care worker, empirical examples cited in the chapter serve to remind us that labour power is the capacity of living labour to labour, thus it is indeterminate. Of course, in the LPT tradition, we need to recognize the control imperative inherent in the labour process and that this indeterminacy may be played out in different ways depending on one's occupation and relative autonomy and discretion.

For example, for many front-line service workers there are very real reasons why selectively packaged emotional displays might be the order of the day. First, most emotion workers and labourers are not offering bespoke services to individual customers and clients – as may fit with the craft work analogy of the professions (Bolton and Houlihan, 2009a; Warhurst, Thompson and Nickson, 2008). Shop-workers, care assistants, waiting staff and telesales agents, who have been described as the 'emotional proletariat' (Macdonald and Sirianni, 1996), dip in and out of routine encounters all day, every day. They neither have the time, nor the inclination, to offer personalized service and view the perfunctory nature of the social exchanges involved in their work as something of a blessing (Bolton and Houlihan, 2005; Leidner, 1996; Paules, 1996). Nevertheless, as with the physical labour process they are able to wriggle and squirm within its confines and, despite processes of deskilling, routinization and control, actually reshape the product in some way (as the examples given above amply display). Second, do we, as consumers, want emotional involvement in every encounter? In fact, it is clear that we do not and management do not set out to create it (Bolton and Houlihan, 2005). Fast and furious is the order of the day and many well-known companies have built their reputation and success on the delivery of routinized niceness. Third, there are ample accounts that show management know their limitations and are quite prepared to work within them (Houlihan, 2002; Taylor, 1998). Turnover in the front-line service and care sectors is high, in some cases reaching more than 50 per cent (*The Sunday Times*, 2005), and whilst organizations might create 'fun' environments in an effort to foster involvement and team spirit it is also recognized that the work is demanding and that tired, bored and disillusioned employees will move to pastures new (Bolton and Houlihan, 2009b). In what Chris Smith describes as the 'double indeterminacy of labour' (Smith, 2006), this certainly represents signs of active agency on the part of employees but also on the part of management as they accept that, despite recruiting for the right attitude, no matter what prescriptions they put in place the material realities of the emotional labour process for employees mean their retention figures will be low (Callaghan and Thompson, 2002; Toynbee, 2007).

Applying LPT to an analysis of the emotional labour process reveals that it is the very absence of structural considerations, such as sector and labour market issues, and lack of acknowledgement of actual workplace experience that renders current analyses of emotional labour ineffectual. The labour process is used to shape our labour power into a commodity form. It is, however, also a social relationship with all of its creativity and also all of its unpredictability. This is never more apparent than when the commodity to be exchanged is our emotional labour power. Contributions to the ongoing emotional labour debate approach the topic in different ways, but ambiguities concerning necessary analytical boundaries around the emotional labour process have tended to reduce the complexity, negotiation and politics involved in the process of work into a one-dimensional focus on the management of identity. No doubt within such a complex debate ambiguities will remain, but it is the hope that developments supported by LPT offer a welcome alternative; drawing our attention to the material realities of contemporary work and putting agency at the centre of an analysis of the emotional labour process.

Note

1   It is true, however, that her account of what is and is not emotional labour tends to be a little contradictory. In *Managed Heart,* she states that jobs such as 'the social worker, the day-care provider, the doctor and the lawyer' are not emotional labourers due to the level of control they have over how emotional labour is performed (Hochschild, 1983: 153) and yet in her afterword to the twentieth-century anniversary edition she talks of nurses, professors and police detectives carrying out emotional labour (2003: 200).

REFERENCES

Ackroyd, S. and Thompson, P. (1999) *Organizational (Mis)Behaviour,* London: Sage.

Anderson, D. and Mullen, P. (1998) *Faking It: The Sentimentalisation of Modern Society,* London: The Social Affairs Unit.

Ashforth, B. and Humphrey, R. (1993) 'Emotional Labor in Service Roles: The Influence of Identity', *Academy of Management Review,* 18: 88–115.

Ashforth, B. and Humphrey, R. (1995) 'Emotion in the Workplace: A Reappraisal', *Human Relations,* 48(2): 97–125.

Ashkanasy, N., Zerbe, W. and Hartel, C. (2002) *Managing Emotions in the Workplace,* London: Sharpe.

Bolton, S. (2002) 'Consumer as King in the NHS', *The International Journal of Public Sector Management,* 15(2): 129–39.

Bolton, S. (2004) 'Conceptual Confusions: Emotion Work as Skilled Work', in Warhurst, C., Keep, E. and Grugulis, I. (eds) *The Skills That Matter,* London: Palgrave, 19–37.

Bolton, S. (2005) *Emotion Management in the Workplace,* London: Palgrave.

Bolton, S. (2007) 'Me, Morphine and Humanity: Eight Days on Ward 8', in Fineman, S. (ed.) *The Emotional Organisation: Critical Voices,* London: Blackwell, 15–26.

►

▶

Bolton, S. (2009a) 'The Lady Vanishes: Women's Work and Affective Labour', *International Journal of Work Organization and Emotion*, 3(1): 72–80.

Bolton, S. (2009b) 'Getting to the Heart of the Emotional Labour Process: A Reply to Brooke', *Work, Employment and Society*, 24(3): 549–60.

Bolton, S. and Boyd, C. (2003) 'Trolley Dolly or Skilled Emotion Manager?', *Work, Employment and Society*, 17(2): 289–308.

Bolton, S. and Houlihan, M. (2005) 'The (Mis)representation of Customer Service', *Work, Employment and Society*, 19(4): 685–703.

Bolton, S. and Houlihan, M. (2009a) 'Work, Workers and Workplaces', in Bolton, S. and Houlihan, M. (eds) *Work Matters*, London: Palgrave, 1–20.

Bolton, S. and Houlihan, M. (2009b) 'Are We Having Fun Yet? A Consideration of Workplace Fun and Engagement', *Employee Relations*, 31(6).

Braverman, H. (1974) *Labor and Monopoly Capital*, New York: Monthly Review Press.

Brook, P. (2009) 'In Critical Defence of Emotional Labour', *Work, Employment and Society*, 24(3): 531–48.

Brotheridge, C. and Lee, R. (2003) 'Development and Validation of the Emotional Labour Scale', *Journal of Occupational and Organizational Psychology*, 73: 365–79.

Bryman, A. (1999) 'The Disneyization of Society', *The Sociological Review*, 47(1): 26–47.

Callaghan, G. and Thompson, P. (2002) 'We Recruit Attitude: The Selection and Shaping of Routine Call Centre Labour', *Journal Management Studies*, 39(2): 233–53.

Carls, K. (2007) 'Affective Labour in Milanese Large Scale Retailing', *Ephemera*, 7(1): 46–59.

Cremin, C. S. (2003) 'Self-starters, Can-doers and Mobile Phoneys: Situations Vacant Column and the Personality Culture in Employment', *Sociological Review*, 51(1): 109–28.

Dutton, J., Worline, M., Frost, P. and Lilius, J. (2006) 'Explaining Passion Organizing', *Administrative Science Quarterly*, 51(1): 59–96.

Edwards, R. (1979) *Contested Terrain: The Transformation of the Workplace in the Twentieth Century*, London: Heinemann.

Fine, G. A. (1988) 'Letting Off Steam? Redefining a Restaurant's Work Environment', in Jones, M., Moore, M. and Snyder, R. (eds) *Inside Organizations: Understanding the Human Dimension*, Newbury Park, CA: Sage Publications.

Fineman, S. (2005) 'Appreciating Emotion at Work: Paradigm Tensions', *International Journal Work, Organisation and Emotion*, 1(1): 4–18.

Fineman, S. and Sturdy, A. (1999) 'The Emotions of Control: A Qualitative Study of Environmental Regulation', *Human Relations*, 52(5): 631–63.

Fredrickson, B. (2003) 'Positive Emotions and Upward Spirals in Organizations', in Cameron, K., Dutton, J. and Quinn, R. (eds) *Positive Organizational Scholarship: Foundations of a New Discipline*, San Francisco, CA: Berrett-Koehler.

Frost, P. (2004) 'Handling Toxic Emotions: New Challenges for Leaders and Their Organization', *Organizational Dynamics*, 33(2): 111–27.

▶

▶

Gatta, M. (2009) 'Balancing Trays and Smiles', in Bolton, S. and Houlihan, M. (eds) *Work Matters*, London: Palgrave, 114–28.

Goffman, E. (1967) *Interaction Ritual: Essays in Face-To-Face Behaviour,* Chicago, IL: Aldine Publishing Company.

Hardt, M. and Negri, A. (2000) *Empire*, Harvard, MA: University of Harvard Press.

Hardt, M. and Negri, A. (2005) *Multitude*, Hamish Hamilton: London.

Harriss, L. C. (2002) 'The Emotional Labour of Barristers', *Journal of Management Studies*, 39(4): 553–84.

Hearn, J. (1993) 'Emotive Subjects: Organizational Men, Organizational Masculinities and the (De)construction of Emotions', in Fineman, S. (ed.) *Emotion in Organizations,* London: Sage, 142–66.

Hochschild, A. (1979) 'Emotion Work, Feeling Rules, and Social Structure', *American Journal of Sociology,* 85(3): 551–75.

Hochschild, A. (1983) *The Managed Heart: Commercialization of Human Feeling,* Berkeley: University of California Press.

Hochschild, A. (2003) *The Managed Heart: Commercialization of Human Feeling* (20th anniversary edition), Berkeley: University of California Press.

Holman, D., Chissick, C. and Totterdell, P. (2002) 'The Effects of Performance Monitoring on Emotional Labour and Well-being in Call Centres', *Motivation and Emotion*, 26(1): 57–81.

Hopfl, H. (2002) 'Playing the Part: Reflections of Aspects of Mere Performance in the Customer-Client Relationship', *Journal of Management Studies*, 39(2): 255–67.

Houlihan, M. (2002) 'Tensions and Variations in Management Strategies in Call Centres', *Human Resource Management Journal*, 12(4): 67–86.

Hughes, J. (2003) 'Bringing Emotion to Work: Emotional Intelligence, Employee Resistance and the Reinvention of Character', *Work, Employment and Society*, 19(3): 603–25.

James, N. (1989) 'Emotional Labour: Skill and Work in the Social Regulation of Feeling', *Sociological Review,* 37(1): 15–42.

Junor, A., Hampson, I. and Robyn Ogle, K. (2009) 'Vocabularies of Skill', in Bolton, S. and Houlihan, M. (eds) *Work Matters*, London: Palgrave, 197–215.

Korczynski, M. (2002) *Human Resource Management in Service Work*, London: Palgrave.

Korczynski, M., Shire, K., Frenkel, S. and Tam, M. (2000) 'Service Work in Consumer Capitalism: Customers, Control and Contradictions', *Work, Employment and Society*, 14(4), 669–87.

Lawler, J. (1991) *Behind the Screens: Nursing, Somology, and the Problem of the Body*, Melbourne: Churchill Livingstone.

Lazzarato, M. (2004) 'From Capital-Labour to Capital-Life', *Ephemera*, 43(3): 187–208: http://www.ephemeraweb.org/journal/4-3/4-3lazzarato.pdf.

Lee-Treweek, G. (1997) 'Women, Resistance and Care: An Ethnographic Study of Nursing Auxiliary Work', *Work, Employment and Society,* 11(1): 47–63.

Leidner, R. (1996) 'Rethinking Questions of Control: Lessons from McDonald's', in Macdonald, C. and Sirianni, C. (eds) *Working in the Service Society*, Philadelphia, PA: Temple University Press.

▶

▶

Lewis, P. (2005) 'Suppression or Expression: An Exploration of Emotion Management in a Special Care Baby Unit', *Work, Employment and Society,* 19(3): 565–81.

Macdonald, C. and Sirianni, C. (eds) (1996) *Working in the Service Society,* Philadelphia, PA: Temple University Press.

Marx, K. (1976) *Capital Volume 1,* London: Penguin.

Meštrović, S. G. (1997) *Postemotional Society,* London: Sage.

Morris, J. A. and Feldman, D. C. (1996) 'The Dimensions, Antecedents and Consequences of Emotional Labor', *Academy of Management Review,* 21(4): 986–1000.

O'Doherty, D. and Willmott, H. (2001) 'Debating Labour Process Theory: The Issue of Subjectivity and the Relevance of Poststructuralism', *Sociology,* 35(3): 457–76.

Parkinson, B. (1991) 'Emotional Stylists: Strategies of Expressive Management among Trainee Hairdressers', *Cognition and Emotion,* 5: 419–34.

Paules, G. (1996) 'Resisting the Symbolism of Service', in Macdonald, C. and Sirianni, C. (eds) *Working in the Service Society,* Philadelphia, PA: Temple University Press.

Ritzer, G. (1996) *The Mcdonaldization of Society* (Revised Edition), California: Pine Forge Press.

Ritzer, G. (1999) *Enchanting a Disenchanted World,* California: Pine Forge Press.

Seymour, D. and Sandiford, P. (2005) 'Learning Emotion Rules in Service Organizations', *Work, Employment and Society,* 19(3): 547–64.

Sharma, U. and Black, P. (2001) 'Look Good, Feel Better: Beauty Therapy as Emotional Labour', *Sociology,* 35(4): 913–31.

Shuler, S. and Davenport, S. (2000) 'Seeking Emotional Labour', *Management Communication Quarterly,* 14(1): 50–89.

Smith, C. (2006) 'The Double Indeterminacy of Labour Power: Labour Effort and Labour Mobility', *Work, Employment and Society,* 20(2): 389–402.

Smith, P. (1992) *The Emotional Labour of Nursing,* London: Macmillan.

Sosteric, M. (1996) 'Subjectivity and the Labour Process: A Case Study in the Restaurant Industry', *Work, Employment and Society,* 19(2): 297–318.

Sotirin, P. and Gottfried, H. (1999) 'The Ambivalent Dynamics of Secretarial Bitching: Control, Resistance, and the Construction of Identity', *Organization,* 6(1): 57–80.

Steinberg, R. and Figart, D. (1999) 'Emotional Labour Since the Managed Heart', *ANNALS, AAPSS,* 561: 8–26.

Sturdy, A. (1998) 'Customer Care in a Consumer Society: Smiling and Sometimes Meaning It?', *Organization,* 5(1): 27–53.

Sturdy, A. and Fineman, S. (2001) 'Struggles for the Control of Affect', in Sturdy, A., Grugulis, I. and Willmott, H. (eds) *Customer Service: Empowerment and Entrapment,* Basingstoke: Palgrave, 140–56.

Sunday Times 100 Best Companies to Work For (2005) Published with the Sunday Times on 6 March 2005.

Sutton, R. I. (1991) 'Maintaining Norms about Expressed Emotions: The Case of Bill Collectors', *Administrative Science Quarterly,* 36: 245–68.

▶

▶

Taylor, S. (1998) 'Emotional Labour and the New Workplace', in Thompson, P. and Warhurst, C. (eds) *Workplaces of the Future,* Basingstoke: Macmillan, 84–103.

The Project on Disney (1995) *Inside the Mouse: Work and Play at Disney World,* Durham: Duke University Press.

Thompson, P. (1989) *The Nature of Work,* London: Macmillan.

Thompson, P. (2005) 'Foundation and Empire: A Critique of Hardt and Negri', *Capital and Class,* 86: 39–64.

Thompson, P. and Newsome, K. (2004) 'Labour Process Theory, Work and the Employment Relation', in Kaufman, B. (ed.) *Theoretical Perspectives on Work and the Employment Relation,* Illinois: Industrial Relations Research Assoc, 133–62.

Thompson, P. and Smith, C. (2001) 'Follow the Redbrick Road: Reflections on Pathways in and out of the Labour Process Debate', *International Studies of Management and Organization,* 30(4): 40–67.

Thompson, P. and Smith, C. (2009) 'Labour Power and Labour Process: Contesting the Marginality of the Sociology of Work', *Sociology,* 43(5): 913–30.

Toynbee, P. (2007) 'Rethinking Humanity in Care Work – Extract from *Hardwork: Life in Low-Pay Britain*', in Bolton, S. and Houlihan, M. (eds) *Searching for the Human in Human Resource Management,* London: Palgrave, 219–43.

Tyler, M. and Taylor, S. (1998) 'The Exchange of Aesthetics: Women's Work and "the Gift" ', *Gender, Work and Organization,* 5(3): 165–71.

Van Maanen, J. (1991) 'The Smile Factory: Work at Disneyland', in Frost, P., Moore, L., Luis, M., Lundberg, C. and Martin, J. (eds) *Reframing Organizational Culture,* California: Sage.

Warhurst, C. and Thompson, P. (1998) 'Hand, Hearts and Minds', in Thompson, P. and Warhurst, C. (eds) *Workplaces of the Future,* Basingstoke: Macmillan.

Warhurst, C., Thompson, P. and Nickson, D. (2008) 'Labour Process Theory: Putting the Materialism Back into the Meaning of Service Work', in Korczynski, M. and MacDonald, C. (eds) *Service Work: Critical Perspectives,* London: Routledge.

Weatherly, K. and Tansik, D. (1992) 'Tactics Used by Customer-Contact Workers: Effects of Role Stress, Boundary Spanning and Control', *International Journal of Service Industry Management,* 4(3): 4–17.

Wellington, C. A. and Bryson, J. (2001) 'At Face Value? Image Consultancy, Emotional Labour and Professional Work', *Sociology,* 35(4): 933–46.

Wharton, A. (1996) 'Service with a Smile: Understanding the Consequences of Emotional Labour', in MacDonald, C. and Sirianni, C. (eds) *Working in the Service Society,* Philadelphia, PA: Temple University Press.

Wharton, A. and Erickson, R. (1993) 'Managing Emotions on the Job and at Home', *Academy of Management Review,* 18(3): 457–86.

Whyte, W. (1948) *Human Relations in the Restaurant Industry,* New York: McGraw-Hill.

Williams, C. (2003) 'Sky Service: The Demands of Emotional Labour in the Airline Industry', *Gender, Work and Organisation,* 10(5): 513–50.

Zapf, D. (2002) 'Emotion Work and Psychological Well-being', *Human Resource Management Review,* 12: 237–68.

Embodying Labour

11

Carol Wolkowitz and Chris Warhurst

Although sometimes featuring in studies of the labour process, embodied labour has not been foregrounded in labour process theory (LPT) – which is in some ways surprising and certainly in need of rectifying. The concern of LPT with workers' perspectives, and its detailed understanding of the ways in which the demands of capital accumulation impact on them, ought to provide ample opportunities for the analysis of embodied labour. Indeed, over the years many accounts of the labour process that draw on workers' own words, from Terkel (1974) to Sennett (2008), convey a vivid sense of the embodied nature of labour and that labour's effects on the body. Perhaps the most vivid is Nichols and Beynon's chemical plant worker who, reflecting on his company's job enrichment programme, stated, 'I never feel "enriched" – I just feel knackered' (1977: 16). Whilst discussion of bodily being and bodily labour in the sociological understanding of employment is growing, in LPT the bodily character of labour and conflicts over the control of the body per se have been given relatively little attention.

While there is no insuperable reason why LPT prevents recognition and analysis of the embodiment of labour, the reasons for its absence first need to be unpacked, as do recent empirical developments that indicate how LPT could benefit from foregrounding that labour. In this chapter we seek to draw attention to the ways in which the organization and control of the labour process are in part shaped around the human body, conceptions of its malleability and the ways that employers seek to profit from workers' bodies. Moreover, we indicate the new labour processes that are emerging as reproductive labour is transmuted into productive labour, which in turn contributes to the blurring of efforts within and outside the labour process to make up workers' bodies.

The attempt to embody labour is made easier, and more necessary, by several developments. First, of course, the apparently escalating commodification of the body – whether in the media, the biological sciences or the labour market – is making the body more visible and more difficult to ignore. No doubt partly as a consequence, there is now a wider attempt (for instance, Orzeck, 2007) to bring together, if not reconcile, the project of historical materialism and an interest in the human body that has hitherto been associated mainly with post-structuralist approaches. Moreover, sociologists of the body, such as Shilling (2005), have begun addressing contemporary employment to a greater extent than hitherto.

The incorporation of embodied labour addresses problems with which LPT has long grappled. Because employers require workers' effort, stamina and many other embodied capacities, focusing on embodied labour necessarily also brings to the fore issues of control, consent and resistance within the employment relationship. However, workers' embodiment is also shaped by, for example, gender, ethnicity, sexuality, and hidden and visible disabilities, so considering labour as embodied labour also means facing the perpetual question of how far the pursuit of profit through the labour process necessarily intersects with other systems of power.

The chapter begins with a brief tracing of the issue of embodiment in the history of LPT. We then outline the contribution LPT can make to understanding embodied labour in the light of current development of the labour process. The chapter shows that recasting 'productive labour' as 'productive bodies' better opens up analysis of the labour process to embodied labour. The chapter then outlines how, as reproductive bodies, workers engage, outside the labour process, in bodily preparation for work, stressing, in addition, how much of this reproductive labour is being shifted into the domain of production. Finally, the chapter signals some key issues that require future research and exploration if embodied labour is to be better understood.

The body in the labour process

At first sight the relative neglect of embodiment in labour process analysis seems related to its interest in the deployment of labour power, that is, a socially constituted capacity (and a very abstract one at that) conceptually distinct from bodily labour. Labour power is generated as a commodity through the social relations of capitalism, whereas bodies, it is assumed, arise 'naturally'. In this line of reasoning, interest in the already-made body exists only in so far as it is positioned in, and in relation to, the capitalist labour process. However, Marx went much further: for him the body constitutes both the source of labour and, as an artefact of labour, its product (Scarry, 1985). Hence, for Marx, bodies are pre-eminently social creations. Harvey (1998) goes further, suggesting that because for Marx the body is a product of worlds without and within – a porous body, Marx's conceptionalization shows surprising parallels with the later post-structuralist rejection of the fixed, natural body. It, too, understands the body to be socially constructed, as Orzeck (2007) states, but through labour rather than through discourse.

The human body also appears in Braverman's (1974) attempt to update Marx's account of the labour process. While neither 'body' nor 'embodiment' appear in the index of *Labour and Monopoly Capital*, the early chapters do address in passing the relationship between the body and labour. Braverman starts with a picture of human labour as inherently different from the instinctual activities of animals because it has an intelligent and purposive character (1974: 31–2). This distinction is important to Braverman because he, as with Marx, conceives the development of industrial capitalism as hinging on the reduction of alienated human labour to mechanical repetitious movement. In tracing the history of Taylorism and Ford's assembly line, Braverman attempts to show that workers lose control not only over the full rewards of their labour but also, through the separation of conception and execution, the direction of the work, which is appropriated by managers. Whilst prior to scientific management the mental processes of conception and the physical labour of execution are integrated – indeed, managers initially access them by observing craftsmen at work – the differences between conception and execution were seen as inherent in purposive action. Hence, once planning and other mental functions are hived off, factory workers are left to carry out physical labour more or less 'blindly' (86). Influenced by Frederick Taylor's engineering background, workers' bodies become emptied vessels, stripped of thought and made to act like machines. And what was true of factory workers at the start of the twentieth century was extended to clerical workers later in that century with the rationalization of the office, Braverman forcibly argues.

Braverman's account has not provided a very hospitable basis for embodying labour. Of course, the mind-body dualism evident in this account (along with the even more fundamental conception of the body as a resource) is not perceived to be entirely 'natural' but, rather, as deeply embedded in the development of the capitalist labour process. However, since Braverman associates skill with the higher functions of mental labour, the body is cast as a lower, and analytically uninteresting, aspect of human existence. Braverman in a sense replicates, rather than challenges, scientific management's view of the mind-body relation. Of course, many labour process theorists never accepted Braverman's view of the total subordination of labour in the production process (see, e.g., Cressey and MacInnes, 1980) but neither do their accounts articulate the embodied character of workers' creativity or resistance.

These views of the body are very different from that projected in many current studies of embodiment, wherein the body is seen 'not just the executant of the goals we frame, nor just the locus of causal factors shaping our representations'; rather, 'our understanding is itself embodied' (C. Taylor, 1995: 170). Body studies explicitly foregrounds the body as the means by which we recognize, and are recognized by, others – as the way we are in the world (Crossley, 2001). Braverman's comparatively 'thin' view of the body may be one reason why some studies of bodies at work, such as Witz, Warhurst and Nickson (2003) or Wolkowitz (2006), have highlighted instead the potential contribution of Bourdieu, who sees knowledges of different kinds literally embodied as habitus, rather than as located in the brain. The issue that emerges, therefore, is the extent to which it is possible to integrate a fuller, richer view of the embodiment of work into understanding of the labour process without losing sight of the particular strengths of LPT.

Some other accounts of the formation of the productive bodies of manual labour have brought the body into view through historical analyses but in a way different from Braverman's, making the body much more central to their understanding of the labour process of the factory system and the discourse of scientific management. This difference is in part because they draw on Foucault's conceptions of power and surveillance. Whereas in Braverman it is the labour process that is controlled by the capitalist employer and which then shapes workers' bodily labour indirectly, the Foucauldian sees power operating directly on the body and, through the body, subjectivity. For instance, Bahnisch (2000) highlights, as did Thompson (1967) much earlier, the ways in which the factory system brought bodies together and organized them in time and space in ways that made direct surveillance possible. Whilst his starting position is similar to that of Braverman, Bahnisch instead considers Taylorism as a 'technology of power' that reflects the fear of, and seeks to discipline, anarchic, dangerous and threatening workers' bodies (2000:55). He sees the revamping of embodiment as lying at the heart of the scientific management of the labour process, arguing that 'Perhaps the most enduring legacy of Taylorism has been the alienation it has caused through reinscribing the binary opposition between the thinking, managerial mind and the working body' (ibid.: 65).

Another history of scientific management and Fordism is Yanarella and Reid's (1996) chapter of a volume devoted to illuminating 'the social and political body'. Whereas Braverman tends to see the distinction between mental and physical capacities as inherent in human labour, Yanarella and Reid see the capitalist labour process as continually constructing and reconstructing what they term the 'mind-body percept'. Yanarella and Reid argue that Taylorism *redrew* the boundaries between the human, the animal and the machine, intensifying work through the construction of a new 'body/machine complex'. Fordist production methods took Taylorism even further, 'dissect[ing] the factory organism into brain (management) and brawn or muscle (worker)' (Yanarella and Reid, 1996: 196). Referencing Gramsci's (1971) 'Americanism and Fordism', Yanarella and Reid also portray Fordism as seeking to contain sexual and other animalistic instincts, and subjecting the worker to careful monitoring, including the worker's personal hygiene and social habits. They then continue by discussing how the 'mind-body percept' has altered yet again, this time reuniting mind and body in what has been termed 'humanware'.

Changes in the labour process thus not only take account of, but also sometimes reconfigure the constitution of the body and embodied activity. However, it has to be said that these Foucauldian accounts of the body in the labour process come no closer to a rounded view of embodiment than Braverman. The reason is because Foucauldian accounts of employment often partake of a more general trend, criticized by Shilling (2005), of concentrating only on constraints on the body from outside it, rather than on the lived body from which we perceive, act and labour in the world. This problem is difficult to avoid even in non-Foucauldian formulations of the productive body.

Productive bodies

Some more recent analysis of the labour process has made reference to the body, some of it explicitly drawing upon LPT. We adopt the term 'productive bodies' in order to emphasize what foregrounding the body adds to LPT. By 'productive bodies' we mean embodied labour intended to produce a profit for the employer, rather than simply work that creates use-values.

This shift in emphasis from 'productive labour' to the 'productive body' highlights from the outset the gendering of both constructions. Moreover, feminist scholarship, has shown that perceptions of gendered bodily difference are involved in the exclusion or inclusion of women and men from particular jobs. For instance, Banta's (1993) historical account of the progressive standardization of workers' (and consumers') bodies in the US points out that American employers feared that women's temperamental 'wayward womanness' – evidenced in headaches, crying and 'the vapors' – could defeat the rational plans of early twentieth century scientific management. A more recent example is Elson and Pearson's (1981) influential account of world market factories' dependence on female labour. In this account, employers have more positive views of women's embodiment but are not less concerned with the bottom line. Elson and Pearson suggest that employers rely not only on the lower labour costs of female labour but are also influenced by 'a widespread belief that there is a "natural" differentiation between the innate [physical] capacities and personality traits of women and men' (92) – especially women's nimble-fingered manual dexterity.

Workers, too, have invested in the gendering of productive bodies and the privileges that this gendering offers them. The most obvious example occurs in Cockburn's (1983) account of the organization of labour processes in the British print industry, which makes explicit reference to bodily difference. In this industry, the labour process was designed around the bodies of the men who did the work. Cockburn's history of the industry notes male workers' (ultimately unsuccessful) struggle to retain the heavy broadsheet hot type and paper presses, which had evolved in relation to male workers' bodies and which therefore excluded the entry of women to the job. Later labour process analyses, such as that of West (1990), recognized that the sex typing of jobs in the industry, as outlined by Cockburn, might have been overcome by redesigning equipment but did not extend the logic of Cockburn's argument in a way that incorporated her appreciation that the existing – and any new – design centred partly on the productive *body*.

It is with the rise of the service economy that employers' use of the productive body, as opposed to simply productive labour, has become more salient in analyses of the labour process. A conceptual and empirical research trajectory is apparent in which it is recognized that employers affect to take control of not only workers' heads and then hearts but now also bodies. The analytical transition can be traced back to Hochschild's (1983) path-breaking *The Managed Heart* in which she identified the emotional labour demanded by many customer-oriented service sector jobs. Emotionality and emotional engagement are capacities previously confined to privatised, interpersonal relations – and a 'specialization' of women, she states. With emotional labour, the private becomes public and commodified, with 'the profit motive slipped in' (119). Whilst much of the subsequent research on emotional labour has focused on the management of feeling, Hochschild was very clear that this management requires 'a publicly observable facial and bodily display' (7). For Hochschild, therefore, emotional labour is also a form of embodied labour.

Hochschild implicitly recognized the existence of what Mills (1951) had identified as a 'personality market', that is, to the way workers in services develop and mobilize their attitudes and appearance in both the labour market and labour process. As Warhurst and Nickson (2009) point out, however, in the inchoate service culture of the 1950s, these workers did so with an absence of managerial intervention. By the time Hochschild published *The Managed Heart* in 1983, employers were clearly intervening more directly. Since then, employers have been increasingly attempting to harness and commodify bodily capacities and features, including the face, bodily comportment, dress and voice of workers in order to signal company product market position through, for example, stylishness and sexual appeal. As such, employers appear to be trying to embody the labour process in a more visible form than hitherto: workers have to be 'the animate component of...the corporate landscape' (Witz, Warhurst and Nickson, 2003: 44). The term 'aesthetic labour' is now frequently adopted to conceptualize employers' mobilization, development and commodification of those bodily capacities and attributes through recruitment, selection and training, and which are geared to producing an aesthetic 'style' of service and sensory experience in the encounter (Warhurst et al., 2000). This performative labour is in addition to the taxing, often skilful, physical bodily labour that many service sector jobs involve (Dutton et al., 2008; Gatta, 2009).

Bryman (2004) cites both emotional and aesthetic labour as 'the primary forms' (127) of the 'performative labour' of 'Disneyization' and recognizes that scientific management now prescribes the embodied interactions required by this labour in routinized service sector work. It is also telling that Bryman makes unreferenced links to labour process analysis in his use of secondary sources to support his claim of Disneyization. The strength of labour process analysis lies in prising open the analytical envelope to include the extent to which bodily display is consciously manipulated by employers. If once employers were exhorted by Frederick Taylor to affect a 'mental revolution' amongst factory workers (Taylor, 1947: 27), now employers seek a strategic 'corporeal (re)form' amongst some service workers. Taking the example of forms of sex at work, Warhurst and Nickson (2009) argue that a careful distinction needs to be made between, on the one hand, employee sexuality that employers consciously and systematically seek to determine in order to provide for a particular customer 'experience', giving employees instructions in comportment, dress and so on; and, on the other hand, forms of employee sexuality that employers sanction or subscribe to, but do not seek to manage. The implication is that only the former kind of sexualized work 'counts' as sexualized labour, and should be carefully distinguished from more general expressions of sexuality at work that simply reflect heterosexualized – for example – relations in the wider society.

This is quite a strong position, emphasizing the continuity of employers' interest in bringing the body under their direct control, albeit now in novel ways. As Lan (2001) points out, in types of work where workers' bodily efforts cannot be managed or enhanced through technological developments, employers must elaborate new 'microphysics of labour control'. But the concept of aesthetic labour goes further than Lan in seeing the management of workers' aesthetic presentation as a feature of waged labour that contributes directly to capital accumulation and not just, as Lan suggests, one which maintains 'symbolic domination by reproducing differences and hierarchies between workers, or between workers and employees' (Lan, 2001: 85).

However, it can be argued that there is a need to give as much attention to the dependence of employers on workers' acquisition, outside the workplace, of the bodily habitus required for particular jobs and occupations, and that much of any habitus is deep-rooted. As Bourdieu (1990: 53) points out, habitus are 'conditionings' of familial socialization that manifest bodily dispositions. Habitus then are acquired over a long period of socialization and are so deeply ingrained in a person that they cannot be easily or speedily inculcated by management. Arguably some bodily attributes and abilities are particularly dependent on long-ingrained, unexamined habit – for instance, the physicality associated with masculine working-class cultures (Willis, 1979) or the capacity for emotional engagement (Payne, 2009) – which are the more effective for being relatively unconscious. As Zimdars, Sullivan and Heath (2009: 661) point out about the acquisition of Bourdieu's cultural capital, 'what matters is a relationship of familiarity, rather than just participation'. They make the point that it is not enough for parents who want their children to attend elite British universities to take these children for occasional visits to a museum; instead the children require a prolonged immersion in a high culture environment. Although Hochschild did not refer to Bourdieu, she makes a similar point, noting that it is within families that the importance of emotional management is conveyed and from which children are then able to 'learn the skills' required of working with people (21). In this respect, as with emotional labour (Callaghan and Thompson, 2002), aesthetic labour can often be easier for employers to recruit than to train (Warhurst and Nickson, 2007).

However, the nub of the issue is whether a sharp distinction can or should be maintained between aesthetic, emotional or sexual labour within the labour process and apparently similar work that takes place within other social relations (Wouters, 1989). This division seems to be challenged by the widespread commercialization of intimacy (as well as the long-standing economics of intimacy characteristic of family interdependencies) (Zelizer, 2005). This debate about delineation and demarcation is one that occurs over emotional labour (Bolton, 2005; Brook, 2009) and can be extended to embodied labour in the service sector more generally. For instance, Folbre and Nelson (2000), as social policy analysts discussing paid care work, reject *a priori* assumptions about inescapable differences between market and non-market care work. Instead, they rightly recognize that 'real people' enter into many different responsibilities that challenge the dualism between self-interested and altruistic motivations or their simple equation with market and non-market (family) relations. However, building on Warhurst and Nickson's (2009) delineation, we could consider whether in so far as there is an overlap between relationships within profit-oriented and non-market care work, this overlap may well be due to the willingness of care workers to exert themselves over and above what is required by the employer.

Both emotional labour and aesthetic labour add much to the understanding of the productive body in the labour process. Moreover, both have become key features of labour process analysis and LPT has done much to develop understanding of both forms of labour (Warhurst, Thompson and Nickson, 2008). Nevertheless, it should not be assumed that the productive body is only relevant to emotional and aesthetic labour. It is important not to get trapped into the assumption that the 'productive body' matters only when it involves interactive service jobs. Creative labour, for example, also foregrounds workers' embodied capital. Whilst Smith and McKinlay (2009) rightly argue that analysis of creative labour needs to get 'behind the hype' about such labour being totally distinctive and always innovative, they recognize that some workers retain considerable power because 'the person-specific nature of much creative talent means that it is sometimes non-substitutable, and thus the standard mobility power of the employer (to switch one troublesome worker with another potentially less troublesome one) is not available' (13). Person-specific talents are highly embodied, in that they inhere in particular bodies and can be lost when that embodied person leaves. The point is that the productive body shifts attention to how labour processes are also embodied processes.

Reproductive bodies

In so far as the productive body is also a flesh-and-blood body, it crosses into and out of the productive domain and so, inevitably, its make up also depends on activities located outside the domain of the labour process. Indeed, embodying labour in a sense *requires* analysts to attend to the reproductive and cultural labour that sustains and modifies workers' bodies, and which usually takes place outside the realm of production. Although some of the 'body work' undertaken on bodies, Shilling (2005) suggests, is job-related, including the work done by workers to manage their own bodies within the workplace, body work also includes the cultural work of making our bodies presentable and acceptable in everyday life (discussed later) and the reproductive work 'people "do" on or for their bodies in order that they can survive and function adequately' (74). This last kind of body work is clearly disproportionately undertaken by women, who are usually responsible not only for the labour of their own reproduction but also much of that required by those people who are unable to (or choose not to) do it themselves. The reproductive body is almost inevitably read as female because of women's roles in childbirth and childcare. Indeed, this equating of the reproductive body with a nurturing female body may be one reason why the body work that most able-bodied adults, men as well as women, do for themselves – eating, bathing, teeth-brushing – has hitherto been invisible as *work*.

Reproductive bodies are less directly constrained by the capitalist labour process than the productive bodies discussed above but neither are they outside the circuits of capital accumulation. As Glenn (2001) states, reproductive labour has long depended on the purchase of household goods (for instance, clothing, toiletries, furnishings and cleaning products). Second, reproductive labour is necessary for the daily and intergenerational reproduction of the 'productive' labour force. Third, under certain conditions, women and others involved in reproductive labour constitute a reserve army of labour available for waged employment at lower cost. In fact, much of the current migrant reproductive labour force has been produced by global economic changes that make it impossible for women in the global south to earn a livelihood in their home countries (Parreñas, 2008). Finally, much of the labour performed in the home by women can ultimately be absorbed by the 'universal market' (Braverman, 1974), where it becomes a source of profit for employers, while continuing to provide – in a transformed way – services that people require for their social and physical care, repair and well-being.

Indeed, Braverman suggests that ultimately households are forced to seek in the market not only 'food, recreation, amusement, and security' but also services for the care of the young, the old, the sick and the handicapped (191). The extent that reproductive work is now undertaken by paid workers, inside and outside the household and, at least in the West, the dating of the distinction between the core male labour force and a female reserve army of labour suggests that the division between productive and reproductive bodies is historically very porous. Moreover, the huge expansion in the employment of paid domestic workers has brought tensions between social classes, previously associated with the realm of production, into the sphere of reproductive labour on a scale not seen since Victorian times (McDowell, 2008).

At present the blurring of productive and reproductive spheres is due in part to the workings of capital accumulation itself. If the hype about the knowledge and creative workers so beloved of the governments of the advanced economies is to be believed – that these workers are cash rich but time poor – then the transmuting of reproductive labour into productive labour is an imperative. To be able to function effectively these workers need the support of a whole army of other workers to provide them with reproductive goods and services that they can no longer provide for themselves – hence the reason why routine services are not displaced but are an integral feature of any putative knowledge and/or creative economies (Sassen, 1991; Warhurst, 2008).

Moreover, in the light of the migration of some manufacturing and extraction industries to low-wage economies, health care and personalized services, which are usually spatially bound (e.g. involving the care and control of bodies), have become key loci for capital investment in the advanced capitalist economies. In Europe, the state is being 'hollowed out', with the provision of health and social care, as the obvious examples, being transferred from the public to the private sector (Meyer, 2006; Player and Lees, 2008). In the US, profit-making corporations have already absorbed much of the non-family care of the aged and infirm. *Making Gray into Gold*, the title of Diamond's (1992) book, suggests that the infirm, ageing body has become a link in the transfer of funds from state to corporation. As Diamond suggests, the labour of many care workers is now structured by tasks that can be numbered, scaled, checked and controlled by people higher in the hierarchy, whether or not they have ever done the work or know how it is really accomplished. For instance, in the nursing home observed by Diamond, what mattered was that the work could be measured in 'the quantitative terms of the charts and its units counted up' and hence 'claimed, managed and owned... To the extent that everyday needs and tending to... [the residents] could be turned into a countable, accountable logic, a bottom line was made possible' (209; see also Lopez, 2006).

However, feminist scholarship has long stressed the gendered dimension of reproductive labour. The undervaluation of reproductive labour is closely related to its naturalization as part of women's family role and it is sometimes not even recognized as work. This lack of recognition is beginning to change with the transformation of much reproductive into productive labour, due in large part to the wider participation of women in paid employment, leaving a 'care deficit' in their wake that is filled by other women workers, often migrant women (Ehrenreich and Hochschild, 2002). Even as reproductive labour shifts from unpaid family labour to the market, it is still women who undertake what is usually undervalued and low-paid labour (England, 2005) and care workers employed in people's homes still struggle to be recognized as workers at all (Boris and Klein, 2006).

Feminist research on paid reproductive labour has been accompanied by intensive discussion of its 'racially divided' character (Glenn, 2001). Over much of the globe the reproductive body is racialized, with paid reproductive labour concentrated among disadvantaged groups of 'racial-ethnic' women and, increasingly, migrant workers. In fact, the regulation of migration and access to training may actually confine migrant women to this kind of work (Meiselas and Human Rights Watch, 2006; Parreñas, 2008). Moreover, as Glenn notes, racialized women are often allocated the heavier, dirtier work involved in running a household and caring for children's needs, while white women retain and celebrate their nurturing roles and quality time with children.

Indeed, the status distinctions between clean and dirty, emotional and physical, is crucial to the division of labour in reproductive labour – and to how the reproductive body is imagined. Precisely because care work is a form of 'body work' on embodied others (Twigg, 2000; Wolkowitz, 2002), the status of the job is often intertwined with the status of the bodies that are the focus of work. Moreover, the particular kinds of 'dirty work' body work involves is associated with status distinctions between workers, and may reinforce other determinants of labour market position. As Widding Isaksen (2005: 124) states, the bodies of paid and unpaid carers of the infirm elderly are stigmatized by association with the abject, ageing 'leaky' bodies of those people for whom they provide care. The 'unsavoury secretions, smells and signs of bodily maturation' and the feelings of disgust they evoke are linked to our society's understandings of femininity and masculinity. The stigma of body work on others' bodies also helps to explain why recruitment to care work depends increasingly on migrant workers, with the 'hatred of the body (somatophobia) and hatred of racialised groups (racism)...played out in the use of racialised female labour to do the work of servicing the body' (Anderson, 2000: 142).

Braverman questioned the distinction between factory production and the provision of services. 'Does the fact that porters, charwomen, janitors, or dishwashers perform their cleaning operations not on new goods being readied at the factory or construction site for their first use, but on constantly reused buildings and utensils, render their labour different in principle, and any less tangible in form, than that of the manufacturing workers who do the factories' final cleaning, polishing, packaging and so forth?' he asked (1974: 249). Braverman does not consider whether, when the cleaning and so on is focused on people's bodies and not just their beds or buildings, there is still no difference. This question is one which researchers are only beginning to address (Twigg et al., 2010; Wolkowitz, 2006). Clearly 'body work' can be organized so as to minimize the differences involved in caring for people and maintaining objects, as exemplified by Diamond's and Lopez's ethnographic data, which document the intensification of labour in residential care institutions, but this is not the whole story. For instance, the Taylorization of care may be accompanied by changes, as well, in the ways that people who receive care are conceptualized. The reconstruction of people as 'work objects' by the labour process means that yet another reconstruction of the body is taking place.

Perfectible bodies, vulnerable bodies, resistant bodies

While (male) productive and (female) reproductive bodies have been the target of both Marxist and feminist analysis, there is a need to consider other constructions of the body which show the interrelation between the body at work and its activities outside work.

Anyone who watches television, shops or goes to the gym has observed the intense longing – in the self or others – to have a makeover. As Shilling (2008: 147–8) notes, 'Where individuals once subjected their bodies to mortification for religious ideals, they are now more likely to endure effort, expense, privation, and pain in the hope of achieving performative goals related to appearance and the accumulation of physical capital.' The 'body projects' (Giddens, 1991) that people undertake, whether tattooing, body building or obesity surgery, are usually associated with the realm of privatized consumption but investment in them is also connected with increasing the exchange value bodies command in the plasticized twenty-first-century 'personality market', previously identified by Mills (1951). Apocryphal stories spill out from the media of middle-aged, usually female, workers using their life savings or remortgaging their homes to pay for facelifts, brow-lifts, botox and other aesthetic interventions to keep themselves employable – the so-called career girl's nip/tuck (de Grunwald, 2006: 80; also Mackay, 2006). These interventions reflect not only the pressures on women to remain young-looking but also depend on a new conception of the body as open to change, rather than as a biological given, and as perfectible. Skeggs (2004) argues that the benefits of investments in the cultural capital carried by the body accrue mainly to the middle class, although when it comes to appearance there is a clear gender dimension: women report being less satisfied with their appearance and more likely to engage in appearance-enhancing behaviour (Jackson, 1992) but also benefit more than men from the 'beauty premium' in their pay packets (French, 2002).

New forms of exchange value in relation to the body figure in the contemporary political economy as a whole and not just in relation to production. As Harvey (1998) puts it, the body has become an 'accumulation strategy'. 'New bodies' – new bodily needs and new uses for the body and body parts – have been taken hold of by capital in its drive for profits (Cooper, 2008; Lowe 1995). Lowe suggests that the commodification of body practices is no longer restricted to labour, but now includes health, sexuality and gender practices involving, for example, organ transplants, assisted reproduction, genomic research, sex reassignment and other body technologies. Some of these developments have been characterized as the 'new enclosure' of the genetic commons, wherein human tissues are being 'fenced off' as a form of commercially profitable bodily property (Dickenson, 2007). Lowe implies a challenge to the labour theory of value, in so far as the body itself, and not merely its capacity to labour, has been given exchange value. The same may be true of sex work and other activities in which it appears that the body itself has been commodified. However, alternative analyses perceive some of these practices in terms of the continuing exploitation of women's reproductive labour, for instance as sex workers (Agustin, 2006) or as surrogate mothers or egg cell 'donors' (Dickenson, 2007).

Perfecting the body also involves what Shilling (2005) calls cultural body *work*. This work has a relation to the productive body, and not just cultural norms, in so far as it is incorporated into aesthetic labour. It usually involves work by the self (which people may hope will be recompensed indirectly in increased self-confidence and a successful career, even when it is not required by employers) and also often the paid work of others – not just the expert cosmetic surgeon but more often the low-paid hairdresser or personal trainer who must negotiate the contradictions of advising the client from a position of low status (George, 2008; Gimlin, 1996).

However, before getting too intrigued by all the ways the body can be 'perfected', there is a need to ensure that the research agenda continues to recognize the 'vulnerable body', that is, the body that is vulnerable to workplace health and safety risks, along with assaults on dignity at work. One of the key reasons for embodying labour is to put workplace health and safety centre stage. As Lawrence Connelly's testimony of a fatal plastic factory explosion in Glasgow illustrates, even in the UK hazardous work can still wreak havoc on the productive body (Taylor and Connelly, 2009). Indeed, the incidence of workplace accidents and injuries, and workers' health and well-being – cut fingers, broken bones and stress – can be a proxy measure for assessing developments in the labour process such as cost-cutting and work intensification.

Keeping workplace health and safety on the agenda depends partly on how the body (and which body) will figure in future debates and research. Constructions of the body have a political significance partly because they affect the visibility of vulnerability and people's willingness to admit to it. As Wendell (1995: 85) asserts, when the body is 'idealized and objectified to a high degree', when 'cultural practices foster demands to control our bodies and to attempt to perfect them', then vulnerability is associated with shame, fear and the failure to control the body. Historically, campaigns for workplace health and safety have been directed mainly towards the protection of women and children, who are seen as vulnerable, rather than the male working body, which is stereotypically portrayed as heroic and powerful (Slavishak, 2008; Williams, 1997). Nevertheless, both men and women suffer from workplace injury and ill health. Men have been much more likely than women to suffer from fatal workplace accidents, and women from non-fatal injuries. Back injuries and pains are not uncommon amongst female hotel room attendants, for example, more so even than in many manufacturing jobs, and cleaners and nurses and other care workers have very high rates of workplace injury (Herod and Agular, 2006; UniteHere, 2006; Wolkowitz, 2006).

Some of the other ways workers' bodies are affected by the organization of the labour process are also sometimes obscured by dominant constructions of the muscle-bound productive body. For instance, the long-term health detriments of night-time working (Atkins, 2009) are insidious rather than dramatic and affect the 'inner' body without any evidence of visible injury or the ingestion of noxious substances. Researchers also need to be more aware of workers' explicit recognition that the absence of dignity at work is not a mere abstraction but closely intertwined with the infliction of poor physical working conditions, long hours and weak provisions for health and safety (Newsome, Thompson and Commander, 2009).

Finally, there is a need to pay proper attention to the 'resistant body' and the embodied activities through which resistance is both carried out and hidden. However, there is a problem here. While the central concern of LPT with struggles over control and autonomy have made it alert to forms of workplace resistance (Thompson and Ackroyd, 1995), its very concern with processes of control may make it harder to notice other kinds of embodied workplace activity. As Shilling (2008) and others have argued in looking at developments in 'body studies' more generally, there is a need to guard against passifying the body, seeing it only as constrained by forces outside it, or even as simply responding to them, and pay more attention to the body as itself a generative force.

However, being attentive is only a first step. There is not always agreement as to what constitutes resistance; because instances of informal resistance can often take the form of outward conformity (Collinson, 2003) or are co-opted by the employer, it is difficult to know whether they represent bodily autonomy or constraint. This problem of conceptualization becomes particularly acute in respect to the issues of dress and appearance discussed above, since workers may have a 'double-edged stance' towards the 'desirable dress' prescribed by employers. Boris's (2006) historical account of American flight attendants suggests that rather than *giving in* to managerial constructions of their bodies imposed on them, many individual women actually came into the profession because they *wanted* to look like stewardesses, while others' deployment of the required sexual appeal used it to support 'a different consciousness of bodily rights' (138). Boris's evidence shows that even though airline workers have sometimes protested against the employers' definitions of beauty and glamour, they have also deployed their glamorous appearance to fight dismissals and to gain publicity for their picket lines.

The embodying of labour, then, is a shifting phenomenon. What constitutes the required productive body is dynamic and adds to the already residual vulnerability of that body in the workplace. How workers react to that vulnerability is yet to be adequately researched, conceptually or empirically, though LPT can have a key role to play in this endeavour, concerned as it is with the perspective of the worker.

Conclusion

Labour process analysis draws attention to the instrumentalization of the body; to its construction as a resource within the labour process; to the ways in which people are involved in reproducing the body outside the labour process, and, in consequence of all these, to the ways workers experience themselves as embodied persons. Perhaps the most interesting questions have to do with the ways in which the constitution of human embodiment (and ideas about embodiment) both feed into and reflect changes in the labour process. Reconfiguring the body-mind relationship in binary terms was central to the evolution of the division of labour in industrial and office employment but the extension of the service sector has potentially brought new binaries, new forms of fragmentation, into play. As research on embodied labour goes forward, there is a need to be careful not to replicate these binaries in an unexamined way.

Here it is useful refer to Leder's (1990) phenomenological account, which builds on Merleau-Ponty (1962), of human beings' perceptions of ourselves as embodied actors. Leder suggests that human beings experience different parts of the body as more or less integral to the self. Arms and legs, and especially, hands, which we can see moving through space and which connect the self to the outer world, he argues, feel less 'inside' the self than the head or the torso. Hence, it could be argued, that when the labour process was organized mainly around manual labour there was a kind of embodied logic that supported the conception of alienated labour as separable from the self. However, when this manual labour is no longer the dominant form of labour, as in advanced capitalist societies, when many people see themselves as working with their heads, emotions and appearance, are workers placed in a different relation to themselves as embodied persons? This is precisely the question that Hochschild (1983) raised all those years ago and if it has 'gone away' it may be partly because people have come to naturalize and accept new conceptions of the embodied self. If true, it also indicates the need for a sociology of work that recognizes the dependence of work on the creation of a habitus, outside the workplace, that make new conceptions and experiences of embodiment sustainable.

We should also note the continuing, but productive, tension between the way LPT talks about bodies in work and body studies more generally. LPT is at its best in analysing the ways that employers identify and commodify *particular* bodily features and activities in response to the indeterminacy of labour, but there is a risk of reproducing the idea that the bodily capacities that employers seek to control are the only ones that matter. Thus, a sociology of work is needed that is also interested in making visible aspects of human embodiment that employers take for granted. As Hockey and Allen-Collinson (2009) suggest, labour involves all the fleshy and sensory capacities that have hitherto been studied by phenomenologists – including movement, rhythm, timing; listening and hearing; occupational vision; olfactory capacities; and the haptic, or tactile, and locomotive capacities. Indeed, phenomenological accounts of embodiment are a reminder that since all 'living labour' is embodied, ultimately recognizing the embodiment of labour has to go beyond considering the physical effort, movement or outward appearance of the physical body and incorporate intellectual practices and artistic talents. As Wolkowitz (2006: 182) suggests, if 'bodies R us', then people's existence as embodied being needs to be integrated into the study of all kinds of employment.

REFERENCES

Agustin, L. (2006) 'The Disappearance of a Migration Category: Migrants Who Sell Sex', *Journal of Ethnic and Migration Studies*, 32(1): 29–47.

Anderson, B. (2000) *Doing the Dirty Work: The Global Politics of Domestic Labour*, London: Zed Books.

Atkins, L. (2009) 'Are Night Shifts Bad for You?', *Guardian*, 17 March. Accessed on 20 August 2009 from http://www.guardian.co.uk/lifeandstyle/2009/mar/17/night-shifts-health.

Bahnisch, M. (2000) 'Embodied Work, Divided Labour: Subjectivity and the Scientific Management of the Body in Frederick W. Taylor's 1967 "Lecture on Management"', *Body & Society*, 6(1): 51–68.

Banta, M. (1993) *Taylored Lives: Narrative Productions in the Age of Taylor, Veblen and Ford*, Chicago, IL: University of Chicago Press.

Bolton, S. (2005) *Emotion Management in the Workplace*, London: Palgrave.

Boris, E. (2006) 'Desirable Dress: Roses, Sky Girls, and the Politics of Appearance', *International Labour and Working-Class History*, 69(Spring): 123–42.

Boris, E. and Klein, J. (2006) 'Organizing Home Care', *Politics and Society*, 34(1): 81–108.

Bourdieu, P. (1990) *The Logic of Practice*, Cambridge: Polity.

Braverman, H. (1974) *Labor and Monopoly Capital*, New York: Monthly Review Press.

Brook, P. (2009) 'In Critical Defence of "Emotional Labour": Refuting Bolton's Critique of Hochschild's Concept', *Work, Employment and Society*, 23(3): 531–48.

Bryman, A. (2004) *The Disneyization of Society*, London: Sage.

Callaghan, G. and Thompson, P. (2002) '"We Recruit Attitude": The Selection and Shaping of Call Centre Labour', *Journal of Management Studies*, 39(2): 233–54.

▶

►

Cockburn, C. (1983) *Brothers*, London: Pluto Press.

Collinson, D. (2003) 'Identities and Insecurities: Selves at Work', *Organization*, 10(3): 527–47.

Cooper, M. (2008) *Life as Surplus: Biotechnology and Capitalism in the Neoliberal Age*, Seattle, WA: University of Washington Press.

Cressey, P. and MacInnes, J. (1980) 'Voting for Ford', *Capital and Class*, Summer, 5–33.

Crossley, N. (2001) The Social Body, London: Sage.

de Grunwald, P. (2006) 'The Rise of the Career Girl's Nip/Tuck', *Eve*, March, 80–3.

Diamond, T. (1992) *Making Gray Gold: Narratives of Nursing Home Care*, Chicago, IL: University of Chicago Press.

Dickenson, D. (2007) *Property in the Body*, New York: Cambridge University Press.

Dutton, E., Warhurst, C., Lloyd, C., James, S., Commander, J. and Nickson, D. (2008) 'Just Like the Elves in Harry Potter: Room Attendants in UK Hotels', in Lloyd, C., Mason, G. and Mayhew, K. (eds) *Low Wage Work in the UK*, New York: Russell Sage Foundation.

Ehrenreich, B. and Hochschild, A. R. (2002) 'Introduction', in Ehrenreich, B. and Hochschild, A. R. (eds) *Global Woman*, London: Granta.

Elson, D. and Pearson, R. (1981)"Nimble Fingers Make Cheap Workers": An Analysis of Women's Employment in Third World Export Manufacturing', *Feminist Review*, 7: 87–107.

England, P. (2005) 'Emerging Theories of Care Work', *Annual Review of Sociology*, 31: 381–99.

Folbre, N. and Nelson, J. A. (2000) 'For Love or Money – Or Both?', *Journal of Economic Perspectives*, 14(4): 123–40.

French, M. T. (2002) 'Physical Appearance and Earnings: Further Evidence', *Applied Economics*, 34: 569–72.

Gatta, M. (2009) 'Balancing Trays and Smiles: What Restaurant Workers Teach Us about Hard Work in the Service Economy', in Bolton, S. C. and Houlihan, M. (eds) *Work Matters*, London: Palgrave.

George, M. (2008) 'Interactions in Expert Service Work', *Journal of Contemporary Ethnography*, 37(1): 108–31.

Giddens, A. (1991) *Modernity and Self-Identity*, Cambridge: Polity.

Gimlin, D. (1996) 'Pamela's Place: Power and Negotiation in the Hair Salon', *Gender and Society*, 10(5): 505–26.Glenn, E. N. (2001) 'The Race and Gender Division of Public Reproductive Labor', in Baldoz, R., Koeber, C. and Kraft, P. (eds) *The Critical Study of Work*, Philadelphia, PA: Temple University Press.

Gramsci, A. (1971) 'Americanism and Fordism', in Hoare, Q. and Nowell-Smith, G. (eds and trans.) *Selections from the Prison Notebooks*, New York: International Publishers.

Harvey, D. (1998) 'The Body as an Accumulation Strategy', *Environment and Planning D: Society and Space*, 16: 401–21.

Herod, A. and Aguilar, L. L. M. (2006) 'Introduction: Cleaners and the Dirty Work of Neoliberalism', *Antipode*, 38(3): 425–34.

►

▶

Hochschild, A. R. (1983) *The Managed Heart*, Berkeley: University of Californian Press.

Hockey, J. and Allen-Collinson, J. (2009) 'The Sensorium at Work: The Sensory Phenomenology of the Working Body', *Sociological Review*, 17(2): 217–39.

Jackson, L. A. (1992) *Physical Appearance and Gender*, New York: SUNY Press.

Lan, P. C. (2001) 'The Body as a Contested Terrain for Labor Control: Cosmetics Retailers in Department Stores and Direct Selling', in Baldoz, R., Kroeber, C. and Kraft, P. (eds) *The Critical Study of Work*, Philadelphia, PA: Temple University Press.

Leder, D. (1990) *The Absent Body*, Chicago, IL: University of Chicago Press.

Lopez, S. (2006) 'Culture Change Management in Long-Term Care: A Shop-Floor View', *Politics and Society*, 34(1): 55–80.

Lowe, D. M. (1995) *The Body in Late-Capitalist USA*, Durham, NC: Duke University Press.

Mackay, M. (2006) 'Danger: Wrinkles at Work', *Independent on Sunday*, 19 March, 9.

McDowell, L. (2008) 'The New Economy, Class Condescension and Caring Labour', *NORA*, 16(3): 150–65.

Meiselas, S. and Human Rights Watch (2006) 'Costly Dreams', Magnum Photos. Accessed on 20 August 2009 from http://www.opendemocracy.net/arts/domesticworkers_3797.jsp.

Merleau-Ponty, M. (1962) *The Phenomenology of Perception*, London: Routledge and Kegan Paul.

Meyer, M. (2006) 'Wie viel Wirtschaft verträgt die Zivilgesellschaft? Über Möglichkeiten und Grenzen Wirtschaftlicher Rationalität in NPO', *Tagung 'Bürgergesellschaft ⊠ Wunsch und Wirklichkeit'*, Wissenschaftszentrum Berlin.

Mills, C. W. (1951) *White Collar*, New York: Oxford University Press.

Newsome, K., Thompson, P. and Commander, J. (2009) 'The Forgotten Factories: Supermarket Suppliers and Dignity at Work in the Contemporary Economy', in Bolton, S. and Houlihan, M. (eds) *Work Matters*, London Palgrave Macmillan.

Nichols, T. and Beynon, H. (1977) *Living with Capitalism*, London: Routledge and Kegan Paul.

Orzeck, R. (2007) 'What Does Not Kill You: Historical Materialism and the Body', *Environment and Planning D: Society and Space*, 25(3): 496–514.

Parrenñas, R. S. (2008) *The Forces of Domesticity: Filipina Migrants and Globalization*, New York: NYU Press.

Payne, J. (2009) 'Emotional Labour and Skill: A Reappraisal', *Gender, Work and Organization*, 16(3): 348–67.

Player, S. and Lees, C. (2008) 'Commodifying Health Care', *Work Organisation, Labour and Globalisation*, 2(2): 9–22.

Sassen, S. (1991) *The Global City*, Princeton, NJ: Princeton University Press.

Scarry, E. (1985) *The Body in Pain*, Oxford: Oxford University Press.

Sennett, R. (2008) *The Craftsman*, London: Penguin.

Shilling, C. (2008) *Changing Bodies*, London: Sage.

Shilling, V. (2005) *The Body in Culture, Technology and Society*, London: Sage.

▶

▶

Skeggs, B. (2004) 'Exchange, Value and Affect: Bourdieu and "the Self"', in Adkins, L. and Skeggs, B. (eds) *Feminism after Bourdieu*, Oxford: Blackwell.

Slavishak, E. (2008) *Bodies of Work: Civic Display and Labor in Industrial Pittsburgh*, Durham, NC: Duke University Press.

Smith, C. and McKinlay, A. (2009) 'Creative Industries and Labour Process Analysis', in Smith, C. and McKinlay, A. (eds) *Creative Labour*, London: Palgrave Macmillan.

Taylor, C. (1995) *Philosophical Arguments*, Cambridge, MA: Harvard University Press.

Taylor, F. W. (1947) *Scientific Management*, New York: Harper & brothers.

Taylor, P. and Connelly, L. (2009) 'Before the Disaster: Health, Safety and Working Conditions at a Plastics Factory', *Work, Employment and Society*, 21(1): 160–8.

Terkel, S. (1974) *Working*, New York: Pantheon Books.

Thompson, E. P. (1967) 'Time, Work Discipline and Industrial Capitalism', *Past and Present*, 38: 56–97.

Thompson, P. and Ackroyd, S. (1995) 'All Quiet on the Workplace Front: A Critique of Recent Trends in British Industrial Sociology', *Sociology*, 29(4): 615–33.

Twigg, J. (2000) 'Carework as a Form of Bodywork', *Ageing and Society*, 20(4): 389–41.

Twigg, J., Wolkowitz, C., Nettleton, S. and Cohen, R. (2010, forthcoming) Special Issue on 'Body Work in Health and Social Care', *Sociology of Health and Illness*, forthcoming.

UniteHere (2006) *Creating Luxury, Enduring Pain: How Hotel Work Is Hurting Housekeepers*, available at http://www.hotelworkersrising.org/pdf/Injury_Paper.pdf. Accessed 2 February 2007.

Warhurst, C. (2008) 'The Knowledge Economy, Skills and Government Labour Market Intervention', *Policy Studies*, 29(1): 71–86.

Warhurst, C. and Nickson, D. (2007) 'Employee Experience of Aesthetic Labour in Retail and Hospitality', *Work, Employment and Society*, 21(1): 103–20.

Warhurst, C. and Nickson, D. (2009) '"Who's Got the Look?" Emotional, Aesthetic and Sexualized Labour in Interactive Services', *Gender, Work & Organization*, 16(3): 385–404.

Warhurst, C., Thompson, P. and Nickson, D. (2008) 'Labor Process Theory: Putting the Materialism Back into the Meaning of Services', in Korczynski, M. and MacDonald, C.L. (eds) *Service Work: Critical Perspectives*, New York: Routledge.

Warhurst, C., Nickson, D., Witz, A. and Cullen, A-M. (2000) 'Aesthetic Labour in Interactive Service Work: Some Case Study Evidence from the "New" Glasgow', *Service Industries Journal*, 20(3): 1–18.

Wendell, S. (1996) *The Rejected Body: Feminist Philosophical Reflections on Disability*, New York: Routledge.

West, J. (1990) 'Gender and the Labour Process: A Reassessment', in Knights, D. and Willmott, H. (eds) *Labour Process Theory*, Houndmills: Macmillan.

Widding Isaksen, L. (2005) 'Gender and Care: The Role of Cultural Ideas of Dirt and Disgust', in Morgan, D. and Brandth, B. (eds) *Gender, Bodies, Work*, Avebury: Ashgate.

▶

▶

Williams, C. (1997) 'Women and Occupational Health and Safety', *Labour History* 73: 30–52.

Willis, P. (1979) *Learning to Labour*, Westmead: Saxon House.

Witz, A., Warhurst, C. and Nickson, D. (2003) 'The Labour of Aesthetics and the Aesthetics of Organization', *Organization*, 10(1): 33–54.

Wolkowitz, C. (2002) 'The Social Relations of Body Work', *Work, Employment and Society*, 16(3): 497–510.

Wolkowitz, C. (2006) *Bodies at Work*, London: Sage.

Wouters, C. (1989) 'The Sociology of Emotional Labour and Flight Attendants', *Theory, Culture and Society*, 6: 95–123.

Yanarella, E. and Reid, H. (1996) 'From Trained Gorilla to Humanware: Repolitizing the Body-Machine Complex between Fordism and Post-Fordism', in Shatzki, T. R. and Natter, W. (eds) *The Social and Political Body*, London: Guildford Press.

Zelizer, V. A. (2005) *The Purchase of Intimacy*, Princeton, NJ: Princeton University Press.

Zimdars, A., Sullivan, A. and Heath, A. (2009) 'Elite Higher Education Admissions in the Arts and Sciences: Is Cultural Capital the Key?', *Sociology*, 43(4): 648–66.

The Globalization of Service Work: Analysing the Transnational Call Centre Value Chain

12

Phil Taylor

The past two decades have seen the call or contact centre emerge as a dominant organizational form which has transformed the configuration and loci of interactive customer servicing. One reason for the wide-ranging debate that it has provoked is the fact that it is a novel form of work organization, characterized by a unique blend of mechanized office/clerical and interactive service work (Boreham et al., 2007) in which developments within the Tayloristic tradition mesh with the performance of emotional labour (Taylor and Bain, 1999). Notwithstanding the value of a diverse literature, a salient criticism has been of a bias towards its 'inner workings' (Glucksmann, 2004), which frequently renders analyses inadequately contextualized. Consistent with Thompson's (2003) observation that a focus on the workplace alone cannot reveal the most significant drivers of organizational change, the author has striven to explore interrelationships between the call centre and political-economic contexts in order to deliver analytical purchase (Ellis and Taylor, 2006). Indeed, it was over how best to overcome the tendency to view call centres sites as self-standing worksites and how analysis should be located in appropriate economic sociology that prompted the engagement with Glucksmann (Taylor and Bain, 2007).

The growth of offshoring, notably from the US and the UK to India (Dossani and Kenney, 2007) and the nature of the Indian call centre labour process, magnify the importance of exploring the interrelationships between the call centre workplace's 'inner workings' and multiple contexts. Self-evidently, overseas migration both exposes further weaknesses in perspectives that treat call centres as self-contained worksites and presents new theoretical challenges. One concrete example relates to the work of Korczynski (2002), who depicts the call centre as an exemplar of a mass customized bureaucracy (MCB) and its work as infused by two equivalent logics, of the need to be 'cost-efficient' and 'customer-oriented'. If the operation of the customer-oriented 'logic' is so influential, then how can it account for companies' decisions to offshore, say, banking and insurance voice provision in the face of profound customer opposition? Surely relocation from high-cost developed countries to lower-cost developing countries demonstrates the dominance of the 'cost-efficient' over the 'customer-orientation' logic. The empirical test of globalization further questions the plausibility of the MCB paradigm.

Prima facie it might be supposed that the ambitious Global Call Centre Project (GCCP) (Holman, Batt and Holtgrewe, 2007), which gathered extensive data on management and employment practices from 2500 centres, based on the implementation of an identical survey in each of 17 countries 'across all regions of the globe', would provide analytical leverage on the dynamics driving remote relocation and the mechanisms by which activities are coordinated transnationally. Implicitly, and explicitly (Holman et al., 2009), the GCCP is informed by the 'varieties of capital' (VOC) approach (Hall and Soskice, 2001) which explains differences in work organization, labour utilization, industrial relations and HR practices through distinctions between national political and economic institutions. Hall and Soskice's key differentiator is between liberal market economies (LMEs) and coordinated market economies (CMEs). The GCCP adds a third, recently industrialized or transitional economies, as categories for understanding how national labour market institutions influence corporate strategies. There is considerable merit in the GCCP's national-level contrasts and comparisons. It is important to know that the call centre generates 'similarities' in markets, service offerings, broad organizational features and workforce characteristics (Holman, Batt and Holtgrewe, 2007: 4–10), suggesting convergence irrespective of national location. It is equally important to appraise divergent national trends and to acknowledge that institutional differences between LMEs and CMEs do significantly shape work organization, HR and industrial relations practices (ibid.: 11–22).

However, the GCCP is not so much a 'global' study as internationally comparative, consisting of contrasts between nationally aggregated data sets. Consequently, the GCCP deals inadequately with the offshoring phenomenon, failing to account for the drivers of the uneven flows of capital and technology across national boundaries, the reasons companies adopt location strategies, locational choice, the transformative role played by Transnational Corporations (TNCs) or nationally based firms acting transnationally, and the manner in which India and 'remote' destinations are integrated into emerging global divisions of service labour. The implications of the dependency of India's international-facing call centres upon corporate decisions in the developed countries are not drawn out. Nor does the GCCP sufficiently explicate coordination across the transnational servicing 'chain' and the ways in which customers in the developed north are entwined with remote sites in the developing south.

The understatement of historical perspective and contextual depth are weaknesses in the GCCP report (Holman, Batt and Holtgrewe, 2007) and in the Indian national study (Batt et al., 2005). The claim that the sector developed in broadly similar ways across all advanced and recently industrialized countries is untenable, for the Indian industry's genesis, development and structure are distinct, not least because its domestic and international-facing segments, the latter preceding the former, are driven by different dynamics (Taylor et al., 2010). Nor is the suggestion that workflows can be routed to different geographic locations with relative ease sustainable given the corporate experience of offshoring. Significant constraints and contradictions render offshoring far more complex than suggested by this generalization (Taylor and Bain, 2005).

Labour as active agency and constitutive of capitalist accumulation, and the nature of the labour process in India, are problematics that lie beyond the GCCP's compass. Simply put, the ready substitutability of value-adding call centre labour at transnational scale cannot be assumed. If managerial attempts to resolve the inescapable indeterminacy of call centre labour take distinctive forms in the developed world, the UK in this study (Bain et al., 2002; Callaghan and Thompson, 2001), then the problematic is exacerbated by the requirement to exercise controls from a distance. To these may be added indeterminacies peculiar to India as a 'place', that cannot be read off from a universal template. To make this conceptual criticism concrete, the GCCP highlight distinguishing features of the Indian sector, including the fact that university graduates dominate employment (Batt et al., 2005: 5), that call-handlers' selection rates are only 7 per cent and that job discretion is outstandingly low by international comparison (Holman, Batt and Holtgrewe, 2007: 11, 16); yet, scant explanation is provided for these 'unique' features.

Methodologically desensitized to the locational dynamics of globalization, the GCCP approach is less helpful for understanding the changes in economic activities, which 'increasingly tend to slice through, while still being unevenly contained within state boundaries' (Henderson et al., 2002: 446). Offshoring challenges the assumption that national geographies are bounded silos into which activity can be isolated for analysis. As Smith and Meiskins (1995) observed, the global economy must be understood as a complex, deeply integrated system, in which production chains are dynamic 'constantly evolving spatial divisions of labour', so that when making comparisons between societies 'in the utilisation of new technology, organisation of work, structure of industrial relations procedures or management styles we should be aware of the inherent tendency to freeze social action within the discourse of national differences' (ibid.: 261). This is especially true where the focus is on 'factory regimes and the labour process because this level ... is particularly dynamic and variegated' (ibid.).

The distinction between the terms international, deriving from a state-centric discourse, and globalization, indicating economic interconnectedness (Dicken, 2007), is pertinent. Arguably, the GCCP pushes to the limits the explanatory potential of an analytical framework predicated on the former of identifying national-level convergence and divergence. The GCCP's authors might point to their finding that only 14 per cent of centres serve international markets (Holman, Batt and Holtgrewe, 2007: 5) as validating such a state-centric analysis. That offshoring is regarded as a peripheral development is suggested by their statement that India and, less demonstrably, Ireland and Canada represent 'exceptions' to the dominant national pattern. Now there is merit in emphasizing that call centres overwhelmingly service customers within national geographies against ill-informed commentary which presumes an offshoring tsunami. A sense of perspective matters, not least because the misconception that call centres are globally footloose can encourage fatalism and passivity in organized labour (Taylor and Bain, 2008).

Nevertheless, call centre offshoring, as the most egregious case of the ICT-enabled transportability of business services (Miozzo and Soete, 2001), deserves serious academic attention. A historical perspective bolsters this case, for the pace of growth is remarkable. When the GCCP gathered data (2003), approximately 100,000 were employed in Indian centres compared with 400,000 by 2009.[1] Moreover, global sourcing now encompasses an expanded range of destinations. The Philippines claimed 227,000 call-handlers by 2009 (BPAP, 2009) and many lesser locations have developed global sourcing hubs.[2] To summarize, Indian call centres and the relocated labour process justify examination, not just because the country remains the pre-eminent remote geography, but also because of the conceptual challenges offshoring poses.

Scope and aims

Since Gereffi and Korzeniewicz's (1994) seminal work on the Global Commodity Chain (GCC), a plethora of studies have adopted this framework or the Global Value Chain (GVC) and Global Production Network (GPN) variants. These commonly attempt to understand the coordination of economic activities at the global scale. First, the chapter provides an overview of their contrasting and complementary approaches and suggests that elements of each provide an effective theoretical resource for understanding significant aspects of the 'globalized' call centre. For while Rainnie et al. (2008) argue that locational and spatial factors are under-theorized in call centre research, their invocation to build on GCC's analytical insights has yet to be followed through. Constraints of space limit the critique of an extensive literature, but the discussion foregrounds the chapter's argument.

Second, the case is made that offshoring and the nature of the transplanted labour process are inexplicable without understanding the development trajectory within the UK that, at a particular conjuncture, led companies to 'externalize' operations organizationally and geographically. Against the GCCP and much of the literature which takes the call centre as a given entity, explanation depends upon situating this constantly evolving ICT-based organizational form and its labour process within dynamic capitalist economic contexts (global, national, local, sectoral, firm). This means we also need to consider political and regulatory frameworks, technological developments and, crucially for present purposes, locational factors. Third, the chapter outlines at *macro* level the broad dynamics of global location and critiques those who assume that the call centre can be located anywhere. The importance of place and locational choice are emphasized. This more focused discussion of political economy leads to the level of the firm and synthesizes 'demand' and 'supply' sides, relating corporate decisions to the capacities of the Indian industry.

Turning to the *meso* level and utilizing insights from the GCC/GVC/GPN frameworks, the objective is to explicate the mode of coordination in the UK-to-India call centre 'chain'. This is an important level of analysis, for it links corporate imperatives of cost minimization, the migratory process and governance with work organization in India. It contributes to understanding the distinctiveness of the labour process at *micro* level. Mutually conditioning relationships interconnect these macro, meso and micro levels.[3]

Sources and methods

The chapter is both conceptual and empirically informed, the argument drawing on primary data from the author's research (since 2002) into UK offshoring to India. In-depth studies examined corporate strategies from the developed country perspective and are based on more than 50 interviews with senior management and on sectoral audits (e.g. Taylor and Anderson, 2008; Taylor and Bain, 2006). Evidence from the demand side is combined with extensive data on the Indian market, consisting of site visits to and interviews with senior management in 25 BPO/call centre companies (Taylor and Bain, 2006). Participation at 12 conferences organized by Nasscom (National Association of Software and Services Companies) generated valuable knowledge of the supply side. This synthetical method allows the call centre 'chain' to be examined from both nodal points. Research on UK trade unions mapped responses to offshoring (Bain and Taylor, 2008) and in India, worker experiences and trade union developments have been analysed (Taylor et al., 2009). Industry, company and union documentation and consultants' reports complement primary sources.

GCC, GVC, GPN theory

As developing countries became important sites for basic manufacturing, the diverse GCC, GVC and GPN frameworks mapped and analysed changing economic activities across different geographies. The eclecticism in this literature reveals terminological variation (chain or network metaphors) reflecting different intellectual orientations (business-management or economic development), but nevertheless, constitutes a loosely integrated tradition (Gibbon, Bair and Ponte, 2008). Given Gereffi and colleagues' original objective to describe functionally integrated and geographically dispersed systems of production, it is easy to see how this theorizing can deliver insights into the globally relocated call centre. Dispersion of economic activity has been accompanied by a significant shift from a situation in which internationalization meant developed country firms establishing branch plants in developing countries, to globalization where capacity is owned by firms in developed countries or developing countries through outsourcing arrangements, to produce commodities (and services including call centres) *for* developed country markets.

In the initial GCC formulation (Gereffi and Korzeniewicz, 1994), governance structure embraced several dimensions along which commodity chains could be analysed. Gereffi's central conception was the division between Producer Driven Commodity Chains (PDCC) and Buyer Driven Commodity Chains (BDCC) in which governance was a function of lead-firm type. BDCCs provoked most interest as novel network forms associated with the organizational externalization and internationalization of production. The usefulness of the chain metaphor lay in the fact that it permitted the highly abstract idea of globalization to be realized concretely in terms of relations organized around tangible commodities. Empirical studies followed which examined the extent to which lead firms dictated conditions to independent suppliers. The expanding field of GCC studies either supported or contested the PDCC and BDCC duality, but one convincing argument was that Gereffi's two ideal types failed to capture the range of governance forms in actual chains. O'Riain (2004), for example, posited a technology-driven chain for the electronics industry.

This variation prompted a re-conceptualization of governance as coordination. Sturgeon's (2002) work on electronics marked a transition. Where

Gereffi's BDCC had shown that only non-core supplies had been outsourced, Sturgeon demonstrated that lead firms relocated and externalized the full range of services. Increasingly, questions of 'governance' within GVCs assumed greater importance, where GVCs consist of 'the set of inter-sectoral linkages between firms and other actors through which this geographical and organisational reconfiguration has taken place' (Gibbon, Bair and Ponte, 2008: 318). If economic globalization is leading to increasing geographical dispersion and differentiation between places, then GVCs should be conceived of as the *integrative* counterpart to these processes. GVC governance focuses on the strategies of particular actors, usually large firms, and the arrangements – in-house, market-based or outsourced – that prevail. Where commodities and services are relocated *and* outsourced to external suppliers, coordination and the maintenance of quality standards become vital concerns.

Gereffi, Humphrey and Sturgeon (2005) then elaborated a theory that specified the determinants of inter-firm governance types. Evaluating three independent variables – knowledge and information complexity, the ease of transmitting information between parties and the existing capacities of potential supply bases – produced a matrix of five possible governance forms. These are market, modular, relational, captive and hierarchy. In this typology, as value chains move from hierarchy to market, the level of explicit coordination and power asymmetry between the actors grows. Governance as coordination (GVC) signified a disjuncture from governance as 'driving' (GCC), narrowing the perspective to the immediate dyadic links in a value chain (Bair, 2008). Gereffi, Humphrey and Sturgeon (2005) scaled down the concept of governance from a characteristic of an entire chain to a description of the mode of coordination prevailing at a particular link.

In response, the GPN framework critiqued the restricted GVC approach and restored a larger analytic picture. The weakness of the chain metaphor lay in its assumption of a vertical and linear sequencing and, consequently, was less useful than the expansive network construct. Global production activities are better conceptualized as being highly complex networks structures, in which there are intricate links – horizontal, diagonal and vertical – forming multidimensional, multilayered lattices of economic activity (Henderson et al., 2002). For GPN theory, the need is to 'grasp the dialectics of global-local' relations, for the firm-centred production networks are deeply influenced by the concrete socio-political contexts in which they are embedded. With the geographical dimension abstracted out of much GCC and GVC analysis (Dicken et al., 2001), GPN restores the 'territorial' of institutional and regulatory contexts and the state as actor. The 'strategic coupling' (Coe et al., 2004) of global production networks with regional assets is important. Henderson et al. (2002) identify three conceptual categories as core to GPN: value (how it is created, enhanced and captured); power (how it is created and maintained within production networks); and how agents and structures are embedded in particular territories. These provide the central tenets of empirical investigation into particular production networks (Johns, 2006).

Just as GVC governance might excessively narrow the focus to dyadic linkages in a value chain in the interests of 'parsimony and intellectual rigour' (Bair, 2008), so, too, might GPN as an explicitly relational approach be too expansive, a totalizing theory lacking explanatory bite. However, rather than regarding them as mutually exclusive, it might be advisable to see them as operating at different analytical levels and as complementary, enabling us to integrate distinct elements of the dynamics and mechanisms of call centre offshoring. As demonstrated below, the key coordinating link is the contractually prescribed Service Level Agreement (SLA), which specifies detailed metrics regarding the volume and quality of calls delivered from Indian sites to UK customers.

However, a myopic focus on dyadic coordination, the *meso* level, deflects attention from how specific linkages are embedded within the logics of capitalist cost reduction and profit maximization. GPN, operating macroscopically, widens the lens to incorporate capital flows, the characteristics of driving firms and the state, institutional, regulatory and labour market influences in destination geographies. GPN also places greater emphasis on value creation than (ironically) GVC analysis. Among the significant issues associated with value creation, Henderson et al. (2002: 448) include 'the conditions under which labour power is converted into actual labour through the labour process'. Issues of employment, skill, working conditions, understated in GVC analysis, are additionally important to GPN.

Call centres – from national to global

Corporate decisions to 'globalize' the call centre are inexplicable without reference to developments from the late 1980s within the UK. First, it is necessary to emphasize technological innovation, whether the advances in information networking technology, the digitalization of telecoms networks, or the massive expansion (and cheapening) of computing capacity facilitating huge increases in information storability and transportability. The key technological development was the ACD switch, which routed calls to available call-handlers within or, latterly, *between* centres (Taylor and Bain, 2007). This distinctive socio-technical system had huge implications for structuring, pacing, standardizing and monitoring work and for expanding the range of services deliverable remotely. Any meaningful analysis must stress the increases in labour productivity and significant cost savings deriving from scale economies and the opportunities to leverage added value from customers. Call centres centralized dispersed – or newly created – services and sales operations and reduced labour costs through increased divisions of labour. Scale was inseparably bound up with space and place as, crucially, servicing sites no longer needed to be located in physical proximity to customers. Distance-shrinking technologies permitted location in and relocation to cities and regions with cheaper but skilled labour and lower infrastructural costs (Richardson and Belt, 2001). So, invoking Massey's (1984) analysis, these newly created spatial divisions of labour were accompanied by corporate restructuring that involved job losses (e.g. bank branches) and process re-engineering, by which largely standardized centres clustered in the UK's peripheral areas (Huws, 2003: 149–50). From this perspective the later drive to relocate overseas might be regarded an extension, albeit at a *transnational* scale, of the same cost-saving, profit-maximizing spatial dynamic that produced concentrations at *national* scale.

However, it is a mistake to overemphasize technology as a driver. The widespread adoption of the call centre must take account of the political and economic environments of deregulation, organizational restructuring, financialization and the broader thrust of neoliberalism. There are important sectoral logics at work. In financial services, the Financial Services and Building Societies Acts (1986) dissolved distinctions between discrete markets, intensified competition and presaged unprecedented merger and acquisition activity. Consequently, call centres became central to organizations' pursuit of competitive advantage. Having become a strategic imperative in financial services, telecoms and utilities, the template was adopted throughout the private sector and increasingly the public sector into the 2000s (Ellis and Taylor, 2006). The dominant paradigm was the mass production call centre in which standardized workflows prevailed, call throughput was prioritized and extensive bureaucratic and technological controls utilized.

This generalization does not imply a universal logic since variation in call centre type and workflow exists. Contingent factors include inbound/outbound differentiation, industrial sector, service complexity, product market, customer segment and depth of knowledge required to handle service encounters. Some centres do deliver professional services such as tele-nursing (Smith et al., 2008), more quality interaction for higher-value customers and relatively complex technical-help activities. Nor does the proliferation of mass production centres mean that customer service representatives (CSRs) are unskilled. The performance of emotional labour is indispensable and organizations' recruitment and training practices prioritize (frequently gendered) social competencies, including conversational and communication skills and customer empathy (Callaghan and Thompson, 2002), attributes which assume exceptional significance in India.

Yet, the call centre is not a static but a constantly evolving organizational form, a fact disregarded in GCCP analysis and more broadly in the literature. In increasingly competitive markets, the established work system was used more rigorously through the combined effects of labour intensification and continued technological innovation. As ACD switches distributed calls between centres, 'virtual' operations allowed management to deepen divisions of labour, constrict the range of tasks and reduce call-handling times. From the mid-1990s, a plethora of CTI (computer telephony integration) applications, including caller-line identity and skills-based routing further intensified labour. Software, such as Blue Pumpkin, with the capacity simultaneously to calibrate staffing levels with call volumes, schedule workflows and monitor performance, had far-reaching consequences. The outcome was a speeded-up and even leaner variant, in which tight flows (Durand, 2007) formed an imperceptible chain of labour subordination. Labour optimization aimed to eliminate 'idle' time through minimal staffing and reducing the gaps between calls with the effect of 'closer filling up the pores of the working day' (Marx, 1976: 534). Performance metrics assumed greater prominence.

Although normative controls are influential (Callaghan and Thompson, 2001), metric-based target adherence is central to labour utilization (Bain et al., 2002). Quantitative and qualitative targets make explicit management's attempt to resolve the contradiction permeating call centre work of providing consistent high-quality service, whilst delivering call volumes of sufficient magnitude that cost reduction is fully realized. The wider significance of targets, that they constitute the tangible link between corporate strategy and workplace productivity, is fundamental to understanding this national-to-global trajectory. As corporate management forecast trends and position their companies against rivals in volatile markets, they formulate organization-wide objectives in relation to anticipated market share, costs and profits, considerations invariably driven by shareholder value. Metrics calculated for business unit are translated downwards to individual call centres as cost and/or profit centres through the mechanism of the SLA. Centre managers disaggregate these figures for workflows, and middle managers and team leaders then drive teams and individual call-handlers to meet targets. This sequence explains supervisory obsession with employees' 'stats' and SLA adherence. Through these coordinating mechanisms, the call centre's 'inner workings' are articulated with the dynamics of capitalist economy.

Consequently, change at macro-economic and sectoral levels can modify or even disrupt corporate objectives which, in turn, can impact on work organization. The wider background was the collapse of the late-1990s speculative boom and the dotcom crash which generated recessionary pressures. The so-called new economy suffered particularly through indebtedness and financialization. The transformation from superheated expansion to supercooled contraction created uncertainty at sector, company and workplace levels, compelling firms to prioritize cost containment. In financial services, further merger and acquisition activity (RBS-NatWest, Lloyds-TSB) represented a structural response to market turbulence, that engendered extreme competition and pushed firms towards the scramble for super-profits that ultimately precipitated the crisis that began with the collapse of Northern Rock in 2007 (Harman, 2009). Aggressive targets became the centrepiece of cost-reduction strategies, not least because labour comprises around two-thirds of call centre costs (Taylor et al., 2005). However, crucially, there were limits in the degree to which economies could be realized through labour intensification in the absence of alternatives such as automation and obvious constraints on extending working hours. In these conditions, offshoring promised to deliver dramatic labour cost savings for UK operators, initially, in financial services. From 2002, this competitive cost-cutting imperative drove firms to migrate voice services.

Global location dynamics

Ritzer and Lair repeat the widespread misconception that the call centre is entirely 'elastic' spatially; 'work can take place anywhere there is a phone line thus making it easy to establish operations nearly anywhere on the globe' (2008: 40). Underlying such assumptions are simplistic versions of globalization: that the world is genuinely borderless (Ohmae, 1990) and that the 'death of distance' (Cairncross, 1997) means that finance, capital and technology can flow uninhibited across a 'weightless world'.[4] In insisting that the 'space of flows' has replaced the 'space of places', Castells' (2000) 'informationalism', which privileges the technologies underpinning global networks, proved hugely influential. However, technology is a necessary, but not a sufficient, condition for enabling firms to offshore. Mobile capital, no matter how apparently weightless, must materialize somewhere (Rainnie et al., 2008). Harvey (2006) emphasizes two contradictory tendencies for capital: the need for sufficient geographical mobility to seek out investment opportunities *and* the need for sufficient geographical fixity so that accumulation can occur. Thus, one of globalization's paradoxes is to heighten the importance of the characteristics of place, notably labour's attributes, in which firms choose to locate facilities (Harvey, 1990: 294). The 'spatial fix' is material and not the 'nothingness' asserted by Ritzer and Lair.

How does this contradiction between mobility and fixity play out in call centre offshoring? Crucially, cost reduction drove UK companies to relocate to India. Synthesizing evidence, cost savings of 40–50 per cent were realizable in early UK offshoring, although recent estimates suggest 25–40 per cent as more typical (Nasscom, 2005; Nasscom, 2006; Nasscom-McKinsey, 2005). There is variability depending on scale and volume, nature of process, degree of standardization, supplier capabilities, precise location, and so on. Labour cost differential at approximately 70–80 per cent which, despite erosion in tight pre-recession labour markets, remains integral to India's comparative advantage, whatever quality rhetoric is spun by companies. Parenthetically, GVC literature, in abstracting the coordinating linkages, understates the importance of such fundamental economic drivers.

Yet, cost arbitrage means nothing without India's other principal 'place' attribute, supplies of university-educated and, indispensably, English-speaking labour. When mapping relocation, it is necessary to emphasize the vital point: that offshoring follows the contours of linguistic and cultural compatibility. While call centre offshoring is an overwhelmingly Anglophonic phenomenon, linguistic congruence also determines lesser migratory trends such as the limited French offshoring to francophone countries, Spanish services from Iberia and North America to Latin America, and even Japanese services delivered from Dalian in China (Taylor, 2010 forthcoming). Capital flows are not merely an abstraction for labour is constitutive of the accumulation process, and labour's language capabilities shape the uneven global landscape. Call centres do not 'slice though' national borders equally. The call centre world is not flat as Friedman (2005) would contend.

Place matters too in respect of diverse institutional, political and socioeconomic factors, includable within GPN's relational compass. The 'strategic coupling' of firms' GPNs with regional economies is important. Migration to India is encouraged by accessible and increasingly reliable telecommunications and technological infrastructures, following the Indian government's National Telecoms Policy in 1999. From the IMF's intervention in 1991, successive Indian governments have adhered to the liberalization, privatization and globalization mantra. Developments remind us that the state is crucial to the offshoring narrative, as governments seek to capture for their territories ever-larger shares of FDI. The success of India's offshored software/IT industry (D'Costa, 2003) prompted national and state governments to promote ITES-BPO[5] as a strategic objective providing various financial incentives. Government responsiveness to the demands of Nasscom helped create the business-friendly environment that reassures overseas investors. Consultants, notably McKinsey, legitimized India as a risk-free and cost-effective destination. This brief account scarcely touches upon the 'lattice' of factors that anchor and territorially embed companies' activities in particular locations.

In adopting a GPN approach, the question arises of how expansive should explanation be? At the broadest level, reference must be made to the neoliberal hegemony of recent decades (Harvey, 2005) and the new institutions of global governance (e.g. World Trade Organization). If the neoliberal economic, deregulatory environment in India attracted UK companies, then consideration must similarly be given to the political discourse within the UK that encouraged migration. Stimulated by the need to respond to first wave of call centre offshoring, the UK government advocated globalization as wholly beneficial in neo-Ricardian terms (DTI, 2004).

Yet, locational choice is hugely constrained. Companies' offshoring decisions are invariably complex and involve evaluating cost benefits against countervailing factors.[6] If lower costs were the sole criterion driving location, then China[7] or states with costs lower than India would be preferred destinations. It is an ensemble of factors, including telecom connectivity, skill, educational levels, linguistic ability and cultural empathy *combined with* lowest possible costs, that provides the basis of comparison between places and informs locational decisions. Arguably then, call centre globalization represents a qualified 'race to the bottom'.

UK company strategy, Indian suppliers and GCC

Just as financial services spearheaded the organizational and spatial transformations involved in telemediated interactive service work within the UK, so too did companies in this sector instigate and subsequently account for the largest share of overseas migration. Second in both chronological and scale terms was and remains telecommunications. British Telecom's (BT) 'remote sourcing' strategy (2003) was followed by Vodafone, 3G and T-Mobile. A sectoral diversity now includes travel/holidays (e.g. Thomas Cook, National Rail Enquiries Service) utilities (e.g. Centrica), media (e.g. BSkyB) and domestic outsourcers (Capita, Vertex). Organizations differ according to inter alia the scale of offshoring, the complexity of the services to be migrated and the timescale for implementation. One element in strategic choice relates to the contractual relationship between the demand and supply sides. At one extreme, there is the situation in which companies own and directly control their overseas operations, subsidiaries known as 'captives' in the Indian context.[8] These include HSBC and Axa. At the other extreme, there lies 'pure' outsourcing, by which companies outsource to third-party providers, whether Indian or multinational. Examples include BT subcontracting to HCL and Infosys or National Rail Enquiries to Sitel. Between 'hierarchy' and 'market' lie diverse forms of co-sourcing and partnership. For example, Barclays developed a joint venture with 51 per cent owned Intelenet and Aviva engaged in Build-Operate-Transfer (B-O-T) with three Indian suppliers (EXL, 24/7, WNS) which established operations later transferred to Aviva's direct control.

Scale influences, but does not wholly determine, choice. For some organizations, small volume prohibits the resource commitment associated with 'captive' operations. Using an Indian or MNC supplier for restricted provision on a single site may be the most appropriate option. Risk is externalized, albeit not mitigated, although the trade-off from subcontracting is weakened control. These are not instances of TNCs reconfiguring the sourcing landscape, but rather UK companies with no or limited global reach seeking tactical remote sourcing. At a larger scale, others such as BT or Aviva pursue multi-vendor, multi-site approaches in order to minimize risk, create inter-supplier competition and capitalize on specialized local knowledge. Barclays' semi-captive model accessed expertise from established specialists to enable a rapid ramp-up in capacity. HSBC is the most notable case of a global transnational corporation, extensively relocating processes to multiple Global Servicing Centres using integrated platforms. Thus, for some firms offshoring has been limited to a single, tactical act, while for others initial decisions presaged unfolding strategic programmes.

Significant variations exist between in-house and outsourced operations. In outsourcing, differences in complexity, contract length, degree of client control, often related to sensitivities to brandedness and quality, produce centrifugal and centripetal tensions. Since the raison d'etre of outsourcing lies in delivering labour cost savings to clients, external financial pressures (Kinnie, Purcell and Adams, 2008) are accentuated. Yet, the difference between captives and outsourcing may be too sharply drawn. Recent Indian evidence indicates that in-house operations are increasingly subject to similar financial stringencies as captives benchmark against the most cost-efficient outsourcers. Whatever comparative financial latitude captives might have enjoyed appears to be eroding.[9]

A complete analysis, consistent with understanding the distinctions between PDCCs and BDCCs, should include the taxonomy of companies at the supply side (Dossani and Kenney, 2007). The early call centre history from the mid-to-late 1990s was dominated by US captives, notably the pioneering GE Capital, whose success hugely contributed to establishing India as a viable location. Subsequently, Indian third-party companies were formed, either as start-ups (e.g. 24/7, EXL) or as BPO arms of IT companies (e.g. Progeon-Infosys), providing credible sourcing solutions. The later arrival of US-based multinational service providers, both generalists (e.g. IBM, EDS) and voice specialists (e.g. Teleperformance), sharpened market competition and further enhanced India's reputation. Subsequently, these MNCs provided templates for Indian third parties as they aspired to become global actors. These variations in capability, expertise and reputation at the supply side differentially impacted on UK companies' offshoring decisions.

Notwithstanding variation, offshored services have tended to be amongst the most standardized and transactional. Extensive evidence supports this cross-sectoral generalization (Taylor and Bain, 2006), a finding confirmed by Batt el al. (2005). In early and often experimental phases, many companies transitioned only overflow and out-of-hours calls, basic customer service, outbound telemarketing, or debt recovery and collections. The intention was to exploit labour cost arbitrage and to have services delivered that would be cost prohibitive if provided from the UK. However, as the scale expanded some greater complexity became discernible, although callflows remain largely routinized. In banking provision typically involves in a manager's words 'the full range of basic banking inquiries', while in insurance it includes claims notification, basic underwriting, policy renewals, and so on. One partial exception to standardization has been the provision of more complex technical help-desk activity.

Most offshoring companies operate UK centres with workforces almost double the industry average (Taylor and Bain, 2005: 270). It is not size per se that matters, but the fact that large operations have the most pronounced scale economies and divisions of labour and callflows are most standardized, characteristics which lend themselves to externalization. Typically, offshoring decisions followed company-wide reviews in response to, or anticipation of, changed market conditions, increased competition and concerns over profitability. The outcome invariably was that the least risk-laden, non-core callflows were identified for migration and were accompanied by a restructuring that recalls Hammer and Champy's (1993) re-engineering revolution. Processes were disaggregated, simplified and recomposed with the focus on cost effectiveness. In addition, offshoring provided opportunities for reconfiguring UK operations, leading to further intensification, downsizing and site closure. Thus, offshoring should be regarded not as a discrete initiative but as interwoven with continuous firm-wide, organizational restructuring.

Several distinct but frequently overlapping approaches to the migratory process are observable, based on whether re-engineering precedes, coincides with or follows relocation. Typical of early phases is 'lift and shift', by which processes are transplanted without modification to ensure transition is as risk-free and damage proof as possible. Re-engineering might precede relocation, but the aim is to replicate process and culture at Indian sites, a transition which constitutes a form of 'Taylorism through export'. However, over time, and particularly where organizations undertake further relocation, re-engineering generally occurs during or following the migratory process, where clients and suppliers collaborate to leverage improvements in speed, flexibility, labour utilization and productivity. The longer a process is migrated, the more the emphasis shifts to continuous improvement, to knowledge and skill accrual and the active engagement of supplier management.

Since the transnational voice 'chain' is decisively shaped by its techno-logical architecture, issue is taken with Henderson et al. (2002) who meth-odologically see ICT as 'an inherent element of [all] GPNs'. Yet, technology cannot be treated as an undifferentiated environmental factor. UK and Indian sites are integrated through common platforms to form 'virtual' call centres. Through 'cloud' technologies, augmented by Blue Pumpkin-type software, call traffic is routed to 'the first available operator irrespective of geography' (*Telephony manager*, quoted in Taylor and Bain, 2006: 160), by which voice services are spatially integrated. Typically, though, calls are not randomly distributed. Given customer segmentation strategies, companies commonly route to India only the 'mass market', with premium or privileged customers' calls serviced domestically. Evidence suggests a dichotomization, by which higher-value calls or those requiring considerable empathy (e.g. cross-selling), deep tacit knowledge or a 'very good understanding of the ver-nacular' are retained onshore as 'core competencies'. Offshoring simplified calls, in which knowledge is rigidly codified, reflects concerns over Indian call-handlers' ability to deliver flexible customer interaction. The following distinction informs most companies' practice.

> Offshoring may be good for very mundane calls, but as soon as calls require greater complexity beyond the script there are problems. I use the Guin-ness analogy of the white head and the black body. Agents in India can deal with the froth but cannot go deep into the body of the call. (*Telephony director*, quoted in Taylor and Anderson, 2008: 71)

Bifurcation is not flawless for, despite call-streaming technologies, segre-gating straightforward from more challenging calls is not always possible. Complex queries that exceed Indian CSR's competence or transcend proced-ure are 'bounced back' or 'escalated' to CSRs in the UK, in what some term 'hands-off'. Such nuances provide additional insight into the detailed inter-place division of labour.

In sum, call centre global chains do not correspond exactly to the in-house PDCC and pure 'outsourcing' BDCC polarities for various forms of disintermediation lie in-between, in which organizational boundaries are blurred. Such diversity invokes Gereffi, Humphrey and Sturgeon's (2005) matrix, but does not exactly map onto it. In the purest market-based BDCC, where 'classic' outsourcing prevails, cost-reduction demand-side influences dominate inter-firm power relationships, making suppliers dependent upon client prescription.

The term 'chain' itself may be questioned for it implies sequential link-ages. If one isolates the call as a service encounter linking UK customers with Indian sites, then the relationship is essentially binary rather than sequential.

Even where UK companies use several suppliers, the nature of the exchange consists of multiple, discrete one-to-one calls, notwithstanding qualifications such as the 'bounce back' loop. More abstractly, Glucksmann's (2004) relational and processual analysis highlights the intermediary function that call-handlers play within broader divisions of labour. At a certain analytical level Indian call-handlers, just as those within the UK, are interconnected upstream and downstream with the activities of other service agents such as motor mechanics or warehousing staff, insofar as calls are part of the 'overall configuration of production/distribution/exchange/consumption' (ibid.: 798). However, this totalizing perspective, however insightful, lacks concrete purchase. These provisos do not contradict the essentially dyadic nature of the 'chain'. That management in both places is preoccupied with the coordinating mechanism at the point of service delivery justifies a narrowing of perspective to consider GVC governance in detail.

Value 'chain' governance and labour process

While 'governance' is multidimensional (legal, financial, regulatory), the focus is on 'operational' governance embodied in contractual SLAs, which are pivotal to the coordination of interaction between Indian sites and UK clients and customers. Generally, SLAs detail the services to be delivered, service and quality management standards, timetables, supplier and client responsibilities, dispute resolution, termination conditions, and so on (de Bruyn and Ramioul, 2006). While embedded in outsourcing as the integrative counterpart to geographical dispersion and organizational disintermediation, they are also utilized, if less obviously, in in-house relationships. Obviously, differentiation exists in specific SLA metrics, contingent upon *inter alia* service complexity, business volumes and call type.

In prescribing quantitative 'metrics' (call volumes, call-handling times, collections/sales targets, abandonments rates etc.), SLAs seek to determine in advance the value that Indian call-handlers will create or 'add', thereby invoking Henderson et al.'s (2002) conceptual category. Call volumes at sufficient scale will enable UK companies to realize the cost-reduction potential implicit in remote provision and, where outsourcing occurs, will ensure that Indian suppliers achieve satisfactory margins. Given the prevailing standardized workflows, these metrics typically specify high-volume, short duration, repetitive calls. Simultaneously, SLAs impose qualitative criteria (customer satisfaction, accent, fluency, rapport, script adherence). Although the customer-oriented logic ultimately is subordinated to the cost-reduction dynamic driving offshoring, companies insist that Indian call-handlers interact sensitively, accurately and fluently with customers. Consequently, qualitative standards are comprehensively implemented and include familiar and distinctively Indian forms, including speech monitoring for accent neutrality. Locutional competencies and the enactment of stylized conversations are critical to governance (Cowie, 2007). Tight scripting reflects not just regulatory requirements, but also management's obligation to deliver consistent call quality in conditions of uncertainty over linguistic capability. Strategic concerns exist over activities that might be considered routine in the UK.

Operational governance at the service delivery interface necessitates continuous performance monitoring and reporting to UK management. While management information systems generate statistics in real time, they are complemented by periodic reports evaluating performance against contract. When call volumes or quality standards fall below prescribed metrics, the result is managerial intervention, including corrective action or dismissal of under-performing CSRs, financial penalties for suppliers, contract renegotiation or even termination in extreme cases. The power asymmetry between client and supplier – the focus of much GCC/GVC – in the outsourced call centre 'chain' is demonstrated by the fact that performance verification resides ultimately with UK senior management.

The widely recognized outcome is an array of bureaucratic, technical and cultural controls (D'Cruz and Noronha, 2009) that are the fundamental source of the uniquely low levels of job discretion the GCCP identifies. They arise not primarily from national institutional factors, as the VOC framework presumes, but from the imperatives of UK companies as their offshoring decisions intersect with the characteristics of labour in its relocated place. From the perspective of labour process theory (LPT), the imposition of SLA metrics represents an attempt to overcome the indeterminacy of call centre labour through detailing exact quantities and qualities of labour power deemed necessary for profitable activity. However, success is only ever partial. Production indeterminacy remains, for even the most stringently enforced SLAs cannot cocoon the transplanted labour process from the consequences of labour as active agency, nor insulate call-handling from potentially damaging quality slippages or quantitative underachievement. If labour indeterminacy unavoidably confronts site and client management alike, it is compounded by wider problematics, some in the sphere of reproduction, that disrupt service delivery and illustrate GPN's 'regional' influences.

First, there is labour power mobility, which constitutes a second labour indeterminacy (Smith, 2006). In conditions of frenetic growth, labour retention became profoundly problematical as call-handlers and managers exploited 'overheated' labour markets in 'Tier 1' cities to move between facilities for better pay and conditions (Budhwar et al., 2009). Although turnover tends to be higher in third-party centres and amongst CSRs on the most volume-driven services, attrition has impacted hugely on recruitment and on service continuity and quality, even in captives and on less standardized services (Taylor and Bain, 2006: 84–100).

Second, and relatedly, there is the relative shallowness of the labour pool. The workforce of international-facing call centres, both captive and outsourced, is exclusively composed of middle-class university graduates. However, English language education does not necessarily equip graduates with the linguistic competence and cultural empathy to interact with customers to standards deemed acceptable by clients and their suppliers. Nasscom-McKinsey (2005: 90) estimated that only 10–15 per cent have the skills for direct employment in an industry that then hires 5 per cent of applicants. Despite the enormous commitment of resources to training, including accent neutralization, successful outcomes are not guaranteed. Companies consistently report linguistic difficulties and misunderstanding as their single most significant problem (Taylor and Bain, 2005, 2006).

Third, although employees possess powerful professional identities and strong career aspirations (D'Cruz and Noronha, 2009), this important socio-normative control may be undermined by the contradiction between employees' expectation and a work intensity that requires many to undertake relentless, routinized work. Fourth, to ensure attendance Indian companies, distinctively, transport staff between home and workplace. Partly control measure, partly intended to mitigate infrastructural chaos and partly stimulated by welfare responsibilities for women employees, the practice stems essentially from operational governance, from the requirement to have prescribed numbers of call-handlers in place at agreed times. Yet, employers' complaints regarding absenteeism indicate difficulties in achieving satisfactory attendance. For many employees travelling and 'waiting around' times contribute to exit decisions (Taylor et al., 2009).

Finally, though beyond the chapter's scope, there is the question of resistance, a central concern of LPT. Employers cannot take labour's consent or compliance for granted. Informal on-the-job resistance, often taking cultural forms, are identified (Mirchandani, 2004). While the immediate prospects for trade unionism may be unpromising, the limited presence of UnitesPro, a union oriented on the call centre/BPO industry, suggests some potential for collective organization (Taylor and Bain, 2008).

Conclusion

GVC governance (Gereffi, Humphrey and Sturgeon, 2005), in emphasizing dyadic linkages in global value chains, helps isolate the SLA as the instrument coordinating the technologically integrated but geographically dispersed call centre 'chain' at the customer servicing interface. Despite contingent variation, the SLA is the common mechanism in sourcing relationships, whether captive, outsourced or in the permutations lying between Gereffi and Korzeniewicz's PDCC and BDCC polarities. It is less important that this 'chain' is best conceptualized as an essentially binary relationship, than to recognize the merit of a focus at this *meso* level of operational governance, which interconnects the *micro* level of work organization with the *macro* levels of capitalist political economy and firm strategy. The SLA is the fulcrum articulating the competitive imperatives of cost reduction and profit maximization, which drive firms to offshore, with the labour process in which site management at the behest of UK management utilize performance metrics to exercise control over call-handlers to meet their mutual corporate objectives.

A criticism of GCC and GVC governance might be that, despite the utility of abstracting inter- and intra-firm coordination, it devalues labour as agency. However, as attempted here, integrating the labour process with GCC/GVC's precepts and elements of GPN's more expansive relational perspective may provide invaluable analytical purchase on concrete global production and servicing chains. Reciprocally, LPT may benefit from future engagement with diverse GCC, GVC and GPN approaches and the insights generated by their efforts to understand inter-firm power relationships, value creating and enhancing processes and the coordination of globally dispersed economic activities.

The qualities of labour are certainly critical in influencing the strategic decisions and shaping the experience of UK companies. Labour has attributes that make India attractive as a location: its cheapness, its relative availability, its education, its putative linguistic capability. Yet, no attempt by capital to use remote location, no 'spatial fix', can overcome the problem of the indeterminacy of Indian call centre labour power. The most intensive managerial controls cannot guarantee for UK firms the seamless substitutability of labour performance from Indian sites. Pursuing the holy grail of SLA conformance can only achieve partial and contingent success. Indian labour as a peculiar commodity presents itself to capital as contradictory, simultaneously a source of value, but inescapably problematic as capital attempts to realize that value.

To re-emphasize, the call centre is a constantly changing organizational form which generates subtle but significant changes in its labour process. Just as macro-economic recessionary pressures of the early 2000s made cost-cutting a central concern for UK firms, contributing to the evolution of a leaner, labour intensified variant, so too will economic crisis have profound consequences. While conclusions are provisional, the emerging Indian evidence suggests that aggressive cost-cutting is ramping-up performance metrics under the rubrics of 'process excellence' and 'performance management', by which reduced numbers of CSRs handle unchanged or increased call volumes and 'underperformers' are dismissed. Thus, articulation between the *macro* level (economic crisis and corporate cost-cutting), the *meso* level (expanded SLA quantitative metrics) and the *micro* level (tighter controls and work intensification) across the transnational call centre 'chain' is a dynamic process, with significant implications for labour and the labour process.

Acknowledgements

Debts of gratitude are owed to Paul Thompson for his encouragement and for the stimulating discussions and to Debra Howcroft and Paul Stewart for their helpful comments. Since this work is based on insights gleaned from research projects over several years, thanks are due to many bodies including Scottish Development International, the Customer Contact Association, Nasscom, the Carnegie Trust, the Royal Society of Edinburgh, Unite the Union, UnitesPro, Union Network International and the International Labour Organization. Thanks are due to Ernesto Noronha, Premilla D'Cruz, Karthik Shekhar, Jon Messenger, Rob MacGregor, Harriet Eisner, Christopher Ng, Jim Mason, Mark Hallan, Anne Marie Forsyth, Al Rainnie and above all to the late Peter Bain.

Notes

1 Figures based on the total of 171,100 employed in the Indian ITES-BPO industry as calculated by Nasscom and the estimate of 60 per cent working on 'voice' services for 2003 and 790,000 and approximately 50 per cent for 2009 (Nasscom, 2009).
2 The caveat is that the scale and capability of many destinations are exaggerated (Taylor, 2009).
3 While call centre offshoring is often interconnected with the relocation of IT/software and diverse back-office processes, this chapter separates out voice services in the interests of analytical clarity.
4 See Huws (2003) for an effective critique.
5 Information Technology Enabled Services-Business Process Outsourcing.
6 For reasons of competitive advantage, some UK companies choose not to offshore voice services, believing that damage to brand and customer confidence outweigh cost benefits.
7 China is not a viable destination for offshored call centres for linguistic reasons.
8 The GCCP describe India as a specialized outsourced location but much of its industry is 'captive'.

9 Significant developments include India's most important captive GE Capital becoming a third-party provider and Dell converting activity into profit centres through 'internal' subcontracting. Presentations by captives to Nasscom Conferences revealed their emulation of third-party 'operational excellence'.

REFERENCES

Bain, P. and Taylor, P. (2008) 'No Passage to India: Initial Responses of UK Unions to Call Centre Offshoring', *Industrial Relations Journal*, 39(1): 5–23.

Bain, P., Watson, A., Mulvey, G., Taylor, P. and Gall, G. (2002) 'Taylorism, Targets and the Pursuit of Quantity and Quality by Call Centre Management', *New Technology, Work and Employment*, 17(3): 154–69.

Bair, J. (2008) 'Analysing Global Economic Organization: Embedded Networks and Global Chains Compared', *Economy and Society*, 37(3): 339–64.

Batt, R., Kwon, H., Doellgast, V., Nopany, M., Nopany, P. and da Costa, A. (2005) *The Indian Call Centre Industry*, Ithaca, NY: Cornell University.

Boreham, P., Parker, R., Thompson, P. and Hall, R. (2007) *New Technology@ Work*, London: Routledge.

BPAP (2009) *Philippines IT-BPO Industry*, Manila: BPO Association Philippines.

Budhwar, P., Varma, A., Malhotra, N. and Mukerjee, A. (2009) 'Attrition in Indian BPOs: The Hidden Cost of Outsourcing', *The Services Industries Journal*, 29.

Cairncross, F. (1997) *The Death of Distance*, Boston, MA: Harvard Business School Press.

Callaghan, G. and Thompson, P. (2001) 'Edwards Revisited: Technical Control and Call Centres', *Economic and Industrial Democracy*, 22(1): 13–37.

Callaghan, G. and Thompson, P. (2002) ' "We Recruit Attitude": The Selection and Shaping of Routine Call Centre Labour', *Journal of Management Studies*, 39(2): 223–54.

Castells, M. (2000) *The Rise of the Network Society*, Oxford: Blackwell.

Coe, N., Hess, M., Wai-Chung, H., Dicken, P. and Henderson, J. (2004) 'Globalising Regional Development', *Transactions of Institute of British Geographers*, 29: 464–84.

Cowie, C. (2007) 'The Accents of Outsourcing: The Meanings of "Neutral" in the Indian Call Centre Industry', *World Englishes*, 26(3): 316–30.

D'Costa, A. P. (2003) 'Uneven and Combined Development: Understanding India's Software Exports', *World Development*, 31(1): 211–37.

D'Cruz, P. and Noronha, E. (2009) *Employee Identity in Indian Call Centres: The Notion of Professionalism*, New Delhi: Sage.

De Bruyn, T. and Ramioul, M. (2006) *Offshore Outsourcing: Handbook for Employee Representatives and Trade Unionists*, Nyon: UNI.

Dicken, P. (2007) *Global Shift*, London: Sage.

Dicken, P., Kelley, P. F., Olds, K. and Yeung, H. (2001) 'Chains and Networks, Territories and Scales: Towards a Relational Framework for Analysing the Global Economy', *Global Networks*, 1(2): 89–112.

▶

▶

Dossani, R. and Kenney, M. (2007) 'The Next Wave of Globalization: Relocating Service Provision to India', *World Development*, 35(5): 772–91.

DTI (2004) *Making Globalisation a Force for Good*, London: Department of Trade and Industry.

Durand, J. P. (2007) *The Invisible Chain: Constraints and Opportunities in the New World of Employment*, Basingstoke: Palgrave.

Ellis, V. and Taylor, P. (2006) ' "You Don't Know What You've Got Till It's Gone": Re-contextualising the Origins, Development and Impact of the Call Centre', *New Technology, Work and Employment*, 21(2): 107–22.

Friedman, T. (2005) *The World Is Flat*, London: Allan Lane.

Gereffi, G., Humphrey, J. and Sturgeon, T. (2005) 'The Governance of Global Value Chains', *Review of International Political Economy*, 12(1): 78–104.

Gereffi, G. and Korzeniewicz, M. (eds) (1994) *Commodity Chains and Global Capitalism*, Westport, CT: Praeger.

Gibbon, P., Bair, J. and Ponte, S. (2008) 'Governing Global Value Chains: An Introduction', *Economy and Society*, 37(3): 315–338.

Glucksmann, M. (2004) 'Call Configurations: Varieties of Call Centre and Divisions of Labour', *Work, Employment and Society*, 18(4): 795–811.

Hall, P. A. and Soskice, D. (eds) (2001) *Varieties of Capitalism: The Institutional Foundations of Comparative Advantage*, Oxford: Oxford University Press.

Hammer, M. and Champy, J. (1993) *Reengineering the Corporation*, New York: Harper Collins.

Harman, C. (2009) *Zombie Capitalism: Global Crisis and the Relevance of Marx*, London: Bookmarks.

Harvey, D. (1990) *The Condition of Postmodernity*, Oxford: Blackwell.

Harvey, D. (2005) *A Short History of Neo-Liberalism*, Oxford: Oxford University Press.

Harvey, D. (2006) *The Limits to Capital*, London: Verso.

Henderson, J., Dicken, P., Hess, M., Coe, N. and Wai-Chung, H. (2002) 'Global Production Networks and the Analysis of Economic Development', *Review of International Political Economy*, 9(3): 436–64.

Holman, D., Batt, R. and Holtgrewe, U. (2007) *The Global Call Centre Report: International Perspectives on Management and Employment*, Ithaca, NY: Cornell University.

Holman, D., Frenkel, S., Sørenson, S. and Wood, S. (2009) 'Work Design Outcomes in Call Centers: Strategic Choice and Institutional Explanations', *Industrial and Labor Relations Review*, 62(4): 510–32.

Huws, U. (2003) *The Making of a Cybertariat*, London: Merlin.

Johns, J. (2006) 'Video Games Production Networks: Value Capture, Power Relations and Embeddedness', *Journal of Economic Geography*, 6: 151–80.

Kinnie, N., Purcell, J. and Adams, M. (2008) 'Explaining Employees' Experience of Work in Outsourced Call Centres: The Influence of Clients, Owners and Temporary Work Agencies', *Journal of Industrial Relations*, 50(2): 209–27.

Korczynski, M. (2002) *Human Resource Management in Service Work*, Basingstoke: Palgrave.

Marx, K. (1976) *Capital Volume 1*, Harmondsworth: Penguin.

▶

Massey, D. B. (1984) *Spatial Divisions of Labour, Social Structures and the Geography of Production*, London: Macmillan.

Miozzo, M. and Soete, L. (2001) 'Internationalization of Services: A Technological Perspective', *Technological Forecasting and Social Change*, 67: 159–85.

Mirchandani, K. (2004) 'Practices of Global Capital: Gaps, Cracks and Ironies in Transnational Call Centres in India', *Global Networks*, 4(4): 355–73.

Nasscom (2005) *Handbook for the ITES-BO Industry*, New Delhi: Nasscom.

Nasscom (2006) *The IT Industry in India – Strategic Review, 2006*, New Delhi: Nasscom.

Nasscom (2009) *The IT-BPO Sector in India – Strategic Review 2009*, New Delhi: Nasscom.

Nasscom-McKinsey (2005) *Extending India's Leadership of the Global IT – BPO Industries*, New Delhi: Nasscom-McKinsey.

Ohmae, K. (1990) *The Borderless World*, New York: Free.

O'Riain, S. (2004) 'The Politics of Mobility in Technology-Driven Commodity Chains: Developmental Coalitions in the Irish Software Industry', *International Journal of Urban and Regional Research*, 28(3): 642–63.

Rainnie, A., Barrett, R., Burgess, J. and Connell, J. (2008) 'Call Centres, the Networked Economy and the Value Chain', *Journal of Industrial Relations*, 50(2): 195–208.

Richardson, R. and Belt, V. (2001) 'Saved by the Bell? Call Centres and Economic Development in Less Favoured Regions', *Economic and Industrial Democracy*, 22(1): 67–98.

Ritzer, G. and Lair, C. (2008) 'The Globalisation of Nothing and the Outsourcing of Service Work', in MacDonald, L. and Korczynski, M. (eds) *Service Work: Critical Perspectives*, London: Routledge, 31–51.

Smith, C. (2006) 'The Double Indeterminacy of Labour Power: Labour Effort and Labour Mobility', *Work, Employment and Society*, 20(2): 389–402.

Smith, C. and Meiskins, P. (1995) 'System, Society and Dominance Effects in Cross-national Organizational Analysis', *Work, Employment and Society*, 9(2): 241–67.

Smith, C., Valsecchi, V., Mueller, F. and Gabe, J. (2008) 'Knowledge and Discourse of Labour Process Transformation: Nurses and the Case of NHS Direct', *Work, Employment and Society*, 22(4): 581–99.

Sturgeon, T. J. (2002) 'Modular Production Networks: A New American Model of Industrial Organisation', *Industrial and Corporate Change*, 11: 451–96.

Taylor, P. (2010, forthcoming) 'Remote Work from the Perspective of Developed Economies: A Multi-Country Synthesis', in J. Messenger (ed.) *Offshoring and Working Conditions*, Basingstoke: Palgrave Macmillan.

Taylor, P. and Anderson, P. (2008) *Contact Centres in Scotland: The 2008 Audit*, Glasgow: Scottish Development International.

Taylor, P. and Bain, P. (1999) ' "An Assembly Line in the Head": Work and Employee Relations in the Call Centre', *Industrial Relations Journal*, 30(2): 101–17.

Taylor, P. and Bain, P. (2005) 'India Calling to the Far Away Towns: The Call Centre Labour Process and Globalization', *Work, Employment and Society*, 19(2): 261–82.

▶

Taylor, P. and Bain, P. (2006) *An Investigation into the Offshoring of Financial Services Business Processes*, Glasgow: Scottish Development International.

Taylor, P. and Bain, P. (2007) 'Reflections on the Call Centre – a Reply to Glucksmann', *Work, Employment and Society*, 21(2): 349–62.

Taylor, P. and Bain, P. (2008) 'United by a Common Language? Trade Union Responses in the UK and India to Call Centre Offshoring', *Antipode*, 40(1): 131–54.

Taylor, P., D'Cruz, P., Noronha, E. and Scholarios, D. (2009) 'Indian Call Centres and Business Process Outsourcing: A Study in Union Formation', *New Technology, Work and Employment*, 24(1): 19–42.

Taylor, P., D'Cruz, P., Noronha, E. and Scholarios, D. (2010) 'Domestic labour – the Experience of Work in India's Other Call Centre Industry', in D. Howcroft and H. Richardson (eds) *Work and Life in the Global Economy: A Gendered Analysis of Service Work*, Basingstoke: Palgrave Macmillan, 99–123.

Taylor, P., Gall, G., Bain, P. and Baldry, C. (2005) ' "Striving under Chaos": The Effects of Market Turbulence and Organisational Flux on Call Centre Work', in Stewart, P. (ed.) *Employment, Trade Union Renewal and the Future of Work*, Basingstoke: Palgrave, 20–40.

Thompson, P. (2003) 'Disconnected Capitalism: Or Why Employers Can't Keep Their Side of the Bargain', *Work, Employment and Society*, 17(2): 359–78.

Go with the Flow: Labour Power Mobility and Labour Process Theory[1]

Chris Smith

Introduction

This chapter expands discussion on the nature of labour power, building on a recent paper (Smith, 2006) where it was argued that the mobility side of labour power within capitalism had been under-theorized and not sufficiently integrated into assessment of workplace conflicts between workers and managers. That paper suggested that mobility power – securing labour services for capital and securing labour processes for labour – provided a terrain of strategy and tactics, which could influence not only the length of stay in any workplace, but also the nature of work – intensity of work, types of authority regime, nature of tasks and so on – as worker controlled exit volition could be used to bargain with employers. This highlighted the more particular nature of labour power within capitalism, that is, the element in the labour process that is uncertain, embodied, external and with an essential duality – the *person* of the worker is not what the employer actually wants, but rather only the labour services (the metaphorical 'hired hand' or 'muscle' in manual occupations) which is the 'property' stored in living labour and carried into labour process by the worker.

Labour processes are both abstract and empirical; the abstract element is valorization – the process where surplus value is created, which is the dominant function of labour processes in capitalism. The commodity form contains use and exchange value; and the worker as a 'special commodity' is hired for both use (their particular skills) and exchange value (their ability to work to create surplus value and profits). The abstract element connects to the capitalist market (for both capitalist products and labour power), ensuring that only firms that remain profitable (and this can have different historical meanings) survive, regardless of the quality or use-value of the

269

products or the skill (or use-value) of labour power in the firm. Capitalism periodically destroys the livelihoods of skilled and unskilled workers as well as companies producing products with high utility. Such products and companies are ultimately judged against exchange or market value which is fickle and crisis-ridden.

The idea of labour power as a *flow* evokes action and movement. Capital is not *naturally* fixed, but possesses certain fixity in some forms which can create the impression of stability. Buildings and machinery are capital with spatial fixity whereas money capital flows through the system in seconds with little apparent sense of a home or spatial identity. Factories and offices have to be constructed, project an appearance of permanence as stable natural structures, even though these very physical aspects of capital are also transitory and embody or represent capitalist social relations (Baldry, 1999, 2010). Labour power can also acquire *fixity*, both through practising one occupation or skill (*task fixity*); or through working for one employer for many years (*temporal fixity*); or through being located in a particular place or community – a sort of *place fixity*. Beynon and Hudson (1993) suggested that capital dominated *space* (something abstract or rootless) and labour *place* (some*where* with cultural meaning or social community). But as I will argue, this understates both the mobility of labour and the immobility of capital.

It is a misreading of the appearance of such fixity or stability to consider labour as a 'resource' for the firm in the same way as fixed capital, as the individual ownership of mobility power by the worker ensures any stay with a particular employer or occupation or skill is always dependent on an exchange bargain – over work effort and mobility opportunities (that is, opportunities to increase the value of labour power, through training, development, career progression etc.) that the exchange facilitates. It is also subject to the human life cycle, which means workers behaving in different ways at different times of their working life – more job changes when young, fewer when middle aged for example. These are qualities that are inherently human, and hence do not apply to fixed capital.

The term *flow* is not used in the sense of an endless and seamless movement of labour power without constraint. As noted in Smith (2006: 407), categories of labour with ascribed differences, 'women or black workers, for example, or certain types of industry (mining, agriculture, with location idiosyncrasies) or traditional forms of labour (such as domestic or household workers)', witness the continued application of employer's coercive controls over labour mobility because workers can't move as easily. But 'with the growth of the labour market, competition and competitive strategies to recruit and retain labour were devolved to employers and workers freedom to quit expanded, which concomitantly reduced employer coercion in the employment contract (Montgomery, 1993: 39–51).'

But 'a constant flow of different individuals through a labour process creates problems when individual differences have a material effect on productivity or profitability for the employer' (Smith, 2006: 408). Hence, the incentives to regularize labour capture and retention for capital and employment security and 'fixity' for workers exist because of the costs of movement for both. But as is argued here, the costs of flow have been declining, as the availability of a global labour pool expands, competition between workers increases, capital movement and trade grows, education and training levels standardize and shared technologies reduce barriers to movement. But such trends are not unidirectional; and place, institutions and state regulations, continue to both facilitate and block movements. It is also the case as Taylor's chapter (Chapter 12) on the offshoring of call centres indicates that the increased mobility of services they provide does not negate the fact that such modern forms of fixed capital are located in particular places for particular logics informed by both capitalist competition, and locational and institutional advantages of certain places.

The chapter begins with a discussion of changes within capitalism and how these changes apply to labour power under new conditions within the global economy. This is accomplished through the double indeterminacy of labour power framework – the dual uncertainties around using and retaining the worker for the employer, and accessing and managing utilization levels for the worker. The chapter concludes by stressing the differences between this view of labour power and that of resource based theory of the firm, and advocating applying a flow perspective to labour process research which has been too workplace or organization-centred, and disconnected from the very dynamic trends within capitalism and capital-labour relations.

Capitalist dynamism over past 30 years

Decentring work from the workplace

We have seen major technological developments since the publication of the *Labour Process Theory* in 1990. ICTs in particular have increased 'virtuality' in work, and stretched the scale and range of communication. Working on the move characterizes many service jobs and a 'workplace-civic society-home' reconfiguration has expanded the porosity of the 'working day' without extending the working day *within* the workplace. Rather, anywhere with satellite access for mobile devices is facilitating the transforming of civic society space (airports, trains, coffee houses, streets, etc.) into a place for the individual to work, but without the social solidarity of a traditional workplace (Felstead and Jewson, 2000, 2005).

Although most service work remains within management control systems and a work*place*, the idea of 'work' as organization-centred is being undermined – de-centred, stretched spatially and temporally, as services move to 24/7 access and labour reserves are sourced by price on an increasingly global scale (see Taylor's chapter in this volume) and professional service workers are accessible on a continuous basis. Recent research on 'train working' noted that '...office professionals now work away from their desks 50–90% of their time'. Such 'mobile teleworkers...spend time travelling and/or working at different locations, use ICTs in work [which] involves some level of knowledge intensity and communication with others either internal and/or external to their organisation' (Axtell, Hislop and Whittaker, 2008: 922). Other studies of specific devices, mobile phones, for example, have found a gender bias (more men reporting frequent use of mobile phones for work purposes) but also that blue-collar workers, especially skilled tradesmen, were significant issuers, thus questioning the bias towards managers and professionals in research on mobile working (Wajcman, Bittman and Brown, 2008: 639). This research emphasizes, however, the control and pleasure dimension of ICTs, and the ability of the individual to manage or control the transgression of work-related calls into the home.

Some writers have suggested that this process of 'decentring work' can be captured in the idea of 'global work' (Jones, 2008). This suggests that 'work' is becoming a practice infused with mobility imperatives, spatial stretching and temporal openness, and the idea of a fixed place of work where the workers go everyday is being transformed into a much more open and interconnected globalized site of work practice. Although not integrated into any idea of capitalism or a capitalist labour process (rather a reified idea of 'work' separated from political economy and capitalist social relations) Jones's empirical work on London's professional service workers does, nevertheless, highlight the increased mobility of workers and the transience of working space for certain occupations.

In a recent review, Felstead (2009: 3) noted that '...time and space have become more compressed and journeys longer' and that 'whereas in 1950 the average person in Britain travelled five miles per day, half a century later it was 28 miles and by 2025 it is forecast to double'. This recent review confirms a gradual move towards work becoming more dispersed, with more intense use of office space (such as hot-desking) and the removal of individual control at work, and continued rise in the use of the home as an extension of the office (see also Baldry, 2010).

Mobility of capital

Alongside the mobility of labour due to changes within the firm, the period has also seen a heightened mobility of capital. In 2006, the UK was the largest recipient country of FDI, followed by the US and China. Members of the EU were well represented as recipient countries; while 9 of the 20 economies with the largest FDI inflows were to developing or transition economies.[2] While capital flow has accelerated, it remains unevenly distributed and hence the effects of transferring different ways of organizing the labour process are also uneven. This means hybridity of some labour processes (especially within China), but retention of national settlement in others (especially Japan) and greater adaptation in others (e.g. the UK).

The period has displayed considerable borrowing, transfer and learning, signified most strongly within the debate on 'Japanization' of production (Elger and Smith, 2005 for review), but also continued Americanization (Edwards and Ferner, 2002; Royal, 2006; Zeitlin and Herrigel, 2000) and the limited impact of foreign investment on the Japanese model (Olcott, 2009). As noted by Deeg and Jackson (2007: 171), 'a growing literature argues that most national economies are actually in a period of hybridization – a process that involves combining institutions adopted from outside a given context with existing ones'. But as Smith (2008: 46–7) has argued, this raises questions about specifying what is being combined, and in the 'best practice' literature, what exact combination of institutional practices produces 'successful' outcomes for capital. From the perspective of this chapter, however, these debates on capitalism and hybridity raise important questions about mobility of capital and labour and how this impacts on actual labour processes, such as conflicts between local and imported ways of working; greater heterogeneity to agents – both owners/managers and workers – and the fracturing of conflicts along nationality lines. The mass movement of 120 million Chinese workers into the export orientated manufacturing industries has destabilized developing countries (Freeman, 2006) as well as sucking in labour intensive (and increasingly capital intensive) production operations from the US, Europe and other parts of Asia, and shifting these countries out of manufacturing and into low-wage service work.

Market access and cost reduction are the primary motives for FDI (see Taylor's chapter in this volume for a discussion of 'quantity' versus 'quality' strategies in the call centre sector). These strategies not only help shape the international division of labour (Frobel, Heinriches and Kreye, 1980) between countries, especially between developed and developing states, but they also show up through intra-country differentiation (Smith, 2008). For example, China has principally sucked in FDI to reduce labour costs from high-wage manufacturing firms, but market access has become *the* driver of recent investment, especially in the service sector (see Gamble, 2006 for a review). While first generation workers in export orientated factories remain dominant, the Chinese workforce is also rapidly becoming better educated, fuelled by the state expansion and international upgrading of Chinese universities, alongside the unprecedented movement of Chinese students into Western universities (especially in the US, UK and Australia) as international educational capitalism expands, with the high fees from overseas students replacing public funding on a huge scale (Slaughter and Leslie, 1997; Slaughter and Rhoades, 2004). The dialectic of this process of internationalization is also producing more fragmentation to *academic* labour – the decentring of the teacher and introduction of new more market-focused functions.[3]

Internationalization and 'globalization' – more labour and more mobility of labour

When Braverman was writing, it was not really feasible to think of a global labour market. American capitalism was king, and hence there was both an explicit and implicit assumption that American business recipes, such as Scientific Management, were somehow systemic to capitalism, and not contingent upon certain varieties of the system. At the time, national and local labour markets dominated the *experience* of most workers and the theoretical horizons of labour process writers. Russia and Eastern Europe allocated labour centrally through the state, and migration between firms was difficult, while flow between societies strictly illegal (Smith and Thompson, 1992). China was just emerging from the isolation of the Cultural Revolution, and Japanese and European stocks of capital were tied to respective national territories. Internationalization was hence a largely US affair, which as the dominant global power signified the hegemonic archetype of the international firm.

Now all this has changed, and the global reach of capitalism has raised the possibility of a global labour market. The global labour reserve expanded, from 1.46 billion workers to 2.93 billion workers – doubling the potential labour pool connected to world economy (Freeman, 2006).[4] A recent ILO report on the question of the existence of global labour market said that: 'Despite limited actual labour mobility, however, the globalization of trade in goods and services, the existence of international network enterprises using global assembly lines for the production of goods, and their recourse to global sourcing of services are all elements that contribute to the emergence of a more integrated global market for labour.'[5] The same report noted on the demand side that different levels of regulation (supranational, regional, national and local) as well as the operation of unofficial norms as networks for the distribution of labour to jobs meant that access to labour was not as straightforward as access to capital and trade (which have been extensively liberalized) and 'therefore...labour mobility is lagging far behind and is still heavily constrained by national regulations.'[6]

Labour flows reinforce patterns of segmentation by race, gender, nationality and citizenship. For example, in oil exporting states, such as the UAE, as much as 90 per cent of workforce are expatriate, non-UAE citizens. In the Gulf states, the foreign workforce has become the dominant labour force in most sectors of the economy (Kapiszewski, 2006). This adds layers of division; it offers opportunities to capital that can globally source labour at both the high and low ends.

While the global workforce has expanded, not all this labour is available to international markets – with over 1 billion workers within the informal economy, as petty traders on subsistence income and excluded from the limited security of being in *waged work* (Davis, 2006). Much of this labour power is therefore unavailable to the world economy, being tied to highly localized markets and largely for subsistence income – but much is also working through contracting chains on products that are for global markets. Informalization is not always due to national economic action. The global efficiency of Chinese labour power has also moved workers in other countries out of more formal sectors, where reasonable wages and conditions were possible, into the informal sectors, where they are not. As Freeman (2006: 4) has noted: 'Employment in Latin America, South Africa and in parts of Asia shifted from the formal sectors associated with economic advancement to informal sectors, where work is precarious, wages and productivity low, and occupational risks and hazards great. The entry of China and India to the world economy turned many developing countries from the low wage competitors of advanced countries to the high wage competitors of China and India.' Such disruption increases migration pressures, moves labour into vulnerable employment and creates labour supply for sectors like prostitution, often tied to parallel expansions of international tourism by countries forced out of manufacturing by global competition.

An interesting feature of the internationalization of Chinese capital (both state and private) is the tendency to bring labour from China to overseas production or extraction sites, thus the firm is acting to retain national labour within its borders, although leakages of labour into local economies are common (Ceccagno, 2003). For example, there are an estimated 750,000 Chinese migrants in Africa – moving with Chinese international firms, illegally or as part of the Chinese government's policy of economic engagement with the continent. Within developing countries, international recruiting agencies are moving labour more extensively than before and hence the labour pool is not only between the sending firm and local workers, but could also be diversified with migrant labour recruited through international employment agencies (Lincoln, 2009; Peck, Theodore and Ward, 2005).

But such freedom of movement is not unrestricted. In fact there has also been new Balkanization (Kerr, 1954) of labour markets with 'fortress Europe' and NAFTA especially policing borders and differentiating labour into legal and illegal categories, with differing implications for labour market access, the segmentation of employment and weakening of unionizing potential, especially in sectors such as agriculture, hotels, restaurants, food production, construction and garments. In the UK, there are an estimated 430,000 illegally resident migrants (Woodbridge, 2005); in the US 12 million; across Europe 500,000 enter illegally annually (Boswell and Straubhaar, 2004: 4). Illegal labour is concentrated in ethnic enclaves and communities, and illegal labour markets are very structured within such communities (Ahmad, 2008: 856). These workers are often well qualified but operate in labour processes that do not utilize their skill, which offers a conversion (see below) benefit to the employer, and disrupts established labour structures for indigenous workers.

Migrant labour is often unsettling of custom and practice within local labour markets. Newsome, Thompson and Commander (2009: 157) show how a different work ethic between Polish and local workers meant that the effort bargain was challenged through rate busting that was internalized as marks of status and identity for otherwise insecure migrant workers in a Glasgow assembly plant. Often within the same corporation, segmentation along race or migrant labour lines can lead to different outcomes for workers in terms of pay, conditions and organization. Holgate's (2005: 467) detailed ethnography of two sandwich factories in the UK noted: 'Workers in the London factory were predominantly BME [black and minority ethnic], whereas at the northern factory they were mainly white. In London, workers had lower pay, no premium pay, less holidays, no sick pay – and no union recognition'. Datta et al. (2007) researching low-paid migrant workers in a fragmented London labour market argue that coping or getting-by are the outcomes of survival tactics used by these workers because organizing and their ability to 'strategize' is difficult given fragmentation of labour power and labour markets. Reliance of kin and ethnic community networks is common bulwark against societal exclusion, and has been highlighted as a means of organizing across many countries (Martínez Lucio and Perrett, 2009). But the network nature of migration, however, means migrants operate in parallel and not directly in competitive labour markets; which often means organizing is not an option.

In general, new labour power is often more desperate to work – to realize itself – and therefore more willing to enter unregulated areas, accept lower wages, worse conditions and more demanding or dangerous jobs. The segmentation of jobs facilitates this, and migration (whether international – Mexicans to Los Angeles – or inter-provincial migration in China) reinforces patterns of segmentation within labour markets and labour processes.[7]

Within China as well, there is a similar locals versus migrants differentiation based on those with urban and rural household registrations. The massive growth of internal migration in China has been circulatory, but this is changing.[8] In terms that I explain below, the external *mobility power* of the employer is stronger than the mobility power of labour and is used to increase labour effort and control workers.

Separation of work relations and employment relations

A final significant trend in the past 30 years has been people doing the same job but on different employment contracts, hence a separation of work relations and employment relations. There has been a systemic growth of different categories of worker on different contracts and the shortening of the length of employment stay within one organization, although rates of tenure vary between say Europe and US, and within different branches of capital (Doogan, 2003).[9] Although flexible work or precarity in work has been much debated in the US and Europe, contract changes have been more dramatic in East Asian societies (Nichols et al., 2004). Contract differentiation has also been strong in the public sector. In higher education, for example, in the US 'in the past 20 years, faculty employment has shifted from being overwhelmingly a full-time position, and on the tenure track, to an occupation in which nearly one-half of the faculty workforce nationwide is part-time, with the majority not being on the tenure track' (Rhoades and Slaughter, 2004: 50). In the UK approximately 40 per cent of positions in higher education are non-permanent (Gold and Brown, 2007).

Therefore, in sectors previously characterized by bureaucratic stability, the value of loyalty (which was typically based on tenure of employment in one organization and hence *immobility* of labour) has diminished as market rationalism has increased. This is partly a response to market uncertainty, but also to government action, and the reduced transaction costs associated with organizations interacting with the labour market (made easier with the rise of generic skills, growth of education and greater standardization of jobs). Put another way 'ownership' of jobs by workers declines and 'employability' and flexibility, the worker as 'free agent' (Barley and Kunda, 2004), expands. While we can read this as the ownership of mobility increasing – workers can move more freely between employers – mobility is built into many jobs (e.g. high churn in service sector jobs), and such job consumerism can also be interpreted as weakening labour power. Thompson and Smith (this volume) discuss the controversy around flexible labour, the apparent cyclical feature of insecure work in the private sector, but they also highlight the impact increased mobility power of capital and labour has had on work effort, namely, increased intensity of work as the fear of job loss increases.

These shifts have also changed companies, disintegrating and disaggregating previously integrated companies with stable welfare regimes and relatively well-paid workers with employment security and pension guarantees, and moving them out of organization-dependency which characterized the large firms that Braverman (and Burawoy, 1979) had used to characterize the good jobs (high wage and high security) in what was a hegemonic, welfarist employment pattern of monopoly capitalism, which was constructed throughout the twentieth century (Gospel, 1992; Jacoby, 1984; Montgomery, 1987, 1993) and now looks increasingly untenable. Final salary pension schemes, the symbolic heart of organization-based welfarism, are no longer available in most large firms in the US and UK and pressures are increasing on such schemes for public sector workers and even unions, such as Unison in the UK, with 1.3 million local government and NHS members, have moved to abolish final salary schemes for their officers.

Theorizing these trends

Back to basics: What is labour power?

Labour process analysis is production centred because it is from within production that labour power starts its conversion into labour and products, before these move into circulation for surplus value and ultimately wages as exchange for the labour power as the 'property' of the worker. However, it is not only in production that our attention needs to focus. Labour power does not enter production as a blank sheet or as raw material, but as prepared human material, formed in mature capitalist societies over several centuries of habituation to industrial and bureaucratic cultures; formed through expanded education systems and formed with expectations of employment and citizen rights. In newly industrializing societies, such as China and India, new generations of labourers are being exposed to the market for the first time – converting from peasant-farmer into workers or quasi-workers (Pun and Chan, 2008); yet expectations of fairness and justice are quickly learnt (Lee, 2007; Pun, 2005).

In all societies labour power is structured through a life cycle – with young workers having to struggle to get into labour processes, and due to age, they are often less enmeshed in customized working patterns, especially where work cultures are no longer sufficiently robust to socialize new workers due to technological change (as in printing) or fragmentation of work – all of which has been enhanced, as noted above, by global trends in capitalism over the past 30 years. Not only is labour power subject to temporal and historical conditioning, it is also subject to different conditions of competition (expanded scales of competition in more globally or regionally stretched labour markets), to different orientations to the market (such as the shift to face-to-face services and extended utilization of 'the whole person' of the labourer) all of which means different requirements for the reproduction of labour power. This can mean a switch in selection criteria in recruitment, an emphasis on attitudes not technical skills for example (Callaghan and Thompson, 2002); or face or look (Wolkowitz and Warhurst – this volume) or the expansion of services requiring emotional labourers (Bolton this volume); or simply attempts to utilize the 'whole person' of the worker in a more 'demanding capitalism' (Green, 2006). But in India and China, entering the labour process can be more intensive *and* extensive – longer working days within more intensive production systems – and exploitation of labour power, especially in the dormitory labour regime, that uses up young bodies, returning broken or damaged ones to society, and replenishing stocks of labour power with new reserves from the countryside (Smith, 2003; Smith and Pun, 2006).

If we look at the character of labour power within capitalism, and not simply the animation of labour power in the labour process, we can get a better perspective on the broad trends outlined above. There are a series of questions or processes that emerge from the nature of labour power within capitalist social relations. These are the *embodiment question, conversion question, duality question* and the *control question.*

The embodiment question

Labour power is not created by a production process for sale in a market like other commodities. Labour power is 'produced' through families, and while a 'labour market' operates in similar ways to other markets, in that it tries to fix the price at which labour is bought, the market is structured in unique ways because labour power is a unique 'commodity'. Labour power is a capacity owned by the individual, rented to the buyer. We cannot separate physically the 'commodity' labour power from the owner – rather we, as individuals, have to present ourselves, even though what we are selling may only engage a fraction of our being and represent a small part of our actual potential as human beings. Because the employer must negotiate through a living individual to utilize their labour services, the employment relationship necessarily involves the *individual qua individual* and therefore emotional, psychological, motivational and other strategies to obtain a definite amount of work effort at a definite price. Regardless of the type of use-value that the employer wants from the labourer – hand, head, sexuality, look, muscle – these fragmented utilities can only come into a labour process within the 'whole person of the worker' and as such, alongside these specialist skills, we also have additional potential, will power, volition, difference, thus requiring consent and negotiation on the part of the employer, especially where such use-values are in scare supply.

Marx quoted Hegel when discussing the differentiation of 'labour power' from bonded forms of labour, such as slavery:

> I may make over to another the use, for a limited time, of my particular bodily and mental aptitudes and capabilities; because in consequence of this restriction, they are impressed with a character of alienation with regard to me as a whole. But by the alienation of all my labour-time and the whole of my work, I should be converting the substance itself, in other words, my general activity and reality, my person, into the property of another. (Hegel, 'Philosophie des Rechts.' Berlin, 1840, p. 104, § 67)[10]

Although Marx sometimes noted that labour power is the 'property' of the worker it is not *like* capital (which has objective, multiple identities independent and external to the individual capitalist) rather labour power is always part of 'the person of the worker', and hence the question of the *embodiment* of labour power is a permanent and essential feature of labour power. The fractioning of labour power into separate elements that match new market demands or segmentations – manual and mental labour, or more recently 'emotional' and 'aesthetic labour' – does not subtract from the embodiment of labour power in 'the whole person'; it merely speaks to the specialization of labour markets and the quality of labour power (its flexibility) within capitalism which is a system that seeks to commercialize or valorize labour power in an infinite variety of ways. New methods of valorization add nothing new to the argument, for as Bolton (this volume) shows the transformation of emotions into 'emotional labour' creates the same control and resistance responses from employers and workers as the former seek to extract exchange value through this monetized asset.

The conversion question

Labour power is variable and plastic. When we buy a TV or packet of crisps, these commodities are quite fixed in terms of their utility. When an employer hires a worker, it is possible to train and retrain the worker, and it is possible for the worker to acquire new skills and qualifications thereby transforming themselves and their 'utility' repeatedly over a working life cycle. This makes labour power an altogether different commodity from other commodities that are purchased through sales contracts in markets. The 'division of labour' expands the productivity of labour power; it also expands choice for workers – especially in the modern era with greater compression in training, extended working life, wider provision of education and training and enhanced value and reduced barriers of mobility between jobs and careers – in some countries more than others. Of course, labour power gets fixed through institutional inertia, specialization, market structures, occupational projects, work cultures, habit and the life cycle, some of which are defences for labour power in order to increase valorization, others are structures to suit capital – to intensify productivity. Specialization creates conversion problems – redundant miners in their 50s might not convert to other jobs, although Elger and Smith (2005) found ex-miners and workers from many other occupational backgrounds working in the new Japanese assembly factories in their Telford research. Thus plasticity of labour power as an asset means there is always a potential *conversion question*, with both labour and capital operating on labour power to convert it into different skills or trades, which means that as an asset it is not 'fixed' or certain (for the employer or worker) – again part of the human quality of labour power.

In the new economy established correspondences are changing – with the graduatization of the labour markets pushing graduates into call centres, retail and work previously occupied by less qualified workers – so-called credential inflation; migrant workers are often overqualified for the jobs they perform (Ahmad, 2008); formally unskilled workers in the Western economies are vulnerable to displacement by internationalization of production (Freeman, 2006); more intense competition within labour markets that are exposed to international migration – including academic labour markets. These changes mean the 'conversion' of labour power is increasing as a process, as individuals are forced to consider changes in jobs and occupations on a more continuous basis. It also means that the calculus of conversion – the choice-constraint issue – is changing.

The duality question

Labour power is the commodity that the worker sells to the buyer – but of course the owner comes with the commodity and this creates empirical confusion that the 'worker is a commodity', when it is only his or her labour power that is the commodity. It can also create the illusion on the part of the worker that only certain bodies – male or white, for example – can deliver certain types of labour power, when capitalism constantly proves it is indifferent to the bodily presentation of labour power, it is only interested in efficient or productive labour power. This is slightly different from the issue of embodiment, but also part of the same question. The empirical presentation of labour within the individual creates a *duality question*. The embodiment of labour power in living labour feeds the illusion and confusion that the capitalist is employing 'people' rather than variable capital. The fact that the worker as a person travels with his or her labour power into the labour process means that dualism and illusion is always a feature of the capitalist employment and labour processes. Marx, in separating labour power from Adam Smith's category of labour, is making this distinction in political economy between a system of slave labour and a system of wage labour (capitalism), and the quote above highlights the difference between selling distinctive labour services and the capitalist demanding more from the 'whole person' of the worker because alongside these labour services there is perpetually present the 'person of the worker' within the labour process. Hence, within the labour process not only does conflict arise because of different interests between capital and labour and the absence of mutuality in effort bargaining (Edwards, 1990; Thompson, 1989), but also because the availability of the asset 'labour power' is not objective or externalized, but requires temporal negotiation through the living person of the worker, who naturally has ups and downs, good and bad days, but is fundamentally not an objective asset in the same way as fixed capital.

The control question

Realization or transfer of labour power from seller to buyer, worker to capitalist, requires of contract or exchange relationship, but this is the formal or legal relationship between apparent equals – the 'noisy' sphere of exchange relations. Proper realization takes place within the 'labour process' – where the skill or effort of the worker meets raw materials, machinery and purpose within a system that can have many forms of labour process organization but within advanced capitalist relations, access to the labour process is controlled by the employer. LPT is centred through the concept of control which is an objective imperative of capitalism. The employee presents him or herself at work as potential. It is up to the employer, through a production or labour process, to extract the labour power or capacity from the worker. Obviously, this process requires consent or agreement, as the worker will not willingly submit to high utilization of work effort without due reward and due respect. Therefore, a management control and consent system is required to extract labour capacity from living labour. The management role is to realize labour power, and this is why management exists as an authority function. If workers were self-managed to produce to the highest productivity levels, the control function of management would disappear, and managers would be left as merely administrative or technical coordinators of work processes. In this role they would be like other workers. But, due to the absence of agreement on the exact relationship between payment and performance, wages and work effort, management as an authority function are required to mediate this relationship and ensure that production is maximized or the needs of the business (whatever they might be, but typically increased output and profitability) are achieved.

Rethinking labour power under new conditions

The features of labour power outlined require theorizing under the new conditions discussed above. Central to all these conditions is renewed mobility of labour and capital, and increased supply of labour power. In my 2006 paper, I attempted to capture some of these features by expanding on the nature of labour power through the concepts of 'mobility power' (MP) and 'effort power' (EP) – being two uncertainties for both capital and labour, requiring both to strategize around the use of labour power, and manage the movement of labour power into and out of any particular labour process. We can look at both MP and EP within the labour process and externally to the labour process – internally is the conventional sphere of labour in production – the animation or realization of labour power through the labour process; externalities relate to reproduction of labour power and attempts by capital and labour to affect MP and EP through institutional action – in the state or market by limiting labour supply, regulating the sale of labour, creating or destroying monopoly rights on labour power (professional credentials around jobs) and so on. As noted by Ellem (2010), 'mobility affects management strategy: firms or operations which are less mobile than others will likely have greater motivation to create conditions conducive to accumulation within particular localities: "capitalists need to develop place-based labour control practices" Jonas 1996, p. 325.'

Mobility power differentials between labour and capital are noted in the literature – the ability of capital to objectify itself in different forms facilitates movement; the embodiment of labour in the person of the worker restricts movement. This creates a power imbalance. But Ellem (2010) notes that 'the "rootedness" of labour can, under some circumstances, become a source of power, when working people and their families create distinctive local communities, cultures and organisations.' Places, especially mining areas discussed by Ellem, can create mutual dependencies. But he also shows how capital can, with strategy and motivation, break down the solidarities within 'places' – in his case-study companies, this meant extending the labour market internationally, and using air transport on a 'fly-in, fly-out' basis and thus undermining place-fixed labour in industrial communities of solidarity. But this is not simply the mobility differential playing out, as suggested in the mobility of capital and immobility of labour thesis,[11] but rather the mobility of some workers versus the immobility of others, and it is always both.

But more positively a community of workers can be established through social networks that can be stretched over long distances – with modern communications available to workers breaking down the place barriers (Lee, 2007; Milkman, 2006).

The geography of labour and capital is more an empirical rather than theoretical question, as in an absolute sense, labour and capital are universals which are, therefore, placeless in that creating capitalist social relations produces the structural features of capital and labour as outlined above. But tactically, the movement of capital and labour can produce particular outcomes for both in particular conditions and the labour process always requires a 'somewhere' – a real site of accumulation (Elger and Smith, 2005: 97) – see also Rainnie et al. this volume.

Externally, representatives of labour and capital appeal to political bodies to regulate labour flow. There are also campaigns to change (enhance or weaken) regulations around labour markets. In Japan, for example, workers cannot be recruited through private employment agencies in *certain* types of jobs, in construction and longshoring work, or security, medicine, and manufacturing in the case of labour dispatch agencies. The existence of these exceptions is political; the existence of three types of employment agencies to supply temporary labour to the Japanese labour market is also due to political external regulation of the mobility power of workers. It is not just at the national level that lobbying for the regulation or deregulation occurs. The internationalization of recruitment agencies themselves have pushed the interests of expanded mobility power for capital – especially in 'actively deregulating economies of the global North – including Spain, Germany, Italy and Japan' (Peck, Theodore and Ward, 2005). The opening up of a niche in the secondary labour market for ethnic Japanese from Brazil to replace stocks of rural Japanese that had historically occupied these positions is also a political process to retain the mobility power of this critical small-firm segment of capital in Japan, by drawing in new labour reserves that fit the ethnocentric character of the Japanese labour market (Higuchi and Tanno, 2003).

By looking at the differences in the 'ownership' of labour mobility comparatively and historically we can appreciate the relative newness of individual controls, that is the devolution of responsibility to the individual worker, who has the freedom and risk to unite his or her labour power with capital in order to convert it into wages. The expansion of wage labour for Marx represented the destructive, de-culturing and de-traditionalizing mission of capitalism, but across capitalist societies there remain cultural or institutional variations in the control of the mobility power of labour. It can be on the side of employers (especially strong in family firms; paternalist employers; company towns and isolated work communities) or the state. In the case of pre-reform China, labour power was a state planned input beyond the control of individual workers. Reform of employment in China, from restricted mobility subject to appeals to supervisory authority, to giving individuals freedom of movement, created profound change. Davis (1992: 1084) noting that: 'In terms of job mobility, the consequences in urban China after 1960 were low levels of inter-firm transfers, high levels of regional and enterprise autarky, and risk averse strategies of advancement that discouraged firm switching.' Managers within state socialist enterprises hoarded labour and were reluctant to let people leave especially skilled labour: 'If individuals at any stage of their working lives could take leave of absence and find employment on their own initiative, the power of the unit to define individual economic and political horizons would greatly diminish' (ibid.: 1064).

The 'footloose capital thesis' is overblown, but it does point to the fact that both developing and developed societies are being remade for new global or regional capital – with export processing zones and service zones and new towns (such as the case of Telford, England or Livingstone, Scotland in the UK, or Tijuana in Mexico or Shenzhen in China, or Prato in Italy). Research by Elger and Smith (2005) on Telford in the UK brings out the way a particular 'transnational social space' (Morgan and Kristensen, 2006; Pries, 2001) is made for international firms – but also how workers remake this space and force adaptations and compromises, not through being organized into trade unions, but disorganized through high amounts of quitting. In this space the social construction of the labour market actively feeds into what is possible in the labour process – how difficult it is for employer to have high selection barriers into firms when finding and keeping workers is a problem; how problematic it is for quality management regimes when there is too much labour churn; and how job enlargements had to be abandoned due to the loss of skills and training caused by high exits and as a result 'fool-proofing' jobs became more widespread. In other words, labour mobility has outcomes for work organization and management control.

Smith and McKinlay (2009: 13) show how employers have objectively significant power reserves over effort and mobility in the creative industries sector and workers have difficulty actualizing effort and mobility power in their favour. But on the other side of the account, the person-specific nature of creative labour means the substitutability of labour is harder despite excessive labour supply; the use of networks for recruitment advantages workers ('in the know'), and the perishable nature of creative products give workers bargaining power.

Mobility power can be for the purpose of the preparation or continued extended reproduction of labour power – for education, training or developmental purposes. In this case employers seek to determine MP in their favour by controlling access to resources that most enhance the value of labour power in contemporary capitalism, namely a continuously trained, educated and knowledgeable workforce. Clearly, such training also increases the open market value of labour power for the worker but through company-specific or mediated training, and not generic packages, it is expected that the MP of workers will be more contained. There are struggles between employers and workers over training labour power – workers might want access to training resources in the firm to maintain their labour power for the market; employers might want to get workers engaged in productive work to increase profitability (Barley and Kunda, 2004). There can also be culture clashes in transnational firms – the Japanese managers in Telford case studies of Elger and Smith (2005) were shocked that local workers did not remain after receiving extended training as would have been the case in Japan. For the workers, converting training into market opportunity was part of the British way.

Mobility can come through types of employment contracts – the growth of agency work increases the movement of labour between employers. The contracting out of work has been seen as positive for the employer in the 'flexible firm' and flexibility debates, which argue, in my terms, that flexibility gave employers more MP by allowing them to determine the employment status of workers and move them off secure contracts into less secure ones or out of the organization altogether – something developed in the 1980s as trade unions lost their power to prevent contracting out work from the firm. The 'flexible firm' ideal type has segments of labour on packages of employment contracts, with different claims on the resources of the firm. Ideologically workers might possess 'freedom' to work through an employment agency rather than being *dependent* on one organization as an employee, but this is often the consequence of a constrained choice (Forde and Slater, 2005). Agency workers experience loss of non-pay benefits and training opportunities, increased insecurity and limited choice over job assignments (Platman, 2004); and the less explicit costs associated with marginalization and the potential experience of being treated as an 'outsider'.

But contracting also positively affects the MP of workers, especially more skilled workers in industries with high rates of knowledge obsolescence – that is where labour power needs more knowledge for realization. Research on the positives of contracting suggests that managing labour mobility power more directly converts or perhaps reinforces the 'free agent' position of waged labour which had been contained through bureaucratization of jobs within internal labour markets of large corporations (see Kunda, Barley and Evans, 2002; and Barley and Kunda, 2004 for the best ethnography on 'itinerant professionals in a knowledge economy' and the movement between employee and contractor status as labour markets fluctuate). Workers receive greater financial rewards through the external labour market compared with internal job ladders – markets pay more than internal promotions under certain conditions. 'Free agents' have greater choices compared with being tied to one employer, aligning MP and EP more within the determination of the worker, although movements in and out of employee status as wages and work for contractors fluctuates (Barley and Kunda, 2004: 319) suggests that going back into the bureaucracy was still the outcome for the minority of the Barley and Kunda's sample of engineers. Other positives of 'free agents' is that work-life balance becomes easier, especially for women workers, who may want to work part-time and going solo or through a temporary employment agency might be the only way to get part-time employment (Meiksins and Whalley, 2002: 86 on women engineers).

Contracting out in the public sector has highlighted the interaction between the degradation of work within the public bureaucracy (through obsessive targets of New Public Management) and changes in the original effort bargain (especially for older public sector workers) which provide the preconditions for workers opting for contracting out as 'free agents'. Grimshaw, Earnshaw and Hebson's (2003: 283) research on supply teachers argues decisions 'to go agency' might be 'interpreted as a form of individualized resistance against the denigration of professional standards'. In my terms using the external labour market means workers getting more determination over their MP, but within a general framework of employers and the state promoting contracting out and deregulations for fiscal and ideological reasons.

Struggles between labour and capital over internal recruitment and selection is often a balance between an employer recognizing that a certain category of worker will move more quickly, but also that they may be more productive or quicker to train when in work – hence a trade-off between efficiency and mobility. Zheng (2009: chapter 6) illustrates this nicely in one of her case studies:

> Let's face it, our employees won't stay long. They are fresh, they are young, and they change their gadgets, their girlfriends and their jobs. But at least they learn things very fast. If we recruit more experienced workers, they will still move but they are much less flexible in accepting how things are done in our factory. (Production Manager, TexA, Chinese, male, 38)

Granovetter's (1995) work on the use of 'job banks' by workers shows how mobility opportunities are accumulated through workplace relationships to help workers navigate through the labour market for strategic purposes.

Skill provides workers with power in the labour process. Hence, when managing skilled workers, employers are forced to confront the *mobility power* of labour in the form of an asset that cannot easily be replaced or removed. Braverman expresses this idea:

> The ideal organization toward which the capitalist strives is one in which the worker possesses no basic skill upon which the enterprise is dependent and no historical knowledge of the past of the enterprise to serve as a fund from which to draw on in daily work, but rather where everything is codified in rules of performance or laid down in lists that may be consulted (by machines or computers, for instance), *so that the worker really becomes an interchangeable part and may be exchanged for another worker with little disruption.* (Braverman, 1994: 24–5, emphasis added)

Faced with the mobility power that skill provides, employers counter worker power by (i) increasing the supply lines through industry-wide or employer-level agreements (along German lines); or (ii) internalizing skill development within the firm, and not within the occupational group or individual, and building competitive barriers between employers (as in Japan). In both strategies, employers are trying to adapt to potential mobility power of skill; and the German and Japanese country level strategies indicate that a zero-sum game suggested by Braverman has too much of an Anglo-American bias, where skills are formed in occupations, accumulated through professions and crafts that act autonomously of large firms and concerted cooperative efforts of employers.

Conclusion – putting mobility into labour power

Capital and labour have mutuality in that profits cannot be made without labour power; and wages cannot be made without labour power being realized within a labour process. The imperative of capture and control of labour power falls to management; the imperative of getting labour power into the labour process (put simply, *of working*) is that of the worker. Indeterminacies of effort and mobility power (finding efficient worker who will stay; finding fair employers and jobs that are regular) creates mutualities that ensure circulation of labour and free flow of labour is not continuous – but that organizations capture, contain and retain for long periods, *particular* workers. Given the scale of capitalism, other agencies develop to institutionalize and facilitate these exchanges (states, large firms, trade unions, employment or labour supply agencies, etc.) but theoretically they act to represent or mediate these two interests and for the purposes of this chapter it has been necessary to retain focus on capital and labour dynamics.

As noted in the introduction to this chapter, labour power acquires *fixity* – by task, temporality and place – by practising one occupation or skill (*task fixity*); or working for one employer for many years (*temporal fixity*); or living in a particular place or community – a sort of *place fixity*. The changes to the labour supply, capital mobility, technological changes and contracts described above have altered these sources of stability or fixity and increased the conversion rates of labour power (the need for job or occupational changes – especially the need to acquire skills to maintain labour power); altered the length of stay with one organization – although this remains comparatively uneven; and stretched the linkages of people to places, either through longer travel to work times, or changing work from *a place to an activity*, or moving work across borders at a higher rate.

Figuratively, labour power is variable capital for the capitalist but not for the worker. The idea of labour power as 'capital' – intellectual capital, skills, assets, resources, property – can only be symbolically capital within capitalist relations of production. The capitalist can liquidate fixed capital, transform it into money and put the money in the bank. Labour power cannot be banked in this way and has utility only in action. Labour power can only be stored at the individual level, in the body of the worker who must actively take it into the world of work in order to secure a wage, or ensure the consumption and valorization of labour power. Labour power can be 'stored' *socially* through occupations (professions with exclusionary rules); organization (large firms with strong internal labour markets); social networks (family, kin and place networks, typical of migrant labour); industrial districts/communities (mining, company towns, industrial communities); social class – workers store of collective identity and organizations – for example, trade unions (craft/work rules of job boundaries, and transfers of jobs through father-to-son dynasties) – London printers before computerization, for example (Cockburn, 1983).

But stores are 'fictive' and vulnerable because labour power is not 'property' like capital and the need to animate labour power through the labour process in order to secure exchange/realization (and wages) forever requires labour power to seek out capital. Stores are also vulnerable to change as a result of class struggle between labour and capital around the double indeterminacy of labour. A *flow perspective* on the labour process developed in this chapter is at odds with popular resource-based views of the firm; versions of HRM, with high commitment workplace perspectives; and with organization-centric models of capitalism. All these approaches represent labour power as fixed, centred and located, rather than moving and dynamic – with mobility-capability that means it is not actually a resource of the individual firm, but the worker. Resource based theories represent the employer's perspective on containing labour mobility as something positive for both workers (guaranteeing access to work) and employers (securing access to labour). A flow perspective brings in mobility, turnover, migration, employment contracts and challenges the orthodoxy of the 'resource-based model' in HR. Future research on the labour process needs to have this broadened conception of labour power.

Notes

1　This chapter was first presented as a rough set of power point slides at the 26th Annual International Labour Process Conference, 18–20 March 2008, University College, Dublin, Ireland. I am very grateful to all the comments received from those that attended my presentation at that conference. The ideas within the chapter have built upon my article, 'The Double Indeterminacy of Labour Power: Labour Effort and Labour Mobility' in *Work, Employment and Society* (2006). That article in turn grew out of projects and debates on labour turnover in the UK and elsewhere with my long-standing research partner, Tony Elger. I have applied the ideas of labour power as having two elements (labour effort and labour mobility) that both workers and employers seek to manage and dominate in a sector analysis through my 2009 joint chapter with Alan McKinlay 'Creative Industries and Labour Process Analysis'. I have also applied it at a national level with work on Chinese migrant workers with Ngai Pun (2007). The aim of this chapter is to restate the utility of the analytical framework for the study of the workplace in the twenty-first century. A *flow* perspective is in contrast to 'resource-based' theories of the firm that seek to make normative judgements about the value and possibility of fixing labour to the firm and employer for the good of both, rather that more dispassionately identifying the permanent tensions between capital and labour over the freedoms of effort and mobility power.

2　http://www.unctad.org/Templates/webflyer.asp?docid=7456&intItemID=1465&lang=1

3　According to a recent paper by Rhoades and Slaughter 'the structure of professional employment on campus is changing in ways that move faculty away from the center of academic decision making and unbundle the involvement of full-time faculty in the curriculum. For example, other professionals (e.g., in teaching centers) are increasingly being identified as "the experts" with regard to pedagogy; the emphasis is on learning, not teaching (making the teacher less central to the process); and the curriculum is being divided into a set of tasks performed by various personnel rather than all being performed by the single faculty member who is developing the course.' http://www.aft.org/pubs-reports/american_academic/issues/june04/Rhoades.qxp.pdf.

4   'The global labour force comprised over three billion workers. Of these, 84 per cent lived in the developing countries of Asia and the Pacific region, Africa, Latin America and the Caribbean, as well as the transition countries of the Commonwealth of Independent States (CIS) and south-eastern Europe (ILO, 2006b).

- Women represented around 40 per cent of the world's labour force (1.22 billion).
- 2.85 billion individuals aged 15 and above were employed. However, about half did not earn enough to raise themselves above the poverty line of two U.S. dollars a day. These figures are the same as those of ten years ago. Agriculture had the highest employment share (40.1%) as compared to industry (21%) and services (38.9%) (ILO, 2006a).
- The global unemployment rate was 6.3 per cent (ILO, 2006a), affecting some 191.8 million people, with young persons accounting for approximately half of the unemployed, a relatively high proportion given that they represented only 25 per cent of the total working age population (ILO, 2006a).
- 86 million persons were identified as migrant workers (ILO, 2006c).
- TNCs comprised 77,000 parent companies with over 770,000 foreign affiliates, the latter employing some 62 million workers (UNCTAD, 2006).
- 66 million workers were employed in Export Processing Zones (EPZs), mainly women (Singa Boyenge, 2007).
- 565,000 jobs were offshore (Farrell et al., 2005).'

Source:http://www.iom.int/jahia/webdav/site/myjahiasite/shared/shared/mainsite/published_docs/studies_and_reports/WMR2008/Ch1_WMR08.pdf.

5   http://www.iom.int/jahia/webdav/site/myjahiasite/shared/shared/mainsite/published_docs/studies_and_reports/WMR2008/Ch1_WMR08.pdf.

6   'Currently, the only free movement regime operating on a large scale is found in a regional setting, i.e. the EU. While labour mobility is covered in bilateral labour or trade agreements or regional integration frameworks, such movement occurs mainly on the basis of unilaterally devised immigration policies.' page 40: http://www.iom.int/jahia/webdav/site/myjahiasite/shared/shared/mainsite/published_docs/studies_and_reports/WMR2008/Ch1_WMR08.pdf.

7   'Circular migration is largely driven by labour market segmentation, as populations in prosperous destination areas are, or become, reluctant to perform low-wage, low-status, seasonal or physically demanding work. More often than not, the dirtiest, most dangerous and most difficult jobs ("3D" jobs) are performed by migrants who belong to the lowest segments of society; lower castes and tribes in the case of India, and ethnic

minorities elsewhere. Segmentation is best captured through in-depth case studies that gather detailed information on ethnicity, occupations and seasonal movements.' http://www.odi.org.uk/resources/details.asp?id=2600&title=managing-labour-mobility-evolving-global-economy.

8 'In 2005, China had the fastest growing economy in the world and also the highest level of economic inequality in East Asia (Balisacan et al., 2005). Such internal regional differences have been an important cause of migration, especially since the mid-1990s (Song, 2004). The number of internal migrants has increased dramatically over the past two decades from about 26 million in 1988 to 126 million in 2004, a majority of whom are circular rural-urban migrants who retain strong links with their rural family. Current projections suggest that between 12 and 13 million migrants will move to urban areas each year over the next two decades, and the actual numbers will depend on the extent to which the household registration (*hukou*) system is relaxed. Around 70 per cent of migrants are aged between 16 and 35, and they generally view migration as an intermediary period in their life between leaving middle school and settling down to marry and having children (Murphy, 2006). Roughly a third of Chinese migrants return to their native homes as it is extremely difficult for them to find permanent white-collar jobs on which they would be able to retire (Murphy, 2006)'. http://www.odi.org.uk/resources/details.asp?id=2600&title=managing-labour-mobility-evolving-global-economy.

9 'In the United States the proportion of the workforce employed long-term [more than 10 years with current employer] is approximately 31% but in the European Union it is approximately 45% (Bureau of Labour Statistics, 2001). Unlike the US where the increase in long-service employment occurs only in women, in the European Union long-term employment has increased for both males and females' (Doogan, 2003: 6).

10 Marx, Vol 1 Capital at http://www.marxists.org/archive/marx/works/1867-c1/ch06.htm#n2.

11 Ellem uses Beynon and Hudson to highlight this dichotomy: 'capital seeks "a (temporary) space for profitable production" whereas for workers spaces are different from and more than this. They are "places in which to live, places in which they have considerable individual and collective cultural investment" (Beynon and Hudson 1993, p. 182). Beynon and Hudson suggest that "space [is] the domain of capital" while places are "the meaningful situations established by labour" (Beynon and Hudson 1993, p. 182).' I would suggest this reading of the power imbalances is rooted in an older industrial era of relative labour immobilities – with increased migration within and between countries, with extended travel-to-work times, with improved communications, with the application of ICTs to disperse work away from a fixed point, there is a displacement

of labour from place, but nevertheless the possibilities of social solidarities developing through these communication devices and through social networks that become more significant in modern work forms. See Elger and Smith (2005: 97–8).

REFERENCES

Ahmad, A. N. (2008) 'The Labour Market Consequences of Human Smuggling: "Illegal" Employment in London's Migrant Economy', *Journal of Ethnic and Migration Studies*, 34(6): 853–74.

Axtell, C., Hislop, D. and Whittaker, S. (2008) 'Mobile Technologies in Mobile Spaces: Findings from the Context of Train Travel', *International Journal of Human-Computer Studies*, 66(1): 902–15.

Baldry, C. (1999) 'Space – the Final Frontier', *Sociology*, 33(3): 535–53.

Baldry, C. (2010, forthcoming) 'Plastic Palm Trees and Blue Pumpkins: Synthetic Fun and Real Control in Contemporary Work Space', in McGraph-Camp, S., Herod, A., and Rainnie, A. (eds) *Handbook of Work and Employment: Working Space*, Oxford: Edward Elgar.

Barley, S. R. and Kunda, G. (2004) *Gurus, Hired Guns, and Warm Bodies: Itinerant Experts in a Knowledge Economy*, Princeton, NJ: Princeton University Press.

Beynon, H. and Hudson, R. (1993) 'Place and Space in Contemporary Europe: Some Lessons and Reflections', *Antipode*, 25(3): 177–190.

Boswell, C. and Straubhaar, T. (2004) 'The Illegal Employment of Foreigners in Europe', *Intereconomics*, 39(1): 4–17.

Braverman, H. (1994) 'The Making of the U.S. Working Class', *Monthly Review*, November: 14–35.

Burawoy, M. (1979) *Manufacturing Consent: Changes in the Labor Process under Monopoly Capitalism*, Chicago, IL: Chicago University Press.

Callaghan, G. and Thompson, P. (2002) 'We Recruit Attitude: The Selection and Shaping of Routine Call Centre Labour', *Journal Management Studies*, 39(2): 233–53.

Ceccagno, A. (2003) 'New Chinese Migrants in Italy', *International Migration*, 41(3): 187–200.

Cockburn, C. (1983) *Brothers: Male Dominance and Technological Change*, London: Pluto Press.

Datta, K., McIlwaine, C., Evans, Y., Herbert, J. and May, J. (2007) 'From Coping Strategies to Tactics: London's Low-Pay Economy and Migrant Labour', *British Journal of Industrial Relations*, 45 (2): 404–32.

Davis, D. (1992) 'Job Mobility in Post-Mao Cities: Increases on the Margins', *The China Quarterly*, 32: 1062–85.

Davis, M. (2006) *Planet of Slums*, London: Verso.

Deeg, R. and Jackson, G. (2007) 'The State of the Art towards a More Dynamic Theory of Capitalist Variety', *Socio-Economic Review*, 5: 149–79.

Doogan, K. (2003) 'Job Insecurity and Long-term Employment in Europe', paper presented to the ESRC's WORKLIFE Seminar Manchester 28 February: www.lse.ac.uk/collections/worklife/Dooganpaper.pdf.

▶

▶

Edwards, P. K. (1990) 'Understanding Conflict in the Labour Process: The Logic and Autonomy of Struggle', in Knights, D. and Willmott, H. (eds) *Labour Process Theory*, London: Macmillan, 125–52.

Edwards, T. and Ferner, A. (2002) 'The Renewed "American Challenge": A Review of Employment Practice in US Multinationals', *Industrial Relations Journal*, 33: 94–111.

Elger, T. and Smith, C. (2005) *Assembling Work: Remaking Factory Regimes in Japanese Multinationals in Britain*, Oxford: Oxford University Press.

Ellem, B. (2010, forthcoming) 'Contested Space: Union Organising in the Old Economy', in McGraph-Camp, S.,Herod, A. and Rainnie, A. (eds) *Handbook of Work and Employment: Working Space*, Oxford: Edward Elgar.

Felstead, A. (2009) 'Detaching Work from Place: Charting the Progress of Change and Its Implications for Learning', Institute for Employment Research, University of Warwick, January 2009.

Felstead, A. and Jewson, N. (2000) *In Work, At Home: Towards an Understanding of Homeworking*, Palgrave: London.

Felstead, A. and Jewson, N. (2005) *Changing Places of Work*, Palgrave: London.

Forde, C. and Slater, G. (2005) 'Agency Working in Britain: Character, Consequences and Regulation', *British Journal of Industrial Relations*, 43(2): 249–71.

Freeman, R. (2006) 'The Great Doubling: The Challenge of the New Global Labor Market', paper to the *Work, Employment and Society Conference*, Aberdeen, July.

Frobel, F., Heinriches, J. and Kreye, O. (1980) *The New International Division of Labour*, Cambridge: Cambridge University Press.

Gamble, J. (2006) 'Multinational Retailers in China: Proliferating "McJobs" or Developing Skills?', *Journal of Management Studies*, 43(7): 1463–90.

Gold, M. and Brown, D. (2007) 'Academics on Non-standard Contracts in UK Universities: Portfolio Work, Choice and Compulsion', *Higher Education Quarterly*, 61(4): 439–60.

Gospel, H. (1992) *Markets, Firms and the Management of Labour in Modern Britain*, Cambridge: Cambridge University Press.

Granovetter, M. (1995) *Getting a Job*, 2nd edn, Chicago, IL: University of Chicago Press.

Green, F. (2006) *Demanding Work: The Paradox of Job Quality in the Affluent Economy*, Princeton, NJ: Princeton University Press.

Grimshaw, D., Earnshaw, J. and Hebson, G. (2003) 'Private Sector Provision of Supply Teachers: A Case of Legal Swings and Professional Roundabouts', *Journal of Education Policy*, 18(3): 267–88.

Higuchi, N. and Tanno, K. (2003) 'What's Driving Brazil-Japan Migration? The Making and Remaking of the Brazilian Niche in Japan', *International Journal of Japanese Sociology*, 12: 33–47.

Holgate, J. (2005) 'Organizing Migrant Workers: A Case Study of Working Conditions and Unionization in a London Sandwich Factory', *Work, Employment and Society*, 19(3): 463–80.

▶

Jacoby, S. M. (1984) *Employing Bureaucracy: Managers, Unions, and the Transformation of Work in American Industry*, Princeton, NJ: Princeton University Press.

Jones, A. (2008) 'The Rise of Global Work', *Transactions of the Institute of British Geographers*, 33: 12–26.

Kapiszewski, A. (2006) *'Arab versus Asian Migrant Workers in the GCC Countries'*, Working Paper, United Nations Secretariat, 15–17 May.

Kerr, C. (1954) 'The Balkanisation of Labor Markets', in Bakke, E., Hauser, P. M., Palmer, G. L., Myers, C. A. and Yoder, D. (eds) *Labor Mobility and Economic Opportunity*, Cambridge, MA: MIT Press, 89–104.

Kunda, G., Barley, S. and Evans, J. (2002) 'Why Do Contractors Contract? The Experience of Highly Skilled Technical Professionals in a Contingent Labour Market', *Industrial and Labour Relations Review*, 55(2): 234–61.

Lee, C. K. (2007) *Against the Law: Labor Protests in China's Rustbelt and Sunbelt*, Berkeley: University of California Press.

Lincoln, D. (2009) 'Labour Migration in the Global Division of Labour: Migrant Workers in Mauritius', *International Migration*, 47(4): 129–56.

Martínez Lucio, M. and Perrett, R. (2009) 'The Diversity and Politics of Trade Unions' Responses to Minority Ethnic and Migrant Workers: The Context of the UK', *Economic and Industrial Democracy*, 30(3): 324–47.

Meiksins, P. and Whalley, P. (2002) *Putting Work in Its Place: A Quiet Revolution*, Ithaca, NY: ILR Press.

Milkman, R. (2006) *L.A. Story: Immigrant Workers and the Future of the U.S. Labor Movement*, New York, Russell Sage Foundation.

Montgomery, D. (1987) *The Fall of the House of Labor*, Cambridge: Cambridge University Press.

Montgomery, D. (1993) *Citizen Worker*, Cambridge: Cambridge University Press.

Morgan, G. and Kristensen, P. H. (2006) 'The Contested Space of Multinationals: Varieties of Institutionalism, Varieties of Capitalism', *Human Relations*, 59(11): 1467–90.

Newsome, K., Thompson, P. and Commander, J. (2009) 'The Forgotten Factories: Suppliers, Supermarkets and Dignity at Work in the Contemporary Economy', in Bolton, S. and Houlihan, M. (eds) *Work Matters: Critical Reflections on Contemporary Work*, London: Palgrave.

Nichols, T., Cam, S., Wen-chi, G. C., Soonok, C., Wei, Z. and Tongqing, F. (2004) 'Factory Regimes and the Dismantling of Established Labour in Asia: A Review of Cases from Large Manufacturing Plants in China, South Korea and Taiwan', *Work, Employment and Society*, 18(4): 663–85.

Olcott, G. (2009) *Conflict and Change: Foreign Ownership and the Japanese Firm*, Cambridge: Cambridge University Press.

Peck, J., Theodore, N. and Ward, K. (2005) 'Constructing Markets for Temporary Labour: Employment Liberalization and the Internationalization of the Staffing Industry', *Global Networks*, 5(1): 3–26.

Platman, K. (2004) ' "Portfolio Careers" and the Search for Flexibility in Later Life', *Work, Employment and Society*, 18(3): 573–99.

▶
Pries, L. (ed.) (2001) *New Transnational Social Spaces*, London: Routledge.

Pun, N. (2005) *Made In China: Women Factory Workers in a Global Workplace*, Durham, NC: Duke University Press.

Pun, N. and Chan, C. K. C. (2008) 'The Subsumption of Class Discourse in China', *Boundary*, 35(2): 75–91.

Rhoades, G. and Slaughter, S. (2004) 'American Capitalism in the New Economy: Challenges and Choices': http://www.aft.org/pubs-reports/american_academic/issues/june04/ Rhoades.qxp.pdf- 151.8KB – *AFT*.

Royal, T. (2006) 'The Dominance Effect? Multinational Corporations in the Italian Quick-Food Service Sector', *British Journal of Industrial Relations*, 44(4): 757–79.

Slaughter, S. and Leslie, L. L. (1997) *Academic Capitalism: Politics, Policies, and the Entrepreneurial University*, Baltimore, MD: The Johns Hopkins University Press.

Slaughter, S. and Rhoades, G. (2004) *Academic Capitalism and the New Economy*, Baltimore, MD: The Johns Hopkins University Press.

Smith, C. (2003) 'Living at Work: Management Control and the Dormitory Labour System in China', *Asia Pacific Journal of Management*, 20(3): 333–58.

Smith, C. (2006) 'The Double Indeterminacy of Labour Power: Labour Effort and Labour Mobility', *Work, Employment and Society*, 20(2): 389–402.

Smith, C. (2008) 'Work Organisation within a Dynamic Globalising Context: A Critique of National Institutional Analysis of the International Firm and an Alternative Perspective', in Smith, C., McSweeney, B. and Fitzgerald, R. (eds) *Remaking Management between Global and Local*, Cambridge: Cambridge University Press, 25–60.

Smith, C. and McKinlay, A. (2009) 'Creative Industries and Labour Process Analysis', in McKinlay, A. and Smith, C. (eds) *Creative Labour, Working in Creative Industries*, London: Palgrave.

Smith, C. and Pun, N. (2006) 'The Dormitory Labour Regime in China as a Site for Control and Resistance', *International Journal of Human Resource Management*, 17(8): 1456–70.

Smith, C. and Thompson, P. (eds) (1992) *Labour in Transition*, London: Routledge.

Thompson, P. (1989) *The Nature of Work*, 2nd ed., London: Macmillan.

Wajcman, J., Bittman, M. and Brown, J. E. (2008) 'Families without Borders: Mobile Phones, Connectedness and Work-Home Divisions', *Sociology*, 42(4): 635–52.

Woodbridge, J. (2005) *Sizing the Unauthorised (Illegal) Migrant Population in the UK in 2001*, London: Home Office.

Zeitlin, J. and Herrigel, G. (eds) (2000) *Americanization and Its Limits: Reworking US Technology and Management in Post-War Europe and Japan*, Oxford: Oxford University Press.

Zheng, Y. (2009) 'Evaluation, Negotiation and Adaptation through Continuity Transition: Expatriates in the Japanese Subsidiaries in China', *PhD Thesis*, Royal Holloway, University of London.

Making Space for Geography in Labour Process Theory

Al Rainnie, Susan McGrath-Champ and Andrew Herod

Introduction

Within capitalism, as Paul Thompson made clear in *The Nature of Work* (1989: 40–1), the labour process becomes specifically capitalist when it is combined with valorization, which involves the creation and simultaneous appropriation of surplus value. As is well known, what is significant within the capitalist labour process is that only living labour can create surplus value. A key element in any capitalist labour process, then, is for employers to determine how to transform potential labour power into actual work and, through that, into realized surplus value. Investigating how this is achieved is an integral element of any exploration of how capitalism works.

At its simplest, we can represent the system of surplus value production and the securing thereof by capitalists in the following terms (see Castree et al., 2004: 28):

$$M\ldots\ldots C \quad \begin{array}{c} MP \\ P \\ LP \end{array} \ldots\ldots C^* \ldots\ldots M + \Delta$$

In this schema, money (M) is advanced by capitalists to purchase commodities (C) of two kinds – MP (the means of production) and LP (the labour power of workers). This results in the process of production (P), leading to a new commodity (C*), which is then sold to consumers for the original amount of money (M) plus a profit (Δ).

Within this process, the buying and selling of labour power is clearly central. There are, however, two important considerations to bear in mind. First, although labour power is bought and sold in much the same way as are commodities like raw materials, because workers are active agents in the accumulation process and so are capable of resisting and transforming it, labour may take a commodity form but it is not a true commodity. Rather, it is a pseudo-commodity, one which is 'idiosyncratic and *spatially differentiated*' (Storper and Walker, 1983: 4, emphasis added). Thus, labour varies considerably across the economic landscape in terms of its conditions of purchase, its performance capacity, its actual performance and its ability to reproduce itself in place. Second, and following from this, as Marxist geographer David Harvey (1982) has argued, raw materials and workers have to be brought together at particular locations so that accumulation may occur (he calls the resultant agglomeration capital's 'spatial fix'). Importantly, this process depends for its success upon these locations' geographical connections with other places, since there are few locations on the Earth's surface where all of the means of production are naturally available *in situ* and in which all of the commodities produced are consumed locally. Equally, workers must also be able to reproduce themselves socially and biologically on a day-by-day and generational basis if accumulation is to occur, a process which requires the economic landscape be structured in certain ways – they must, in other words, be able to come back to work day after day sufficiently fed, clothed and rested to be able to work, which will require that the economic landscape is laid out in certain ways (they must have shelter, they cannot live too far from their work, etc.). As a result of these geographical considerations, Harvey has argued, any analysis of the capitalist mode of production must be understood not in terms of a historical materialist analysis but, rather, of a historical-*geographical* one.

Significantly, although the manner in which labour's spatial differentiation affects the accumulation process and efforts to develop a historical-geographical materialist analysis of capitalist accumulation have been well explored within the geographic literature, such considerations are only now beginning to intersect with labour process theory (LPT) at a theoretical level. Hence, in their recent review of LPT within the literature on the sociology of work, Thompson and Smith (2009, 5: emphasis added) observed that '[t]he orientation of LPT to the waged workplace, and to some extent case study methods of analysing that workplace, [have] meant that [LPT has been] less equipped to address…issues such as the varieties of (often informal or unwaged) types of work, [and the] temporal *and spatial dimensions*' of work. We could not agree more. Indeed, we would argue forcefully that a geographically informed approach to understanding the workplace and evolving economic landscape of capitalism is essential to achieving LPT's goal of 'reach[ing] beneath institutional, formal patterns…to discover and explore hidden or informal realms of industrial relations and workplace conflict' and to understand the 'total social organisation of labour' (Thompson and Smith, 2009: 4–5). In particular, we argue that understanding the labour process requires understanding that what occurs on the shop floor is shaped by what goes on outside the factory or office gates, for the perpetual reconstitution of capital-labour relations is fundamentally shaped by the spatial contexts within which this occurs.

Given these claims, we have organized the chapter as follows, drawing upon themes outlined in McGrath-Champ, Herod and Rainnie (2010). First, we lay the foundation for how a spatially informed approach can enrich LPT. Second, we explore three specific sets of processes which have implications for thinking about the labour process and the relationships between places which can affect it. Finally, we offer a brief conclusion.

Thinking geographically about the labour process

Although the micro-geography of the workplace and the spatial layout of assembly lines or desks can have a significant impact upon the labour process (Baldry, 1999), in this chapter we wish to focus upon how the broader economic landscapes and geographical relationships within which workplaces are located can have important effects upon what goes on within the factory or office. Specifically, we suggest that how workers reproduce themselves socially and biologically, such that they can keep coming back to their workplaces on a daily basis, is fundamentally spatially structured, as is the way in which workers and labour markets are regulated and the way in which accumulation literally 'takes place'. In order to do so, we explore several key aspects of how labour power is regulated geographically and how this shapes the ways in which the labour process operates. Although there is not enough space here to do anything except delve into such matters briefly, we hope that such an exploration will illustrate our point that a geographical approach to LPT adds important insights that are missed by aspatial approaches (see Herod, Rainnie and McGrath-Champ, 2007; Rainnie, Herod and McGrath-Champ, 2007 and McGrath-Champ, Herod and Rainnie, 2010).

First, as intimated above, the economic landscape of capitalism must be constructed in certain ways to ensure that accumulation can occur. Hence, collectively capital must invest in 'factories, dams, offices, shops, warehouses, roads, railways, docks, power stations, water supply and sewage disposal systems, schools, hospitals, parks, cinemas, restaurants – the list is endless' (Harvey 1982: 233) so that surplus value can be extracted and realized. Through doing so capital embeds itself – sometimes for long periods, sometimes for shorter ones – in particular places. This embedding is at the heart of the production of the unevenly developed landscape of capitalism. There are, though, three sets of issues which emerge from such embedding.

The first of these issues is that capitalists always face a conflict between the need to be fixed in place so that accumulation can occur and the need to try to remain sufficiently mobile so as to take advantage of opportunities that may emerge elsewhere. The resolution of this geographical tension, though, manifests itself differently amongst different segments of capital – large steel mills are generally more spatially fixed than are footloose textile manufacturing sweatshops, for instance. In turn, this has implications for how the labour process is organized and how workers behave. In particular, workers who see their work as not very spatially mobile may be more willing to be militant than if they believe it to be highly mobile, as they may view militancy as cause for capital to leave a community. The second issue is that there is often a conflict between capital and labour over how the landscape should be configured. In particular, whereas capital may prefer to create one type of economic landscape, a landscape that perhaps maximizes profits by ensuring a particular 'spatial fix' is developed (such as having workers live next door to a factory so that they might always be on call for work [see Pun and Smith, 2010]), workers may prefer a quite different landscape, one which more readily facilitates their social and biological reproduction on their own terms (such as being able to live at some distance from their place of work so that they might not always be under the watchful eye of their boss). Finally, different groups of workers are differentially able to cross space so as to access paid work, which can affect how the labour process is organized – domestic responsibilities mean that married women with children, for instance, frequently have less spare time in the day than do their husbands, which leads them to have to work closer to home than do their spouses because they have less travel-to-work time available to them (Hanson and Johnston, 1985; Hanson and Pratt, 1995). Put more bluntly, although an essential element in the production process is ensuring that workers show up to work each day, and although they cannot do this unless the landscape is broadly made in such a way as to allow them to access work geographically, within these constraints different groups of workers and capitalists may have quite different ideas as to how the economic landscape should be made. This may lead them to agitate for different spatial configurations of capitalism which, in turn, shapes how the labour process is organized. For example, better transit routes with which to more easily cross space may allow married women either to seek jobs that are further away from their homes or to work increased numbers of hours, since they will have to spend less time commuting and will more easily be able to fit this in with their domestic responsibilities (we highlight women here because, in the present domestic division of labour, they usually do most domestic work).

If the first major concept to consider is that of how the creation of various spatial fixes can shape how the labour process unfolds, the second concerns how particular types of activities are deliberately located in different places, such that, say, manufacturing may occur in one region but corporate headquarters may be concentrated somewhere else. In other words, we must recognize that there is not just a social division of labour but also a spatial division of labour. This also has important implications for the labour process, for even though the production process may be split up over significant geographical distances, it can remain organizationally quite integrated. Hence, in the case of the North American automobile industry, although General Motors assembles vehicles in plants within the US, many of the components used on those vehicles are actually manufactured in Mexico and China, a geographical structuring which allows GM to take advantage of low-wage workers and other local conditions in various parts of the world yet still claim that its vehicles are 'built' in the US. The creation of such spatial divisions of labour through the geographical partitioning of various elements in the production chain, then, has significant implications for how the labour process is organized and how workers might organize to resist capital.

Second, not only might individual corporations develop particular sets of spatial divisions of labour for various reasons, but it is important to recognize that the collective spatial division of labour created under one era of capitalist accumulation may be quite different from that created under another. Hence, industrialization in nineteenth-century Britain created booming manufacturing regions in the north of England, southern Scotland and South Wales, regions which began to go into decline by the 1960s. However, as Massey (1984) showed, there is a dialectical relationship between spatial divisions of labour laid down at different historical moments. Thus, the large pools of unemployed labour created when these older industrial regions began to wane proved attractive to other investors, who subsequently began establishing new manufacturing and service-sector activities in them – the extant spatial divisions of labour, in other words, helped shape subsequent rounds of capital investment and their associated labour processes. This highlights two interconnected things. The first of these is that whilst it is common for labour to move to capital it is also not uncommon for capital to move to where labour is, as in the case of Japanese and other foreign firms choosing to locate in places like Telford, England (Elger and Smith, 2005) or South Wales (Cooke and Morgan, 1998), largely on the basis of abundant labour supply. The second is that the economic landscape's extant spatial structure can dramatically shape patterns of new capital investment, with all the implications this has for how labour processes are organized (in the case of Britain's old industrial regions, for instance, women rather than unemployed men were often hired in the new firms). The shifting spatial division of labour, then, can have important implications for how the labour process within and between workplaces is organized and subsequently evolves.

Third, workers' and capital's varying degrees of spatial embeddedness play important roles in shaping how cultures of work emerge in particular places, which in turn affects how labour processes develop. Thus, as Ellem (2010, 7–8) notes, although its mobility is often a source of power for capital, 'the "rootedness" of labour can, under some circumstances, become a source of power [for workers, as] when working people and their families create distinctive local communities, cultures and organisations'. Hence, in his work on the Pilbara mining region in Australia, Ellem (2003, 2006, 2010) has shown how strong unionism grew out of workers' concentration in communities located close to the iron ore mines in which they worked, to such an extent that the multinationals who own the mines sought to disembed and de-localize workers by implementing 'fly-in/fly-out' work arrangements. This geographical reorganization of the relationship between workplace and place of residence, with miners now living thousands of miles away in places like Perth or Sydney but being flown in for fortnightly blocks to labour in the mines, has made it much more difficult for unions to organize workers – with their homes now dispersed over an entire continent, workers cannot now engage in the kinds of informal activities (like meeting in pubs or churches) which are often central to developing strong bonds of unionism. Equally, though, the rootedness of certain types of capital – typically, those with large sunk costs whose investments are not easily moved elsewhere (utility companies come to mind) – may lead them to engage with the local state in 'boosterist' coalitions designed to bring investment to their communities by, for instance, relaxing environmental and other regulations, offering tax breaks and other subsidies, and so forth, all under the belief that if such capital cannot flee elsewhere then it needs to bring circulating investment to it (Cox and Mair, 1988). Such boosterism may also encourage various firms to put added pressure on their workers to be quiescent for fear that any worker militancy may scare off potential investors, a fear which is often greater than for firms that themselves are more geographically mobile, or to 'work harder' to show their 'business-friendly nature' (with all of the implications that has for how work is organized locally).

At the same time, however, it is important to recognize that labour's rootedness does not always lead to militancy in the way in which it did with Pilbara mineworkers before fly-in/fly-out was instituted. Rather, workers strongly rooted in place (perhaps because of kinship ties or an inability to sell their homes) may sometimes dampen their militancy for fear of scaring off potential investors, with such tendencies towards militancy or quiescence perhaps reflecting whether their local economy is booming or in recession at a particular moment (a booming economy may make rooted workers more willing to be more militant, whereas one in recession may lead those same workers to reconsider their militancy). The point, then, is that rather than seeking to use the concept of spatial rootedness as a *predictor* of behaviour (rootedness = militancy *à la* Australian mineworkers; mobility = quiescence), it helps instead to explain *post hoc* why certain groups of social actors may engage in particular types of behaviour.

Putting all of this together, it is evident that local labour control regimes and how work is organized are shaped significantly by the manner in which workers and capitalists are differentially embedded in the economic landscape (Peck, 1996). This is important, because when capitals and workers are relatively fixed in particular places within the landscape, it is likely that certain traditions of work and ways of organizing the labour process will become congealed in those places, at least until massive economic restructuring and the creation of new spatial divisions of labour begin to erase them. Thus, when contrasting Japanese foreign direct investment in Telford in the British West Midlands with that in South Wales, Elger and Smith (2005) show that Japanese firms have succeeded in establishing 'union free' workplaces in the former but not in the latter, where all but one firm eventually recognized a union. Systematically discounting simply a 'new town effect', they explain this as a result of Telford's failure to preserve its earlier union traditions and institutions and to insert these into the new workplaces as they opened. This is quite different from the case of South Wales, where such traditions were maintained in place and provided the unions and community political and economic resources upon which to draw when seeking to organize the firms.

It is equally important to recognize, though, that whereas geographical fixity can help congeal traditions of work in particular places, the geographical mobility of workers can also bring to new locations traditions of militancy developed elsewhere, such that their arrival can serve as the catalyst of radical change in formerly quiescent and/or non-unionized labour forces and lead to the 'invention' (Hobsbawm and Ranger, 1983) of new traditions. Worker mobility can also bring to new places expectations of work standards and rights developed elsewhere. Hence, Merkle's (1980) work on the origins of Taylorism showed how British workers who migrated to the US in the late nineteenth/early twentieth century to work on imported British machinery brought with them particular attitudes towards labour standards which affected how the labour process was organized. Thus, Frederick Taylor's efforts to speed up these workers came into conflict with long-standing British craft practices, and it was only after these immigrant workers were dismissed and Taylor trained rural migrant labour that he was able to massively increase the British equipment's productivity. In yet other cases, however, even if workers themselves remain fixed in place, traditions may be transmitted geographically through what Wills (1998) calls a 'demonstration effect', as workers in one place are inspired by learning about successful struggles of those in more distant places. Although this latter does not require the physical movement of workers themselves, it does necessitate the spatial diffusion across the economic landscape of information about disputes elsewhere – a fact which raises interesting questions about how the economic landscape's spatial structure may help or hinder the transfer of knowledge from place to place (thus, even in today's world of information hyperflow, rural areas without access to the internet or television may receive information much more slowly than those places which are more plugged in to global media). The point, then, is that the mobility or not of both capital and labour and the geographical connectedness between places can have significant impacts upon how work is organized and how workplace traditions may develop in particular places and/or be transmitted across space from one community to another.

What the above discussion highlights is that the invention and sustenance of workplace tradition and rules (whether formally laid out or not) is itself spatially embedded and structured. But it also underscores the fact that migrating militants are likely to need a supportive milieu of local institutions and ways of living within which to become embedded if they are to be successful, as do local militants who may either be inventing their own traditions *ex nihilo* or drawing inspiration from those they see being articulated elsewhere. The manner in which the labour process is structured within the workplace, together with how workers are regulated and resist such regulation, is shaped to an important degree, then, by how particular workplaces are geographically embedded within the communities in which they are located (how easily are workers able to get to work, for instance?) and how they are geographically tied to communities which may be hundreds or thousands of miles away (what does a strike in a components producing factory in Mexico mean for how work may have to be reorganized in a GM assembly plant in Kansas?). Having thus outlined in broad terms some key geographical concepts and how these help us think about how the labour process is organized, we now briefly turn to three specific practices, all of which have geographical dimensions, to see how they impact the ways in which labour processes may be organized and/or conceptualized, these being issues of: (i) the production and representation of geographical scale; (ii) labour migration; and (iii) community unionism.

Producing and representing scale

The spatial scales at which social life is organized are significant for understanding how the labour process is structured. For instance, whether workers labour under local collective bargaining contracts or national ones has important consequences for how work is controlled – do local or national directives prevail? Equally, how spatial scales of social organization like the local or the global are represented discursively can play an important part in efforts to understand both how work is organized and social actors' praxis in response to this. Thus, the relationship between local, regional, national and global scales of organization is frequently represented in terms whereby each scale is considered to be a rung on a ladder, with actors understood to move 'up' the scalar hierarchy from the local to the national and then the global when they globalize themselves, or 'down' it from the global to the local, as when transnational corporations embed themselves in local communities. However, it is also common to see the relationship between local, regional, national and global scales of organization portrayed in terms of a series of concentric circles, in which one moves 'out' from the local scale to scales like the global. What is important here is that these two ways of conceptualizing scales – as rungs on a ladder or as sets of concentric circles – lead workers and capitalists to think of the relationship between different scales in diverse ways. Hence, in the ladder metaphor the global appears above other scales, whereas in the circle metaphor it is larger than others and encloses them (see Herod 2008 for more details). Such matters of how we think about scale relationally are important, for they deeply affect how we conceptualize what it means to talk about rescaling work and/or institutions' organizational capacities. Consequently, if unions seek to 'scale up' or 'scale down' their collective bargaining practices, how they understand the relations between, say, the local and the national can have important implications for the kinds of strategies in which they engage. Hence, if they internalize a vertical/hierarchical view of the world they may feel more compelled to work through their national organization, which is seen to sit at the top of the scalar ladder and is presumably viewed as the peak of scales and the focal point of action, than if they internalize a horizontal view in which 'national' power is seen as more diffuse – the national scale 'encompasses' other scales rather than 'sits atop them'. The reason such apparently abstruse considerations are important is because both unions and firms are constantly 'confronted by demands at different scales...and by scale-specific arguments about [economic and work] processes' (Ellem, 2010: 9), as when, for example, the mantra of 'global competition' is used as the rationale for calls for local workplace restructuring. Indeed, how the relationship between the global and the local is understood can have signal consequence for workers' abilities to resist work reorganization – is 'the global' seen to bear down on 'the local' from above, making it difficult to imagine opposing mantras about how work *must* be restructured so that factories can maintain 'global competitiveness', or is the relationship between the two scales viewed in more equal terms?

The issue of spatial scale is also implicated in questions concerning the geographical resolution – the local or, say, the national – at which workers should organize themselves to seek to shape the labour process. As Castree et al. (2004: 8) argue, the increasingly stretched nature of social relationships between place-based workers across national and supranational space can take a variety of forms, which may differ in time and across space. This generates for workers a complex landscape of geographical difference and interdependence, which in turn creates such scalar dilemmas concerning at what level(s) accommodation or resistance are best organized. The conclusion to be drawn from this, as Holgate (2007: 99) argues, is that the geographical scale at which action should be taken to defend working conditions is always relative and contingent. In most cases, worker or union activity will be place-based, originating from the workplace. However, the increasing scale(s) of economic activity demand(s) new spatial structures be developed by labour to counter the power of capital's (often) superior command of space. Shifting from the local to the global, therefore, has to mean more than simply upscaling forms of action, since the process is more dialectical than the phrase suggests. It is not a linear process, nor is it an either/or choice. Rather, it is dependent on the situation in which workers find themselves and may involve a mix of organizing approaches which have quite different spatialities embedded in them.

For their part, and drawing insights from the activities of a range of transnational companies across contract cleaning, catering and security industries, Anderson, Hamilton and Wills (2010) have suggested that globalization has altered the scalar architecture of capitalism and that this is having important implications for trade unions. Specifically, they show that the emergence of TNCs, global cities and new transportation nodes are challenging the limitations of long-standing trade union organization, which typically focuses upon workplaces and national trade union structures. Based on an analysis of the Service Employees' International Union in the US and living wage campaigns in London, they highlight the need to develop multiscalar approaches to organizing workers that include the strategic targeting of corporate power centres, organizing across geographical zones rather than within just workplaces, and the development of extra-workplace networks (such as those created by the Indian Union for Information & Technology Enabled Services [UNITES] to link workers in Indian call centres with British workers and British unions' efforts to facilitate Indian unions' organizing efforts in such centres [Taylor and Bain, 2010]).

Migration

Labour migration can take a number of forms: temporary or permanent, internal and external, legal and undocumented, skilled and unskilled, voluntary and forced (Castree et al., 2004: 187). At its heart, however, all migration is a geographical process, one that involves not only the movement of workers across space but also the geographical tying together of places (the origin and destination communities) that may be quite distant from one another. Consequently, labour migration can have significant impacts on labour markets and the organization of work in both the origin and destination communities. Hence, often it is the youngest and most skilled workers who leave communities for pastures greener. Given the gendering of skills and of domestic responsibilities, frequently these are male workers (as with the *braceros* who historically migrated from Mexico to the US to work in agriculture or construction), although in some cases migration streams may be made up overwhelmingly of women (as with Filipinas who leave for jobs in North America or the Middle East as domestic workers, a migration facilitated by their government [Kelly, 2010]). With younger or more skilled workers leaving, labour processes in the origin communities may need to be transformed – employers might have to invest in labour-saving technologies as their workforce leaves or might themselves have to relocate and seek out new pools of labour in other locations. Migration, though, can also have significant impacts upon how the labour process is organized in the destination community – Hardy and Fitzgerald (2008: 7), for instance, argue that large-scale labour migration has produced low-value and less technologically advanced production in central Europe. Equally, with the arrival of large numbers of new migrants, local workers' abilities to demand higher wages or better working conditions may be undercut, with the result that their employers may delay investing in labour-saving technologies and/or may choose not to relocate to other communities in search of cheaper labour, with the outcome of both decisions having dramatic impacts upon how the labour process is organized. At the same time, however, it is also the case that the migration of skilled workers may stimulate a technological upgrading of local jobs, thereby also transforming how the labour process is organized (Wadhwa et al., 2009).

Migration, though, can also have dramatic impacts upon the organization of the labour process in terms of how migrant workers are slotted into particular jobs. Indeed, the concentration of migrant workers from a particular ethnic background within an industry or sector is quite common. Hence, in the construction industry in Sydney, Australia, Koreans/Asians are concentrated in the tiling industry, Lebanese and Koreans in plastering and Italians disproportionately work in formworking. Tracing the shifting ethnic composition of the tiling sector in the post-war period, Shin (2009) has documented the establishment of a unique Korean ethnic system of control, autonomy, wages and skill formation. This has had important implications for how particular jobs are conducted. Specifically, although they coexist within a broader working environment of collectively (and commonly 'pattern') bargained agreements and industry-wide regulation in an industry which remains one of the top two union strongholds in Australia and in which many aspects of job conduct are highly regulated by contract, Korean workers have nevertheless engaged in informal redesigns of the labour process which are having impacts upon other workers' work practices. Thus, deploying a squatting position whilst laying tiles rather than the more typical Western/Anglo-style kneeling position, Korean immigrants have managed to achieve a faster pace of work than have other ethnic groups in the industry.

Equally, influenced by practices in Korea, such immigrant tilers, many of whom are illegal or undocumented, have tended to focus on total earnings rather than formal hourly wages, thereby unwittingly colluding with capital in expending long hours of work to maximize earnings. 'Pyramid' subcontracting, whereby a contract is parcelled out over and over, has also been common and has enabled 'middlepersons' to enter the subcontracting chain. These middlepersons have both Korean and English language skills (though no tiling skills) and facilitate communication, but they also exert searing control between English-speaking subcontractors and non-English speaking, self-employed Korean tilers. The result is that contracts are let with margins so tight that labour costs are squeezed relentlessly. Consequently, the tilers, whose poor English-language skills give them little capacity to articulate objection to these control measures, often put hours and earnings above health and safety and enhance their 'screeding' (floor levelling) skills by practising in their own time in the beach sand. In doing so, they both contribute to, and are victims of, the derogation of the industry's skills infrastructure (see Toner, 2003).

Community unionism

So far we have considered two ways in which geographical processes and structures operating beyond individual workplaces impact how the labour processes within them are organized: (i) through the production of new scales of workplace regulation and discourses thereof, as with the upscaling or downscaling of collective bargaining; (ii) through labour migration into or out of particular communities. A third way concerns how practices of community unionism have implications for the workplace. Of course, at a certain level unionism has always relied upon the broader community within which workplaces are located for its success. Historically, community has been constructed by both capital and labour. Hence, unions have often developed out of, for instance, fairly closed industrial labour markets (e.g. the rail yards in places like Crewe or Swindon in the UK) or closed communities (company towns in many countries), whilst communities have also developed around paternalist employers like Cadburys in the UK. However, instead of unions being simply 'embedded in' particular communities, as in the historical instances above, what is different about contemporary 'community unionism' is that it very self-consciously focuses upon developing linkages between the workplace and the broader community, that is, society at large. It quite consciously recognizes and acts upon the fact that workers live their lives beyond the workplace as well as within it, and that there can be commonality of interest and greater strength when 'workplace' issues are taken up and supported by individuals and organizations outside the workplace. Hence, the focus of praxis is not always the workplace itself but may be the broader community, in the belief that organizing the community can have significant impacts upon workers' lives and the organization of work within the workplace.

Within this context, Tattersall (2005, 2008, 2010) conceptualizes community unionism as a particular form of coalition building. Cautious of innumerable and inconsistent interpretations of 'community', and avoiding the error of perceiving the term as referring to simply a particular social or ethnic enclave, she defines community unionism as having three discrete but mutually reinforcing elements: it is focused on non-workplace organization; it seeks to develop a common interest identity; and it largely takes place in local neighbourhoods or communities. The term 'community unionism', however, is important, she proposes, as it is a catch-all phrase which describes a new range of strategies for union growth and power that connect workplace action to new spheres of action in the non-workplace realm. It follows from the above, then, that there is no 'single' version of community unionism.

Drawing similarly upon an encompassing notion of community unionism, Wills (2001: 466) argues that there are four advantages to unions of forging common cause with community groups and political campaigns:

- community initiatives are able to tackle issues of justice that stretch beyond any particular workplace;
- unions are able to reach non-union workers who have been traditionally marginalized from trade unions;
- unions are often able to reach low-paid, contingent manufacturing and service workers who are employed in small workplaces, workers who have been difficult to reach with traditional organizing methods; and
- the community can be invaluable in defending traditional workplace trade union organization.

Certainly, community unionism has been criticized for having serious weaknesses. These include that there are relatively few instances of it, that it has sometimes been limited to an 'agonized liberalism' which seeks to appeal to the moral conscience of business and political elites rather than securing its goals through building and exerting political power, and that the models developed in North America (where community unionism has tended to be concentrated) may not be that applicable elsewhere (Taylor and Mathers, 2008). Furthermore, Clawson (2003) suggests that community unionism may lead to the abandonment of rank-and-file participation and solidarity. However, what is central to the practice of community unionism – and why we focus upon it here – is that it is about breaking down the mental and organizational fences which have separated worker action in the workplace from that beyond it. Put another way, it seeks to shape labour practices in the workplace by switching organizing's geographical focus to the spaces beyond the workplace. Consequently, it highlights how developments outside the workplace can have significant impacts upon processes within it. In this regard, then, our interest is not that the examples below represent campaigns in which unions have been involved. Rather, we explore community unionism for the theoretical insights it can give us for thinking about how the labour process is shaped by the ways in which various social actors engage with the spatial contexts within which they find themselves, with all of the implications this has for thinking about what shapes the labour process.

One example of seeking to organize beyond the workplace so as to shape what goes in within it is that detailed by Johns and Vural (2000). Specifically, they explored the 'Stop Sweatshops Campaign' initiated in 1995 by the US UNITE union and the National Consumers League (NCL). Although UNITE had long sought to address sweatshop conditions in garment factories by focusing upon the workplace, the union found such tactics rather ineffective, for as soon as they had improved conditions in one workplace another would spring up to take its place. Consequently, UNITE reconfigured their geographical tactics to focus attention on organizing not the spaces of the workplace but the spaces of consumption. In particular, they organized consumers to bring pressure to bear on retailers to not sell clothing sourced from sweatshops. Given that the retail outlets were much easier to identify than were the sweatshops (which were often located in secluded buildings in places like New York City), UNITE and the NCL were able to avoid the problem of having to organize each individual sweatshop. Through coercing the retailers to not buy from sweatshops that did not respect certain work conditions and wages, then, UNITE and the NCL were able to effect changes in the labour process within the industry. Certainly, this strategy still required the union to seek out sweatshops so as to make sure that retailers were living up to their side of the bargain, but this was a much easier task than was seeking to organize each one.

The Service Employees' International Union (SEIU) in the US has employed similar tactics of shifting their organizational focus from the spaces of work to those of consumption. This change in tactics relates to how the structure of the janitorial industry in which SEIU organizes has changed over the past three decades. Thus, whereas it used to be the case in cities such as Los Angeles that janitors were typically hired directly by building owners, beginning in the 1970s owners increasingly began to contract this work with janitorial companies. This has had two important consequences (see Milkman, 2006). First, in any given shift individual janitors may now clean several different buildings located across the city, rather than a single one or a cluster of buildings owned by the same company. Second, the legal employment relationship for janitors has changed – typically, janitors are no longer employed by the building owners themselves but, instead, by the janitorial company contracted by them to clean. These situations – workspaces spread out across cities and a change in the legal employment relationship – made it increasingly difficult for the union to engage in traditional workplace-based organizing practices. As a result, the SEIU shifted its geographical focus from organizing on a building-by-building basis and instead began to use street theatre and other activities in the public space of the streets to coerce building owners to, in turn, pressure the janitorial companies with which they contract to provide better wages and working conditions for the janitors (Savage, 1998). Again, as with the UNITE/NCL campaign, by shifting their geographical focus SEIU's goal was to impact the labour process to give workers better working conditions in the workplace.

For sure, community unionism is not a universal prophylactic nor an instant remedy to declining union strength and density. Nevertheless, it does illustrate how the walls around the workplace are not as impervious to social practices and relations beyond it as we perhaps sometimes might intimate through focusing our attention more directly upon the labour process and the extraction of surplus value in the workplace.

Conclusion

By outlining a range of concepts that help us think about how the labour process is organized within the broad landscape of global capitalism, along with specific associated practices that provide illustrative grist, this chapter has shown that a spatially informed perspective enhances LPT. Neither workers nor capital are merely passive elements in the geographies of social relations, for both actively construct the world around them. The control of space and place is crucial to the way that jobs are created, exported, lost and fought over, and to the labour processes within which such jobs and production are founded. We have argued the need for a geographically informed reading of the labour process, given that labour, an 'idiosyncratic and spatially differentiated' pseudo-commodity (Storper and Walker, 1983), varies so dramatically across the economic landscape. In this regard, we hope to have more fully opened up theoretically the category of labour, which lies at the centre of LPT.

In terms of the chapter's specifics, we have outlined several key concepts that help us think about how the labour process is organized. The need of both capital and labour to create appropriate 'spatial fixes' – one to ensure that accumulation can occur, the other to ensure that it can reproduce itself daily and generationally – shapes the unfolding labour process. Likewise, the development of a particular 'spatial division of labour' not only reflects how the labour process is organized but also then shapes its further development – the geographical splitting up of the various parts of a production chain may allow for continued functional integration, even as it helps divide workers spatially and so reduces the kinds of contacts between them that might facilitate oppositional politics. Further, the economic, social and political landscapes that ensue from the conflicts between capital and workers have repercussions for the labour process long after the social relationships that initially produced them have disappeared. All this highlights the fact that the relative spatial embeddedness of workers and capital, the kinds of community that do or do not emerge, workers' opportunities for solidarity within and beyond the workplace and a host of associated practices like engaging in local boosterism are amongst a myriad of geographically situated dimensions that impact the labour process.

In terms of specific geographical practices, in discussing the scaling of economic life and the discursive representation of its scaled nature we suggested that if scales are understood as horizontal or networked, rather than exclusively hierarchical, it is much easier to see the simultaneity of the global and the local, the possibility of more imaginative ways of operating through and across multi-scaled networks, and the impact of this on the workplace and labour processes. Stepping on from the discussion of scale, the phenomenon of labour migration illustrates that the movement of people involves the geographical tying together of places and significantly impacting the labour process through changing the amount of labour available. It also changes the skills, expectations and organizing capacities of workers at both the receiving and sending places. Finally, through examples of the 'Stop Sweatshops' and 'Justice for Janitors' campaigns, we suggested that community unionism illustrates the connectivities between the spaces of the workplace and those beyond, especially with regard to how organizing in either of these spaces can impact what goes on in the other.

In sum, we have sought to take Thompson and Smith's (2009) admonition about how a spatial sensitivity is missing from much theorizing concerning the labour process, and both to make the geographical visible but, more significantly, to show how geographical concepts and thinking can better help us understand how labour processes develop. The key point established by this chapter, then, is that the world of work and capitalist production is geographically structured and that we need to be aware of this as we seek to understand the labour process. It is our strong conviction that a geographical perspective has the capacity to strengthen and enhance this enduring body of theory and will 'expand the scope and explanatory power' of LPT by forming one of a range of new 'resources for resilience...and innovation' (Thompson and Smith, 2009: 5).

REFERENCES

Anderson, J., Hamilton, P. and Wills, J. (2010, forthcoming) 'The Multi-scalarity of Trade Union Practice', in McGrath-Champ, S., Herod, A. and Rainnie, A. (eds) *Handbook of Employment and Society: Working Space,* Cheltenham: Edward Elgar, 383–97.

Baldry, C. (1999) 'Space – the Final Frontier', *Sociology,* 33(3): 535–53.

Castree, N., Coe, N., Ward, K. and Samers, M. (2004) *Spaces of Work: Global Capitalism and Geographies of Labour,* London: Sage.

Clawson, D. (2003) *The Next Upsurge: Labor and the New Social Movements,* Ithaca, NY: ILR Press.

Cooke, P. and Morgan, K. (1998) *The Associational Economy: Firms, Regions, and Innovation,* Oxford: Oxford University Press.

Cox, K. R. and Mair, A. (1988) 'Locality and Community in the Politics of Local Economic Development', *Annals of the Association of American Geographers,* 78(2): 307–25.

Elger, T. and Smith, C. (2005) *Assembling Work: Remaking Work Regimes in Japanese Multinationals in Britain,* Oxford: Oxford University Press.

Ellem, B. (2003) 'Re-placing the Pilbara's Mining Unions', *Australian Geographer,* 34(3): 281–96.

Ellem, B. (2006) 'Scaling Labour: Australian Unions and Global Mining', *Work, Employment and Society,* 20(2): 369–87.

Ellem, B. (2010) 'Contested Space: Union Organising in the Old Economy', in McGrath-Champ, S., Herod, A. and Rainnie, A. (eds) *Handbook of Employment and Society: Working Space,* Cheltenham: Edward Elgar, 349–67.

Hanson, S. and Johnston, I. (1985) 'Gender Differences in Work-Trip Length: Explanations and Implications', *Urban Geography,* 6: 193–219.

Hanson, S. and Pratt, G. (1995) *Gender, Work, and Space,* New York: Routledge.

Hardy, A. and Fitzgerald, I. (2008) 'Cross Border Trade Union Collaboration in the Context of Competition and Arbitraging Labour in an Enlarged Europe', Paper presented to ESRC Research Seminar Series 'Changing Cultures of Competitiveness', University of Manchester, July.

Harvey, D. (1982) *The Limits to Capital,* Oxford: Basil Blackwell.

▶

▶

Herod, A. (2008) 'Scale: The Local and the Global', in Holloway, S., Rice, S., Valentine, G. and Clifford, N. (eds) *Key Concepts in Geography*, 2nd edition, London: Sage, 217–35.

Herod, A., Rainnie, A. and McGrath-Champ, S. (2007) 'Working Space: Why Incorporating the Geographical Is Central to Theorizing Work and Employment Practices', *Work, Employment and Society*, 21(2): 247–64.

Hobsbawm, E. and Ranger, T. (1983) *The Invention of Tradition*, Cambridge: Cambridge University Press.

Holgate, J. (2007) 'Producing: Changing Patterns of Work', in Douglas, I., Huggett, R. and Perkins, C. (eds) *Companion Encyclopedia of Geography: From Local to Global*, 2nd Edition, London: Routledge.

Johns, R. and Vural, L. (2000) Class, Geography, and the Consumerist Turn: UNITE and the Stop Sweatshops Campaign, *Environment and Planning A*, 32(7): 1193–213.

Kelly, P. (2010) 'Filipino Migration and the Spatialities of Labour Market Subordination', in McGrath-Champ, S., Herod, A. and Rainnie, A. (eds) *Handbook of Employment and Society: Working Space*, Cheltenham: Edward Elgar, 159–76.

Massey, D. (1984) *Spatial Divisions of Labour: Social Structures and the Geography of Production*, London: Macmillan.

McGrath-Champ, S., Herod, A. and Rainnie, A. (2010, forthcoming) *Handbook of Employment and Society: Working Space*, Cheltenham: Edward Elgar.

Merkle, J. A. (1980) *Management and Ideology: The Legacy of the International Scientific Management Movement*, Berkeley: University of California Press.

Milkman, R. (2006) *LA Story: Immigrant Workers and the Future of the U.S. Labor Movement*, New York: Russell Sage Foundation.

Peck, J. (1996) *Work-Place: The Social Regulation of Labor Markets*, New York: Guilford.

Pun, N. and Smith, C. (2010) 'Dormitory Labour Regimes and the Labour Process in China: New Workers in Old Factory Forms', in McGrath-Champ, S., Herod, A. and Rainnie, A. (eds) *Handbook of Employment and Society: Working Space*, Cheltenham: Edward Elgar, 228–46.

Rainnie, A., Herod, A. and McGrath-Champ, A. (2007) 'Spatialising Industrial Relations', *Industrial Relations Journal*, 38(2): 102–18.

Savage, L. (1998) 'Geographies of Organizing: Justice for Janitors in Los Angeles', in Herod, A. (ed.) *Organizing the Landscape: Geographical Perspectives on Labor Unionism*, Minneapolis and London: University of Minnesota Press.

Shin, J. S. (2009) Immigrant Workers, the Labour Market and Skills Formation in the Sydney Construction Industry, Ph D thesis, Faculty of Economics and Business, University of Sydney, Australia.

Storper, M. and Walker, R. (1983) 'The Theory of Labour and the Theory of Location', *International Journal of Urban and Regional Research*, 7(1): 1–42.

Tattersall, A. (2005) 'There Is Power in Coalition: A Framework for Assessing How and When Union-Community Coalitions Are Effective and Enhance Union Power', *Labour and Industry*, 16(2): 97–112.

▶

▶

Tattersall, A. (2008) 'Coalitions and Community Unionism: Using the Term Community to Explore Effective Union-Community Collaboration', *Journal of Organizational Change Management*, 21(4): 415–32.

Tattersall, A. (2010, forthcoming) *Power in Coalition*, Ithaca, NY: Cornell University Press.

Taylor, G. and Mathers, A. (2008) 'Organising Unions, Organising Communities', Working paper University of West of England.

Taylor, P. and Bain, P. (2010, forthcoming) ' "Across the Great Divide": Local and Global Trade Union Responses to Call Centre Offshoring to India', in McGrath-Champ, S., Herod, A. and Rainnie, A. (eds) *Handbook of Employment and Society: Working Space*, Cheltenham: Edward Elgar, 436–54.

Thompson, P. (1989) *The Nature of Work*, 2nd edition, Houndmills: Macmillan.

Thompson, P. and Smith, C. (2009) 'Labour Power and Labour Process: Contesting the Marginality of the Sociology of Work', *Sociology*, 43(5): 913–30.

Toner, P. (2003) 'Supply-Side and Demand-Side Explanations of Declining Training Rates', *Journal of Industrial Relations*, 45(4): 457–84.

Wadhwa, V., Saxenian, A., Freeman, R. B. and Gereffi, G. (2009) 'America's Loss Is the World's Gain: America's New Immigrant Entrepreneurs, Part 4', Available at Social Science Research Network: http://ssrn.com/abstract=1348616. Accessed 20 September 2009.

Wills, J. (1998) 'Space, Place and Tradition in Working-Class Organization', in Herod, A. (ed.) *Organizing the Landscape: Geographical Perspectives on Labor Unionism*, Minneapolis: University of Minnesota Press, 129–58.

Wills, J. (2001) 'Community Unionism and Trade Union Renewal in the UK', *Transactions of the Institute of British Geographers*, 26(4): 465–83.

Beyond the Blank Slate: Identities and Interests at Work

Abigail Marks and Paul Thompson

Identity has become the focal point of concern across the social sciences and with reference to a range of issues and fields of study (Cornelissen, Haslam and Balmer, 2007). Papers on identity have long been a feature of the International Labour Process Conference (ILPC) and the 2009 event had its largest stream on that topic. What is the point of interest and connection for labour process analysis (LPA)? Historically, it has been focused on the so-called missing subject debate. This is a well-trodden territory that we do not want to repeat in any detail here (though see chapter by Jaros in this volume). Suffice to say, the central issue has been how to fill the hole originally left by Braverman's objectivism – his self-limiting choice to omit consideration of worker action and attitudes in relation to what he regarded as the long run tendency to work degradation. In one sense, this is a wholly misleading frame for debate in that few ever agreed with Braverman's position, for the simple reason that the 'subjective factor' is part of the objective picture. All subsequent research in a labour process tradition has, therefore, examined and theorized worker agency in one way or another. For mainstream LPA, the subjective factor is addressed through consideration of issues of resistance (and more recently misbehaviour), creativity (such as the significance of tacit skills and knowledge to labour and capital) and consent (notably the games and discretionary practices that help to tie workers to the workplace order). In broad terms, such emphases are consistent with the Marxian tradition of writings on the self-activity of labour (without the teleological belief in the historical mission of the working class) and literatures of industrial sociology that focused on informal self-organization of workers.

The 'missing subject' debate was, however, largely driven by something else: the view, originally taken by two of the prime movers of ILPC – David

Knights and Hugh Willmott – that a particular *view* of subjectivity was missing. From the mid-1980s they developed an argument that to account for the
reproduction of work relations and capitalism itself, the precarious, insecure
nature of human identity had to be put centre stage (Knights, 1990; Knights
and Willmott, 1989; Willmott, 1990). These accounts of the supposed self-
defeating search for a secure identity drew on Giddens, critical theory and
latterly, Foucault. Despite the references to the labour process and capitalism,
this was a perspective focused on projects of self-exploration inherent to the
existential nature of human conduct, rather than the dynamics of actors
within the employment relationship. At best, certain tendencies in capitalism, notably individualisation, could trigger or accentuate the existential
anxieties that lie at the heart of identity formation. The core propositions
of the 'Manchester School' with respect to identity have not sub-stantially
changed, as can be seen from a recent paper from a later entrant on the scene
(O'Doherty, 2009).[1] O'Doherty talks of the 'basic anxieties and insecurities
associated with the "primordial" and existential nature of being-in-the-
world' (110) and the 'recursive practices of social agents preoccupied with
questions pertaining to existential matters' (116).[2]

Credit has to be given to the Manchester School for pushing the issue of
identity and linking it to normative controls (see chapter by Sturdy, Fleming
and Delbridge in this volume). But, the main outcome of their intervention
was that subjectivity *became* identity and identity seemingly obliterated an
interest in anything else. Take the recent statement from Thomas in her
overview of critical management studies and identity, 'Subjectivity is a term
used to denote an understanding of individual identity as the product of
discourse, ideology and institutional practices' (2009: 180). However, by
the mid-1990s, the focus on identity had become associated with particular
claims about processes and outcomes. With a much heavier dose of Foucault
added to the mix (Casey, 1995; Townley, 1993; Willmott, 1993), subjectivity
had become the subjected self. In essence, this wave of theorizing promoted
the idea of a coincidence of influence between the identity shaping strategies
of organizations and the identity seeking concerns of individual workers,
with some commentators adding the dimension of surveillance technologies
and self-discipline through teams (Barker, 1993; Sewell, 1998). The outcome –
designer employees and colonized identity, with resistance (informal and
formal) either written off as disappeared or where existing, illusory and (as
before) self-defeating.

Readers will no doubt be aware of the debate and the mainstream LP critique of such claims and once again we do not want to cover old ground (see
May, 1999; Thompson and Ackroyd, 1995). We do, however, want to note
an unfortunate by-product that is relevant to this chapter. Such claims and
their refutation became entangled with judgements about the validity of an

interest in identity itself. Arguments such as Thompson and Smith's view that the 'indeterminacy of labour had been replaced by indeterminacy of identity' (1998: 562) tended to marginalize mainstream LP interest in the issue. Fortunately, that has now changed and there are signs of the development of perspectives on identity that can bring something different to the debate and which are compatible with traditions of LPA. Webb's recent book *Organisations, Identities and the Self* seeks a 'renewed sociological perspective on the interconnections between personal biography social identities and organisations' (2006: 14) and avoids the contemporary predilection for over and under-socialized conceptions of human action. In her very useful review of writings on identity and work, Leidner (2006) also explores how the issues can be understood by combining insights from the micro-sociological, labour process and related theoretical resources.

Meanwhile, researchers sympathetic to a labour process tradition have been outlining more empirically driven accounts of:

> ...the ways in which identities are ascribed and achieved within different workplace contexts which allows an understanding of the cultural and economic features of the labour process and a broader examination of debates concerning the inter-relationship between agency and structures. (S. Jenkins, 2007: 3)

Related work takes this further by examining the fracturing of identities and interests in the context of the uneven impacts of high performance work practices (Delbridge and S. Jenkins, 2006). A further stream of research, that Jaros (2009) labels 'contextualist', has combined insights from LPA and social identity theory to produce accounts of the varied outcomes of identity construction amongst technical and knowledge workers (Marks and Scholarios, 2007; Marks et al., 2007). This chapter should, therefore, be seen as a contribution to this emergent attempt to develop materialist readings of identity.

Before we examine the relevant concepts and theoretical resources that can enhance such understandings, a further layer needs to be added to the scene setting. The explosion of interest in identity outside its traditional social-psychological heartlands rested on an additional development – the discursive turn. The original arguments of the Manchester School and the Foucauldian wave merged into and were modified within a much broader literature that has come to dominate much of the recent post-structuralist writing on identity. If a concern with subjectivity became focused on identity, identity became even more strongly linked to discourse. The next section gives a critical evaluation of this latest and most significant turn in the identity debate.

Discourse, identity and organizations

Contemporary critical writing, mostly influenced by post-structuralism and the 'linguistic turn' takes as its starting point a rejection of the idea that identity has an 'essence' or is fixed, stable or enduring. Individual and organizational identities are treated as fluid, multiple and unstable social constructions (Collinson, 2003; Gergen, 1991). To refer to identity as a social construct is, for most purposes, non-contentious, but from what is it socially constructed? The answer for most scholars in this tradition is – discourse. 'We are nothing but the discourses through and in which we live' (Calas and Smircich, 1987: 4). In one sense, there is nothing special about identity, given that post-structuralism asserts that discourses constitute the social world by bringing all kinds of phenomena into being. However, a particular conception of identity is given force through the idea of the 'death of the subject'. The purposeful, rational subject manifested in a stable, unitary self is displaced by discursively constructed, fluid and fragile selves (Ainsworth and Hardy, 2004: 155).

In general terms, post-structuralist approaches to discourse focus on their supposedly constructive effects, with individuals or organizations conceived of as 'sites' or 'fields' within which their identities are shaped and regulated. Rather than a more traditional view that identity is a biographical narrative in which the individual moves through the world developing a sense of coherent personal identity, if there is no 'true' self, identity is the outcome of narration through multiple discourses (Phillips and Maguire, 2000). At a different level, *organizational* identity is also frequently treated as a 'narrative construction' (Chreim, 2005) – in this case, through corporate and business press texts. When the processes of organizational and individual identity formation are brought together, they are seen as mutually constitutive rather than separate. There can be little doubt that some organizations have taken a greater interest in the values and normative behaviours of their members in recent years. That in itself, tells us little about the likely effects of 'cultural' initiatives.[3] However, post-structuralists tend to assume identity shaping outcomes for one or other of two reasons. First, because of the earlier noted assumption of congruence between the identity 'needs' of the organization and the individual: 'Individuals subscribe to or are motivated to engage with organizational objectives and ethos through identification with organizational identity' (Davies, 2006: 7).

Second, because the a priori assumption is that discourses constitute the world – in this instance acting on individual identity. A prominent example is Casey's (1995) claim of how new organizational discourses, manifested through quality initiatives, teams and cultural engineering, produce designer employees whose 'corporatized selves' collude with managerial requirements. What is particularly significant about her argument for our purposes is the assertion that discursively produced organizational selves displace occupation, profession and class as primary sources of self-identity. The only mediating factor tends to be other discourses. Given that the individual is essentially treated as a blank slate, the emphasis can only be on the dynamics *between* discourses.

Amongst the problems with such approaches are the a priori attribution of causal powers to discourse and the elision of differences between individuals and organizations as empirical objects. So, for Ainsworth and Hardy (2004: 155), individual identities are the materials from which larger, social identities are built. Individuals and organizations (and indeed other entities), however, have different emergent properties. The former, whilst potentially juggling a variety of social identities, also has a continuous sense of self. A work organization lacks that self-consciousness and it is dubious whether any unitary organizational identity could be said to exist. One of the reasons is that organizations are sites for contending interests and identities, from professions and occupations, to gender and ethnicity. Corporate identity is a much more specific phenomena, but one that is clearly assembled from quite different 'materials' from that which constitute individual identities or other social identities. The differences are elided because only discourse is seen as the formative power and the empirical objects are not accorded properties in their own right.

However, the most widely observed problem is an inherent danger in constructing an explanation of identities in and of organizations from such texts where the agent is either absent or treated as a passive receptor of the (dominant) narrative. Such concerns echo long the previously noted critiques of the substantive removal of agency in Foucauldian and post-structuralist writings (Thompson and Ackroyd, 1995), but are re-articulated with reference to discourse and identity by Reed:

> As a result, the potential for people to influence, much less control, the construction and reconstruction of the discourses which define their lived realities, identities and potentialities is virtually extinguished by a sui generis process of discursive reproduction in which they become the biological and cultural 'raw material' to be 'worked on and through' by the latter's constitutive practices. We become enterprising and/or calculating and/or colluding and/or disciplining 'selves' because we are the subjects/objects of discursive formations... (Reed, 1998: 209)

There is a potential escape hatch within the dominant perspectives and a partial corrective to a socially determinist view – that of identity work. Identity work has a variety of formulations, but all seek to develop a notion of reflexive action that highlights the active aspect of engagement with the

process of identity construction – 'Interpretive activity involved in reproducing and transforming self-identity' (Alvesson and Willmott, 2002: 627).
Manchester School perspectives contained an early version of an identity
work argument that they have maintained (Collinson, 2003; Knights and
Willmott, 1989). As outlined earlier, drawing on existential perspectives,
insecurity and anxiety become the driving force and identity work becomes
the search for a secure and stable sense of self. This is argued to be never
feasible and is becoming less feasible in the more fragmented conditions of
post-modernity, but it is believed to explain the attraction of corporate cultures to some employees.

A broader version of identity work allows those sympathetic to post-structuralism to reconcile the idea that the self is a result of contending discourses
with some notion of interpretation and self-reflection. Though Alvesson and
Willmott's (2002) primary (and perfectly reasonable) motive in their paper is
to incorporate notions of identity regulation into perspectives on managerial
control, they are aware of the limitations of theorizing about identity that
emphasize the vulnerability of subjects to discourses and counter-emphasize
the precarious and contested processes of identity work. Buy-in to managerial discourses is conditioned by other elements of life history, whether other
sources of identity to material conditions, cultural traditions and relations of
power. This analysis is certainly compatible with a more materialist reading
that sees that the 'possibilities of using language to make differentiations
and to structure (social) reality are not limitless' (Alvesson and Willmott,
2002: 628). Yet, the authors find it hard to escape the web of discourse. It
is through attending to, mobilizing and engaging with discourses, that we
'embellish or repair our sense of identity as a coherent narrative' (ibid.: 627).
A recent application of this perspective to organizational change at a Swedish
Volvo plant (Schaeffer, Huzzard and Sommereng, 2009) confirms the pattern
of argument and its limitations. Widespread changes in the workplace are
interpreted solely through the lens of disruption to and repair of the self,
whilst 'managerial discourses' underpinning regime changes are said to 'fuel'
or 'induce' identity work (ibid.: 2 and 4).

It is also worth recognizing that many post-structuralists have consciously
drawn back from earlier Foucauldian excesses concerning disciplined selves
and now seek to examine how individuals actively engage with discourses
and through that engagement, construct alternative identities within and
potentially resistant to forms of domination (Thomas, 2009). In their work,
Thomas and Davies (2005) examine resistance to the discourses of new public management (NPM). Resistance, in typical Foucauldian terms, is stimulated by the contradictions, weaknesses and gaps between alternative subject
positions. In turn, individuals respond to categorizations and classifications
by struggling to appropriate and transform the discourse of NPM. Or as

Ainsworth and Hardy put it, 'disciplinary techniques and normalization produce embodied identities and create limited subject positions from which only certain identities can speak' (2004: 166). Whilst well-known studies such as those by Kondo (1990) and du Gay (1996) do utilize a reflexive language whereby employees construct or 'craft' a variety of selves, it is still presented primarily as a process of interpreting and/or internalizing dominant organizational discourses.

Whatever insights generated, it is not enough to confine identity work as primarily a 'choice' of subject positions offered within competing discourses. Within such perspectives, no consistent framework is developed that can adequately describe and explain the other drivers, dimensions or non-discursive features of identity work and managerial regulation.

Rethinking identity and identity work

Having briefly reviewed some of the theoretical trajectories amongst critical scholars, it is our contention that the increased attention paid to identity in a range of literatures, whilst welcome, is flawed in two decisive respects. First, its explanatory power is oversold – as MacInnes notes, 'how can one concept do all this work?' (2004: 533). Even prominent promoters of identity theorizing such as Alvesson (2007) and du Gay (2007) have recently observed that there has been an 'overconsumption' of self and identity in recent social science and that identity is inevitably moving down the 'intellectual hit parade'. Second, it is under and mis-conceptualized. Too much theorizing on identity either fails to discuss what motivates or drives identity work (other than discourse), appearing to assume that the self is a blank slate on which anything can be written; or interprets such work in a highly restrictive fashion with the sole focus on self-identity and the individual as a unit of analysis. As we noted earlier, all entities potentially involved in identity work – organizations, groups and individuals – are assumed to be equivalent and have the same emergent properties.

Part of the solution to these problems can be addressed by reinserting conceptions of interests into explanations of behaviour at work. Put more precisely, we need to develop a conceptual schema that treats the pursuit of identity and interests as equally plausible explanations of behaviour. Such a perspective was outlined in Ackroyd and Thompson's *Organization Misbehaviour*, but its conceptual basis was underdeveloped:

> Interests and identities are not opposites. They reciprocally and discursively form one another…For us, this combination of 'self' – interest and self-identity is the bedrock of employee action in the workplace…(1999: 55)

Discussion of interests has become the big taboo in much of social science as it invokes images of the rational, sovereign subject. A growing number of theorists now either ignore or explicitly rule out a consideration of interests, as the following quote from Contu and Willmott's new media case study indicates. Referring to employee actions, they say

> Any antagonism and resistance...is not intrinsic and necessary to the actors as exploited economic categories (the exploiting owner-capitalist v. the exploited wage labourer). Rather, antagonisms arise out of the relationship of subordination when this operates to impede the realization of identities that are fundamental for the self-understanding of LMA staff. (2001: 10)

Yet, studies of human behaviour in general and the employment relationship in particular are inconceivable without a conception of interests. Though divergent interests still require articulation to become activated, one of the essential features of core theories of the labour process is that given the dynamics of exploitation and control, the social relations between capital and labour in the workplace are of 'structured antagonism' (Edwards, 1990). We have too often allowed such considerations to be silenced or at best left as a silent partner in a wider analysis. But what are interests? Our preliminary definition would be: a socio-economic position that generates a propensity to act in defence or pursuit of scarce material resources.

Operationalizing this definition does not require a belief in a population of perfectly rational utility-maximizers but it does mean that we have to allow for the possibility that people can purposefully pursue their perceived interests, even when they clash with aspects of their identity, as the following example illustrates:

> I feel very guilty about the decision I took. I feel I've done what's best for my children but not what's best for the community. I think it's awful, immoral and unjust that people can do this in order to get their children into certain good schools. It's the system that is corrupt. It's a way of allowing selective education within a state-funded education system. If I were in charge of the education system, I'd stop it. But I'm not, so I have taken this decision for my children – because I think they will get a better education this way. (A parent talking about going to church in order to get their children into a particular school – *The Guardian*, 13 July 2006)

Such guilt could be said to be a form of cognitive dissonance or as Goffman (1968) would describe, *stigma*. It is possible that over a period, parents in such a position may seek to reduce that dissonance by adjusting their identity.

However, we should not assume a process of alignment, in part because interests and identities are multiple, and also because identity can be the dominant driver of behaviour, submerging or negating potential interests. There are numerous examples that could be drawn from voting behaviour. Thomas Frank (2004) gives an extensive account of why many of the poorest citizens of Kansas vote for a right-wing Republican agenda. He argues that the conservative movement has managed to turn class differences into a cultural war that involved a 'systematic erasure of the economic', providing a 'ready-made identity in which class is a matter of cultural authenticity rather than material interests' (259).

At the core of developing more adequate accounts of behaviour in and out of work is to start from a conception of individuals and groups who, across a life course form identities and interests in the context of available symbolic and material resources, institutional constraints and obligations (MacInnes, 2004). Without this notion of navigation and adaptation to discursive and extra-discursive social relations, we are left with a predominantly voluntarist and individualized picture of identity work, 'entailing a kind of individualised "pick'n'mix" choice, where people may play identity games and reinvent themselves perpetually, in line with a shifting, expanding and incoherent network of relationships' (Webb, 2006: 18).

One means of linking interests and identities would be to conceptualize identity work as *interaction with and appropriation of symbolic resources*.[4] Such a way of thinking was briefly articulated by Thompson and Findlay and more recently picked up and supported by Leidner (2006). Referring to identity work, the argument is that:

> ...our starting point is simply that we can observe that workplace actors as knowledgeable agents draw on symbolic resources in their relations of contestation and co-operation. They may do so for a variety of reasons, including: to assert their own identities or shape others within struggles over power and resources, to legitimate their own actions or de-legitimate others; or as a means of surviving and developing satisfactions from particular conditions of work and employment. (Thompson and Findlay, 1999: 176)

Such symbolic resources may, in particular contexts, include status and esteem; favourable self-concepts; and sense of belonging. Reference to resources is, in part, an attempt to move away from the blank-slate error and draw attention to *drivers* of identity work. Discourse may be one of these resources but by making it the sole focus, post-structuralists produce a partial and under-powered account. In order to build on the above insights, we need to consider contributions from a wider range of theoretical resources.

Theoretical resources for rethinking and reconnecting identity work and interests

In a useful and innovative paper, Alvesson (2007) rightly notes that much of the debate in organization studies about identity has proceeded on the basis of a post-modernist inspired false polarity between (bad) notions of fixed and stable selves, and (good) fluid and fragmented subjectivities. In practice there are a variety of theoretical resources that escape such limitations. The impact of the argument is undermined somewhat by the fact that most of the six positions Alvesson outlines are variations on post-modern themes. Only one – social identity theory (SIT) – could be said to be truly outside that box. Elsewhere (Ashcraft and Alvesson, 2007), SIT is also used to acknowledge the material component of identity work. However, this is not the only alternative perspective that can help inform understandings of the relative balance of identity and interests. We also look at the contributions of critical realism and related perspectives (particularly the work of Margaret Archer), and the input from established sociological theories on class consciousness and occupational groupings.

Identity, class and the sociology of occupations

Many of the classic sociological studies of work and workers, class and manual work, such as Beynon (1975) and Nichols and Beynon (1977) were written without explicit reference to identity. Terms such as ideology and consciousness were used, without diminishing the capacity of such accounts to illuminate peoples' experiences and actions. What was then referred to as consciousness is now often replaced by identity. But an underlying assumption tends to remain – that of a short or long run alignment between objective class and subjective class identity. That assumption is not wholly unreasonable. Collective interests, though structurally embedded, are always latent – they require articulation in order to become active. Identity plays arguably *the* crucial role in this process given that without shared meanings, grievances deriving from divergent interests are unlikely to be translated into collective action. In this sense we can treat social identity as a form of what Marxists used to call collective or class consciousness.

Contemporary work on class identity continues to focus on the division between 'objective' and 'subjective' class. Although it could be argued that economic activities are always, to some extent, culturally embedded, a dual systems perspective would distinguish between the 'objective' outcomes of class processes, for example, material differences in income and the social relations associated with both the 'objective' and the 'subjective' and culturally determined (or mediated) experiences of class relations (Crompton and Scott, 2005). In this sense, it could be argued that subjective understandings of class relate to class as an identity. That is, an attachment to a group that represents cultural (and political) security and is bounded with self-esteem. Objective class location is closer to the observations of structural reality depicted by occupational group or income and both manifests and represents material interests. In their study of redundant steelworkers, MacKenzie et al. (2006) note that although thinking in class terms may not necessarily be one and the same as the class consciousness necessary for the creation of political action, it does reveal an awareness of class as a reality and can be based within objectively based phenomenon such as occupational groupings and income.

Within this way of thinking the only goal of identity work is to achieve shared meanings that are aligned to the objective position. Identity, however, needs to be treated as more than a collective outcome of interest articulation, and the 'work' associated with it as a distinctive set of practices in its own right. Moreover, by acknowledging a dynamic interaction between two sets of resources – symbolic and material – there is no reason why there should be an alignment between the two, particularly where there are multiple sources of cleavage. Recent research in the field of class identity parallels our perspective on social identity and in particular, its relationship with interests. Crompton and Scott call for a re-conceptualization of class that includes a 'closer investigation of both interests and identities' (2005: 5).

Indeed, one reason that class is a notoriously difficult concept is that it can be, and has been, used as a fundamental concept for analysing social structure but is also recognized as an important part of that bundle of loyalties, shared experiences and common values that comprises an individual's social identity. As Marks and Baldry (2009) argue, people rarely judge themselves relative to other groups in society by their economic relationships alone, often more explicit and more immediate are all those fine gradations offered by comparisons of occupation, income, consumption and lifestyle and other dimensions of perceived status. All these factors can be elements of an individual's social identity as well as representation of or component of their interests. Class identity can consist of a complex bundle of symbolic and material resources, reflecting personal histories, shared experiences and perceived social status. Such meanings are sometimes revealed when there are tensions between the two. For example, a study of IT employees (ibid.) found that whilst many recognized their 'middle class' occupational position, they 'felt working class'. Such employees were choosing a form of identification were in effect, making a statement about their own personal value and sense of esteem associated with particular political and cultural associations.

Within a parallel body of work, the sociology of professions and occupations mirrors the theorizing of class identity, with a focus on both the material and symbolic underpinnings of collective identities. Early conceptualization and research on the professions focused on the supposed traits of professionalism, including trust and altruism. Inherent in these definitions is the notion of a professional identity and such conceptions are given priority over interest-based motivations (Saks, 1995). As part of the radicalization of social science and the society at the time, theorists switched from notions of serving the public, collegiality and trust (as hallmarks of a strong identity) to explanations emphasizing self-interest, occupational controls and extrinsic rewards (Friedson, 1970; Larson, 1977). More recently, some post-modernists have argued that amongst the multiple sources of contemporary identity, class, occupational and professional groups are of increasingly marginal significance to identity (Bauman, 2001; Casey, 1995). Whilst the observation of multiplicity is surely right, other evidence points to the continuing centrality of work to identity formation (Hall, Briscoe and Kram, 1997). Moreover, with falling trade union density, the professional unit or body becomes an ever more central forum for collective action and representation (Baldry et al., 2007). In this manner, the occupational group is seen to be a medium for symbolic power and citizenship, as well as more formal interest-based activities (Derkzen and Bock, 2007). As with class, contemporary research illustrates the balancing act between identity and interests. In comparing two groups of software workers, Marks and Scholarios (2007) noted that those employees that were more qualified and undertaking complex work 'invested' in a strong professional identity and saw little value in organizational identity. In contrast, the less qualified, lower skilled group had fewer external opportunities and developed a stronger identification with the organization.

Professional/occupational esteem does not in itself require identity work, as membership of some groups, for example, the legal profession, automatically confers it. However, if an individual does not hold the values of the profession or fails to make an investment in their professional identity they are likely to be gaining self-esteem from other identities. This is more likely for employees who do not belong to a high-status occupational group. Ashforth and Kreiner (1999) examined a group of 'dirty workers', including sewage workers and cleaners. For them, the availability of externally derived occupational prestige (Treiman, 1977) – status, power, quality of work, education and income – is a limited resource. Yet, they invest in a different kind of identity work that challenges the stigma and develops pride in the activities, supported by a strong occupational culture. In all these examples, there is a complex interplay, both discursive and non-discursive, between identities and interests.

The boundary between the group and the individual

As we indicated earlier, identity work takes place across a number of territories, implying varied units of analysis. SIT allows for a shift of focus to boundaries between the individual and the small(er) group. A search for self-esteem is seen as a key driver of behaviour and as long as membership of a group enhances self-esteem, one will remain a member of that group (Tajfel, 1978). Alternatively, as Tajfel (1978) argues, if the group fails to satisfy this requirement the individual may try to change the structure of the group (social change); seek a new way of comparison which would favour his/her group, and hence reinforce his/her social identity (social creativity); or leave/abandon the group with the intention of joining the 'better' one (social mobility). There are clear connections to interests here. For those with high social change beliefs, and hence high social identity salience, there is the assumption that the only way to improve negative conditions lies in collective accomplishment via group action that may include trade union membership.

'Identity work', in this formulation, is largely a pragmatic choice based on the reality of available resources. People generally desire a positive self-image (ibid.), consequently they prefer to identify with high-status groups (Ellemers, 1993) and organizations (Mael and Ashforth, 1992). The identity work process, nonetheless, would be senseless if the target is unattainable, or unrealistic expectations that would damage self-esteem. Whether individuals make a choice, or are allocated by default to a group, they develop a collective cognition that develops with the intensity of identification and leads to group members defending the properties and attributes associated with their group.

A clear strength of social identity approaches is that it provides both theoretical and empirical evidence for individual factors that determine identification, providing a compelling indication that individuals are more than inert receptors of organizational narratives, or are merely positioning themselves amongst rival discourses. Indeed, studies show that employees can make a conscious decision – a deliberate itinerary of identity work – to engage with an entity even if they are not directly exposed to relevant discourses. Wiesenfeld, Raghuram and Garud (2001) found that employees who are isolated from their employing organization – on client sites or satellite office – and therefore less exposed to antecedents of organizational socialization, rituals and symbols, may still identify with the organization as a consequence of their need for affiliation. Moreover, the minimal group studies (Ashforth and Mael, 1989; Tajfel, 1982; Turner, 1984) indicate that in cases where members have little or no contact with each other they still exhibit identification to the collective.

Despite evidence to the contrary, SIT makes no explicit concession to the idea of interests as a driver or mediator of identity formation. Although it could be argued that one factor that determines the desirability of a target is its status in terms of material benefits and resources, the key function of attachment to a group is deemed to be the provision of social identity information which helps the development and maintenance of a favourable self-concept (Tyler and Blader, 2001). So, although a valuable theoretical resource, SIT lacks sufficient explanatory power on its own. One further resource that could add insight with respect to the individual-group boundary is the Impression Management (IM) perspective, mostly associated with Goffman (1959, 1961). IM argues that the process of establishing social identity becomes closely allied to the concept of the 'front', described as 'that part of the individual's performance which regularly functions in a general and fixed fashion to define the situation for those who observe the performance' (Goffman, 1959: 22). As a 'collective representation', the front establishes a proper 'setting', 'appearance', and 'manner' for the social role assumed by the actor, uniting interactive behaviour with the personal front (ibid.: 27). It explains how identity work is carried out by employees creating, defending and performing identities in their own eyes and those of others through a process described by Hughes (1951) as 'the social drama of work'. IM and the broader body of work from which it emerged – symbolic interactionism – counteracts the limitations of SIT by demonstrating the multiple and fluid nature of identity. Identity is not limited to the influence of one group, but is created and amended as a response to the whole range of people that workers engage with.

There are a number of limitations identified with this approach. It pays little attention to broader social contexts and the structures of power and collective interests that frame micro-level identity work. Of equal relevance for our purposes, it has also been argued that symbolic interactionism is not sufficiently microscopic as it has a tendency to ignore psychological factors (e.g. Gergen, 1999). The approach is thus rendered vulnerable to criticisms that there is no recognition of a core self and that, in line with post-structuralist writers, there is a belief that selves are purely socially constructed and discursive (Leidner, 2006). A final set of resources can help to offset that weakness.

The boundary between the self and social identity

Whilst SIT literature is littered with the term (e.g. self-categorization, self-stereotyping, self-concept), there is no actual mention of the self. Yet, in our view, a conception of the self is a necessary dimension to a full account of identity work. The challenge, as Richard Jenkins (2004) and Archer (2000a,b) argue, is to pilot a course between the tendency of the dominant European intellectual tradition to see the self as either 'autonomous' or 'plastic'; producing accounts of human agency that are either over or under-socialized. With reference to the currently influential post-structuralist perspectives, Archer observes that they involve, 'subtracting our human powers and accrediting all of them – selfhood, reflexivity, thought, memory, emotionality and belief – to society's discourse' (2000b: 12).

From a micro-sociological perspective, Richard Jenkins (2004: 69) resolutely engages with the concept of the self and views the self as an entity clearly separate from identity. It is the core of who we are and it is the self that enables us to navigate our way through identities. Identity, whether personal or social, connects the self to social structures. Unlike Goffman, Jenkins sees identity at this level as being more than constituted uniqueness, but an internal understanding of social identities. As both he and Tajfel (1971) suggest, personal identity (or as Jenkins describes it, selfhood) is the process by which individuals compare themselves with others rather than groups. However, personal identity is also an extension of the self. It is the point at which social identities merge to form the self. Whilst the self is largely reflective, personal identity is how individuals project who they are.

Critical Realist work also engages with the relationship between the self and identity. The focus is on a more usable conception of human agency (see also the chapter from Thompson and Vincent in this volume). Sarah Jenkins draws on the writings of organization theorists (Ackroyd and Fleetwood, 2004; Fleetwood and Hesketh, 2006) to assert a notion of reflexive performance in which agents identify structures and resources that constrain their action, but also construct strategies to use them to pursue their personal goals: 'Here, individual agents identify their own interests and align the situations in which they find themselves in some way with their own agential projects' (2007: 5). She says that critical realists have paid little attention to issues of identity but, as O'Mahoney (2005) notes, in Archer's *Being Human* (2000a,b) we are provided with a notion of a continuous sense of self 'prior and primitive to our sociality'.

Archer restores agency through a focus on human purposes and powers developed through an active process of reflection on practices and engagement with social reality. This is consistent with the earlier observations of MacInnes (2004: 541) that self-definitions and other forms of identity work reflect how individuals make sense of and reconcile conflicting opportunities and aspirations. For Archer, though fluid, a coherent and (to a degree) stable personality emerges with some continuity of consciousness. Archer suggests that through a process of internal and materially grounded conversations, rather than discourse, people make sense of their identity. To some extent, this is compatible with SIT in that these conversations lead to identity formation based on which group provides an individual with the most social confirmation. Moreover, from this perspective, selfhood or personal identity is neither fragmentary nor wholly inscribed by discourse. Drawing on Archer, Webb describes this as 'a personal awareness of a continuity of being, which is unique, physically embodied and in common with others, shares a capacity for agency' (2006: 9). A personal identity is based on what we care about in the world and builds upon 'interior conversations' connected not just to discourse but emotions, memory and self-worth.

This approach may affirm the primacy of practice, but that becomes more complex when we consider a broader sense of social identity. As Webb points out, we have multiple and fluid social identities, which are different in alternative contexts. To make sense of this, identity must be the bridging concept between self and social structure. Archer argues that social identity is the capacity to express what we care about in social roles that are appropriate for doing this. There is a dialectical relationship between personal and social identities. We bring our individual sense of self to the process of role selection but we cannot choose roles without negotiating social constraints. There is a form of calculation of opportunity costs involved in how we learn what is desirable and feasible to identify with.

> Those who have experienced enough of a role to wish to make some of its associated interests their own have also changed to the degree that they know that they do indeed find such activities interesting. (Archer, 2000b: 17)

Archer describes the formation of social identities as emerging from a process of 'progressive individuation' in virtue of 'relations to society's scarce resources'. This is only a schematic understanding, but it is compatible with insights from SIT and a broader conception of an interaction order. This perspective is also compatible with R. Jenkins (2004) who argues that, without the self, an individual wouldn't know who they are and therefore would be unable to act.

Whilst we have made no attempt in this chapter to integrate these varied perspectives, the purpose of such exploration is to highlight more adequate resources that are sensitive to the different entities (individuals, groups, organizations) that are involved in identity work; the different contexts (including the labour process and employment relationship) it is undertaken in; and the inter-relations between identities and interests.

Conclusions

Academic interest in identity – its shaping and diversification – reflects real changes in society and work. These include changes in the balance of visibility and power in the voices of capital and labour; the widening of the labour market and restructuring of employment to accommodate new types of workers; and shifts to service work that often requires aspects of the individual self to be part of product that is being sold. So, identity matters, but we have argued in this chapter for a conception of identity that does less, but explains more. Though alternate theoretical resources to the dominant post-structuralist readings add explanatory power, primarily through identifying drivers, conditions and contexts of identity work, problems of weak explanation cannot be addressed solely within conceptions of identity. This is particularly the case when attempting to address the behaviour of actors in the employment relationship, where, as we have argued, interests are fundamental. Even those who write about identity seldom explicitly disavow interests as a motive force. Most of the time, as we have illustrated in this paper, interests are a hidden script in identity explanations. This sometimes happens when trying to explain the choice of subject positions (post-structuralists), the salience of context-driven self-categorizations (SIT), or to the formation of social identities being determined by having to negotiate society's resource distribution (Archer, 2000a). As a result, a key task is to integrate or at least seek to explain the interactions between interests and identities – the pursuit, appropriation and defense of material and symbolic resources. In a world of multiplicity, this might also help to explain why some identities are chosen or favoured over others; as well as the often fragile and transactional nature of cultural norms promoted by management, but disposable in tougher times (Kunda and Ailon-Souday, 2005).

A second dimension of doing less is to accept that identity is part of subjectivity, but not all of it. The other parts include the range of agential practices associated with the self-activity of the labouring subject. Mainstream LPT seeks to articulate a notion of purposeful, if not always knowledgeable, economic agents, negotiating the contours and constraints of capitalist relations of production. As Armstrong argues:

> A more constructive approach to the 'missing subject' of the labour process would appear to call for rather more respect for these subjects...Instead of approaching workers as instantiations of some prefabricated theory of individuation concocted in the thought-laboratories of academe, it might be better to adopt an hermeneutic approach in which they are treated as industrial sociologists in their own right, with their own theories of the social order and of the potentials of their own place within it. (2008a: 27)

We need a framework that provides a better and a more balanced account of agency and its structural constraints that recognizes, 'It is through identity work that the conditions of being a subject and being subject gain substance for managers and workers alike' (Thompson and McHugh, 2009: 405). LPT is well equipped to explain these kinds of behaviours and their contexts, not only for its concepts, but also because the tradition of qualitative and ethnographic case studies foregrounds worker voice and experience. However, its concepts are primarily interests-oriented. That's why we have emphasized in this chapter the need to combine with other theoretical resources – from sociology, social identity and critical realism – that can illuminate processes of identity formation and work. Closer attention to these resources can help LPT to better address issues such as the mobilization of work-based grievances; the development and effectiveness of normative controls; the social construction of skills; and the motives for some kinds of organizational misbehaviour.

This would undoubtedly allow LPT to 'explain more', but, we have argued a more differentiated understanding of identity and identity work would have broader analytical value. In particular, we have emphasized two arguments. First, a more materialist reading that focuses on valued and contested symbolic resources (that moves beyond the individual as a blank slate to be inscribed by discourse).[5] Discourse is an important influence on the shaping of identity and the better post-structuralist studies have been useful in illustrating how this might work. However, we should not assume, a priori, that discourse is the driver or determinant. Instead, we should treat discourse as both a medium and category of symbolic resources. The second argument we have emphasized is one of disaggregation. In other words, the need to take the distinctive dynamics and dimensions of identity work undertaken by particular entities (organizations, groups, individuals) and at different levels (the self, personal and social identity) – seriously and not assume, as is often currently the case, that we can understand or describe them in the same way. Such a framework clearly needs considerably more work. But for LPT it may help us to move on from the 'missing subject'. No doubt, our post-structuralist critics will dislike or disagree with some of these arguments, but missing, the subject ain't.

Notes

1 What *does* change are the sources of theoretical inspiration and language. O'Doherty lets us know that conceptions of subjectivity and identity are now to be advanced by drawing upon Laclau and Mouffe and post-Lacanian psychoanalytical alternatives to Foucault (2009: 113).

2 A detailed and persuasive critique of the Manchester School's concepts and evidence with respect to subjectivity is provided in recent papers by Armstrong (2008a,b).

3 Space precludes an extended critique of the assumption that such cultural initiatives have been successful. For reviews from a labour process perspective, see Thompson and Findlay (1999) and Armstrong (2008b).

4 Compare that with the longer but narrower definition of Alvesson and Willmott (2002: 626), for whom identity work is where 'people are continuously engaged in forming, repairing, maintaining, strengthening or revising the constructions that are productive of a precarious sense of coherence and distinctiveness'.

5 There are also, obviously, biological and social factors (that help make up the personality, for example), that also militate against the blank slate. But they are beyond the scope of this chapter.

REFERENCES

Ackroyd, S. and Fleetwood, S. (2004) 'Developments in Critical Realism in Organisation and Management Studies', in Fleetwood, S. and Ackroyd, S. (eds) *Critical Realist Applications in Organisation and Management Studies*, London and New York: Routledge.

Ackroyd, S. and Thompson, P. (1999) *Organization Misbehaviour*, London: Sage.

Ainsworth, S. and Hardy, C. (2004) 'Discourse and Identities', in Grant, D., Hardy, C., Oswick, C. and Putnam, L. (eds) *The Sage Handbook of Organizational Discourse*, London: Sage.

Alvesson, M. (2007) 'Shakers, Strugglers, Story-tellers, Surfers and Others. Varieties of Perspectives on Identity', Paper delivered to workshop at University of New South Wales, Sydney, 8 March.

Alvesson, M. and Willmott, H. (2002) 'Identity Regulation as Organizational Control: Producing the Appropriate Individual', *Journal of Management Studies*, 39(5): 619–44.

Archer, M. (2000a) *Being Human: The Problem of Agency*, Cambridge: Cambridge University Press.

Archer, M. (2000b) 'Realism and the Problem of Agency': http://www.journalofcriticalrealism.org/archive/JCR(A)v5n1_archer11.pdf.

Armstrong, P. (2008a) 'Subjectivity as Entrapment: Knights, Willmott and the Consciousness of the Working Class', Paper presented at the Conference of Practical Criticism in the Managerial Social Sciences, Leicester University Management School, 15–17 January.

Armstrong, P. (2008b) 'Existential Struggle and Surplus Value: Hugh Willmott on Managerial Subjectivities', Paper presented at the Conference of Practical Criticism in the Managerial Social Sciences, Leicester University Management School, 15–17 January.

Ashcraft, K. L. and Alvesson, M. (2007) 'The Moving Target of Dis/identification: Wrestling with the Reality of Social Construction', Presented at the 23rd EGOS Colloquium, Vienna, 5–7 July.

▶

▶
Ashforth, B. and Kreiner, G. (1999) 'How Can You Do It?: Dirty Work and the Challenge of Constructing a Positive Identity', *Academy of Management Review*, 24(2): 413–34.

Ashforth, B. E. and Mael, F. A. (1989) 'Social Identity and the Organization', *Academy of Management Review*, 14(1): 20–39.

Baldry, C., Taylor, P., Hyman, J., Scholarios, D., Marks, A., Watson, A., Gilbert, K., Gall, G. and Bunzel, D. (2007) *The Meaning of Work in the New Economy*, Houndmills: Palgrave.

Barker, J. (1993) 'Tightening the Iron Cage: Concertive Control in Self-Managing Teams', *Administrative Science Quarterly*, 38: 408–37.

Bauman, Z. (2001) *The Individualised Society*, Cambridge: Cambridge University Press.

Beynon H. (1975) *Working for Ford*, Wakefield: E.P. Publishing.

Billig, M. (1996) *Arguing and Thinking*, 2nd edition, Cambridge: Cambridge University Press.

Calas, M. and Smircich, L. (1987) 'Post-Culture: Is the Organizational Culture Literature Dominant but Dead?', Paper presented at the 3rd *International Conference on 'Organizational Symbolism and Corporate Culture'*, Milan, June.

Casey, C. (1995) *Work, Self and Society: After Industrialism*, London: Routledge.

Chreim, S. (2005) 'The Continuity-Change Duality in Narrative Texts of Organizational Identity', *Journal of Management Studies*, 42(3): 567–93.

Collinson, D. (2003) 'Identities and Insecurities: Selves at Work', *Organization*, 10(3): 385–409.

Cornelissen, J. P., Haslam, S. A. and Balmer, J. M. T. (2007) 'Social Identity, Organizational Identity and Corporate Identity: Towards an Integrated Understanding of Processes, Patternings and Products', *British Journal of Management*, 18(1): 1–16.

Crompton, R. and Scott, J. (2005) 'Class Analysis: Beyond the Cultural Turn', in Devine, F., Savage, M., Scott, J. and Crompton, R. (eds), *Rethinking Class: Culture, Identities and Lifestyle*, Basingstoke: Palgrave Macmillan.

Davies, C. A. (2006) 'Imposing Organizational Identities: A Means of Regulating Behaviour?', Paper presented at the biennial *Conference on Organizational Discourse*: Amsterdam, July.

Delbridge, R. and Jenkins, S. (2006) 'Disconnected Workplaces: Interests and Identities in the "High Performance" Factory', *Academy of Management Symposium*, Atlanta, 14 August.

Derkzen, P. and Bock, B. B. (2007) 'The Construction of Professional Identity: Symbolic Power in Rural Partnerships in The Netherlands', *Sociologia Ruralis*, 47: 189–204.

du Gay, P. (1996) *Consumption and Identity at Work*, London: Sage.

du Gay, P. (2007) *Organizing Identity: Persons and Organizations 'After Theory'*, London: Sage.

Edwards, P. K. (1990) 'Understanding Conflict in the Labour Process: The Logic and Autonomy of Struggle', in Knights, D. and Willmott, H. (eds) *Labour Process Theory*, London: Macmillan.

▶

►

Ellemers, N. (1993) 'Influence of Socio-structural Variables on Identity Enhancement Strategies', *European Review of Social Psychology*, 4: 27–57.

Fleetwood, S. and Hesketh, A. J. (2006) 'Prediction in Social Science: The Case of Research on the Human Resource Management-Organisational Performance Link', *Journal of Critical Realism*, 5(2): 228–50.

Friedson, E. (1970) *Professional Dominance: The Social Structure of Medical Care*, Chicago, IL: Aldine.

Gergen, K. J. (1991) *The Saturated Self: Dilemmas of Identity in Contemporary Life*, New York: Harper Collins.

Gergen, K. J. (1999) *An Invitation to Social Construction*, London: Sage.

Goffman, E. (1959) *The Presentation of Self in Everyday Life*, Garden City, NY: Doubleday.

Goffman, E. (1961) *Asylums: Essays on the Social Situation of Mental Patients and Other Inmates*, Garden City, NY: Doubleday.

Goffman, E. (1968) *Stigma. Notes on the Management of Spoiled Identity*, Harmondsworth: Penguin Books.

Hall, D. T., Briscoe, J. P. and Kram, K. E. (1997) 'Identity, Values and Learning in the Protean Career', in Cooper, C. L. and Jackson, S. E. (eds) *Creating Tomorrow's Organizations. A Handbook for Future Research in Organizational Behavior*, New York: Wiley.

Hughes, E. C. (1951) 'Mistakes at Work', *Canadian Journal of Economics and Political Science*, 17: 320–27.

Jaros, S. (2009) 'Identity and the Workplace: An Assessment of Contextualist and Discursive Approaches', Paper at 27th International Labour Process Conference, Edinburgh, April.

Jenkins, R. (2004) *Social Identity*, London: Routledge.

Jenkins, S. (2007) 'Identities, Gender and Power: A Critical Realist Examination of Agency in the Workplace', Unpublished paper, University of Cardiff.

Knights, D. (1990) `Subjectivity, Power and the Labor Process', in Knights, D. and Willmott, H. (eds) *Labour Process Theory*, London: Macmillan.

Knights, D. and Willmott, H. (1989) 'Power and Subjectivity at Work: From Degradation to Subjugation in the Labour Process', *Sociology*, 23(4): 535–58.

Kondo, D. K. (1990) *Crafting Selves: Power, Gender, and Discourse of Identity in a Japanese Workplace*, Chicago, IL: The University of Chicago Press.

Kunda, G. and Ailon-Souday, G. (2005) 'Managers, Markets and Ideologies – Design and Devotion Revisited', in Ackroyd, S., Batt, R., Thompson, P. and Tolberts, P. (eds) *The Oxford Handbook of Work and Organization*, Oxford: Oxford University Press.

Larson, M. S. (1977) *The Rise of Professionalism: A Sociological Analysis*, California: University of California Press.

Leidner, R. (2006) 'Identity and Work', in Korczynski, M., Hodson, R. and Edwards, P. (eds) *Social Theory at Work*, Oxford: Oxford University Press.

MacInnes, J. (2004) 'The Sociology of Identity: Social Science or Social Comment?', *British Journal of Sociology*, 55: 531–43.

►

▶

MacKenzie, R., Stuart, M., Ford, C., Greenwood, I., Garder. J. and Perrett, R. (2006) ' "All That Is Solid?": Class, Identity and the Maintenance of a Collective Orientation amongst Redundant Steelworkers', Sociology, 40(5): 833–52.

Mael, F. and Ashforth, B. (1992) 'Alumni and Their Alma Mater: A Partial Test of the Reformulated Model of Organizational Identification', Journal of Organizational Behaviour, 13: 103–23.

Marks, A. and Baldry, C. (2009) 'Stuck in the Middle with Who? The Class Identity of Knowledge Workers', Work, Employment and Society, 23(1): 49–65.

Marks, A. and Scholarios, D. (2007) 'Identifying a Profession: The Creation of Professional Identities within Software Work', New Technology, Work and Employment, 22(2): 98–117.

Marks, A., Scholarios, D., Baldry, C. and Hyman, J. (2007) 'The Identity Construction of Knowledge Workers: A Study of the Call Centre and Software Industries', Presented at WES conference, Aberdeen, 11–13 September.

May, T. (1999) 'From Banana Time to Just-in-Time: Power and Resistance at Work', Sociology, 33(4): 767–83.

Nichols, T. and Beynon, H. (1977) Living with Capitalism, London: Routledge.

O'Doherty, M. (2009) 'Retrieving the "Missing Subject" in Labour Process Analysis: Towards Emancipation and Praxis', in Alvesson, M., Bridgman, T. and Willmott, H. (eds) The Oxford Handbook of Critical Management Studies, Oxford: Oxford University Press.

O'Mahoney, J. (2005) 'The Limits of Identity Construction: Anxiety, Trust and Change at Gearco', Unpublished paper, University of Cardiff.

Phillips, N. and Maguire, S. (2000) 'The Dynamics of Trust and Identity in Intraorganizational Relations: A Discursive Perspective', in Combes, C., Keenoy, T. and Grant, D. (eds) Organizational Discourse: Word-views Work-views and World Views, London: KCM Press.

Reed, M. (1998) 'Organisational Analysis as Discourse Analysis: A Critique', in Grant, D. and Oswick, C. (eds) Discourse and Organisation, London: Sage.

Saks, M. (1995) Professions and the Public Interest: Medical Power, Altruism and Alternative Medicine, London: Routledge.

Schaefer, S., Huzzard, T. and Sommereng, I (2009) 'Volvo for Life? An Investigation into identity Work at Volvo Cars Torslanda', Paper at 27th International Labour Process Conference, Edinburgh, April.

Sewell, G. (1998) 'The Discipline of Teams: The Control of Team-based Industrial Work through Electronic and Peer Surveillance', Administrative Science Quarterly, 43: 397–428.

Tajfel, H. (1971) Social Comparison and Social Change: Studies in Inter-group Behaviour, London: Academic Press.

Tajfel, H. (1978) 'Social Categorization, Social Identity and Social Comparison', in Tajfel, H. (ed.) Differentiation between Social Groups, London: Academic Press.

Tajfel, H. (1982) 'Social Psychology of Intergroup Relations', Annual Review of Psychology, 33: 1–39.

▶

▶

Thomas, R. (2009) 'Critical Management Studies on Identity: Mapping the Terrain', in Alvesson, M., Bridgman, T. and Willmott, H. (eds) *The Oxford Handbook of Critical Management Studies*, Oxford: Oxford University Press.

Thomas, R. and Davies, A. (2005) 'Theorizing the Micro-politics of Resistance: New Public Management and Managerial Identities in the UK Public Services', *Organization Studies*, 26(5): 683–706.

Thompson, P. and Ackroyd, S. (1995) 'All Quiet on the Workplace Front? A Critique of Recent Trends in British Industrial *Sociology*', *Sociology*, 29: 615–33.

Thompson, P. and Findlay, P. (1999) 'Changing the People: Social Engineering in the Contemporary Workplace', in Sayer, A. and Ray, L. (eds) *Culture and Economy after the Cultural Turn*, London: Sage.

Thompson, P. and McHugh, D. (2009) *Work Organisations: A Critical Introduction*, Houndmills: Palgrave.

Thompson, P. and Smith, C. (1998) 'Re-Evaluating the Labour Process Debate', *Economic and Industrial Democracy*, 19(4): 551–77.

Townley, B. (1993) 'Performance Appraisal and the Emergence of Management', *Journal of Management Studies*, 30(2): 27–44.

Treiman, D. J. (1977) *Occupational Prestige in Comparative Perspective*, New York: Academic Press.

Turner, J. C. (1984) 'Social Identification and Psychological Group Formation', in Tajfel, H. (ed.) *The Social Dimension: European Developments in Social Psychology*, Cambridge: Cambridge University Press.

Tyler, T. R. and Blader, S. L. (2001) 'Identity and Co-operative Behaviour in Groups', *Group Processes and Intergroup Relations*, 4(3): 207–26.

Webb, J. (2006) *Organisations, Identities and the Self*, London: Palgrave.

Wiesenfeld, B. M., Raghuram, S. and Garud, R. (2001) 'Organisational Identification among Virtual Workers: The Role of Need for Affiliation and Perceived Work Based Social Support', *Journal of Management*, 27: 213–29.

Willmott, H. (1990) `Subjectivity and the Dialectics of Praxis: Opening up the Core of Labour. Process Analysis', in Knights, D. and Willmott, H. (eds) *Labour Process Theory*, London: Macmillan.

Willmott, H. (1993) `Strength Is Ignorance, Slavery Is Freedom: Managing Culture in Modern Organisations', *Journal of Management Studies*, 30(4): 515–52.

Appendix: Guides to Further Reading

Most influential journal articles informed by labour process theory

The list below was generated initially by nominations from authors in this book and members of the ILPC Steering Group, with the 'influence' aspect tested by Google Scholar citations (via Publish or Perish). The articles are listed in descending order of citations. Obviously that means recently published papers are less likely to be listed, but the number from the last decade is surprisingly high. 'Informed by Labour Process Theory' excludes articles that are just critiques of or commentaries on.

Marglin, S. A. (1974) 'What Do Bosses Do? The Origins and Functions of Hierarchy in Capitalist Production', *Review of Radical Political Economics*, 6: 60–102.

Sewell, G. and Wilkinson, B. (1992) 'Someone to Watch Over me: Surveillance, Discipline and the JIT Labour Process', *Sociology*, 26(2): 271–89.

Taylor, P. and Bain, P. (1998) 'An Assembly Line in the Head: The Call Centre Labour Process', *Industrial Relations Journal*, 30(2): 101–17.

Pollert, A. (1988) 'The Flexible Firm: Fixation or Fact?' *Work, Employment and Society*, 2(3): 281–316.

Ackroyd, S. and Thompson, P. (1995) 'All Quiet On the Workplace Front: A Critique of Recent Trends in British Industrial Sociology', *Sociology*, 29(4): 1–19.

Hyman, R. (1987) 'Strategy or Structure? Capital, Labour and Control', *Work, Employment and Society*, 1(1): 1–25.

Bain, P. and Taylor, P. (2000) 'Entrapped by the Electronic Panopticon? Worker Resistance in the Call Centre', *New Technology Work and Employment*, 15(1): 2–18.

Ramsay, H. (1983) 'Cycles of Control: Worker Participation in Sociological and Historical Perspective', *Sociology*, 11(3): 481–506.

Delbridge, R., Turnbull, P. and Wilkinson, B. (1992) 'Pushing Back the Frontiers: Management Control and Work Intensification under JIT/TQM Regimes', *New Technology, Work and Employment*, 7: 97–106.

Armstrong, P. (1985) 'Changing Management Control Strategies: The Role of Competition between Accountancy and Other Organisational Professions', *Accounting, Organizations and Society*, 10(2): 129–48.

Taylor, P., Mulvey, G., Hyman, J., and Bain, P. (2002) 'Work Organisation, Control and the Experience of Work in Call Centres', *Work, Employment and Society*, 16(1): 133–50.

Callaghan, G. and Thompson, P. (2002) 'We Recruit Attitude: The Selection and Shaping of Routine Call Centre Labour', *Journal Management Studies*, 39(2): 233–53.

Berggren, C. (1993) 'Lean Production: The End of History?', *Work, Employment and Society*, 7(2): 163–88.

Brighton Labour Process Group (1977) 'The Capitalist Labour Process', *Capital and Class*, 1: 3–22.

Thompson, P., Warhurst, C. and Callaghan, G. (2001) 'Ignorant Theory and Knowledgeable Workers: Interrogating the Connections between Knowledge, Skills and Services', *Journal of Management Studies*, 38(7): 923–42.

Vallas, S. P. (1999) 'Re-thinking Post-Fordism: The Meaning of Workplace Flexibility', *Sociological Theory*, 17(1): 68–101.

Callaghan, G. and Thompson, P. (2001) 'Edwards Revisited: Technical Control and Call Centres', *Economic and Industrial Democracy*, 22(1): 13–37.

Fuller, L. and Smith, V. (1991) 'Customers' Reports: Management by Customers in a Changing Economy', *Work, Employment and Society*, 5(1): 1–16.

Burawoy, M. (1983) 'Towards a Marxist Theory of the Labor Process: Braverman and Beyond', *Politics and Society*, 8(3&4): 247–312.

Thompson P. (2003) 'Disconnected Capitalism: or Why Employers Can't Keep Their Side of the Bargain', *Work, Employment and Society*, 17(2): 359–78.

Bolton, S. and Boyd, C. (2003) 'Trolley Dolly or Skilled Emotion Manager?' *Work, Employment and Society*, 17(2): 289–308.

Graham, L. (1993) 'Inside a Japanese Transplant', *Work and Occupations*, 20(2): 147–73.

Cressey, P. and MacInnes, J. (1980) 'Voting for Ford: Industrial Democracy and the Control of Labour', *Capital and Class*, 11: 5–37.

Ezzamel, M., Willmott, H. and Worthington, F. (2001) 'Power, Control and Resistance in "The Factory That Time Forgot"', *Journal of Management Studies*, 38(8): 1053–80.

Dawson, P. and Webb, J. (1989) 'New Production Arrangements: The Totally Flexible Cage?' *Work, Employment and Society*, 3(2): 221–38.

Witz, A., Warhurst, C. and Nickson, D. (2003) 'The Labour of Aesthetics and the Aesthetics of Organization', *Organization*, 10(1): 33–54.

Harley, B. (1998) 'The Myth of Empowerment: Work Organisation, Hierarchy and Employee Autonomy in Contemporary Australian Workplaces', *Work, Employment & Society*, 13(1): 41–66.

Leidner, R. (1999) 'Emotional Labor in Service Work', *Annals of the American Academy of Political and Social Science*, 561(1): 81–95.

Blair, H. (2001) ' "You're Only as Good as Your Last Job": The Labour Process and Labour Market in the British Film Industry', *Work, Employment and Society*, 15: 149–69.

Parker, M. and Slaughter, J. (1988) 'Management-by-Stress: The Team Concept in the US Automobile Industry', *Technology Review*, October: 37–44.

Taylor, P. and Bain, P. (2006) 'India Calling to the Far Away Towns: The Call Centre Labour Process and Globalisation', *Work, Employment and Society*, 19(2): 261–82.

Hodson, R. (1995) 'Worker Resistance: An Underdeveloped Concept in the Sociology of Work', *Economic and Industrial Democracy*, 16(1): 79–110.

Shaiken, H., Herzenberg, S. and Kuhn, S. (1986) 'The Work Process under More Flexible Production', *Industrial Relations*, 125(2): 167–83.

Thompson, P. and Wallace, T. (1996) 'Redesigning Production through Teamworking', *International Journal of Operations and Production Management*, 16(2): 103–18.

Smith, C. and Thompson, P. (1998) 'Re-Evaluating the Labour Process Debate' *Economic and Industrial Democracy*, 19(4): 551–77.

Houlihan, M. (2002) 'Tensions and Variations in Call Centre Management Strategies', *Human Resource Management Journal*, 12(4): 67–85.

Elger, T. (1979) 'Valorisation and Deskilling: A Critique', *Capital and Class, 7*: 58–99.

Elger, T. (1990) 'Technical Innovation and Work Reorganization in British Manufacturing in the 1980s', *Work, Employment and Society*, special issue, May: 67–101.

Vallas, S. P. (1990) 'The Concept of Skill: A Critical Review', *Work and Occupations*, 17(4): 379–98.

Gottfried, H. (1991) 'Mechanisms of Control in the Temporary Help Industry', *Sociological Forum*, 6(4): 699–713.

Taylor, P. and Bain, P. (2003) 'Subterranean Worksick Blues: Humour as Subversion in Two Call Centres', *Organization Studies*, 24(9): 1487–509.

Armstrong, P. (1989) 'Management, Labour Process and Agency', *Work, Employment and Society*, 3(3): 307–22.

Thompson, P. and Smith, C. (2001) 'Follow the Redbrick Road: Reflections on Pathways in and out of the Labour Process Debate', *International Studies of Management and Organization*, 30(4): 40–67.

Grugulis, I., Dundon, T. and Wilkinson, A. (2000) 'Cultural Control and the "Culture Manager": Employment Practices in a Consultancy', *Work, Employment and Society*, 14(1): 97–116.

Smith, C. (1989) 'Flexible Specialization, Automation, and Mass Production', *Work, Employment and Society*, 3(20): 203–20.

Sinclair, J., Mike Ironside and Roger Seifert (1996) 'Classroom Struggle? Market Oriented Education Reforms and Their Impact on the Teacher Labour Process', *Work, Employment and Society*, 10: 641–61.

Fantasia, R., Clawson, D. and Graham, G. (1988) 'A Critical View of Worker Participation in American Industry', *Work and Occupations*, 5(4): 468–88.

Tinker, T. (2002) 'Spectres of Marx and Braverman in the Twilight of Postmodernist Labour Process Research', *Work, Employment and Society*, 16: 251–81.

Lloyd, C. and Payne, J. (2002) 'Developing a Political Economy of Skill', *Journal of Education and Work*, 15(4): 365–90.

Danford, A. (2003) 'Workers, Unions and the High Performance Workplace', *Work, Employment and Society*, 17(3): 569–73.

Twenty most cited articles from labour process series books[1]

J. Kelly, 'Union Militancy and Social Partnership' *The New Workplace and Trade Unionism (1996)*

D. Knights and T. Vurdubakis, 'Foucault, Power and Resistance and all That' *Resistance and Power in the Workplace (1994)*

S. Taylor, 'Emotional Labour and the New Workplace' *Workplaces of the Future (1998)*

C. Warhurst and P. Thompson, 'Hands, Hearts and Minds: Changing Work and Workers at the End of the Century' *Workplaces of the Future (1998)*

D. Knights, 'Subjectivity, Power and the Labour Process' *Labour Process Theory (1990)*

M. Korczynski, 'The Contradictions of Service Work: Call Centres as Customer-Oriented Bureaucracy' *Customer Service: Empowerment and Entrapment (2001)*

A. McKinlay and P. Taylor, 'Power, Surveillance and Resistance: Inside the Factory of the Future' *The New Workplace and Trade Unionism (1996)*

N. Bacon and J. Storey, 'Individualism and Collectivism and the Changing Role of Trade Unions' *The New Workplace and Trade Unionism (1996)*

P. Thompson, 'Crawling from the Wreckage: The Labour Process and the Politics of Production' *Labour Process Theory (1990)*

C. Baldry, P. Bain and P. Taylor, 'Bright Satanic Offices: Intensification, Control and Team Taylorism' *Workplaces of the Future (1998)*

H. Willmott, 'Subjectivity and the Dialectics of Praxis: Opening Up the Core of Labour Process Analysis', *Labour Process Theory (1990)*

L. McArdle, S. J. Proctor, M. Rawlinson, J. Hassard and P. Forrester, 'Total Quality Management and Participation: Employee Involvement or the Enhancement of Exploitation?' *Making Quality Critical (1994)*

S. Clegg, 'Power Relations and the Constitution of the Resistive Subject' *Resistance and Power in the Workplace (1994)*

T. Manwaring and S. Wood, 'The Ghost in the Labour Process' *Job Redesign: Critical Perspectives on the Labour Process (1985)*

A. Tuckman, 'Ideology, Quality and TQM' *Making Quality Critical (1994)*

E. Wray-Bliss, 'Representing Customer Service: Telephones and Texts' *Customer Service: Empowerment and Entrapment (2001)*

A. Felstead and N. Jewson 'Flexible Labour and Non-Standard Employment: An Agenda of Issues' *Global Trends in Flexible Labour (1999)*

P. Armstrong, 'Management Control Strategies and Inter-Professional Competition: The Cases of Accountancy and Personnel Management' *Managing the Labour Process (1986)*

T. Elger and C. Smith, 'Global Japanization? Convergence and Competition in the Organization of the Labour Process' *Global Japanisation (1994)*

R. Milkman, 'The New American Workplace: High Road or Low Road?' *Workplaces of the Future (1998)*

Note

1 For a full list of the books, see http://www.ilpc.org.uk/BookSeries.aspx

Name Index

Subject Index